BOOK OF
BUFFS, MASTERS, MAVENS AND UNCOMMON EXPERTS.

BOOK OF BUFFS, MASTERS, MAVENS AND UNCOMMON EXPERTS.

by the Editors of
The World Almanac®
Henry Doering, Editor

WORLD ALMANAC PUBLICATIONS

NEW YORK

Cover design: Elke Raedisch and John Lane

First published in 1980.

Paperback edition distributed in the United States by Ballantine Books, a Division of Random House, Inc. and in Canada by Random House of Canada, Ltd.

First American hardcover edition printed by Prentice-Hall, Inc., 1980

Library of Congress Catalog Card Number 79-56154

Library of Congress Catalog Card Number (hardcover edition) 80-81179

Newspaper Enterprise Association, Inc. ISBN 0-911818-13-8

Ballantine Books ISBN 0-345-29178-6

Prentice-Hall, Inc. ISBN 0-13-967836-0

Printed in the United States of America.
Newspaper Enterprise Association, Inc.

World Almanac Publications
Jane D. Flatt, Publisher
200 Park Avenue, New York,
New York 10166

CONTENTS

CIVIL WAR

Timothy Burgess, **Confederate Army**/100; William Frassanito, **Civil War photographs**/101; Charles Klein, **Battle reenactments**/103; Paul Loane, **GAR Uniforms & equipment**/105; Richard Mudd, **Lincoln assassination**/106; Seward Osborne, **20th NY State Militia**/108; Lloyd Ostendorf, **Abraham Lincoln photographs**/109; Jerry Russell, **Battlefield preservation**/111; Joseph Rzotkiewicz, **Gettysburg**/113; Stan Schirmacher, **Service records**/114; John Walter, **Regimental histories**/116

MILITARIA

Neil Crowley, **Toy soldiers**/119; Craig Herbert, **World War I ballooning**/120; Vincent Kehoe, **18th Century British Army**/122; Robert Klinger, **Militaria restoration**/124; Richard Mundschenk, **Imperial German artifacts**/125; George Woodbridge, **U.S. military clothing**/127

VEHICLES

Noland Adams, **Corvettes**/129; Bill Barth, **Model T restoration**/131; Donald Bougher, **Pontiacs**/132; Ken Brock, **Gyrocopters**/134; Bruce Comstock, **Hot air balloons**/136; James Dworshak, **Nash automobiles**/137; Warwick Eastwood, **Horseless carriages**/139; Walter Gosden, **Auto history**/140; Glenn Hansen, **BMW 700s**/142; John Hoschek, **Buses**/143; Richard Knudson, **MG sports cars**/145; Ruth Landesman, **Houseboats**/147; Dave Newell, **Corvairs**/148; Perry Piper, **Edsels**/150; Don Ricardo, **Vintage autos**/152; Wally Scott, **Soaring**/153; Bob Smiley, **Jaguar XK series**/155; Kenneth Soderbeck, **Fire trucks**/156; Horace Sowles, **Horse-drawn vehicles**/157; Jim Sykes, **NSU autos**/159; John Thomas, **Hudson Motor Car Co.**/160; John Voelcker, **Morris Minors**/161

PEOPLE

Jack Bales, **Horatio Alger**/164; Tyra Berry, **Hank Williams**/165; Samuel Burr, **Aaron Burr**/167; Sandor Burstein, **Lewis Carroll**/169; Mario DiGiovanni, **Christopher Columbus**/170; John Gable, **Theodore Roosevelt**/172; Pearl Hodges, **Rose O'Neill & Kewpies**/174; William Hogarth, **Richard III**/175; Loudilla, Loretta & Kay Johnson, **Loretta Lynn**/176; John McCabe, **Laurel & Hardy**/178; Sue McCasland, **Elvis Presley**/180; Christe McMenomy, **Dorothy L. Sayers**/182; Don Reed, **Dracula**/183; Julian Wolffe, **Sherlock Holmes**/185

HISTORY

Robert Alotta, **Philadelphia history**/187; John Baeder, **Diners**/188; Jess Barrow, **Naval aviation**/189; Fred & Betty Beals, **Old Buildings & bridges**/191; Cuesta Ray Benberry, **Quilts**/192; Barbara Brown, **Genealogy**/194; Elizabeth Brownell, **S.Arizona history**/195; Errett Callahan, **Primitive technology**/197; Alexander Cook, **Great Lakes**/199; Isaac Davis, **Maine town histories**/201; Thomas Dixon, **C&O Railroad**/202; Philip Gardner, **Custer Co., Nebraska**/204; Thomas Hahn, **Canals,** /205; Eugene Huddleston, **Railroad photography**/207;

NATURE AND SCIENCE

ARTS AND CRAFTS

AND SO FORTH

INDEX

FOREWORD

HENRY DOERING

BUFFS, MASTERS, MAVENS, AND UNCOMMON EXPERTS

IT NEVER OCCURRED to Henry Doering that he himself qualified as a buff, master, or expert, until the notion was suggested to him shortly before he finished this book. Doering, who interviewed and wrote the stories of the experts who appear here, has become a master of the worlds of hobbyists, craftsmen, amateur historians, collectors, plant and animal fanciers, adventurers, and dozens of other enthusiasts. In short, Doering is now an expert on experts.

This book was begun in early 1979 when *The World Almanac* launched a search for widely recognized experts and the fascinating areas of their expertise. We wanted them to describe the satisfactions they derive from their hobbies and to tell us how and why they got started.

Why? Because we've been irritated with ourselves lately. It seems like the more leisure time we have, the less we do with it. We thought that if we could talk to a group of individuals who live life to its fullest, and find out what spurred them into action, that it just might prove contagious.

We don't think we're alone. We believe that thousands of Americans would gladly use their free time more constructively if they could be exposed to the pleasures that other folks enjoy, and had specific facts on how they, too, can blossom into buffs, masters, and experts.

Doering, a 29-year-old assistant editor of *The World Almanac*, did not find the hunt an easy one. Endless hours of telephone interviews alternated with days of frustration, as he tried to locate busy buffs. To reach a California master at home after work meant Doering was toiling at midnight in his New York office or apartment. Hundreds of weekend hours, too, were spent on the telephone or sorting out notes.

Does our buff of buffs have any personal observations? In fact, Doering found himself most interested by the personality traits common to specific hobbyists.

You might think, for instance, that master stamp and coin collectors would be a lot alike. Not so, says Doering. "Coin collectors seem to be more outgoing than philatelists. Perhaps the stamp collectors worry about revealing too much about their valuable collections. They're very reticent."

Doering found car buffs to be the most talkative. "What they love is the contact with other collectors," he explains. Artists and craftspeople are among the least talkative, he learned. "They get a satisfaction out of their activities that often can't be explained to someone who doesn't share them. And they don't seem introspective about why they do what they do. They don't need a reason."

Cat and dog lovers are most alike, says Doering. Each contends that his or her animal is the best of them all. Fitting the stereotype, these experts do tend to perceive their pets as considerably more human than other animals.

Doering's own favorite? It's no surprise that he found the adventurers the most interesting to talk with. Racer, flyer, or explorer — they were exceptionally enthusiastic. "But they're also very calm and unflappable, quite practical about the risks they take," says Doering. "After all, their lives depend on a cool analysis of risk. Rash, excitable people probably wouldn't live long enough to become experts in one of these fields."

But all the buffs, masters, and experts — from bonsai plant grower to kite flying aficionado — had one thing in common, Doering points out. "Each was curious about what the other folks I'd spoken with were doing. I think curiosity about the world around them is what really gets them started as hobbyists."

Now that the book is finished, will Doering continue to collect experts? "I haven't even scratched the surface," he admits. "There are easily 20 experts out there for every one I've contacted, and doubtlessly hundreds of specialties I haven't even thought of."

"I enjoy these people's enthusiasm and their stories. They have something to tell us about how to live a full life. Yes, I'll probably keep on collecting," he says.

We hope when you read this book your curiosity will be aroused. Just like Henry Doering's was.

COLLECTIBLES

WILL ANDERSON
BREWERIANA

WHEN WILL ANDERSON was a senior at Cornell University in 1961, he was, like a lot of his fellow students, an avid beer drinker. Anderson and his fraternity house roommate even started a collection of beer cans.

Today, the 40-year-old associate publisher of Scholastic Magazines, is a nationally-known collector of "breweriana," and an expert on U. S. breweries and beers.

Among the several thousand items Anderson has in his collection are beer bottles and cans, serving trays, calendars, posters, tap knobs, lithographs, old letterheads, and "just about anything" relating to the brewing of beer in the United States. An addition to his Croton Falls, N.Y. home, set up like a small museum, houses the collection.

Anderson says the most popular items in his collection are the beer cans. "When people come to the house," he says, "they immediately gravitate to the cans." One of the most interesting of his estimated 2,000 cans is a 1905-vintage can from the Haffen Brewery in the Bronx. It was designed for a beer they put out called Neffah: "That's Haffen, spelled backwards; a pretty dumb way to name a beer, in my opinion," says Anderson.

He's also particularly fond of a 7-foot-by-4-foot chromolith picture on metal of the Frank Jones Brewery in Portsmouth, New Hampshire. This piece, which is worth about $800-$900, is valuable because it shows the brewery on it, and not just a buxom woman or other advertising artwork.

Anderson is not only interested in the artifacts left behind by breweries of the past, but he has an interest in the history of the beer industry, as well. For example, he says there were five brands of beer over the years named Budweiser. In addition to the famous brand made today by Anheuser-Busch, there were others preceding it because "Budweiss is a place in Czechoslovakia where they made a particular kind of beer, which became a generic term" for this type of brew.

It is vital that "small and regional breweries have help in their struggle to survive," in order to provide the beer-drinking public with "alternatives to mass-produced, bland national brands," says Anderson. There are only 45 small breweries left today, of the more than 2,000 that existed at the turn-of-the-century in the U.S. Anderson serves these more obscure beers in his home, instead of the more popular national brands.

"I pride myself on having these small breweries' beers and introducing people to them," he says. "When they drink them, they really like them because they have more body and bouquet than the pap that passes for beer today." While he realizes he "can't preach to people to stop drinking" the major national brands of beer, Anderson wishes that they would realize that it is a misconception that "beer made locally is no good. Actually, the fresher the beer, the better."

As a founding member of the Eastern Coast Breweriana Association (ECBA) in 1970, Anderson has kept busy as an officer of the 550-member organization. The ECBA has a convention on the grounds of a different East Coast brewery each year: "it gives an historic meaning and significance" to the proceedings, he says.

Anderson has written five published books: *Anderson's Turn-of-the-Century Brewery Directory* (1968); *Beers, Breweries & Breweriana* (1969); *The Beer Book* (1973); *The Breweries of Brooklyn* (1976); and *The Beer Poster Book* (1976).

For the novice collector of breweriana, Anderson advises joining one of the several breweriana clubs in the U.S. as a great way to meet fellow collectors and learn something about the field. Also, by attending the meetings of the breweriana collectors, the novice will be able to find items to add to his collection. "The meetings are veritable flea markets," says Anderson, adding that most of the collectors who are selling or trading items are very honest and won't try to take advantage of the novice collector. In addition, the collector should be prepared to dig around a great many flea markets and antique stores to find what he is looking for.

Anderson will be glad to advise anyone on breweriana, and provide information on the various collectors's organizations or on U.S. beers or breweries. He can be contacted at PO Box 352, Croton Falls, N.Y. 10519.

LILLIAN BAKER
HATPINS

TIME WAS WHEN THE well-dressed lady wouldn't be seen anywhere without a hat. Since these hats were large, heavy and frequently had to fit securely on a substantial amount of hair, hatpins were a necessity. As richly varied in design as the hats which they secured, hatpins today are artistic reminders of a more formal time.

For Lillian Baker, however, hatpins are a part of everyday life. The Gardena, California, journalist is an avid collector of hatpins. In fact, she has so many, "I stopped counting at 500." And she has written the definitive collector's reference book on the subject.

Miss Baker's interest began with her career. As a newspaperwoman, she covered many antique shows, and became fascinated by the variety and artisanship of hatpins. In addition, she had some that belonged to her mother, and she was curious about them.

"I soon discovered that there really wasn't anything written about hatpins or hatpin holders," she said. Miss Baker decided to do some research. Her 12 years of research led to her publication of *Hatpins and Hatpin Holders*, the first comprehensive work on the subject.

According to Baker, "The first symbol of women's emancipation was the hatpin and the hat. When the British suffragettes were ordered to remove their hatpins in the coutrtoom as dangerous weapons, American women were outraged, and adopted as their symbol the hat — the bigger the better." With a varied background in writing and publishing (her first job was as a wartime continuity writer for WINS-Radio in New York City), Miss Baker has continued to work as a columnist, reporter, reviewer and public speaker, collecting new hatpins and an assortment of other hat-related jewelry all the while.

Because of their value, Miss Baker is reluctant to be specific about many of the hatpins in her collection. However, she is particularly proud of her collection of jet hatpins made by Queen Victoria's jeweler ("it's a finer collection than in any museum"), and two transparent enamel hatpins probably made by the renowned designer Lalique. Another of her interesting hatpins dates from the discovery of King Tut's tomb in Egypt in the early 1920s. It features a brass scarab with a plastic image of the Pharoah. "I just love that," says Miss Baker.

She feels hatpin collecting is particularly rewarding because of the amazing variety. "They're really little works of art," she says, "made by fine jewelers."

"I bet I've seen 100,000 hatpins over 20 years, and seldom have I seen any two alike...They were individually made, many for a particular person" and, thus, are unique.

In 1977, Miss Baker founded the International Club for Collectors of Hatpins & Hatpin Holders, the first organization of its kind. Working out of her home, she provides the club with a monthly newsletter, *Points* and a quarterly, *News and Review of Hatpins and Hatpin Holders*. There are 168 members; Miss Baker wants to limit the number to 200, as she does most of the work herself and "any more would be just too much."

A beginning hatpin collector will be able to find a great many hatpins to choose from, but Miss Baker warns of replicas. "I have no objection to them," she says, "as long as the people know that's what they are." She says that with the increasing popularity of hatpin collecting, many companies are now putting out copies of pins by famous jewelers.

Hatpin collecting, like most other things, is getting increasingly costly. "There was a time when if I paid $10 or $12 for a hatpin, it had to be pretty special," she says. "Now, paying $35 or $40 is common." The best sources for buying hatpins, she says, are reputable dealers and or fellow collectors.

Miss Baker is interested in assisting beginners (or established collectors, for that matter), and in gaining new members for her organization. She can be contacted at 15237 Chanera Ave., Gardena, CA 90249.

STANLEY BAKER
RAILROADIANA

EVER SINCE I WAS a kid," Stanley Baker says, "I've been fascinated with railroads." And he is one of those lucky people whose adult life has fulfilled a childhood dream.

Baker lived in northeast Minneapolis as a child, near the yards of the Great Northern, Northern Pacific, and Chicago & Northwestern railroads. He would go down to the Great Northern depot and watch passenger trains come and go. "And the freight trains," he remembers. "I had a favorite spot where I'd sit. I was just a little kid, and I was just interested in trains."

He collected toy trains as a youngster, buying worn-out toys from second-hand shops and fixing them up, constructing elaborate layouts of track on the living room floor or in his backyard, and pretending he was an engineer. He also began collecting "railroadiana," all kinds of items relating to the railroads.

"Not many people realize what railroadiana consists of," he says. "Many people don't understand about the finer things, all of the little treasures, the railroad gave away." The railroads were like planes today, and distributed "many beautfiul items" as advertising come-ons.

Not content with merely collecting and dreaming about the railroads, Baker used to hop rides on outbound freights with a couple of pals when he was a teenager. "We'd grab a freight at Minneapolis and take a trip anywhere in Minnesota or even the Dakotas," he recalls. "If we couldn't get a connection to come back that night, we'd sleep in a boxcar or find some hobo jungle where we could bed down in the grass."

While "most collectors specialize," according to Baker, "I've been picking up most everything pertaining to railroads." He can endlessly list the items he collects. Among them: switch keys ("they're rare, scarce, hard to come by"), railroad pocket watches, jewelry, lapel emblems, lodge pins, china from dining cars ("that's a big thing now, bringing fantastic prices"), silver services, linens, advertising souvenirs, train parts, lanterns, and so on.

"Whenever I saw something to do with railroads, I couldn't refuse. I just fell in love with it all," he says.

Among Baker's favorite items is his collection of wax sealers. These were used by railroad agents and depots to seal special communications and money packages. "It was something akin to registered mail today," says Baker, noting that the seal, with a metal "matrix" embossed with the agent or depot name, was widely used by the railroads.

"There's a lot of railroad history" connected with these sealers, according to Baker. They were first used in the early 1800s, and went out of fashion after World War I. "After their usefulness ended, " says Baker, "they were called in by the companies to their home offices and no one knows what happened to them after that. Often, they were junked; but many were just shoved into the back of a drawer, where they can still be found today."

Baker has about 400 of the sealers, which he has been collecting since he was a child. "I made the rounds of a lot of railroad stations, asking the agents if they had any," he recalls. "Every once in a while I would pick up two or three." Most are worth about $50, though some have been valued at $500 or $1000.

Baker finds his treasures in many places. He haunts antique stores, flea markets, auctions and sales, as well as train depots, to find items to be added to his collection.

The bulk of his railroadiana (of "many thousand items") is in storage. "And it's really costing me to keep it there, I can tell you." Someday, he would like to open a museum, preferably in a converted railroad depot. But there never seems to be enough time for him to do so.

The 63-year-old former insurance safety engineer (he retired in 1965 to devote full-time to his hobby) became the nationally recognized authority on railroadiana in 1976, with the publication of the definitive reference book, *The Collector's Book of Railroadiana*, which he co-wrote with Virginia Brainard Kunz. With photographs of his own collection, Baker's book outlines and illustrates all the collectibles pertaining to railroads. He also wrote *The Railroadiana Collector's Price Guide* (1977), and is presently working on a comprehensive book that will provide research and documentation of all known railroad artifacts.

For the novice collector of railroadiana, Baker advises first making a study of the categories "you plan to specialize in, to acquaint yourself with authentic railroad items." He urges that collectors know their subject well before going out to buy, "so you don't get stuck with a reproduction or a fake."

JEFF BOUCHER
ORIENTAL RUGS

ART, FOR JEFF BOUCHER, is like a magic carpet flight over the Middle East, and that carpet is undoubtedly one from his stunning collection of peasant and nomad Oriental rugs.

The 65-year-old industrial engineer, a career Army man born in Lingleville, Texas, might seem an unlikely person to be a scholar and expert in such an area. How then did he get started in collecting these exotic beauties?

Boucher traces the beginning of his interest to his many visits to various tribal, village, and city bazaars while on special U.S. Army assignment in the Middle East from 1960 to 1963. When he was assigned as a project engineer for a World Bank-funded flood control project in Pakistan from 1964 to 1966, he also scoured the local markets for additional treasures. Today that initial collection of rugs and tribal weavings has been replaced by the "older pieces that form my current collection, which were obtained in Europe and America from estate sales or other collectors."

Boucher is particularly well-known for his work as vice-president of the 500-member International Hajji Baba Society, a worldwide organization of Oriental rug collectors. Hajji Baba, Boucher explains, is the "patron saint" of the Oriental rug society, the hero of an 1824 novel called *Haji Baba of Ispahan*. The major goal of the society, Boucher says, is "the promotion of knowledge and appreciation of Oriental rugs as an art."

But there is a special, more mystical quality about these textiles that interests Boucher. "Rugs made by a people for their own use, and woven in the traditional colors and designs of their ancestors, especially those woven as dowry pieces or to be presented to an important person, are said to have a soul derived from past generations of weavers." Such rugs, carefully handmade from the finest wool and dyed in complementary natural dyes, "acquire a fascinating patina with age that seems to speak to the observer." Finding and obtaining such rugs, says Boucher, "gives me the greatest thrill and pleasure. I find something new in each piece every time I examine it."

A particular specialty of Boucher's expertise is the work of the Baluchi tribes of Iran and Afghanistan. In 1974, he was instrumental in mounting a major exhibition of these rugs in London, one of the few such exhibitions ever held. He wrote the catalogue for the show (as he as done for several other of the Hajji Baba Society's major shows). He also lectures around the world on the subject.

Now the deputy director of installations and services for the U.S. Army Materiel Development and Readiness Command based in Washington, Boucher continues his collecting and rug society activities at a steady pace.

Boucher has much advice on how to avoid the pitfalls that frequently trap the novice collector. He is most concerned that beginners not rush headlong into the business of collecting Oriental rugs and tribal weavings, without some basic knowledge of the field. Before even beginning such a collection, he advises, the enthusiast must visit museums and other collections "where you can see and handle fine rugs," to get an understanding of what kinds of rugs there are, what to look for in a rug, and what has value. Then, he urges the novice to join a club or society where knowledgeable people are willing to further his education. Finally, the beginner should obtain and study several good books in the specific area of your special interest within the field.

Then — and only then — "you may collect rugs. But be careful! Buy the best you can afford. You will never regret it." Thus, should a collector want to change the focus of his collection as he develops more expertise, "he'll be able to do so at a profit."

Boucher will be happy to counsel novices in the Oriental rug field. He can be contacted through the International Hajji Baba Society, Inc., 7404 Valley Crest Blvd., Annandale, VA 22003.

MARIAN BOYCE
SALT & PEPPER SHAKERS

WHO SAYS COLLECTING has to be expensive? Marian Boyce doesn't think so ... and she has the collection to prove it!

Mrs. Boyce began collecting salt and pepper shakers in the 1930s, and today, the Watkins Glen, New York, executive secretary has 800 pairs of them, of which very few cost much money. What is the secret to all this collecting and economy too?

"A few are rare sets," she says, "but most are what the average collector can find. In other words, they're not museum pieces."

That's not to say, however, that Mrs. Boyce doesn't have some impressive items in her collection. For example, she has a set of the first salt and pepper shakers ever patented. They're called "Hobbs Hounds," and they are two lead hound dogs looking skyward, with amber glass eyes. They were made in 1869, and Mrs. Boyce purchased them for $15 from a fellow collector. She says that one week after she bought them, another collector called and offered her $75 for them. "So you see, part of the technique to collecting is knowing when to buy," she says.

Mrs. Boyce also collects salt and pepper shakers with advertising motifs. For example, she has sets of penguins advertising Kool cigarettes, a milk glass replica of an old General Electric refrigerator (complete with a motor on top), and a set of Philip Morris bellhops. "The advertising sets are really very interesting," she says. "A lot of the companies are no longer in existence, so it's of historic interest to have these shakers."

Other theme salt and pepper shakers she collects are nursery rhymes (she has Old King Cole and the Three Bears, among others) and famous people: Uncle Sam, John F. Kennedy, Lyndon Johnson, and the Nixons, to name just a few. In addition, she has about 200-300 single shakers of different types.

Unlike many collectors, Mrs. Boyce is able to display her entire collection. She has a floor-to-ceiling, glass fronted cabinet, which was specially built in her dining room, where many of the shakers are displayed. In addition, she has "two china closets stuffed full of them." At holiday time, she will often take out shakers with appropriate designs and make displays or use them on festive tables. She likes the idea of using them whenever possible, because people seem to enjoy seeing and handling them. "Of course, there are some I wouldn't let anyone touch."

Mrs. Boyce began her collection in 1938 after her paternal grandmother died. She was the only grandchild in the family, and her uncles gave her many of her grandmother's belongings. Among them were about 20 sets of hand-painted salt and pepper shakers.

"They fascinated me," she says, "and it soon grew into a habit to collect them. Friends and relatives began giving them to me. And later, after I got married, I began to write to people listed in various collectors' magazines. My collection just grew."

Salt and pepper shakers are quite inexpensive to collect. Mrs. Boyce says it is still possible to obtain shakers for a dollar or two per set though they're starting to get scarce." The beginner can read advertisements from other collectors in any of the numerous hobby magazines to get a good idea of what is available.

"I really enjoy my collecting because it's still pretty much an open field and there are frequent opportunities to acquire unique and attractive items," she says. She feels that she has one of the prime salt and pepper shaker collections in existence, because of the number. "You don't hear of too many people who have even 500 sets," she says.

"The exciting part is the hunt, looking for the shakers everywhere. But you do come to the point where you have to limit yourself. You can't just go out and buy everything you see," says Mrs. Boyce.

Mrs. Boyce says her family "doesn't understand why I do it," but for her, a great deal of the pleasure of her collection is "looking at my shakers, and the memories they conjure up are just fantastic. I can remember the person who gave them to me or the occasion when I got them."

Interested salt and pepper shaker collectors (or would-be collectors) can reach Mrs. Boyce at RD 2, Watkins Glen, NY 14891.

BOB BUFFALOE
COCA-COLA MEMORABILIA

THINGS DO GO BETTER with Coke — especially if you're Bob Buffaloe!

The 38-year-old special education teacher from Memphis, Tennessee, began collecting old soda pop bottles in 1972 ("reminiscent of childhood days," he says), but it wasn't until he visited Florida in 1973 that he found his true calling as the leader of the "Cola Clan."

Driving near Panama City, Florida, one afternoon, he and his wife spied two vandalized Coke machines sitting outside an apparently abandoned building. Looking inside the building, he saw dusty cartons. They drove to the nearby Coca-Cola bottling plant to ask permission to rummage through the building, which Buffaloe had guessed could be a storehouse.

Permission granted, they went back and spent a few happy hours discovering such interesting items as a 1910 advertising postcard for Coca-Cola (now worth $100) and piles of old signs, calendars from the 1930s, napkins, seltzer bottles, and more, all dealing with Coca-Cola.

Now, Buffaloe's home is crammed with thousands of advertising items relating to Coke, from a 5-foot tall model bottle beside the TV set in the living room, to his fully outfitted 1930's soda fountain in the den. Advertising signs hang everywhere, competing for space with trays and calendars.

"We started out just to get some nice signs to put on our kitchen wall," says Buffaloe. "But it spread into five rooms."

Isn't living with all of this advertising material a bit tedious? "Not at all," says Buffaloe. "It's very interesting to display and we haven't grown tired of it...It's a unique art form of high esthetics that's purely American. And it turned out to be a good investment, too."

Among the prizes of Buffaloe's 2,000-piece collection: two advertising cut-out displays for Coke, one from 1925 and one from 1930. Both are the only ones known to exist outside the firm's archives. The 1925 display features a lovely young woman dressed in a white fur, while the 1930 model shows a giant rounded bottle of Coke. They're worth about $600 apiece. Buffaloe says, "Items that are that rare are almost impossible to set a value on. A collector will pay much more than a piece is worth sometimes because he really wants it."

In 1974, Buffaloe founded an association with some other Coke collectors, which they called "The Coke Clan." When they ran into trouble with Coca-Cola corporate headquarters in Atlanta, they changed the name to "The Cola Clan." From an initial membership of 50 people, the group has grown to over 2,300 members all over the U.S. and in several foreign countries.

The Coca-Cola Company was so pleased with the formation of the club, that it endorsed it, Buffaloe says, and thus the Clan is the recognized official collectors organization for memorabilia relating to Coca-Cola. Buffaloe originated the Cola Clan's monthly newsletter *The Cola Call*. The Clan also has an annual convention.

Fortunately for Buffaloe, he acquired the bulk of his collection before this memorabilia became so popular. Presently, however, Buffaloe and his fellow fanatics are finding it "difficult to compete with three very wealthy collectors" in the field, who are buying up many of the choicest items, at high prices.

"Part of the thrill of collecting is the unknown," says Buffaloe. "There is such an infinite amount of stuff to collect because no one really knows for sure what's out there."

Among the most sought after items, Buffaloe says, are trays from 1898-1906, any metal signs or advertisements showing the straight-sided bottle (prior to 1915), a 1929 toy delivery truck with tiny cases of the beverage on the back, a 1934 tray with Johnny Weismuller on it ("it has gone way beyond retail value, to $400"), and a 1931 calendar that featured art by Norman Rockwell.

Though Buffaloe says that the economics of collecting memorabilia of Coca-Cola today has made it "almost too late" to begin a collection. He suggests collecting reproductions of memorabila relating to Coke. This is a rapidly growing area of collecting, because the items are relatively plentiful and quite well made. They're also much less expensive.

New members of the Cola Clan are always welcome. Membership is $12 annually. Write to Buffaloe at 3965 Pikes Peak, Memphis, TN 38108.

GEORGE CEARLEY
AIRLINE MEMORABILIA

GEORGE CEARLEY'S HOBBY has really taken off! If it has anything to do with commercial aviation, and especially with Braniff Airways, Cearley's probably got it.

Any items relating to the operation of airlines are of interest to the 32-year-old biological sciences instructor from Dallas, Texas. Cearley has one of the largest and most complete collections of commercial aviation memorabilia in the United States. From airplane models to airline schedules, his collection is a unique and colorful conglomeration that is a revealing history of the adventure of commercial flight.

Ever since he was a small boy growing up in Dallas, and particularly with the advent of the jet age in 1958, Cearley has been avidly interested in commercial aviation. Since Dallas was (and is) the homebase for Braniff Airways, it is not surprising that his greatest interest has been in Braniff.

Cearley has a gigantic collection. It includes 5,000 individual issues of airline schedules, dating back to 1926; 130 small plastic models of commercial planes;16 display models ranging from two to six feet in length and 2,000 postcards and numerous posters, photos and publications from various airlines.

Among the highlights of his collection: a 54-inch long model of an American Airlines Lockheed Electra prop jet, with flashing wing lights, formerly used as a promotional model in travel agencies and the airline's ticket offices. He also has Western Airline's first schedule, vintage 1926, and an original 1928 Pan American schedule of service to Key West, Florida.

One of the unique parts of his collection is his library of 5,000 original flight announcement recordings, from Dallas's Love Field between 1958 and 1974. Cearley found these in 1974 when, as part of his work with the Texas Aviation Historical Society, he took a tour of the airport. There, in a former P.R. office on one of the old concourses, "I found a stack of metal records with all the flight announcements recorded on them."

Through research, Cearley discovered that Dallas was one of the few cities to utilize this automatic system to make flight announcements. They were recorded in a studio in Dallas, and were played in the airport on a jukebox-like system.

Someday, Cearley will give his collection to a museum. "There is nothing like this in the country...even the Smithsonian doesn't have a collection of commercial aviation materials," he says. He plans to donate his collection to a museum recently begun at the Universtiy of Texas-Dallas.

With all of this history at his fingertips, Cearley has begun writing articles on airlines and aircraft for aviation hobbyist publications. Among the recent articles he's written have been histories of Capital Airlines, National Airlines, and Eastern Airlines, the Boeing 707 and 720, and several articles on the surprisingly fascinating topic of airline schedules. His history of Braniff Airways, in honor of the firm's 50th anniversary in 1978, appeared in *Captain's Log*, an aviation history publication.

He has also written a book on the airline's 50-year history, which was published by Bryan-Tompkins, a London aviation publishing firm. It is a 208-page compendium of facts and photographs about Braniff and all the airlines it has acquired over the years. The book even contains a "fleet history of every aircraft operated by Braniff: where it was obtained and what happened to it," Cearley says.

He recommends that novice collectors of aviation memorabilia (or any commercially-related memorabilia field) collect "what currently available memorabilia there is, as it may become more valuable in the future." It is also possible to get material from dealers and other collectors. But, Cearley cautions, "people have been paying much too much" for the materials. "A timetable an airline gives away free, is sometimes sold for $30. That's way too much."

Finally, Cearley recommends joining an organization or hobbyist group in the field and corresponding with fellow collectors. He particularly recommends the World Airlines Hobby Club, 3381 Apple Tree Ln., Erlanger, KY 41018.

Cearley will be glad to answer queries from airlines buffs, addressed to him at PO Box 12312, Dallas, TX 75225.

WILLIAM DARRAH
STEREOGRAPHS

B EFORE RADIO, MOVIES, and television made them obsolete, one of the most popular and appealing uses for photographs was stereographic slides. The double-imaged, postcard-sized pictures were viewed through a special viewer (a stereoscope), a system most well-appointed American homes couldn't do without from 1851 to 1930. Scenic views of famous places were available, and views of the owner's family, home, or vacation could be made, much as today's inexpensive cameras provide everybody with the opportunity to create their own photographs.

William Darrah recognizes the intrinsic value of these pictures as not only an essential part of the development of today's advanced photographic technology, but as a very real and timeless way of preserving history. In fact, he has become something of an expert on the subject.

Stereographs first came to Darrah's attention in 1944, while he was researching the American West of the 1870s for a biography of John Wesley Powell, the first modern explorer of the Grand Canyon. Much of the illustrative material was contained on stererographs.

He began by collecting stereographic views of the West. Then, he focused on collecting stereographs that showed the development of American technology. He realized that the period from 1850 to 1860 represented an important era in the development of photography. Thus, his interest in the history and development of photography as it could be seen through these pictures was born.

Cartes-de-visite form an important part of the early history of photography too, says Darrah. These small photos, attached to a 2-inch-by-4 inch card, were common from 1857 to 1900 in the U.S. These "photographic visiting cards" originally were portraits, but eventually had "every conceivable subject."

They originated in France in 1854, when the photographer Andre-Adolph-Eugene Disderi patented a four-lensed camera which made eight photographs simultaneously on one large plate, Darrah says. From this plate, the large print that was developed was used as a regular portrait, while the remaining smaller pictures were mounted and used as visiting cards. The fad really took off when the French emperor, Napoleon III, had a *carte-de-visite* made at Disderi's studio. Soon, the custom spread all over Europe and into the United States. They were popularly exchanged on holidays and birthdays, or as a remembrance of a special occasion. Often, the pictures (somewhat akin to today's snapshots) were displayed in albums, he says.

According to Darrah, these pictures "of ordinary people are gems. And they were the bread and butter for every serious working photographer in the U.S."

Even in small towns, he says, "there were photographers of great skill who had enough pride to turn out good quality work." The cartes-de-visite "created photography as a profession, giving the average photographer a means of earning a living by developing a market for his more serious work." He explains that most of the photographers ran one-man operations, doing all the work themselves, without assistance, except for an occasional helper who did menial chores. For Darrah, there is "great pleasure to be derived from looking at these actual pieces of the work" of the photographers.

At its peak, Darrah's collection of stereographs totalled over 105,000 different items. In 1978, however, he sold the bulk of his collection to Rimhart Galleries in New York City. He now has more time to pursue the study of the cartes-de-visite, and his many writing projects.

A former professor of biology at Harvard University, Darrah is the author of 14 books. Among them, *Stereo Views: A History of Stereography in America* (1964), and *The World of Stereographs* (1977), which received the 1978 Rudy and Hertha Benjamin Book Award from the New York Photographic Historical Society. He is presently working on a book about *carte-de-visite* photographs from the period 1858 to 1900.

Stereographs and, most particularly *cartes-de-visite* are still quite plentiful on the market, according to Darrah. The novice collector, if he will comb flea markets and antique sotres, should be able to assemble quite a collection. The average price of a *carte-de-visite* these days is anywhere from 10 cents to one dollar. Darrah cautions, "Have patience and ingenuity in building a collection. Learn as much as you can about the things you are interested in; build slowly and enjoy your results."

There is a national organization for people interested in stereographs. The National Stereographic Aossication (PO Box 14801, Columbus, OH 43214) will be able to provide much helpful information. In addition, Darrah recommends the collector join one of the numerous photo history societies around the country.

Darrah can be contacted at RD 1, Gettysburg, PA 17325, for further information or assistance.

HERMAN DARVICK
AUTOGRAPHS

ELVIS PRESLEY'S BRINGS only $75, but Greta Garbo's is worth $675. You can sell Farrah Fawcett-Majors's for $3, but Franklin D. Roosevelt's will bring $75. And yours is probably worth nothing at all!

Autographs — whose is worth how much and why — are Herman Darvick's specialty.

Darvick, a 34-year-old New York City public school teacher from Rockville Centre, has been after other people's signatures for a long time. "I used to get autographs of baseball players outside Yankee Stadium," he recalls. " I was also interested in the President of the United States, so one day when I was 16, I wrote to former Presidents Hoover and Truman and they each sent me their autographs." Inspired, Darvick also wrote to Dwight Eisenhower, John F. Kennedy, Lyndon B. Johnson, Carl Sandburg, Eleanor Roosevelt, and Pablo Casals. They all sent him their autographs, too, and "I was on my way!"

Now, Darvick has a collection of autographs, letters, and other documents of every U.S. Vice President while he was in office. Another specialty that Darvick wants to continue adding to is a collection of letters and notes written by Theodore Roosevelt while he was vice-president.

His most unusual autograph is a piece of stationery from the Office of the Vice President, with the Vice President's oath of office typed on it. He sent it to Vice Presidents Nixon, Humphrey, Agnew, Ford, Rockefeller, and Mondale, and all signed it.

Darvick is also called upon frequently to authenticate the autographs of the famous, and in this capacity has discovered an unusual situation.

It is impossible to sign your name exactly the same every time, says Darvick. However, a lot of celebrities are trying it with a device called the Auto-Pen, a machine that reproduces signatures. The chief user. of this device in recent history has been the President of the United States. Jimmy Carter's office uses one, but that is not where the controversy arises.

Darvick and other experts have discovered that a personal assistant to President Carter, Susan Clough, signs the President's name to letters and other documents with great regularity. Chances are, if you write to the White House you will get a letter from the President with his signature made by Miss Clough.

Carter's signature changed while he was in office, too, Darvick says. Until he became President, his signature was basically the same: the "r's" looked like undotted "i's." In 1978, it changed, and the "r's" in "Carter" became more like backwards "3's."

Says Darvick, "Susan Clough changed her forgeries. Now her "r" resembles his "r," but she doesn't do it quite right." A search at the National Archives discovered she had signed three official proclamations, something it was traditionally thought a President would do for himself.

Carter does have a penchant for hand-writing letters, says Darvick, so those have become the most valuable autograph collectibles from his administration. Not only that, Darvick adds, but Carter refuses to sign autographs at personal appearances, saying "The Secret Service doesn't allow it."

Darvick checked with the Secret Service and was told they knew of no such policy. Why won't the President sign? "Either he has a thing about not wanting people to profit off his valuable signature, or he just doesn't want to."

Darvick says the most sought-after, but so far undiscovered, autograph is Julius Caesar's. It's worth at least $2 million, which is what the Las Vegas hotel, Caesar's Palace, has offered to anyone who obtains it. The other most valuable autographs are those of Shakespeare (only six known) and Christopher Columbus (only eight known). They're each worth in the neighborhood of $1 million, and are all in museums or university libraries. Of the autographs that are still in general circulation from time to time, the most valuable is probably that of Button Gwinnett, a signer of the Declaration of Independence. It is worth $100,000 on the market, as is an original manuscript of "The Star Spangled Banner."

Anyone can start an autograph collection, says Darvick. All you need is 15 cents postage. Simply pick out someone you want to get an autograph from and send them a handwritten request. "It shows your sincerity. Someone famous is going to think more about you if you take the time to handwrite the letter." And it doesn't hurt to mention how much you liked the person's last book, or that you voted for him in last election, "something that indicates you have some real interest in that person."

"Autograph collecting is the only hobby where you can create your own collectible, one that didn't exist until the person puts pen to paper to give it to you," Darvick says.

Above all, "don't give up." Sometimes it takes a lot of ingenuity and persistence to achieve a successful result.

Autograph collecting appeals to Darvick because "I feel that if you have someone's letter, you have a frozen moment of that person's time. You know what he was thinking. Part of his life or thoughts are on that paper."

Darvick is president of the Universal Autograph Collectors Club, which has over 1,000 members in every state and in Canada, England, France, and Scandinavia. The organization is branching out all the time, says Darvick, by holding mini-conventions in cities where there are a profusion of members. At these conventions, members have a chance to meet each other and autograph dealers, as well as display their collections.

Darvick says that the main contact with the membership is the bimonthly newsletter of 28 pages, *The Pen and Quill*, which he edits. The newsletter is a useful compendium of information and news for autograph collectors, frequently including addresses of famous people, facsimilie signatures ("that's the only way you can authenticate a signature: have two of them") and so forth. The club's $9 annual dues include the magazine.

"The greatest thing is, no one cannot be interested in collecting autographs. Everybody has to like someone."

Both Darvick and the UAC can be contacted at PO Box 467, Rockville Centre, NY 11571.

JERRY DE FUCCIO
COMIC BOOKS & ART

IT'S PROBABLY NOT an understatement to say that comic books are a way of life for Jerry DeFuccio. They provided the first sparks for his adolescent creative urges, they led him to his lifetime career, they even proved to be a profitable investment. Besides all that, DeFuccio unabashedly loves comic books — and the artists, stories, and artwork of the so-called "Golden Age" of the 1930s and 1940s.

With a bit of irony, DeFuccio tells how he came to be caught up in the world of comic books. "My humanitarian-physician father, Dr. Charles P. DeFuccio, made house calls in the traditional Italian section of Jersey City, while his docile young son waited in the car. Kindly local merchants provided ice cream and comic books on the hour." Thus, says DeFuccio, "I soon recognized the potential of panel-to-panel continuity as a trenchant story-telling form."

Unfortunately, DeFuccio says, his father didn't share his enthusiasm for comic books, and tore up large amounts of young Jerry's collection. He managed to save some 600 comic books by hiding them at his grandmother's house.

He credits comic books with getting him involved in his lifetime career. De Fuccio, an associate editor of *Mad Magazine*, has been working with comic art and artists for all of the 25 years he's been with the publication. De Fuccio "blames" his success on his dad's disparagement of comic books as a serious art form. "That's how I got forced into this business," he laughs.

DeFuccio's taste in comic books has always been specific: "I didn't like the homespun stuff. I was into avengers, people who left their calling cards," who righted wrongs and did good deeds. He always disdained the "funnies"-type comics.

"The Sunday papers were populated with goofy people. I respect people better than myself. And there was the romantic idea of committing a noble act, or saving someone, then leaving your calling card and disappearing. It was straight out of *Beau Geste*," he says.

"God knows why they wanted to help society," he says. "They were playboys, but they had all this money and hardware to dabble around with."

Who was DeFuccio's favorite? Somebody called The Spirit, who wore a "black mask and a blue suit. He got beat up a lot, but he always came out of it" to emerge triumphant at the end of the story.

DeFuccio's collection of the 600 comic books he saved from his childhood (he has collected very few others over the years) has proven to be a valuable investment. They are all in mint condition, which makes them highly desirable to other collectors, and can sometimes be sold for what impresses even a seasoned expert like DeFuccio as astounding prices. A couple of years ago, he sold his *Marvel Mysteries* #1 comic book for $2,000. Currently, the same book is listed in the *Overstreet Comic Book Guide* (the comic book collector's Bible) at $10,000. The first comic book to feature Superman (*Action Comics* #1, 1939), which DeFuccio also owns, is currently worth $8,400 on the open market.

DeFuccio considers the Golden Age of comic books "something like Camelot — it lived for only a short time." A particularly compelling aspect was the artwork. Each comic book was done by one artist, who did the story, the drawing, and the lettering himself. Thus, each comic book "was very distinct and had its own personality." DeFuccio searches for the old-time comic book artists and, when he finds them, commissions them to redraw some of the classic stories for him. He now owns a number of original reproductions of great comic books, reproductions that will last far longer than the already-fragile originals.

"I'm a dyed-in-the-wool comic book collector," DeFuccio says. "There is an association of ideas when I look at an old comic book. Something unlocks in my head and I recall the circumstances when I first saw the book."

A friend who collects more gentle comic books of Walt Disney characters and the like, once tried to interest DeFuccio in collecting that kind of comic. DeFuccio turned him down. "I always wanted to be Batman. But Donald Duck! I didn't like the costume."

DeFuccio will be glad to hear from comic book collectors and fans of the Golden Age of comic books. He can be contacted at Mad, 485 Madison Ave., New York, NY 10022.

SIBYL DE WEIN
"BARBIE" DOLLS

IN 1980, "BARBIE" WAS 21 years old. She was already a great success for one so young. In fact, says Sibyl DeWein, more than 120 million of the Mattel fashion dolls have been sold, making "Barbie" one of the most popular toys of all time.

Mrs. DeWein, of Clarksville, Tennessee, has a special reason for knowing all about "Barbie": she has a collection of 1,346 of the dolls (including "Ken," "Skipper," and other "Barbie" friends) that is a complete representation of the toy's fascinating history.

"In 1960, I bought a couple of 'Barbie' dolls and made outfits for them, as Christmas gifts for my cousin's daughters," says Mrs. DeWein. "Creating those miniature fashions was so enjoyable I couldn't stop." Neighborhood children, as well as the offspring of friends and relatives, sought out Mrs. DeWein to make clothes for their "Barbie"s.

In 1963, Mrs. DeWein bought her first "Barbie" doll, to use as a seamstress's dummy for the tiny garments. "By 1965, I'd become an avid collector, researcher, and record keeper," she says.

With all that research and record keeping, along with collecting each new doll in the "Barbie" line, Mrs. DeWein has become a noted buff in the "Barbie" doll field.

Mrs. DeWein's collection represents 49 different dolls in Mattel's line. "I have one of each of the different kinds, and one of all the variations on each doll," she says. "Mattel changed 'Barbie' a little each year, keeping her hairstyle and hair color in fashion with the times, as well as improving the technology in the manufacture of the doll."

"I have one bedroom that has nothing but 'Barbie' things in it," she says. "It has overflowed into a second bedroom, and is rapidly filling that one up, too." To clothe her collection of "Barbie" dolls, Mrs. DeWein also has over 1,000 of the special outfits manufactured by Mattel.

The history of "Barbie" has been fascinating, ever since the doll was the hit of the 1959 New York Toy Fair. "Barbie" was invented after Ruth Handler, the wife of Mattel's president "came up with the idea. She noticed that her daughter preferred playing with paper dolls which had adult clothes." Mattel had been trying since 1947 to get into the doll market, and was looking for something innovative and unusual.

"Mrs. Handler thought, 'Great, we'll put out a doll with a high fashion wardrobe,'" says Mrs. DeWein. After two years of planning, testing and manufacturing, "Barbie" came into being in 1959. "Barbie," by the way, is named after the Handlers' daughter; "Barbie's" boyfriend "Ken," when he came along in 1961, was named after their son.

Mrs. DeWein's collection of "Barbie" dolls indicates the major changes made in the manufacture of the product. "The first change was in 1964, with the 'Fashion Queen Barbie,'" she says. "This doll had a sculpted hairdo and came with three interchangeable wigs, instead of the traditional rooted hair."

In 1964, the first bendable-knee doll appeared — "Miss Barbie" — which was "also the only doll to have opening and closing eyes. She's very rare"; in 1966, "Barbie" had "hair you could change the color of." A major change, in 1967, brought the first "twist and turn Barbie," and "Barbie's first 'face-lift,'" when the doll's face and hairstyle were changed to reflect the longer-haired, youth conscious look of the time. Mrs. DeWein says that from 1968 to 1972,"'Barbie' talked, with a string-operated device in her chest."

Mattel had its first "Barbie"-related flop in 1967, with a black doll called "Francie." The doll had appeared the year before, "as 'Barbie's' cousin "Francie" who was, of course, white; the next year they used the same doll, but made her black, and the children just weren't ready for a black doll with the same name the next year." But, in 1968, when the company introduced "Christie," "Barbie"'s "black is beautiful friend" (as countless TV ads proclaimed),"she was instantly popular," Mrs. DeWein says.

In 1970, there was "Living Barbie," with almost human movement of wrists, ankles, elbows, waist, and so forth. "Malibu Barbie," a suntanned version, first appeared in 1971. When "Barbie" first came out, and for many years afterward, there was some concern voiced by parents that she was a little too mature for their children to play with. But, says Mrs. DeWein, "I doubt that she'll ever lose her substantial bosom."

"Barbie" and her friends have kept up with the times. "There's even an unauthorized imitation of 'Ken' put out, called 'Gay Bob,'"says Mrs. DeWein. "The joke in 'Barbie' circles is that when you put'Gay Bob' on the same shelf with 'Barbie' and 'Ken,' he takes 'Ken' away from 'Barbie.'

"'Barbie' was always a hit. The children adored her right from the start." The popularity of the doll can only be attributed to what Mrs. DeWein calls "the 'Barbie' mystique, that indescribable quality the doll has." She thinks it has a lot to do with "the fact that she's a perfect miniature fashion model. Even her clothes are beautifully designed and made fashions, not just doll clothes."

Mrs. DeWein really doesn't know "why I like collecting and researching 'Barbie.' I've never been able to tell why I find a hobby interesting." For many years, she was a wildflower buff, with the same passion now reserved for "Barbie." "Whatever I do, I do with gusto. I have to know everything about a subject."

She has used her store of knowledge in two "Barbie"-related books. *The Collector's Encyclopedia of Barbie Dolls* (Crown Publishers, 1976) was written in collaboration with Joan Ashabraner, another "Barbie" enthusiast, and is the complete story of "Barbie" dolls from their inception. A second book, *Collectible Barbie Dolls 1977-79* was published in 1980.

Mrs. DeWien isn't the only person out there who collects "Barbie" dolls. There are two newsletters, *The Barbie Gazette* and *Barbie Bulletin*, which reach over 1,000 readers nationwide. And, Mrs. DeWein says, there are at least 2,000 collectors who are members of the "Barbie" Collectors Club of California.

Because so many "Barbie" dolls have been made, there's a plentiful supply for collectors. It needn't cost a lot of money to begin a collection, either, says Mrs. De Wein. "Start where you are. Go to yard sales or flea markets and buy every 'Barbie,' 'Ken' or other related doll you can find for under $5. You can always trade your duplicates with another collector for something you really want," she says.

The most valuable "Barbie" product to collect is a 1959 mint condition (in the original box and unused, that is) "Barbie." "If you could find one, they're now worth about $850," she says. Other valuable collector's items are the "Barbie" with the movable eyes, the black "Francie" doll, and a 1965 "Barbie" "with her hair parted on the side. This is unique because most of the "Barbie"s made that year had their hair in a dutch bob," she says.

Mrs. DeWein will be happy to give advice on the collecting of "Barbie" and her friends, or to give information on the value, collectibility, or history of the dolls. She can be contacted at 1696 Valley Rd., Clarksville, TN 37040.

MAUDIE EASTWOOD
DOORKNOBS

Some PEOPLE COUNT sheep," cracks Maudie Eastwood. "I count doorknobs: brass ones, iron ones, glass ones; cast, blown, moulded, pressed, pleated; fire polished, wheel polished, glazed, silvered, Wedgewood, and Bennington."

All that counting has paid off for Mrs. Eastwood: she's the maven of American doorknobs, and has written the definitive reference book on the subject.

Mrs. Eastwood, who terms her interest in hardware "an outgrowth of an inner interest in things technical," has gathered doorknobs most of her life. It wasn't until 1972, when she had to retire from her beauty shop due to arthritis, that she really became a serious collector and historical researcher into these fascinating, everyday items that most people overlook as works of art.

Talking to Mrs. Eastwood, it's possible to get a sense of the many and varied delights of doorknob collecting. She has 1,500 of them in her eclectic collection, ranging from the more conventional, though highly attractive, brass, bronze, cast iron, wood, and glass knobs, to the exotic knobs made of abalone, ivory, horn, and hoof. The earliest knob in her collection is from 1827, and she doesn't have any more contemporary than 1920.

She is particularly proud of a "glorious 'bubble cushion'" doorknob, an octagon shaped-knob, roughly 3¼ inches across, made of colored glass and with silver bubbles inside. It was made around 1880, she says. Another pride and joy is an 1878 doorknob that came from the U.S. Capitol. "It's just such a fine knob," she says. "It's cast in bronze, with what we call a rope design. It's what you'd expect: elegant, but not tremendously ornamental."

Mrs. Eastwood's "original method of collecting was to stop in everywhere I could — antique shops, flea markets, and so on. Then, of course, when your friends find out you have a collection, they start looking around for you." But the greatest boon to Mrs. Eastwood's collecting came from a "good friend who traveled extensively around the United States. She was so well-acquainted with my collection, and with what I needed or wanted, that she was invaluable in picking up specimens for me."

"The fact that I have this collection isn't the most important thing," Mrs. Eastwood says. "I am a historian, and my interest in artifacts is minimal." She uses her collection of doorknobs as the basis for extensive research into the history and manufacture of these fascinating items.

According to Mrs. Eastwood, the earliest patented doorknob was manufactured in England about 1670. "They didn't issue patents before that time, but I imagine there were doorknobs, perhaps not as we know them, prior to then." Doorknobs probably originated in Germany, where "they had very fine ornamented locks in the 1400s. They were beautiful things, and had knobs of some kind, but not like ours today."

A lot of people credit Mrs. Eastwood with breaking ground in the hobby with her book *The Antique Doorknob*, published in 1976. It was the first compendium of information for the collector and sold well, Mrs. Eastwood says. "I had been collecting bits and pieces of information for five years without any idea of publishing," she says. "I was just trying to make a catalogue for my own use." She was prevailed upon to publish her work, and "in too great haste, I sat down and put the whole book together in six weeks time, which was not a sensible way to handle it at all."

Another soon-to-be-published book, three years in the making, will delve further into the history and collecting of doorknobs for both the individual and museum collector, she says.

Mrs. Eastwood feels it is still possible for someone to begin a doorknob collection, and fairly economically, too. "The market prices on doorknobs haven't really settled yet," she says, "because it's not known how many were made and which kinds are most desirable."

Among the most sought-after knobs by collectors: enameled, egg-shaped, or emblematic metal knobs; millefiori; cut or colored glass;hand-painted Limoges; Bennington doorknobs (but not the "mineral kind commonly passed off as Bennington"); hand-tooled wooden knobs; and knobs of exotic materials, she says.

She has sage advice for would-be collectors: "Pay attention to the inner voice and strike the words 'can't' and 'won't' from your vocabulary. Recognize opportunities. But if you are not naturally equipped with a deep interest, forget it."

Mrs. Eastwood has derived great pleasure from both the collecting and researching of her doorknobs. "At this point, she says, "the greatest benefit has been a greater understanding of my fellow man. I also find that it's been a marvelous way to improve my capacities after the age of 50. I've regained a certain sharpness and perception. It's been a means of developing more self-value."

Mrs. Eastwood is always glad to hear from fellow doorknob buffs — or offer advice to novices. She can be contacted at 3900 Latimer Rd. N., Tillamook, OR 97141.

CARL FAUSTER
LIBBEY GLASS

ONE MIGHT THINK that after 39 years as an advertising and marketing executive with the Libbey Glass Division of Owens-Illinois Corporation, Carl Fauster would be tired of glass when he retired in 1969. Instead, in his collecting of the product of his former employers, Fauster has become more than ever involved with the world of glass.

For 150 years, beginning in 1818, Libbey's fine, hand-cut lead glass (and that of its predecessor, New England Glass Company) was the standard of excellence in American glassmaking. Though the demand for hand-cut glass died gradually during this century, a legacy of artistry and true quality remained, and Fauster is one of the people responsible for keeping that artistry alive.

Fauster began collecting glass in 1951, after he had arranged the publicity for an exhibition of Libbey glass commemorating the Toledo Museum of Art's 50th anniversary. The museum was founded in 1901 by Edward Drummond Libbey, the president of the glass company.

"My personal interest in collectible glass began rather strangely," says Fauster. "I first collected glass 'whimseys,' novelty objects of glass made by the old-time glass blowers who made whatever suited them at a particular moment." Usually, Fauster says, these items were made during a slow time at the glassworks. The more popular whimsey items included canes, bells, pipes, spittoons, and paperweights. The history of the whimseys so fascinated Fauster, that he began collecting in earnest.

With this solid basis for his collection, Fauster branched out over the years into the more substantial pieces of Libbey cut glass (goblets, plates, chalices, vases, bowls, etc.), specializing in the so-called "brilliant period" glass from 1890-1915. Today, Fauster has nearly 300 pieces in his collection, and is considered one of the country's leading experts on Libbey glass.

The "crown jewel" of Fauster's collection is a brilliant-period cut glass punch bowl, the twin of one made in honor of President William McKinley in 1891. The original bowl was apparently accidentally destroyed by the White House, Fauster says. The bowl, 18 inches in diameter and weighing 75 pounds, was the largest single piece of cut glass ever made up to that time, according to Fauster.

With its special design of shields, stars, and stripes, the duplicate bowl was the hit of the 1904 St. Louis world's fair, and was promptly thereafter sold to a private collector.

The bowl disappeared from sight until 1967, when Fauster was organizing the activities for Libbey's 150th anniversary celebration. The owners of the bowl contacted Libbey with an offer to sell it back to the company. When the company indicated it was not interested in purchasing it, Fauster bought it for his own collection.

Incidentally, Fauster says, it was standard practice, "with a presentation bowl of this kind, to keep a backup piece" in case anything should happen to the original.

As a result of all the research Fauster did for his collection, he wrote and published a book on the subject. The book, *Libbey Glass Since 1818*, which was published in 1979, covers the history of the oldest, continuously operating glassmaking concern in America from its beginnings as New England Glass Company to the present day. Included in the 450 pages of text and photographs, are over 1,300 illustrations of items from Fauster's collection and other private and museum collections.

Glass collecting is currently the number two collecting hobby after stamps in the United States, Fauster says, attributing its popularity to the great variety of glass that can be collected. "Today's current escalation of interest in brilliant-period cut glass is just one facet of the general interest in glass of all makers, types, and colors," he says. And it is still possible, "for a small amount of money, to find a signed, authentic piece of brilliant-period cut glasss" which will only increase in value with the passage of time. "It's not as collectible as Tiffany yet, but some of the items available are coming pretty close to Tiffany's value," he says.

In general, Fauster urges beginning cut glass collectors to "discover and follow your basic interests." Don't try to collect everything, but narrow down your collecting to a manageable level.

Glass is "very, very appealing as a collectible because it is beautiful to look at, and the craftsmanship cannot be duplicated today," says Fauster. explaining why he enjoys collecting Libbey glass.

Fauster's book is available from the publisher, Len Beach Press, PO Box

7269 R.C., Toledo, OH 43615, at $30 per copy, plus $1.75 postage and handling.

Fauster is happy to counsel beginners, or hear from other Libbey glass collectors. He may be contacted at PO Box 7413, Toledo, OH 43615.

JIM FOX
LICENSE PLATES

I HAVE BEEN A collector of one thing or another since I can remember," says Jim Fox. That collection of "one thing or another" has grown into 20,000 license plates.

Fox, 33, who lives in Mentor, Ohio, has had a passionate interest in automobile license plates ever since he was seven years old. In 1954, a man who lived across the street from Fox in Cleveland Heights gave him a 1938 Ohio plate that was lying around in his garage. Fox started collecting plates then, "picking up a wagonful from gas stations in March and April" when the old license plates were changed for new ones. He had about 200 plates from Ohio and some other states when he lost interest at 10 and "discovered music."

By 1970, Fox was the drummer for The James Gang rock band, and was traveling all over the country. "I wondered if I could get a car plate from each state in the union." He managed — very well, indeed. He has gotten within 18 plates of having a complete collection of every year issued by every state.

Fox's main goal is to finish his collection of U.S. passenger car plates. But, "it has never been done," in the annals of license plate collecting, he says.

His favorite license plate of all was given to him by the Sheik of the Arab emirate of Abu Dhabi. It was in London, in 1971, where The James Gang was performing, that Fox spotted the plate. It was lying in the backseat of a Lamborghini in front of the hotel in which Fox was staying, a silver on red metal plate with "Abu Dhabi 4" on it.

"I just had to have it," says Fox. But how was he going to get it?

"I asked at the hotel desk who the car belonged to, but there was such heavy security they wouldn't tell me," he recalls. Finally, an Arab bellhop sidled up to him and let him know that it was the sheik's car. So, Fox called the sheik's suite on the house phone.

"After speaking with about four guys, someone got on the phone and said, 'This is the Sheik. Do you want that old thing? I'll be happy to give it to you.'" And soon, Fox said, the sheik stepped out of the elevator "with a greasy blonde on each arm and half a dozen bodyguards" and presented the astounded Fox with the license plate.

Getting the plate is a coup, say Fox, because "you could write to Abu Dhabi for a hundred years and get no answer."

It was during this time, too, that Fox discovered the Automobile License Plate Collectors Association, the national hobbyist organization of license plate collectors. "That was like popping the cork" on his interest. "because I discovered I was not the only lunatic collecting the things. It was like a candy store through the mail" when he discovered he could trade license plates with other collectors.

In addition to trading, it is also necessary to purchase plates to build a collection, Fox says. "A guy with a little perserverance and a few dollars to spend" can usually get almost any plate he wants. They range in price from $5 up, although certain hard-to-get specimens are frequently not available at any price.

"The price is 100 percent related to what someone wants and how much he wants it," says Fox. He cites as an example a 1921 Alaska license plate. There are only two known to exist, one of which is on the kitchen wall of an elderly fellow's house in Anchorage. "I don't think $100,000 would do it, " he laughs.

For the beginning plate collector, Fox advises, "Collect the choicest pieces available. Don't be afraid to ask anyone, anywhere!" Many times, he says, he wouldn't have gotten the plates he has if he hadn't "hit a junkyard in my knee boots and bothered" to wade through piles of rubble to get at a plate.

Fox will be happy to counsel license plate collectors. He can be contacted at 10176 Page Dr., Mentor, OH 44060.

ROBERT FRATKIN
POLITICAL CAMPAIGN MEMORABILIA

WITH THE ELECTION comes the end of the political campaign. After the tumult and shouting have died down, there isn't much call for all the buttons, badges, ribbons, banners, pamphlets, posters, and other flotsam and jetsam of the campaign...or is there?

For Robert Fratkin and more than 3,000 members of the American Political Item Collectors (APIC), every election is a win, regardless of the outcome, for they can obtain important and valuable items to add to their collections.

Fratkin, 41, is an investment executive who lives in Washington, D. C. For the last 20 years, he has been collecting campaign memorabilia relating to U. S. presidential elections.

He first became interested in political collecting in 1960 when he worked in the Adlai Stevenson and the John F. Kennedy campaigns in Los Angeles."I just liked the artifacts," Fratkin says, "I realized that all those things are very important. You can learn a great deal about the history of U.S. society and culture by examining them."

It's possible, Fratkin says, to trace the development of presidential campaign strategies through campaign buttons. For example, in 1930, the buttons were smaller, with lots of words crammed onto them. Today, the buttons are bigger, with just a couple of words, and they're less attractive and less of them are made.

"People used to be proud to wear campaign buttons," Fratkin says. "They were excited about politics, and you could tell where someone stood by the button he was wearing. Then you'd either agree and shake hands" or have a political argument.

"One of the great banes of American civilization was the invention of air-conditioning," Fratkin feels." Now people just sit home and watch TV and don't want to get involved." So, politicians are turning more and more to TV as the major campaign aid, and less and less to the use of buttons, pamphlets, and the like.

The dividing line in the collection of campaign memorabilia begins in 1896 with William McKinley, as he was the first president to serve in the 20th century. Fratkin collects from 1896 forward, and estimates that he has over 20,000 items of all kinds in his collection. Perhaps his most interesting piece is a 1¼-inch Hoover-Curtis red, white, blue and gold "jewgate" campaign button. A jewgate is a yoke-like double button with the pictures of both a presidential and vice-presidential candidate on it.

What's the one item every collector would like to have in his collection? Probably a James Cox-Franklin D. Roosevelt jewgate from the 1920 presidential campaign. Fratkin estimates that it would be worth about $3,000 if it were available.

Another interesting aspect of this kind of collecting is the potential investment value. Political items have been recognized by investors and financial publications as being a good investment, Fratkin says, because "over the last 10 years, their value has outpaced the rate of inflation." Something that might have sold for $100 10 years ago, now brings $400-500 on the market.

How does someone get involved with collecting these items? The best way is to do some research. Once a person has a feel for the field, then it makes it a lot easier — and more fun — to be a collector. Among the presidential candidates, Fratkin feels that the campaign paraphernalia of Dwight Eisenhower, Thomas E. Dewey, Wendell Wilkie, William H. Taft, and Lyndon Johnson are probably the most undervauled and therefore most reasonable to collect. But, it can be fairly expensive. He emphasizes,"Don't buy cheap; buy the best you can afford. Cheap things are common and are likely to remain common."

Campaign materials can be found almost anywhere — in attics, basements, flea markets, antique shops — and at almost any price. Interestingly, the age of a particular item does not necessarily guarantee its value. For example, an 1896 McKinley button might only bring $5, while a similar item for the Cox campaign in 1920 would be worth $50.

Fratkin has been president, since 1978, of APIC, which is the nationwide organization for collectors. He suggests that people interested in collecting these items join the organization, as it gives them an opportunity to learn quickly about the field through the group's publications and other members. Memberships, at $12.50 per year, are obtainable from Joseph Hayes, 1054 Sharpsburg Dr., Huntsville, AL 35803.

MYRON FREEDMAN
CIGAR BANDS

WHEN MYRON FREEDMAN was growing up in Chicago, he had a large stamp and coin collection. But, in 1959, it all went up in smoke — cigar smoke. That's when Freedman acquired the small collection of cigar bands that became his burning passion. Today, Freedman, an aerospace engineer in Tucson, is an authority on cigar bands, cigar box labels, and other kinds of seals and labels.

"I was an avid coin and stamp collector. But I reached a point where I had all the stamps I needed to complete my collection, except for the expensive and hard-to-find ones," he says. "I don't like to buy and don't like to compete with a thousand other people, so I sold both collections," he says.

Freedman "happened on an old collection of my father's that he had put together in 1937, with some 200 bands. I held on to it." That formed the basis for his present collection, which today he conservatively estimates at 60,000 cigar bands, covering the years 1890 to the present. "That's not a large collection" he says. "There are a few 300,000 band collectors." He specializes in United States, Cuban, Canadian, and Mexican cigar bands, and some antique European sets, all displayed in albums like stamps.

Cigar band collecting is very popular in Europe, and "since World War II, European manufacturers have been making special sets of cigar bands just for collectors." But the heyday of the cigar band, says Freedman, was from the turn of the century to just prior to the 1920s. "The bands were beautiful works of art. What you see on a cigar today is nothing but printing. The old ones had lithographed pictures. I appreciate the artwork."

Among the highlights of his collection, say Freedman, is a 1910 set of all the state seals of the United States, and five different sets of U.S. Presidents, which he says "were a popular subject for cigar bands."

According to Freedman, the lithography company would either develop the design and sell it to a cigar company, or patent and register it and use it for themselves. Many lithographers also made cigar boxes and/or cigars. "There's no clear-cut line as to who was a box maker, label maker or cigar band maker."

"In the early days, the cigar bands were what sold the cigar." He says the cigars were stacked on a saloon bar or a cigar counter, and people would buy certain brands because "Teddy Roosevelt or Anna Held, or some great musician, artist, actor, or racehorse was pictured on the band."

Freedman is executive secretary of the International Seal, Label and Cigar Band Society. The society, which includes collectors of cigar box labels, liquor labels, and such items as Christmas and Easter seals, has about 200 members. Freedman says the group is "not close-knit at all. We've never had a convention and never will." It was started in 1956, by a former member of the defunct International Cigar Band Society that had flourished in the 1930s, who decided to reinstitute a collector's organization.

Freedman is also the publisher of the first cigar band catalogue ever printed in the U.S. With another cigar band collector, Harry Copleston, he wrote *The Cigar Band Catalogue* in 1975. It covered the history of the manufacturers that were then still in business. Freedman says about 125,000 different cigar bands were identified and discussed in the volume. The book was privately printed and sold out two printings.

Cigar band collectors are what Freedman terms "secret collectors. They don't let other people know about what they collect. I can't quite understand why. Maybe they feel people will think it's odd. I am a collector by nature. If I wasn't collecting cigar bands, it would be something else."

Cigar band collecting is generally an inexpensive hobby, says Freedman.

"Most collectors like to trade between themselves, although I sometimes do buy particualrly interesting ones." He says cigar band collectors "try to keep the hobby on this trading basis. The minute you push up prices, you attract people who are not interested in collecting but in investing. Too many hobbies have been ruined by investors."

It would be difficult, but still possible, to start a cigar band collection today, says Freedman. "Go to flea markets, antique stores, and the like. You never know where they'll turn up. Also, talk about your interest. Often people will give you an old collection that's just sitting around their attic."

To the novice cigar band collector, Freedman advises, "Go slow, and acquire early material from smokers in your family or among your friends." He also suggests joining the International Seal, Label and Cigar Band Society. Both Freedman and the organization can be contacted at 8915 E. Bellevue St., Tucson, AZ 85715.

PAT HAMMOND
KITES

MY THEORY of aerodynamics," says Pat Hammond about kite flying, "is 'name them, they fly better.'"

There must be something to it, because her delta-wing, red nylon kite "Red Tails on the Sunset" soared to first place in the Smithsonian Institution's National Kite Competition in 1972.

"That was my first and last kite competition," adds Mrs. Hammond, who's known around San Antonio, Texas, as "the Kite Lady." But she's found her niche in the kite world, as the owner of the largest collection of kites in the U.S., as an expert on kite construction, lore, and design, and as a warmly winning philosopher on kites and the human experience

According to Mrs.Hammond, "The kites found me. I didn't find them." She started with a collection of 50 or 60 kites, displayed on the gallery walls of her home. Many of them had come to her from her brother, who was a doctor in Vietnam. The family lived next door to the mayor of Alamo Heights, Texas, and when Mrs. Hammond found out about the kite contest, she asked him if she could fly a kite in the competition named after their community. "I was going to call it "Alamo Heights," if it flew, 'The Fall of the Alamo' if it didn't," she laughs. The mayor was so taken with the idea "he issued a proclamation about it."

The kite flew — even when she changed the name. "Oh, it was just a magic kite. When it won, that was a sign to me to look at kites in a bit of a different way," she recalls.

She began collecting kites in earnest — and learned how to build them herself. "The more I fooled with them, I discovered there was more than meets the eye — or more than meets the sky." Soon she had 500 kites, and is collecting and making more all the time.

"As a collector, I never feel I possess a kite before I give it back to the sky. I feel as though I've borrowed them from the sky," she says.

Where do kites come from? There's no such thing as an antique kite, says Mrs. Hammond, "because they aren't meant to last. What first gives the kite life is the air. What you see is a means to understanding the unseen."

No one really knows when the first kite was flown, but it must have happened when "man had the desire to become something more, the desire to fly. It came long before man could leave the ground," she says.

Her favorite kite was one she saw in a small village in Mexico. As she was driving through the interior of the country, "a boy suddenly appeared, flying a kite made from the back pages of a funny book, with struts made of turkey or chicken feathers. The string was a collection of scraps, all tied together. But that kite was the most responsive kite I've ever seen."

"That little boy had never heard of anything theoretical" about kites; "it was an experience he had for himself."

Mrs. Hammond not only collects kites; she collects anything and everything concerning them: blueprints of early box kites, children's books, photographs, scientific monographs, and the like. She also teaches school children and other groups how to make and fly kites.

But Mrs. Hammond is most at home with the spiritual nature of kites and kiteflying. "If you want to use a kite as a metaphor," she says, "it is this: no two kites have ever been alike, no two kites have ever been flown in the same wind."

She loves kites because "they're dependent on the wind that is invisible to give them life. They're basically just string, sticks, and paper, yet with the wind they become something more."

It is the wind that truly fascinates Hammond. "In Latin, Hebrew, Greek and about 35 other languages, the word for wind and spirit are the same." And it is that invisible essence of spirit that she tries to capture in her building, studying, and flying of kites.

Kites are important to the human experience, she feels, because "they literally fly across barriers. Everybody responds to them."

Mrs. Hammond is high on anyone learning about kites. "Try it or fly it...you'll like it." she enthuses. "A flight in the mind's eye is just as valid as one 10 miles up."

"The persistence is more enduring than the failures. Man pulled his way to the moon by his kite strings," she says.

RON HARTMANN
JAPANESE SWORDS

Y OU CAN COLLECT them all of your life and still not be an expert," says Ron Hartmann. And that is one important reason why he enjoys collecting Japanese samurai swords.

Since the proper understanding and appreciation of valuable art swords from

Japan requires much detailed study, and many of the research materials are in Japanese or unavailable in the United States, the 43-year-old project engineer for Anheuser-Busch has found his interest to be a challenging one.

Hartmann "always enjoyed edged weapons, and collected swords when I was a kid." When he obtained his first two Japanese samurai swords (one from the early 1600s and one of World War II vintage) in 1965, the subsequent research "captivated my somewhat eccentric thinking, and soon I was captured by this field of collecting."

He soon discovered there were other people who had been "captured" by the unique and interesting swords, and that there was a national organization, the Japanese Sword society of the U.S., the largest group of its kind in the world, outside of Japan. He joined, became involved with the group, and today serves as treasurer, as well as the editor of the Society's newsletter (which goes bi-monthly to some 250 people in the U.S. and abroad).

For Hartmann, "perfection is the key to collecting Japanese art swords." Therefore, his own collection contains only about 25 at the present time. Though he is reluctant to describe any of them in detail, or put values on the swords he does have ("the rash of burglaries of sword collectors lately makes me hesitant"), Hartmann is clearly proud of what he has collected, and has constructed a special sword room in the basement of his St. Louis home to display them. Not only does Hartmann collect the swords, but also related objects such as hilt ornaments, armor and sword guards.

To perfect the swords he has collected, it is frequently necessary to have the blades polished. This is a time-consuming, costly process that can only be done in Japan. "You have to find someone you can trust" to do the job, says Hartmann.

According to Hartmann, there are still a great many of the swords available, though in recent years "the Japanese have bought and taken back literally truckloads." However, it is still fairly easy to come across fine swords, mainly of the World War II vintage, at prices ranging upward from $200.

The best way to get started with a collection, Hartmann says, is to buy a sword or two. And the best place to buy swords is from another collector. The Japanese Sword Society can help in this, because of its list of members (which every new member receives) and its publications, which frequently advertise swords for sale. Once a collector has several swords, he can utilize them to trade up in quality and price.

"Avoid being influenced by the Almighty Dollar, which quickly becomes evident in this field of collecting," Hartmann counsels. " It is expensive, and profits can be made, but maintaining a 'pure' attitude toward this art form can give great pleasure through the enjoyment of something unique, beautiful and rare."

Hartmann would "like to offer my services to anyone who wishes to research a Japanese sword or dagger." Obviously, he is always eager to puchase items for his own collection. But, if research is the request, "that is handled as such, without any pressuring on my part." For further information on the swords or the Japanese Sword Society in the U.S., contact Hartmann at 5907 Deerwood Dr., St. Louis, MO 63123.

JAY HICKERSON
OLD-TIME RADIO

BEFORE TV TOOK over the American consciousness, imaginations were stimulated, creativity inspired and a whole generation entertained by radio. Along with the great stars of stage and film who brightened the airwaves, an entirely new batch of personalities developed directly as a result of their performances and appearances on radio.

Alas, this world of imagination limited only by the listener's mind, was limited itself to relatively few short years. But Jay Hickerson, and others like him, still hear those long-ago voices and keep them sparklingly alive, through the collection of old-time radio shows.

Hickerson, 45, has been collecting since 1970. As a professional pianist, he collected theme songs of radio and TV shows to use in his act. He would play them and ask his audience to identify them. Through a friend, he acquired four reels of tape, with about 100 old original radio broadcasts on them. He liked what he heard and, armed with those shows, a primitive catalogue, and two tape recorders, he "invaded the world of experienced collectors."

He now has tapes of approximately 6,000 programs, spanning the entire Golden Age of Radio in the 1930s and 1940s. He claims to have the largest collection of Jack Benny radio broadcasts (some 305 of them) in existence, including Benny's very first show in 1930.

Hickerson also specializes in the "Suspense" and "Lux Radio Theatre" shows. He has every episode of "Suspense," which was a program devoted to chilling plays and horror stories, from 1942-62. His collection of "Lux Radio Theatre" tapes spans the entire existence of the show (1935-53) which presented adaptations of films and plays, often starring the actors who originally appeared in them on stage or screen. Over 150 different bandleaders are represented in his collection of big band braodcast tapes.

A most intriguing characteristic of radio show buffs is that they all trade their shows with each other, usually without any financial remuneration. Hickerson says it's "all done on the honor system;" each old time radio buff has a catalogue of the items that he owns and wants to own, and collectors trade around in this fashion.

"Old-time radio is not as popular as comic books," says Hickerson "mainly because there's no money value to the broadcasts." As a result, he says, it is one of the least popular of the "fan" hobbies. There are only about 1,000 people in the country who actively collect and trade.

There are always new transcriptions of shows being discovered, says Hickerson, so there is plenty of material to collect and trade.

Hickerson hasn't been content with just collecting all of these radio shows. He has been publishing a monthly newsletter, *Hello Again*, (the phrase was the popular catchword of Jack Benny) since 1970. These few mimeographed pages, with news about radio show collectors and the personalities of that bygone era, along with information about collectors' wants and needs, has become the oldest, most respected, and most widely read in the hobby, with 300 subscribers all over the United States.

For the last 10 years, Hickerson has run annual old-time radio conventions near his Orange, Connecticut, home. These weekend-long affairs feature seminars on various aspects of old-time radio, and provide opportunities for buffs to meet each other, trade shows, and meet some of the stars of old-time radio whom Hickerson always manages to have present. According to Hickerson, "This is the only convention of its kind in the country, and it's getting more and more popular each year."

Hickerson has gotten a great deal of pleasure from his hobby. "I tend to be somewhat nostalgic, so I enjoy listening to and collecting the programs," says Hickerson. "And I also enjoy the correspondence with people around the country and meeting them at conventions."

For Hickerson, a fascination with old radio shows is easily explainable. "It is something you hear, not see. I have a vivid imagination, and the shows appeal to it. Also they are a reflection of society at the time of the show."

The old radio shows are important historic documents, too, Hickerson feels. "There are many visual records of Jack Benny, but we need to know what he sounded like, too."

All in all, "just using your imagination is the most important. Many people today don't know how to do that."

The novice radio show collector need only have a reel-to-reel tape recorder and contact with other collectors, to begin in the hobby. Hickerson can supply information on reputable dealers in radio show broadcast tapes, and a list of all hobbyist clubs and publications on request. He also suggests subscribing to his newsletter. A sample copy will be sent if he receives a stamped, self-addressed envelope.

To contact him, or to subscribe to *Hello Again* ($6 for a one-year subscription), write PO Box C, Orange, CT 06477.

LEO & LUETTA HIRTZ
HAND-WIND PHONOGRAPHS

THE INVENTION OF THE phonograph by Thomas Edison in 1877 started a new era in entertainment. Soon, hand-wound phonographs, using wax cylinders or metal discs, were making music in the parlors of many an American home.

Today, some of those phonographs are still playing their old songs, thanks to Leo and Luetta Hirtz, a Bernard, Iowa, couple who collect and restore the machines and the recordings that were played on them.

Hirtz, 65, a farmer and farm equipment dealer, says, "I lived in the days before radio, when the phonograph was our main source of home entertainment." Thus, he had an old cylinder phonograph from his family, and his wife had a disc machine that had belonged to hers.

"We didn't know for many years there were still any spare parts around," Hirtz says. But they did find some, and decided to fix up the two machines they had.

"They sounded so good again after about 50 years of silence" that Hirtz says he and his wife were inspired to continue collecting and restoring old phonographs. After their family of eight daughters was raised, "we had a little extra money to pursue this hobby...and are thoroughly enjoying it."

At present, the Hirtzes have a collection of 150 hand-wound phonographs, including some 40 or 50 external horn machines dating from the turn of the century. The most common of the machines was the Edison Standard, a wax cylinder model, which first had two minutes, and later, four minutes, of recording per cylinder. These machines, which sold for $20 when they were new, had a 14-inch horn as an amplifier. The first disc machines were made in 1912-15, says Hirtz.

Among the machines Hirtz is especially fond of — a 1909 Edison "Amberola," a large phonograph that used both two- and four-minute records. "It has an ugly cabinet," says Hirtz, "but it's quite a piece of mechanism." This was one of Edison's deluxe models.

"Out here in the Midwest, we farmers all bought the cheapies," he says. "The Easterners all bought the deluxe models." So, when an Eastern phonograph enthusiast comes out Hirtz's way, "he's excited by all our cheapies...and our hearts beat a big thump when we see the deluxes back East."

In addition to the cylinder and disc phonographs, the Hirtzes also own 20 Edison "long-playing phonographs." These machines, which Hirtz says were "highly unsuccessful" when they were manufactured, had 12-inch discs that played for 20 minutes, using a tiny pointed needle.

With such a collection of machinery, the Hirtzes naturally needed something to play on all the phonographs. They obtained their first 100 recordings from a woman in Dubuque, Iowa, who sold them with a phonograph for $100 in 1958. Now, their collection has grown to some 600 discs and 1,900 wax cylinders, as well as 1,000 78-rpm records, and includes some "personality" cylinder recordings of William Howard Taft, William Jennings Bryan, Thomas Edison, Sophie Tucker, Theodore Roosevelt, and others.

Though it might seem a problem to have 150 phonographs around the house, Hirtz says it's not so bad. "It's a good thing I have an understanding wife," he laughs. They only keep one phonograph in the living room at a time, the rest are scattered around the house, the attic, and in Hirtz's workshop. Hirtz is proud of the fact that "all of the machines can be played."

"Our aim is to restore them, but not so well that they look like new," he says, adding that their desire is to make the machines authentic, but giving the appearance of having been used. He estimates that it takes about 25 hours of work, on the average, to put an old phonograph into working order. He has been busy over the last few years doing restoration jobs not only on his own machines, but for other phonograph collectors from all over the United States.

Hirtz does the mechanical repairs, while his wife restores the woodwork of the cabinets. Hirtz is able to obtain original parts for his machines, which gives him "the satisfaction of knowing that most of our machines are strictly original," he says.

Hirtz is enthusiastic about the collection and restoration of the old machines, and encourages people to become interested in the hobby. He says that the Midwest is still the best place to find the "cheapies," adding that many phonographs can be purchased through collectors' and dealers' advertisements in such magazines as *Antique Phonograph Monthly*.

Phonograph buffs gather annually in Union, Illinois, for a weekend of exchanging ideas and parts for machines. "It amazes me that so many younger people really are enthusiastic over the old music machines," says Hirtz.

For the novice phonograph collector/restorer, Hirtz advises, "Don't pay a big price for this stuff unless you know for sure it's rare and worth it."

The biggest satisfaction Hirtz gets from his restoring and collecting is "taking an old piece of equipment that hasn't talked in 40 or 50 years, and making it talk again."

Will his collection of phonographs be passed down to his children or grandchildren? "It's 100 percent O.K. with my kids that I'll enjoy them [the phonographs] while I'm here, and when I croak, they can have the biggest auction in the country."

Hirtz will be happy to counsel restorers or collectors of hand-wound phonographs. He can be reached PO Box 6, Bernard, IA 52032.

DOUG HODGE
WORLD WAR II RADIO

DURING WORLD WAR II, radio brought the realities of war into people's homes for the first time. Just as television would bring the sights of the Vietnam War into America's living rooms a couple of decades later, radio in the 1940s provided an earlier generation with their first sounds of battle.

To Doug Hodge, those broadcasts provide a fascinating mirror of the past. He has acquired a collection of over 20,000 World War II-vintage broadcasts, the majority of them documentaries, the actual history-making sounds recorded during the conflict.

Hodge's interest developed while he was a Hollywood cinematographer, working on commericals and a few films which brought him in contact with many of the people involved in the golden age of radio. In 1970, a former radio actor gave him a tape of an old show. Hodge was so interested in it that he soon began collecting and swapping entertainment programs with other buffs.

"As I listened to some of the old programs," he recalls, "I found the relation of the broadcasts to actual events fascinating. History had always seemed so dry in school, but these recordings made it real, as if I were actually a witness to the events as they happened."

Hodge thinks these broadcasts are superior to TV or filmed journalism. "It was actually more vivid than visual accounts, for the radio newsmen were required to describe the event with words. From there, the mind forms the images." Striking ones they were, too.

When he moved to Hawaii in 1977, he went to the *U.S.S. Arizona* monument. He was surprised to discover that there were no recordings about the Pearl Harbor attack of December 7, 1941 on sale. So, working in his Honolulu studio, he created the record album "December 7, 1941 — Day of Infamy," which is now sold, among other places, at the monument.

This recording sparked a demand for more records about various aspects of World War II, using the actual voices, sounds, and personalities of the era. He is now working on six more World War II-related albums. "Prelude to Global War" will concern itself with Europe prior to the commencing of hostilities. He also plans to issue other albums on the European Theater, as well as on the Pacific Theater, D-Day, VE-Day, and VJ-Day.

As a spinoff of his interest in World War II broadcasting, Hodge has amassed a collection of wartime songs. This was music geared "to encourage the civilian population" to greater participation in the war effort. He also conducts oral history interviews with eyewitnesses to the Pearl Harbor bombing, as well as with participants in other important Pacifc battles.

One of his most valuable and interesting broadcasts is an eyewitness account of the Pearl Harbor bombing, transmitted by phone from Honolulu to New York City at the height of the attack. On the tape, a local NBC radio correspondent, on the roof of the *Honolulu Advertiser* building describes what he is seeing. "I've never been able to locate the man who made the broadcast," says Hodge, "or learn anything about him. The broadcast was interrupted by the telephone company disconnecting the line so that emergency calls could be placed."

Hodge has turned his oral history interest to preserving Hawaiian history and culture. He is working on a series of recordings of legends of Hawaii, utilizing Islanders who will tell legends and play native music on traditioanl instruments. He's also collected some interviews relating to the 1924 explosion of Kilauea volcano.

Hodge has the distinction of being the first person ever to record the Kilauea volcano while it was erupting. In 1979, when the last eruption of the volcano occurred, the National Park Service allowed Hodge to record it. "I've got over 24 hours of recording with spectacular sounds," he says. His soundtrack will be used on a *National Geographic* special about volcanos. "Up until now, the volcano sounds you hear in most films have been manufactured by the filmmakers."

He feels having an interest, and making that interest truly a part of a person's daily life, is very important. "Find something that you like to do so well that you'd do it for free — and then dedicate yourself to it," Hodge says. For the person who thinks he might be interested in oral history or the collection of recorded moments from the past, he urges, "Ask questions. There are people in this world who have an incredible amount of information stored in their minds, that they will willingly share if someone would simply bother to ask."

Hodge finds his avocation (which has now become a full-time pursuit) rewarding. "One of the nicest rewards of attempting something innovative is receiving a favorable response," he says. He has received many letters from young people saying that they never actually realized what happened at Pearl Harbor and how, "after hearing the album, they had some idea of what their parents must have felt during the first days of World War II."

Contact Hodge at PO Box 25851, Honolulu, HI 96825 for further information.

NEAL HOSPERS

HOTEL/MOTEL MATCHCOVERS

M Y LIFE CAREER was determined through matchcover collecting," Neal Hospers says. Not only has he had a 38-year career in the hotel and motel industry — he now owns the world's largest collection of hotel/motel matchcovers as well.

At the age of 11, Hospers took a Christmas holiday trip with his parents from Flint, Michigan, to New Orleans. "We stopped at eight different hotels on our trip down and back," Hospers recalls, "and I picked up everything from post cards, wrappers, matchcovers, and stationery, to ashtrays at each of the hotels we visited."

Once he got home, he stored them in the basement. But the following summer, "when matchcover collecting became the neighborhood fad, I remembered that I had collected match folders on the trip, so I dug them out. Since they were all from hotels, I decided right then and there to collect only hotel covers."

Soon, Hospers started playing hotel, and when friends and relatives stayed at his home, "I made them register and pay a penny per night for their accomodations." He even played bellhop, and had a guest register for them to write their comments in as they left. He was also expanding his matchcover collection by corresponding with hotels in the Caribbean, England, Canada and Mexico, the only countries outside the U.S. producing advertising matchcovers at that time.

His first job was as a summer bellhop at the famous Santa Maria Inn in Santa Maria, California, in 1942. From there, it was on to Cornell's School of Hotel Administration, and a career in hotel and food service management that eventually brought him to Ft. Worth, Texas. Today, he's the operator of a restaurant, a real estate concern, and the Ft. Worth Grey Line Tours franchise. All along the way, he's collected matchcovers.

Hospers has an astounding 37,000 covers in his collection, including matchcovers dating back to early in the century. The covers (he always removes the matches for safety's sake) are mounted in over 250 albums in his study, all catalogued and cross-referenced. Among his favorite items is a 1911 matchcover from Atlantic City's famed Chalfont-Haddon Hall Hotel, with a picture of the venerable hotel as it looked at the time. His 1,900 Texas covers present "virtually a history of lodging throughout the state."

He joined the Rathkamp Matchcover Society (RMS), the premier organization for matchcover collectors, in 1942 and is now the 21st oldest member in length of membership in the club. His association with the RMS has put him in touch with over 3,000 other matchcover collectors in the U.S. and Canada.

Hospers was the host for the RMS national convention in Ft. Worth in 1978. One of the highlights of the convention was a tour, arranged by Hospers, of the nearby Atlas Match Factory, one of the nation's leading suppliers of matches.

Hospers credits the popularity of the matchcover hobby to several factors. First, and foremost, it is inexpensive and easy to begin a collection. He acquired a lot of his matches simply by trading covers with other collectors, as well as picking up covers while traveling and relying on friends to do the same. In addition, matchcover collecting is "kind of a folksy thing. Lots of collectors spend time corresponding with each other and getting together to swap covers and talk about their collections."

"I have the most fun with my collection when someone visits and says, 'I bet you don't have a matchcover from Flin Flon, Manitoba,' for instance, and I'll go look in my collection and inevitably I'll have one from there. People get a kick out of that," he says.

Hospers is always glad to hear from fellow hotel/motel matchcover collectors, and will be happy to counsel beginners in the field. He can be reached at 316 Ridgewood Rd., Ft. Worth, TX 76107.

TONY HYMAN
CIGAR BOXES

IN THE LAST 100 YEARS, there've been 500,000,000,000 cigars made — and almost all of them have been sold out of a box. In that same period, there have been over 2,000,000 different brands of cigars, and many times that number of different styles of boxes.

Surprising as these statistics might be, for people like Tony Hyman of Elmira, N.Y., they represent the almost limitless possibilities for collecting cigar boxes, which Hyman terms "the greatest as-yet-undiscovered hobby that exists today."

Hyman was attracted to cigar boxes at the age of 12 because of his desire to collect something and "because of their cost — free!" The first two boxes he collected were for King Edward and Red Dot cigars. "They represented the two great traditions of cigarmaking: the East and the South," he says. He used to pick up his boxes at liquor and drug stores in California when he was a youngster. Later, while traveling in the service, he would find cigar boxes that were "particularly unusual" and send them home to his parents to store for him.

Today, an entire room in Hyman's house is devoted to his collection of 4,000 boxes. He only displays about 300 items at a time (the rest are all packed in carefully labeled cartons), for the room also contains a desk, typewriter, his research materials, and an extensive library of other historical items about the industry. "I consider myself a very serious amateur historian of the industry," he says. He has photos, trade catalogues, and every book since the 1830s on the cigar industry. "I collect anything that will help fill in the giant jigsaw puzzle that is the cigar industry," he says.

Hyman collects cigar boxes from three different perspectives: One category is the cigar box as three-dimensional sculpture ("it's the answer to a design problem of packaging a certain quantity of three-dimensional products"). This includes boxes shaped like beer steins, bottles, mailboxes, log cabins, and made of inlaid wood, serpentine, pressed glass, and other unusual materials.

He collects other boxes for the advertising content of the label. "The exotic labels were not created to sell the full box, but to attract the guy with a couple of nickels in his pocket," Hyman says. So, the labels featured highly artistic lithography picturing nudes, sports figures, generals, and other personages;sometimes jokes and puns were illustrated.

Finally, Hyman collects boxes that can be viewed as "historic artifacts," for they tell something about the times in which they were made. Among these boxes are labels from 1865-90 with Negro humor, anti-Chinese labels from the 1870s, boxes that held "health cigars" and "chlorophyll cigars." The treasure-hunting aspects of cigar box collecting are "very appealing," he says. "The variety is, for practical purposes, virtually endless. I've handled 50,000 boxes and learn something new monthly."

During the heyday of cigar production in America, there were 100,000 U.S. factories. In addition, cigars were produced by wholesalers, retailers, and private individuals. At one time a person could have his own private cigar brand, with a picture of his home, his family, his yacht or a favorite pet for $3. "These were throwaway items that people put a lot of thought into. I'm fascinated with the ingenuity that results when a lot of people are let loose on the same problem," says Hyman.

The cigar was a phenomenon of industrialization and urbanization, says Hyman, and replaced chewing tobacco, because it was "difficult to deal with chewing, spitting, and drooling" in the more sophisticated society that emerged after the Civil War.

Cigar box collecting is "still a wide open field," says Hyman, adding that good and interesting cigar boxes can be had in flea markets, antique stores, and the like for an average of $3-$5 per box. And everyone, in a very short time, can have an interesting collection. "I've never met a box collector who didn't have really fine items in his collection, items that I would like to have in mine," Hyman says.

In 1978, Hyman was asked to be the curator of a major exhibition at Elmira's Arnot Art Museum titled "The Cigar Box, A Century of Packaging Art, 1860-1960." He designed the exhibit and selected the material to be presented, depicting the best of the known examples of cigar box design and cigar label printing, as well as displaying some cigar production equipment.

As an offshoot of the exhibition, Hyman wrote and published, in cooperation with the museum, *The Handbook of American Cigar Boxes*. The book, which sells for $27.50, is a compendium of historical data on the cigar industry, illustrated with pictures of many notable cigar boxes. Hyman says the book has already, in the one year it has been out, become the standard for cigar box collectors.

In addition, Hyman has also become an authority on the value of cigar boxes. He has appraised cigar boxes in the collections of the Smithsonian Institution, the American Antiquarian Society, and museums. He will usually do appraisals of cigar boxes at no charge, if the questioner will send complete details and a self-addressed, stamped envelope for reply. He needs to have the brand name, box size in inches, description of the inner label, the date of the tax stamp (or its length if date is unknown), the factory number, and the tax district on the box in order to give an accurate appraisal.

Oh yes, Hyman smokes cigars. "I like the cheap domestic ones," he laughs.

Hyman can be contacted through the Arnot Art Museum, 235 Lake St., Elmira, NY 14901 for further information on cigar box appraisals or to purchase a copy of his book.

JAY KETELLE
AUTO AD POSTCARDS

THE PICTURE POSTCARD has been one of the most popular (and effective) tools for advertising new model cars and trucks. Annually, the manufacturers issue advertising postcards, depicting the newest models, inviting the consumer to stop by his nearby dealership and test-drive the car of his choice. This has been a popular practice since the very beginnings of the commercial auto industry, and Jay Ketelle, of Amarillo, Texas, has become an avid collector of, and expert on, the advertising postcards.

Ketelle, 45, has been collecting since 1975. He was always interested in cars and started accumulating books about automobiles at an early age. "I never knew anyone collected the cards," he says, until he was given 30 of them. Then he found out that, indeed, a lot of other people were interested in the same thing.

His collection has grown to around 3,000 cards. That's small, he says, but it is small because he specializes. Ketelle only collects cards advertising convertibles, station wagons, and trucks, plus a special series of 1,777 different cards made in 1940-1958 for car dealers.

These special cards, featuring a variety of popular models, were "made for new car dealers. They could order by model and year, and when a car was traded in on a new car, they used this card to inform potential buyers that this particular used car was available." The company that manufactured the cards, Dealer Supply Co., is still in business, and Ketelle was able to talk with its original owner and president. He was given an order blank listing all of the cards the firm produced in this series, which he uses as a checklist in building his collection. Thus far, Ketelle reports, he has been able to collect most of them.

Some of the cards in Ketelle's collection are quite unusual — and different in concept from the more traditional advertising postcard. While he has a few going back as far as 1902, it is the cards of somewhat later vintage that are most unusual. For example, he has a card for the 1956 Ford that could be played as a 45-rpm record. Santa Claus and Rosemary Clooney sing Ford's praises on the recording.

Another card, advertising DeSoto for 1958, is many pieces of a puzzle. The receipient could cut it out, put it together, and a picture of the car would appear.

Ketelle keeps the bulk of his collection in photo albums, under plastic, 12 to a page. Though this is rather expensive, he feels it keeps the cards looking fresh. "When I started collecting, I really looked for cards that had not been mailed," he says. "The quality was better"

Not only has Ketelle collected advertising postcards, he has written about them, as well. He publishes a monthly newsletter of 6 to 12 pages, sent free to over 500 of his fellow collectors. He founded the newsletter "just to build my collection,"but it has become a thriving operation, because it features advertisements from collectors, indicating items they wish to trade or sell to other collectors. According to Ketelle, his newsletter is the only one in the field. And it's very popular. "When that newsletter comes out, Ketelle says, "people call day and night."

Ketelle finds his hobby a good way to relax from the pressures of his occupation as a Chevrolet salesman. "I really like the work, and I'm successful at it," he says, "but sometimes it can drive me crazy. With my collecting, I've gotten to travel, and meet a lot of good people." He's never received a bad check from a fellow collector, either, he says.

"It's kind of like going back to the old days, where people's word was good," he says. "I deal with a lot of real nice people."

It's easy to begin collecting auto advertising postcards, Ketelle says. Most of the cards for the last few years can be obtained from auto dealers or manufacturers free of charge. Ketelle advises the beginner to collect cards of all types first, then specialize later. "This way, you'll have cards with which to trade." Ketelle also suggests the novice peruse his newsletter; about 90 percent of the cards offered for sale in it are $2 or less.

"I'm willing to talk to anybody, anytime" about the hobby, says Ketelle. "I don't consider myself an expert, but I am very knowledgeable. There are new collectors coming along everyday, and I'm sure eager to be in touch with them."

To contact Ketelle or obtain a subscription to the newsletter, write to him at 3721 Farwell St., Amarillo, TX 79109.

ROBERT KUNTZ
ANTIQUE GOLF CLUBS

BEFORE YOU CHUCK out that old set of golf clubs gathering dust in your attic, garage, or basement, you'd better think twice. Robert Kuntz did — and he found an antique club that led him into an exciting kind of collecting, and made him a nationally-known expert.

While sorting through some junk in his attic one day in 1968, Kuntz, a 65-year-old industrial sales engineer from Dayton, Ohio, rediscovered a wood shaft golf club that he had used to teach golf to his two children years earlier.

Thinking he had "found the last wood club there was" by unearthing this "cleek" (the equivalent of a present-day two iron), he took it out to the local golf course. The old pro there "laughed at me and took me out to the pro shop, where, in a rack hanging from the ceiling, he had dozens and dozens of the old clubs stored, gathering dust."

What Kuntz did discover was that a lot of other people enjoyed collecting the old clubs — and many things relating to the game of golf. And he found it a great way to learn the history of the game "that I'd played all my life."

With one of these collectors, Joseph Murdoch (see page 49), Kuntz founded the first hobbyist organization in the field, The Golf Collectors Society. Founded in 1970, the club has grown from 35 to 720 members. Kuntz and Murdoch didn't try to make the organization grow, but it did anyway. "We have no president, no officers, no bylaws, no dues. It's a unique organization, run by a couple of benevolent dictators," Kuntz quips.

He estimates the group's members own a total of 150,000 to 200,000 old clubs. His own collection numbers 4,000, which he says is not really a lot. He knows some men who have double or triple that number.

A system of racks along the walls of his basement and his golf den displays the most valuable and interesting clubs. The rest are packed neatly in storage boxes.

Each golf club is slightly different from the others, since they were hand-crafted, Kuntz says. "You learned to play by feel." So, the golfer had to learn the characteristics of each shaft. For example, Bobby Jones had to "go through sets and sets of clubs" to find the set he could most accurately and easily play with.

According to Kuntz, the old clubs were very different from those made today. For one thing, they were (with a few exceptions) all woods and had longer heads. One of the best clubmakers was U. Philip in Scotland. Collectors still look for his clubs," Kuntz says. He spent much more time on crafting the clubs than many of his contemporaries. "It was the same as today: there were good — and not so good — craftsmen," says Kuntz.

Among the unusual clubs Kuntz has is an 1870s vintage U. Philip "rut iron," used to knock balls out of the wagon ruts on the commons where the game was played in Scotland. "In those days, the rules required that you had to play the ball from where it lay," says Kuntz, so a variety of special clubs for various natural hazards had to be invented.

Kuntz has become proficient in the restoration of the old clubs, which often have been neglected for many years. His expertise in the restoration and history of the golf club led to an appointment as a consultant on golf clubs to the United States Golf Association (USGA). He also restores clubs for the USGA Golf House Museum, in Far Hills, New Jersey, and for the Royal Canadian Golf Museum.

Kuntz really enjoys his hobby. He talks volubly and knowledgably not only about his collection and the crafting of golf clubs, but also on the history of the game.

Golf had its origins in Scotland in the 13th century, and has been played ever since. A succession of Scottish kings in the 1400s tried to outlaw the game in favor of the militarily useful sport of archery, but Kuntz says golf remained consistently popular. The game appeared in the American colonies in the 17th century, but its popularity in the U.S. had its genesis during the late 1800s.

"While we call it a Scottish game, it evolved from something else," says Kuntz. "Nobody just invented it. There were many kinds of games with balls and sticks that preceded golf."

Antique golf clubs are becoming quite valuable now, Kuntz says, with some having sold at auction for $1,000. The average club, though, can still be bought for around $10. Some of the long-nose clubs go for $500 to $1,000.

The best way for someone to get involved in collecting old clubs, or other golfiana, Kuntz says, is to talk to other golf collectors, and old-time golfers. Since there is little reference material on the subject of old golf clubs in particular, Kuntz recommends this personal contact (and visiting antique stores, pro shops and garage sales) as the best method for starting a collection.

Why has Kuntz devoted so much time to the collecting and restoring of old golf clubs? "I've played golf all my life, as well as being mechanical, so I've enjoyed working to tune them up. When you find an old, rusty, beat-up thing, it's good to get it working again." He makes the clubs playable but not perfect when he restores them, seeking to return them only to the condition they might have been in after having been used for a time.

Kuntz also has a large library of golfing literature and books, which he consults frequently for information on the origin and value of the clubs. "Reading is my winter hobby out here in snowbound Ohio," he explains, adding, "I sit down every evening when I'm home and read the old books I have on golfing."

Kuntz is happy to answer questions and give advice on golf club restoration and collecting, and the Golf Collectors Society. He can be reached at the J. R. Kuntz Co., 235 E. Helena St., Dayton, OH 45404.

MARK LASKY
SPORTS AUTOGRAPHS

HE ONCE CHASED Willie Mays's car — and almost got hit by a taxi. Centerfielder Bob Allison threatened to punch him in the face. And basketball player Don May tried to give him an iguana in a shoebox.

These hair-raising, whacky experiences (and plenty more) happened to Mark Lasky in his vigorous pursuit of his favorite leisure-time activity: collecting the autographs of sports figures.

Lasky, a 26-year-old artist and cartoonist for United Features Syndicate in New York City, has been collecting baseball players' autographs (though he's branched out into other sports) since he was 14 years old. Growing up in the New York metropolitan area has meant there's been no dearth of autograph-gathering opportunities, either.

"I started doing it because all my friends were," says Lasky. "I enjoyed it. It gave me a chance to meet in person the athletes I admired and emulated."

Lasky got his first autograph practically by accident. He was hanging around Shea Stadium with a friend one autumn afternoon, trying to gain admittance to a New York Jets football practice session.

"I wasn't able to get in, for a reason I don't even remember now," he says, "but I spotted Mets shortstop, Bud Harrelson, coming out of the stadium. I just went up to him and asked for his autograph."

From that first autograph in 1967, Lasky's built a collection that now includes over 1,500 athletes' autographs. He has become an expert in the fine art of obtaining them with a minimum of fuss and bother.

But Lasky is also ready to exert himself to get an autograph he wants. Witness the day he chased Mays's car down Madison Avenue. "I saw him driving by in his car," Lasky recalls, "and along with a mob of kids, ran down the street after him. I almost got hit by a cab, but he stopped at a stoplight, and one other kid and I were the only ones who got his autograph."

Fortunately, not all of Lasky's pursuits have been as hazardous. He apparently charmed May, a former New York Knicks forward — so much so that he offered Lasky a no-longer-wanted pet iguana that was staring malevolently out of a shoebox. Lasky declined the honor.

For Lasky, autograph collecting has been a matter of hanging out in the right hotel lobby, or standing by the team bus waiting to take the players to the stadium. "The way to succeed in collecting autographs," he says, "is to try not to do what the fans do." Thus, he emphasizes the importance of doing some research about where the teams are staying, and the players' habits, and learning the best opportunities to get autographs.

Lasky's collection has been compiled largely on three-by-five index cards, although many of his baseball players' autographs are on baseball cards, with the star's picture. He also has autographs on scorecards, photographs, baseballs, and team yearbooks. Among the many autographs he has collected: Hank Aaron, Casey Stengel, Mickey Mantle, Luis Aparicio (a very difficult one to obtain, says Lasky), Dizzy Dean, Peewee Reese, Gil Hodges, Jackie Robinson, Billy Martin and Reggie Jackson.

Obtaining some autographs is "easy, because the players are friendly and amicable; others are tough to get," he says. "The friendlier players assume it is part of their responsibility to cater to fans. The others act like it's an extra burden."

Some players, says Lasky, "have been really crass to me." Bob Allison, whom Lasky encountered in the lobby of New York's Hotel Roosevelt, threatened to punch Lasky in the face when he asked for his autograph. When Lasky asked Norm Cash, then a Detroit Tigers player, to autograph an old baseball card, Cash said, "Where do you kids get all this (expletive deleted) from anyway?," to which the ingenuous Lasky meekly replied, "In stores."

It is the friendly players, naturally, who Lasky remembers most fondly. Bob Shawkey, a pitcher and manager who was active in baseball from the Babe Ruth-Lou Gehrig era until today, "was very friendly with kids. Some of my best memories are of the stories he'd stand and tell us as we were all standing around," says Lasky. Today, he says, superstars Pete Rose, Steve Garvey, and Bobby Hull are probably the three most accomodating pros to autograph seekers.

Though the passing years have somewhat dimmed Lasky's enthusiasm for collecting autographs, he feels it is a great hobby for youngsters. "I think it's healthy for kids," he says. "For one thing, it's inexpensive; but it also gives kids a chance to come in contact with the athletes they idolize, and to develop their social skills."

Lasky recommends that anyone interested in collecting sports autographs should "go where the teams are." If the collector doesn't live near any professional teams, there's always the U.S. mail. In fact, Lasky says he has gotten some of his best autographs that way. Lasky says he was aided in his autograph collecting through the mail by looking up the addresses for all the professional baseball, hockey, football, basketball and soccer teams in *The World Almanac.*

Lasky's greatest enjoyment in collecting sports autographs has been in getting the autographs in person. "I am one of those who does this for fun," he says, "so I always wanted to get the autographs in person. I wasn't about to go buying autographs," so he has concentrated on contemporary stars in his collecting, leaving historical collecting to others.

Lasky has a word of advice for youngsters and others who collect autographs: "Remember, the players are human beings with the right of privacy. If you assume that the player has a responsibility to the fan, it's also true the fan has a responsibility to the player. Be polite and appreciative, and don't expect too much."

Lasky can be contacted c/o United Features Syndicate, 200 Park Ave., New York, NY 10017.

JAMES LOWE
POSTCARDS

Ο**NE OF THE FASTEST** growing hobbies in America is the collection of picture postcards, and one of the country's most prestigious collectors, with over one million postcards, is James Lowe, pastor of the Spruce Street Baptist Church in Newton Square, Pennsylvania.

Lowe, 50, began collecting postcards in 1944, as an offshoot of his interest in stamp collecting. "I discovered that not too many people collected postcards at that time," he says. "It was an uncharted field that I wanted to explore."

He began with "just a handful but albums and shoeboxes of the old cards kept showing up in attics, and eventually, in the antique shops throughout the country." He built his collection steadily.

"I started out collecting views of cities," he says, "the farther I could got back in time the better." After doing this for some years, he decided to specialize in cards of specific publishers and artists. "It made my efforts more highly rewarding, and my collection better," he says.

A major focus of his collection is a line of postcards manufactured by the London firm of Raphael Tuck. Their cards "were some of the best received in the consumer market between 1900 and 1915," says Lowe. Tuck was most renowned for its "oilettes," reproductions of oil paintings, utilizing a special lithography process that provided unusual quality. Lowe's collection includes 52,000 of those cards.

The Tuck process required as many as 15 different printing plates for colors. "It was expensive, nothing like the chrome printing process used today. The quality of the workmanship was much better, too," says Lowe. Each card was an individual (although mass-produced) work of art.

Another of Lowe's favorite items is the so-called "garbage postcard." Originally printed by the U.S. government as a memorial to President William McKinley, the cards didn't turn out well, so they were destroyed. One box of 500, however, got into the hands of a New York City garbage disposal service. Each day, for 500 days, the captain of the firm's garbage scow mailed one of the postcards to his main office to report how much garbage he had hauled out to sea that day. One of those cards, thought to be worthless in 1901, is worth $650 today. That card, along with 399,999 other cards, are sorted and filed neatly in Lowe's basement. The remainder of the cards in his collection are stored in boxes, awaiting their collector's attention..

Owning all those postcards made Lowe curious about their history. He's done extensive research into the history of the postcard and the many artisans and manufacturers, particularly from the picture postcard's "Golden Age," 1907-1915.

According to Lowe, the picture postcard originated at the 1893 World's Columbian Exposition in Chicago, where government-issue postcards with pictures of the various buildings at the fair were extremely popular. Prior to May 25, 1901, Lowe says, no one was allowed to make postcards but the government. But on that date, new regulations allowed commercial postcards for the first time. They quickly got a firm hold on the American public."

Suddenly, he says, there were picture postcards of all kinds: views of cities and scenic sights, greeting cards for all the holidays, joke cards, and more. America went picture postcard crazy for a few years. "The cards were ubiquitous," Lowe says. "Everyone used them. It was a form of entertainment as much as anything else."

But, like many a fad, the bubble was doomed to burst. Lowe credits our entry into World War I and the break in trade with Germany as the reason for the decline of the picture postcard. "The Germans were making the best, and the cheapest, postcards," he says. "The Americans just could not produce the same high quality at a low price."

Since 1966, the man often referred to as "Mr. Postcard of America" has been president of Deltiologists of America, an international organization of postcard collectors. (Deltiology, incidentally, is the new name given to postcard collecting.) It is the largest of several postcard collectors' societies in the United States, Lowe says. The Deltiologists' bi-monthly newsletter, which Lowe once edited, goes to some 1,800 members in the United States and abroad. First year membership in the Deltiologists of America costs $7.50, which buys a membership packet of information and a year's worth of the newsletter.

Lowe advises beginners to join Deltiologists of America because it is the best way to obtain information about what's available at what price and it provides the guidance of expert collectors. Lowe also suggests starting with a particular category of interest (a geographic area, a specific holiday, a certain person), and searching for cards in that category. Most towns have flea markets and antique stores which are good sources for the cards, as well as other collectors, so the novice should be able to get a foothold in the hobby with comparative ease, he says. In addition, Lowe says, it isn't a bad idea to "get one of the several basic books about postcard collecting" and read about the various ways in which one can collect the cards. A standard book on antique postcards is Lowe's own *The Standard Postcard Catalgoue*, published in 1968, the first of its kind.

Deltiology is satisfying to Lowe "from the artistic view as well as the historical. Postcards cover every major historic period and event. They were a sociological phenomenon, a flourishing fad that came and went. And I don't think it will ever happen again."

Lowe is always happy to give beginners a helping hand, and would like to hear from established postcard collectors, too. He can be reached at 3709 Gradyville Rd., Newton Square, PA 19073. Lowe would appreciate correspndence that includes a stamped, self-addressed envelope for reply.

JACK LOWENSTEIN
BEER STEINS

THE GERMANS, IN THE 13th Century, discovered an interesting technique for creating pottery: high temperature firing. One of the first uses to which they put this new "stoneware" (as we know it today) was for drinking vessels.

Along came the 16th century, and with it, the growth in Cologne, Germany, of the art of creating what came to be known as "beer steins" from this same pottery. Ornate, decorative, and useful lidded mugs, steins have been an inseparable part of the beer drinking culture ever since.

To Jack Lowenstein, a chemical engineer from Kingston, New Jersey, beer steins represent "an exciting hobby that satisfies the urge to collect, while at the same time presenting a challenge to discover the raison d'etre for these articles." Lowenstein knows, because he has one of the most complete and unusual collections of beer steins around.

Lowenstein started his collection about 30 years ago, with one stein, an old, lidless mug his father gave him which he used as a pencil holder. Then he got a couple more steins, and before he knew it, "I was hooked."

There are so many beer steins in the world, Lowenstein says, "that I had to specialize." So, he decided to concentrate on collecting only those steins which have as their motif "the Munich Child," the symbol of Munich, Germany. The "child" is really a monk, in honor of the settlement of monks who founded the German city. "Over the years, it has changed into looking like a little girl, holding a stein of beer in one hand and a bunch of radishes in the other. It has become the fun symbol of Munich, and is often shown in humorous poses on the steins," he says.

Since he started specializing in 1970, Lowenstein says that he has discovered that "it makes it much easier in any collection to have some central items that tie it all together." Now, he can go into an antique shop, see a beer stein, and know instantly if it is one that he wants to add to his collection. He has 250 Munich Child steins in his collection.

Of the other 150 steins Lowenstein has collected, he is most intrigued by those made by Faience between 1750 and 1790. They are earthenware with a tin glaze and "they're reasonably valuable, somewhat primitive, and have a certain beauty," he says.

He also owns beer steins made by the famed firm of Villeroy and Boch, a Saar Valley firm that operated between 1880 and 1910. "These are the 'Cadillacs' of beer steins," he says. "They're artistic, well-made and well-designed. After you've seen your first one, you can spot another across a room."

"To the dismay of my wife," says Lowenstein, "I display my steins on shelves all over the house. Someday, I'll have a room just for myself."

For Lowenstein, much of the joy in collecting steins comes from his extensive research into their origins. He likes to find out "why they were made in the first place, how they came to be produced, who were the artisans, what is the story behind the many illustrations used on steins, and so on." And, he says, the research isn't easy.

Fortunately, he is fluent in German, so he is able to read a lot of the manufacturers' literature and other materials on the history of steins with comparative ease. It is finding the material in the first place that presents the most challenge in his research.

Much of his research has involved the steins from Creussen, a small town on the Rhine River. For a brief period in the late 17th century, the town was a pottery center, with artisans from Bohemia in residence. The local potters and the Bohemian artisans collaborated on the steins, which Lowenstein describes as being dark brown in color, "short and squat like British tankards, with pewter lids, and decorated in relief in motifs of the Apostles, German electors, or planets."

"These are very, very unique," Lowenstein says. "And very obscure. But, with a little bit of work on my part, I find I'm the U.S. expert on these steins."

The new collector of old steins should really join Stein Collectors International, says Lowenstein. This organization, founded in 1965, now has some 1,000 members in the United States and Germany. Lowenstein is the executive secretary of the organization, as well as the editor for its quarterly magazine *Prosit*.

"Only through association with another collector can you learn what to look for and what to avoid," he says. "You can't read up on how to collect." The $20 membership in Stein Collectors Internaional "is really a very small investment, considering the price of steins, to get the kind of education we can give to members."

Lowenstein says that old steins are still quite plentiful today, although, like most collectibles, the prices have risen to considerable heights. Fifteen years ago, when the stein collecting hobby wasn't so well established, many steins could be purchased for $5 and $10 Now, steins fetch anywhere from $40 to $1,000 and, as Lowenstein puts it, "we collectors did it to ourselves;" because so much information has become available to collectors, largely through Lowenstein's research efforts, the prices have been driven up.

"We don't want to hide information from others," says Lowenstein, "so we have to take our lumps on the money" aspect of collecting.

"Most true collectors don't worry about the vaule. I don't. But steins have been a good investment."

And steins are still very much a big business. The manufacturers in Germany "are going hot and heavy. I've been to two factories that are turning out steins as fast as we do aspirin tablets."

Lowenstein is enthusiastic about stein collecting. "Deep down, maybe they're a reflection of my German background," he says. "They are very artistic. The clay body is the perfect canvas for a good designer to let his imagination fly.

To obtain further information about stein collecting or to join Stein Collectors International, contact Lowenstein, PO Box 463, Kingston, NJ 08528.

BRUCE MANSON
TOY TRAINS

I T'S A SURE BET that not many 51-year-old men spend their day playing with electric trains — but Bruce Manson does.

As the curator of The Toy Train Museum in Strasburg, Pennsylvania, 80 miles from Philadelphia, Manson is responsible for the collection of toy trains that has made the museum an attraction for more than 30,000 visitors a year.

"I always owned trains as a kid, " says Manson. They were largely forgotten, until about 20 years ago, when he noticed toy trains were starting to have some value as collectibles. It was then, he says, that "I realized the toys were a manifestation of the period of their manufacture as well as being, in many cases, a distinct form of art."

The museum, a replica of the Santa Fe train depot in Ferris, California, was built in 1977 by the Train Collectors Association, the national organization for collectors of toy trains. Manson, a former realtor and investment executive from California, has been the museum's curator since 1978.

What prompted a successful business man to give up his job and come to a small town to run a train museum? "I had done well in business and had investments, so it was just a lot more pleasant to be involved full-time with my hobby, making my avocation my vocation," he says.

The museum displays toy trains from 1880 to the present, made of all kinds of material from wood, paper, and glass to contemporary metal and plastic models. Manson says a big attraction of the museum is the train layouts which depict different eras in the history of trains.

The community surrounding the museum has "become the center for this growing hobby," according to Manson. In addition to the train museum, Strasburg boasts its own steam railroad that operates regularly, as well as the Pennsylvania State Railroad Museum. "It's kind of a Mecca for people interested in railroads," he adds.

In addition to his work with the museum (which is closed during the winter), Manson also has his own museum at home. His collection of toy trains and other toys is housed in a large converted barn behind his house.

Manson specializes in collecting the trains made by American Flyer, for many years one of the two major manufacturers of electric trains (the other is, of course, Lionel). Formerly produced by the A.C. Gilbert Co., the American Flyers are now made by Lionel, which has apparently cornered the market in standard "O"(as opposed to HO) gauge electric trains.

In his collection are some 2,000 trains ("that's small," he says), including engines, cars, and accessories, along with a fairly extensive collection of model buildings, many from the early 1900s. Since toys and trains are inseparable in the view of Manson and most other collectors, he also has 1,200 mini-autos made in the 1920s by Tootsie Toys.

Currently, Manson is in the process of building a 900-square-foot train layout in his barn, which will become the centerpiece of his collection .

Among the unique American Flyer trains in Manson's collection is a pre-production model from the early 1930s. This experimental model steam engine was the first to have a mechanism in it that made real smoke puff from its smokestack. Since the company didn't mass-produce these engines until 1946 and 1947, Manson says his train is possibly the only one in existence from the Thirties.

Another of the pieces Manson particularly enjoys is a small lead figure, about the size of a toy soldier. It is a rumpled, somewhat strange looking man, "the town idiot," he says, made somewhere between 1940 and 1950. A comparable figure was sold at auction in London for $150. Manson says.

While the popularity of standard O-gauge toy trains made by American Flyer and Lionel has declined, except for collectors, HO-gauge trains are still very popular. However, Manson says, don't think there's necessarily a goldmine in your kid's train set. "At the moment, HO is not particularly collectible, because so many sets have been cranked out in plastic," he says.

But don't despair. "You just can't tell what will be valuable in the future. It depends a great deal on the old law of supply and demand: how many were made, how many survived, how desirable is the item." There's really no way the would-be collector can confidently evaluate the future worth of a contemporary train or other toy, he adds.

Even the trains made by Lionel or American Flyer between 1920 and 1960 aren't of guaranteed value as collectibles.

"Some, it's really sad to say, just haven't become valuable," says Manson. Other, perhaps unlikely, toy trains have become extremely valuable. For example, Lionel in the mid-1950s tried a train set with a pink engine and pastel cars for girls. The trains didn't go over with girls — or anyone else, for that matter — so the company painted them all black and sold them as regular sets. If a collector owned one of those pink sets today, Manson says, he could sell it for $1,000 or $1,500; the black engines for that same year are worth only about $100.

Novice collectors should limit themselves to one particular manufacturer or one particular era, Manson feels. "You would have to have a lot of patience, and a great bank account, to try to get all of everything made." And, he counsels, not just trains, but any kinds of toys, are interesting, and relatively easy, to collect.

Manson also recommends the new collector join the Train Collectors Association. Not only will he receive the *Train Collectors Quarterly*, the association's informative official magazine (which Manson edits), he will be able to get in touch with other train collectors and participate in the group's events. A major event of the association is its twice-yearly "train meet," in York, Pennsylvania, where more than 6,000 people turn out "just to talk trains, sell, and swap," he says.

Manson will be glad to answer questions or exchange information about toy trains or the Train Collectors Association. He can be contacted at The Toy Train Museum, PO Box 248, Strasburg, PA 17579.

EUGENE MORRIS
FIRE MEMORABILIA

If EUGENE MORRIS' daughter hadn't made him angry enough to attempt to kick her — and break his foot on a bathroom fixture instead — he might never have become an expert on fire memorabilia.

It was at Christmastime some 25 years ago, and, as Morris puts it, "She did something naughty." She escaped, but he hit his foot against the bathroom sink, and wound up in bed. "At that time, I made models as a hobby," he says, "and the first one I worked on while I was laid up was an antique fire engine."

His interest "just grew from there." The fact that he is an executive in the insurance business "made it a natural" for him to become involved in collecting fire memorabilia.

Today, Morris has one of the largest collections of fire memorabilia in existence. He is also the founder and director of a national museum devoted to preserving these artifacts, honoring firefighters, and recording the history of American firefighting. The New England Fire and History Museum, located in Brewster, Massachusetts (near Cape Cod), has become a popular tourist attraction during the six months a year that it is open. With its six buildings on four-and-a-half acres, the museum is a Mecca for firefighting enthusiasts and historians alike.

Items in the museum collection of which Morris is particularly proud include 43 fire engines, and the frontispiece, or decoration, from the famous "Live Oak 44" fire engine in New York City. Carved of one piece of oak, the frontispiece was the emblem of the "Terrible Turks," a volunteer fire company made up of a ship's captain and other men associated with shipping. These men, dressed in uniforms suggesting the Mideast, became the basis for the Civil War Zouave regiment, according to Morris.

For his own part, Morris has been involved in recent years with collecting "fire marks." These pieces of metal were the trademarks of insurance companies in the late 1700s and early 1800s, and were affixed to the buildings of people who were insured. When the building caught fire, the volunteer fire department would come to the insured house, put out the fire, and get a reward from the insurance company. These marks have become collector's items because they have been extinct since the Civil War, when paid fire departments came into being.

In 1972, Morris founded a national group, the Fire Marks Circle of America, which now includes 300 collectors. He says the interest in this sort of collecting is growing at a phenomenal rate.

Many of the fire marks now sell for over $1,000, says Morris, emphasizing that even the reproductions that have been made for many years bring good prices among collectors. But, he says, the novice should join the Fire Marks Circle so "he doesn't get clipped on the fakes. Only the most practiced eye can tell whether or not one of these things is authentic."

Another project that Morris has been involved with, in connection with the museum, is a search for living descendants of the O'Leary family, who were traditionally thought to have been responsible for starting the 1871 Chicago Fire, the nation's most famous fire disaster.

While Morris has heard from some people claiming to be related to the O'Learys, "most of them are just publicity seekers. They don't have the facts." What is complicating the search, Morris feels, is that there is "still a great deal of reticence on the part of people to discuss what actually happened."

It is now known, "for sure, that the O'Leary family didn't cause the fire," Morris says. There are many theories, the most probable among them being that a peg-legged tramp named O'Donnell had come to the O'Leary's back door asking for a handout. The tramp was, perhaps, sent away empty-handed, vowing revenge, or was housed in the family's barn, where he started the fire, either accidentally or on purpose. After the fire, only his clay pipe and peg leg were found; his fate has remained a mystery to this day.

Morris's most notable achievement was the construction of a diorama, "The Burning of Chicago, 1871." Based on pictures from the archives of the Chicago Historical Society, the huge diorama (at half-inch scale) is a popular attraction at the New England Fire Museum. "It's historically correct," says Morris, "but not esthetically perfect." There is still work to be done on the exhibit, including installing mechanisms to make the ships on the Chicago River move. Morris was awarded a Freedoms Foundation Medal in 1969 for his construction of the diorama.

Despite all the work involved, Morris is definite about his interest: "I love it. It's a hobby that's taken me over completely. I'm engrossed. I've met so many interesting and nice people through this hobby."

Morris urges anyone interested in collecting fire marks to get in touch with Henry Kroll, 1708 Highland Dr., Silver Spring, MD 20910, for information on the Fire Marks Circle of the Americas. Morris will gladly answer queries about collecting fire memorabilia or the New England Fire & History Museum, addressed to him at 159 Main St., Chatham, NJ 07928.

JOSEPH MURDOCH
GOLF BOOKS

H E COULD BE CALLED "golf's number one bookworm" for he has golf's number one collection of books about the sport, well over 2,500 of them.

Golf comes naturally to Joseph Murdoch of Lafayette Hill, Pennsylvania. He is the child of Scottish parents, and has played golf since he was eight years old. "I developed a life-long enthusiasm, bordering on passion, for the game," he says.

Murdoch also has been an avid book collector for much of his life. In 1959, he became curious about how many books had been published relating to his favorite sport. "So, I decided to browse the book shops, thinking I'd pick up a couple of dozen or so. Before I knew it, I had a couple hundred."

"Since I've been playing the game for 50 years, I rarely need a book of instruction, but I am quite a nut on the history and tradition of the game," he says.

He estimates that he now owns virtually all books ever published about the game. His oldest is a poem in book form, *On Golf,* which was published in 1743.

A number of Murdoch's books were originally published in limited editions, which enhances their value as collector's items. "Many of the books are unusual, from the standpoint of production," he says. "The making of books intrigues me, and quite a few of the ones I own are rather handsome."

The first instructional golf book, by a student at St. Andrew's University, Scotland, the cradle of golf, was published in 1857. Murdoch has a copy, as well as copies of the first U.S. golf book, published in 1893 by the Spaulding sports equipment company. In fact, Murdoch has all the golf books published in the United States before the turn of the century.

"I don't work at my collecting nearly as hard anymore. But I've covered a lot of miles tracking down books," he says. Once, Murdoch heard of a book called *Golf in East Africa,* published in Nairobi, Kenya. He, inquired about the availability of the book, and several weeks later got a reply that the company was out of business. After writing to a Capetown, South Africa, publisher he knew, Murdoch got the address of the author, a civil servant who had returned to England. Murdoch wrote to the author who, it turned out, had moved. But the letter was forwarded to him and "he was so flattered somebody would want his book and go to all the trouble to track him down that he gave me the last remaining copy."

As should be evident from all of this, "Collecting is a peculiar form of madness within the nutsy world of golf," Murdoch chuckles. "Besides, it keeps me out of bars."

One book that Murdoch has sought for years, with no success, is *Golf in the Year 2000,* which he describes as a satirical book, published around the turn of the century in Britain. "I guess if there was one book I wish I had, that would be it," he says.

Not content with merely collecting the books, Murdoch has used them as a basis for extensive bibliographic research. He has read all 2,500 of the books ("anyway, most of them"), and has also catalogued, cross-referenced, and studied them. From this work (much of it involving painstaking copying of information onto three-by-five index cards), Murdoch was able to create a volume called *The Library of Golf.*

"I did it for my own amusement," Murdoch says, "to help me in finding books that I was lacking in my collection." But a Coral Gables, Florida, bookseller saw Murdoch's list and suggested that he make it into a book. The volume, published by Gale Research Company in 1968, is a bibliography of golf-related tomes published between 1743 and 1966. It is still available.

"It has become the Bible for golfers interested in this subject," Murdoch says. A companion volume, taking the booklist through to 1977, was privately printed in 1978, but Murdoch's supply of only 150 copies was quickly exhausted.

With a fellow golf maniac, Robert Kuntz, whose forte is collecting antique golf clubs (see p.38), Murdoch founded the Golf Collectors' Society. That organization, boasting over 500 members who are collectors of all aspects of "golfiana," is operated out of Murdoch's home.

Murdoch suggests anyone interested in collecting golf literature haunt used-book stores, flea markets, yard sales and antique shops. "The ideal thing to do is find a used-book dealer you trust, and if you have him on your side, he can do an awful lot of good for you."

To collect books in the first place, says Murdoch, "You have to be a ratpacker at heart. I get a lot of satisfaction in seeing my library grow and I know that I have picked up a lot of knowledge from reading the books."

Murdoch is happy to counsel beginners in the field of golfiana, especially in the collecting of golf literature. He can also supply membership information about the Golf Collectors' Society. Contact him at 638 Wagner Rd., Lafayette Hill, PA 19444.

DAVID & BETH PENNINGTON
SPINNING WHEELS

THE GOOD COLONIAL or pioneer housewife was never without her spinning wheel. It was the most necessary part of the family's textile and clothing making. as well as being an important piece of household furniture.

Today, most clothes are made in factories utilizing machines many times larger and faster than the spinning wheel. But with the revival of interest in traditional crafts, spinning is returning to prominence, and David and Beth Pennington, of Ann Arbor, Michigan, are two of its most ardent advocates.

Beth, who teaches traditional crafts, developed an interest in weaving after being in the Peace Corps in Colombia from 1962 to 1964. Back in the States, her weaving instructor suggested she learn to spin as well, "and one day in 1967 we found a spinning wheel in an antique shop. It looked lonesome, so we bought it."

"At this point," David says, "I became involved and made a fatal discovery: all spinning wheels are not alike"

"David became intrigued with how they looked and worked, " Beth says. "Some had manufacturer's names on them, and he began tracking them down." Thus began their collection, which now numbers more than 150 spinning wheels, and includes other textile-related tools as well.

"All of our wheels are interesting, each has something unique about it," says Beth. One wheel that fascinates both the Penningtons was made about 1864 by J. Green of New York, who attempted to make the woman's task easier — and ended up with a rather strange device.

This wheel is not like the small wheel that is traditionally thought of when talking about spinning wheels, says Beth. "That's actually called a 'flax wheel' and it's operated by sitting down and pressing a treadle, with a continuous bobbin taking up the thread." With big 5-foot wheels, like Green's, the traditional method of handling the wheel (which really only operates as a flywheel) was to hold the spindle and walk away from the wheel while it turned. The operator added fibers as she walked away. "In any event, she could only walk back so far before having to come back to the wheel," says David.

What Green invented and patented was a spindle that rode on a small car on rails about six feet in length. With this machine, the operator sat down, and used a treadle to keep the wheel moving, while the little car went back and forth. "This probably saved the woman about 20 miles a day in walking," says Beth. "And it's a very pretty wheel, with a red pinstripe all around it."

While Beth has concentrated primarily on the actual craft of spinning, David has been researching extensively the history and manufacture of the wheels in their collection. The oldest wheel he can verify is circa 1790, "but other pieces may be much older." Most of the collection covers a period from the early 1800s to 1920, he says. The first part of the 19th century is considered the heyday of the spinning wheel in America.

"The thing I've found most interesting," says David, "is the different ways people around the country found to solve the same problem. The spinning wheel basically does one thing: twists fibers together. But the manufacturers and inventors came up with so many innovations they thought improved that basic job. I try to get into their minds and fathom why they did these things. Man is fascinated with minute technical changes, and people were attempting to keep making them right up to the 1900s, when the spinning wheel was, for all practical purposes, dead."

The Penningtons have found most of their spinning wheels in the Northeast, though they say that later pieces may be found in the Midwest. "It's getting more difficult to get rare pieces," David says. "But wheels are always around, and, like everything, the prices have escalated." When they started collecting, David says, a good wheel could be had for $35 or $40, mainly because "they were considered a pain to handle by many antique dealers." Now, with the revival of interest in crafts, and their popularity as decorative accessories, David says a good wheel often costs $200-$300, or more.

All this makes the Penningtons despair of beginners getting into collecting. "The lack of availability of unusual wheels, as well as the high prices, combine to make it difficult for a beginner to put together an extensive collection today."

With Dr. Michael Taylor, the Penningtons wrote *A Pictorial Guide to American Spinning Wheels* (The Shaker Community, 1975), which is the only book on American spinning wheels, at present.

The Penningtons are always happy to answer inquiries about spinning wheels. They request that the writer supply them with a picture, if possible, along with a rubbing of any names or marks on the wheel, and a stamped, self-addressed envelope, for a reply. They can be contacted at 1993 W. Liberty, Ann Arbor, MI 48103.

FRED PFENING
CIRCUS MEMORABILIA

GONE FOREVER are the great days of the circus, when every city, small, medium or large, could count on an annual visit from one of the great circuses that crisscrossed the country. They conjured up magic for a dime, the exotic for a night, and memories for months.

For Fred Pfening, the circus hasn't been reduced to the few extravaganzas that appear in coliseums, auditoriums, and convention halls in major cities. He can still hark back to the days of bareback riders, sawdust, and the big top, for his large collection of circus memorabilia has made him a leading expert on the shows, performers, and technology of an exciting time in American history.

Ever since he was taken to circuses by a childless neighbor, Pfening's world has been the circus. At 10, he produced a backyard circus, at 16 he spent the summer working for a small Ohio circus, and at 17 he joined Ringling Brothers and Barnum & Bailey as an usher for a season.

"I was always fascinated with the mechanical aspects of putting a circus on," says Pfening. "The logistics of its movement, the business side, all fascinated me." He began collecting memorabilia, and researching the history of circuses, their performers and equipment.

Pfening's collection is huge. In fact, it threatens to take over his house. " I recently expanded my basement, so I would have more space to store everything, and tore up my wife's wisteria tree to do it," he says wryly. Included in his collection are well over 60,000 photographs of circus acts, performers, trains, animals, and the like. Since that's too many to display in any kind of orderly fashion, Pfening has most of them neatly stored, but "I have to go digging into piles to find pictures."

There are more than pictures in Pfening's collection. He has a large number of "route books," for instance. There were 250 of these souvenir books, like a school yearbook in composition, published by American circuses as far back as 1850. And Pfening has all but 19 of them. Among Pfening's other interesting and important memorabilia: all of Barnum & Bailey's programs from 1872 to the present; posters, lithographs and woodblock window ads from Rickett's Circus; Christmas cards, special menus, tickets, passes, letterheads, handwritten letters from P. T. Barnum, route cards, route sheets, and more.

Pfening is also extremely knowledgeable about circus history. The first United States circus was Rickett's, which began in 1800. At that time, says Pfening, the circus consisted "mostly of horseback acts and acrobats; later they added a traveling menagerie." From 1871 on, of course, the prevailing force in the circus was P.T. Barnum. Although not strictly a circus man, Barnum's entreprenurial genius was the impetus behind many circus acts and innovations, according to Pfening.

During 1890-1910, the heyday of the circus, there were as many as 25 shows operating from trains, and 50 more that traveled overland. Today there are only the two traveling companies of the Ringling Brothers and Barnum & Bailey Circus left. The decline of the circus, which began in the 1930s, was nearly complete by the 1950s, when TV and the problems of finding tent locations sounded a death knell for most traveling shows, Pfening says.

"The circus provided, particularly in the golden days, an opportunity for a family outing," he says, in noting the importance of the circus to American life. "It always had clean entertainment for the whole family, thus making a unique cultural contribution."

Since 1960, he has been the editor of *Bandwagon*, the quarterly magazine of the Circus Historical Society. Many of the articles resulting from his research have been printed in that magazine. He was also the president of the 1,400-member group from 1956 to 1962.

For the person interested in starting to collect circus memorabilia, Pfening suggests "clip today's ads and take your own pictures when the circus visits your area." The escalation of prices for the older circus memorabilia "is just unbelievable." At a recent auction in New York, the original agreement between Barnum and Bailey, along with a check of Barnum's, was sold for $1,600, Pfening says.

The older material is still fairly plentiful. It is possible to find it, sometimes, at auctions, flea markets or antique stores. And collectors frequently trade or sell to each other.

Pfening urges people interested in collecting circusiana, or in the history of circuses, to join the Circus Historical Society (800 Richey Rd., Zanesville, OH 43701) or the Circus Fans Association of America (PO Box 69, Camp Hill, PA 17011). This will put them in touch with veteran collectors and historians.

WINIFRED ROWE
SOUVENIR SPOONS

NOT EVERY COLLECTION begins with a lifelong fascination. Frequently, a collector wants to have a collection that will fill a special need. Winifred Rowe is a perfect example.

While she collected "a lot of things" over the years, she needed to find a hobby that would take up less space in her house, and wanted a collection that wouldn't require a lot of special care. Souvenir spoons seemed to fit the bill. "Besides," she says, "they were interesting and beautiful on display."

Mrs. Rowe began collecting souvenir spoons in 1957, and now has nearly 400 in her collection. They range from "plain cheapies," the kind that can be found at almost any contemporary souvenir stand, to more valuable and interesting antique spoons.

She is particularly devoted in her collecting to spoons that come from her home state of Wisconsin and the surrounding states. She has traveled all over the region, searching for spoons. Among the interesting Wisconsin spoons she has, for example, is one commemorating the courthouse in her home county.

But Mrs. Rowe doesn't confine herself to such a specialized area. "Basically, I collect anything that really appeals to me," she says. She is particularly proud of a silver spoon of Little Tommy Tucker, the nursery rhyme character, who can be seen in three dimensions on the spoon handle.

According to Mrs. Rowe, souvenir spoons were originally made of sterling silver or silver plate. They started to become popular in the 1890s, when they were frequently sold or given away as advertising premiums or as commemoratives of some special event, person, or place.

Today, says Mrs. Rowe, those sterling spoons are worth anywhere from $15 to $100. And they can be found everywhere — in antique shops, stores, attics, garage sales, or flea markets — which makes collecting them particularly easy for the enthusiast.

In 1959, Mrs. Rowe decided to form a club "getting together spoon collectors from near and far." She began to publish a newsletter, called *The Spooner*, devoted to news and information about spoons and spoon collecting. Mrs. Rowe writes, edits, and mimeographs it herself. It is distributed to nearly 130 people monthly.

Mrs. Rowe really enjoys her collection. Collecting has given her a chance to do some traveling. "Mostly, it's just a lot of fun to have spoons of the places you have been or of places or events that mean a lot to you: your church, your courthouse, your town's centennial celebration." Collecting souvenir spoons has also helped Mrs. Rowe "learn a lot of history and geography, so it's not only a pleasurable hobby, but educational, too."

Mrs. Rowe will be happy to give further information about souvenir spoon collecting, and invites subscriptions to *The Spooner*. She may be contacted at RR 1, Box 61, Shullsburg, WI 53586.

CLARK SECREST
TOBACCO & COFFEE TINS

I'm crazy. That's my excuse," says Clark Secrest, in explaining why he's spent more than 10 years collecting old tobacco and coffee tins.

Crazy he may be, but the Denver newspaperman has gathered a fascinating collection of these tins, and founded a nationwide organization for fellow collectors, all since 1970.

Secrest began collecting the tins after he found a Log Cabin syrup tin from the 1930s in a junk shop in the Colorado mountains. "I paid $5 for it at the time, and it's worth a great deal more than that today," he says. Something about the tin fascinated him, and he began collecting other food containers, before finally settling on the more interesting tobacco and coffee tins.

Currently, Secrest has 200 items in his collection. "That's small," he says, "but I stress quality not quantity. Many of my pieces are one-of-a-kind items."

Among his unique and interesting tins is a pocket-sized Peggy O'Neil tobacco tin from 1915. "It has a lovely lithograph of Peggy, a sort of 'Little-Bo-Peep' character derived from the then-popular song 'Sweet Peggy O'Neil,'" says Secrest. Another prize of his collection: a set of "six little tobacco tins, shaped like people." Among them are a singing waiter, a Dutchman, a mammy, a Scotland Yard detective, and "a satisfied customer." The heads all come off, and the insides were filled with one of four different brands of tobacco, he says.

The tins which Secrest and other collectors look for are from the period 1895 to 1920, when tobacco and other manufacturers used them as important means of advertising their products. "The tins feature marvelous lithography," says Secrest, "and were meant to be so attractive that they would be used for a secondary purpose." Once the tobacco was used, "a tin box could be very useful around the farmhouse. Many were made like canisters, and designed to be so attractive the housewife wouldn't throw them away."

The tobacco industry "was very competitive, and all of the manufacturers tried to outdo each other" in elaborate design, says Secrest. The tins depicted all manner of subjects, from U.S. Presidents to farm scenes, pretty women to steam engines, from dogs to wild animals. "Most were lithographed in eight colors and they're just beautiful," he says.

Secrest "refuses to take all this very seriously," and says he's collecting only for his own amusement. Alas, he says, it is becoming difficult for other people to have a similarly pleasant experience.

"The tobacco tins, particularly, are hard to find and very expensive. It's kind of a shame, because the prices are keeping a lot of people away from the hobby." As an example of how prices have gotten out of control, Secrest says, his Peggy O'Neill tobacco tin was purchased for $1 in 1973. Now, he says, he's had an offer of $1,500 for it. "It's the law of supply and demand," he says, adding that the average tobacco tin sells today for $15 to $30.

In determining the desirability of a tin, three major factors are considered by the collectors — "rarity, fine graphics, and excellent condition of the tin." "To be truly collectible, the tins must meet all three conditions, though some of the rarest ones do happen to be pretty ugly," he laughs.

Secrest is most serious about research in the hobby. "I do a lot of research into the history of the manufacturers of these tins," he says. He has concentrated his research on several of the major companies. A typical example is the thorough study he made of Somers Brothers. This Brooklyn, New York, firm was active from 1870-1901. "They manufactured highly elaborate lithographed tin cans, " he says, which are some of the finest examples of the art ever made.

Secrest prefers collecting tobacco tins because "they have the best graphics, generally. The pictures are more interesting, the colors more vivid." The coffee tins are less artistic and, therefore, are less appealing to him.

In 1971, Secrest started the Tin Container Collectors Association, which now has 900 members worldwide. He edits and publishes *Tin Type*, the monthly 20-page illustrated club newsletter which contains information on the history and current values of the collectibles.

"We're crazier than mousetrap collectors. We have no sense," says Secrest. "We've lost all sense of the value of a dollar. Imagine paying all this money for these tins. None of them are really worth $10, let alone $500 or $1,000."

In addition to tobacco and coffee tins, other food tins and talcum powder tins are becoming highly collectible. "There are some talcum powder tins from the '20s and '30s that are really neat," he says, adding that it's still possible to get good ones at a fair price.

For the beginner in the hobby, Secrest suggests looking "everywhere you can think of" to find the tins. It also helps to read some of the books written about tin cans as collectibles. Joining the Tin Container Collectors Association is also valuable.

Secrest and the Tin Container Collectors Association can be reached at PO Box 4555, Denver, CO 80204.

JESSE SHEREFF
GILBERT & SULLIVAN MEMORABILIA

EVEN THOUGH HE'S MATTER of fact about it, Jesse Shereff is the very model of the studious Gilbert and Sullivan buff.

The 40-year-old computer engineer from New York City has been immersed in the lives and operas of those turn-of-the-century geniuses William Gilbert, and Arthur S. Sullivan, since his childhood. "I grew up listening to their music and loving it. It was something that grew in me," he says.

About 1965, Shereff started to turn his appreciation for the music of the two men into a more tangible form, and began collecting books and other memorabilia relating to Gilbert and Sullivan and the performances of their operas.

Shereff is one of an elite group of collectors in the field. "Most Gilbert and Sullivan buffs are interested in their music and the literature about them," he says. "My interest lies there, too, but in my collection I go far beyond that."

Among the items in his extensive collection are books, model theaters with settings from the operas, figurines, plates, cups, records, advertising cards, programs, magazine clippings, sketches, and more. For example, Shereff says, he has the Three Little Maids from *The Mikado* on a hand-tooled leather painting that was sold as a souvenir at the original Madison Square Garden around 1886 or 1887. "It's just a tremendous collection," he says. "I couldn't even begin to estimate how many thousands of items I have."

Shereff's collection does not include manuscripts, scores, or other such items. "They're all in museums," says Shereff.

The Pierpont Morgan Library, in New York City, has "a fabulous Gilbert and Sullivan collection of original manuscripts, books, and artifacts. But, when they don't want to be bothered with queries, they send the person on to me," says Shereff.

"Pretty much all of my stuff is mass-produced things." And mass-produced they were, in profusion, when the Gilbert and Sullivan operas hit the shores of America in the 1880s. "There were no copyright laws in America at the time," says Shereff, "and in the case of *H.M.S. Pinafore* and *The Mikado*, there's practically no end to these early American artifacts. When *Pinafore* and *The Mikado* were new, there was a mass of unauthorized stuff put out to capitalize on them."

Despite the apparent profusion of material, Shereff says, "the supply is dwindling. Gilbert and Sullivan collecting has become so popular that items get snapped up right away when they come up for sale."

Not only are Gilbert and Sullivan items disappearing from the shops as rapidly as they appear, but prices are climbing at very hefty rates, according to Shereff. "Books are an important part of my collection, and the prices have gone way up," he says. "When I was building up my collection, I could go down to a bookshop and pick up secondhand books for $3.50 to $7.50 apiece. Now, prices have gone wild, because the dealers have gotten wise to the popularity of this material." Thus, when Gilbert and Sullivan books, even of the most ordinary sort, come into the secondhand bookshops, Shereff says "they're marked up extensively, to as much as $20 or $25."

Books are not the only victims of Gilbert and Sullivan-induced inflation, Shereff says. In England, for example, he's seen a copy of dance music arrangements from the operas selling today for 40 or 50 pounds — "and they were mass produced by the thousands and sold for four shillings apiece," says Shereff.

American advertising trade cards are another example, he says. These cards, which were in common use everywhere, featured characters from the operas endorsing everything from corsets to candies. "You could get piles of these cards a few years back for 25 cents to $1," he says. "Today, they cost $6 to $10 apiece."

Shereff credits this dramatic rise in price to the fact that the operas of Gilbert and Sullivan continue to be greatly popular, even after 100 years of existence. "They wrote immortal things," he says.

Shereff is an active member of the New York City Gilbert and Sullivan Society. The society is associated with the many other local chapters nationwide and in England, "although we all think of oursevles as independent," says Shereff. About half of the Gilbert and Sullivan Societies are performing groups, he says, who present Gilbert and Sullivan operas on a regular basis. The 400-member New York Society, on the other hand, is primarily geared toward "appreciation and collecting," he says. Most of the members are book and record collectors, however, and haven't gone in for collecting memorabilia as Shereff has. He only knows of about 12 other people in his group who are also collectors of memorabilia.

Shereff is happy to encourage people to become Gilbert and Sullivan buffs, but feels it is probably no longer possible to get into collecting, at least for the average person. "How anyone is going to start building a collection at prices like these, is beyond me. I couldn't do it," he says.

Shereff will be happy to give further information to anyone who contacts him at 185 West End Ave., Apt. 20F, New York, NY 10023.

DON STEWART
ANTIQUE KEYS

Back in the '40s when I got out of the service," Don Stewart recollects, "I was a great believer in collecting all kinds of unique junk. At that time, anyone who gathered all that stuff was looked on as a little crazy by most people."

Well, he was crazy — like a fox — for today, Stewart, who lives in Phoenix, Arizona, has a world-renowned collection of antique keys, and he's become the leading expert in the history of the manufacturers who made them.

Stewart was a construction worker after World War II, and frequently came in contact with old locks and keys. "Some were so pretty and interesting, I kept them," he says. "I just kind of locked in on the hobby, you might say."

When he made a vacation trip to Europe some years ago, "My goodness, there were keys all over the place. I just loaded up, and took them home."

He doesn't really know how many keys he has collected. "Everyone always asks that," he says, "and I don't have the foggiest notion." He does know that there are over 2,000 of the keys displayed on the walls and in other parts of his home.

"My poor wife is complaining that I'm crowding her out into the street," he chuckles. "I've got so many buckets and boxes full of keys you wouldn't believe it." He also has his entire garage crammed full of old catalogues and literature from lock and key manufacturers, which he uses for reference.

"I know more about those old keys and locks than most of the manufacturers," says Stewart. "They come to me for information. You'd be surprised what they don't know until I tell them. It's all news to them." Most of the firms never even kept files of their obsolete catalogues or literature. The material was simply thrown away. "It's just one of those things nobody ever thought of," he says.

Putting a monetary value on the keys is pretty impossible, says Stewart. For one thing, most of them have no intrinsic value, unlike a lot of other collectibles (unless they are very, very old — Roman Empire-vintage, for example). Also, 90 percent of the keys were individually handmade, says Stewart, so "they're all unique, one-of-a-kind items." In addition, "keys are a tough thing to date. You have do to it in 100-year lumps."

The keys *are* interesting, however. Among the fascinating keys Stewart has in his collection, for example, is a key from an assayer's safe in an Idaho mining town. The safe was rigged with an explosive device so that if someone used the wrong key, it would explode the lock and the safe could not be entered. He also has some pocket watch keys from around 1900. In addition, Stewart has a set of casting plate keys. These were master keys used in the factory to make the rest of the keys.

"I have so many interesting keys I can't keep track of them all," Stewart says.

That there are so many keys around to collect is not surprising to Stewart. He says that up until World War I, "everyone, even so-called poor people, had hired help. So, they had to keep their things locked up or the help would steal them blind." Hence, each household had a huge ring of keys for all manner of locks.

Though he's "just a retired bum now," Stewart keeps himself busy with a small retail stamp and coin store. He also has a complete printing shop, which he resurrected from a construction site in Idaho. He's used the equipment to publish several books about keys and their manufacture.

His most notable work, *Standard Guide to Key Collecting, United States, 1850-1975*, has become the bible for key collectors. "I did everything on that book. I researched, wrote, edited, set type, printed and bound it," he says proudly. Because the first printing, in 1976, has been long sold out, Stewart is in the process of preparing a second edition. He has done four other books, mainly reproductions of old catalogues for use by collectors, who want all the original research material they can get their hands on.

In 1978, Stewart founded, and remains the executive director of, Key Collectors International, the major hobby group. The 294 members all over the country and abroad, are all kept well-informed with the latest news in the world of keys with *Key Collectors Journal*, published by Stewart.

Keys are appealing to him because of their "history and beauty. The fact that everyone has to use them during the course of life and totally ignores them is interesting to me. People guard and treasure keys until they no longer need them — then they throw them away."

Not only that, "but the inventiveness of the people who spent all their waking moments designing and making them" is important to Stewart. Besides, there's "just the sheer joy of searching out information about a key and finding out all about it."

A membership in Key Collectors International, at $15 for the first year ($10 thereafter), will bring novices "a whole wealth of information that's invaluable for starting out." Stewart recommends that anyone interested in collecting keys contact him at P. O. Box 9397, Phoenix, AZ 85068.

GIL SHAPIRO
STORE FIXTURES

WHEN GIL SHAPIRO was a senior in high school in 1961, he sold his family's furniture to buy a used drugstore.

Today, Shapiro is the proprietor of New York City's Urban Archaeology, a unique retail outlet that deals solely in artifacts from commercial establishments. Shapiro has sold the pieces of many a dismantled drugstore, bar and restaurant since 1978, when "Urban Archaeology" opened its doors in the chic SoHo section of Manhattan.

But, back to that first drugstore. It was in Manhattan Beach, Brooklyn, and he bought it for only $500 ($100 for the interior of the store, $400 to have it removed and placed in the Shapiro home). Naturally, Shapiro's parents were a bit surprised to find a complete drugstore in the living room.

"You can imagine what they said," Shapiro says. Fortunately, they were able to get their furniture back — and still let young Gil keep the drugstore. It turned out to be a pretty good investment, too. Among the items in the store were 32 signed Tiffany wall sconces (which Shapiro still owns), valued today at $5,000 to $8,000 apiece.

Even now, Shapiro lives with the objects he collects. He has three residences: an apartment in SoHo, and houses in Queens and Woodstock, New York. In his Queens home, for instance, he has a drugstore in one of the bedrooms, a complete soda fountain in the recreation room, and a barber shop and saloon breakfront elsewhere in the house. A cast iron billiard table with an elephant head design, made in 1884, serves as his dining room table.

Most of what he collects (and what Urban Archaeology sells) dates from 1880-1920. "This is the way I've always decorated, even before I had the business," he says. "Everybody always thought I was out of my mind. Maybe I was, but now they all want what I have."

In addition, these pieces are a good investment, Shapiro says. "Many people are buying them for the investment alone." He cites slot machines, which he has been selling and collecting for the last several years. There has been an average increase in their value of 10 percent per month or over two years. The high prices of slot machines and other commercial artifacts, are, in fact, threatening to drive the average collector out of the market.

"If someone had bought these things several years ago, when I started, he would be in good shape today," Shapiro feels. But the collector "without a large bankroll" is pretty well stymied by today's costs.

In addition to their investment value, and their unusual characteristics, urban artifacts impress Shapiro with their beauty. "I just like the look and feel of old places — and the talent of the people who created these things."

Shapiro is a tireless crusader in his quest for new and unusual items to add to his collection or his retail business. For example, he saw a picture in *National Geographic* of a soda fountain that had been operating in Columbus, Indiana since the 1880s. "It was just a question of hopping on the plane" and buying the complete soda fountain from the flabbergasted owner.

Shapiro believes the dedicated collector of urban artifacts can get virtually anything they want "depending on how badly you want to have it and whether you're willing to go right into the lion's den and come out with the treasure."

For Shapiro, "This is better than going to a movie, eating out or watching TV."

Always glad to give advice, and assist buyers, sellers, or the curious, Shapiro can be contacted at Urban Archaeology, 137 Spring St., New York, NY 10003.

PAUL VAVERCHAK
PADLOCKS

WHEN I WAS A KID," Paul Vaverchak remembers, "I had an uncle who worked on the railroad. If he went on a trip to another part of the country, he would bring home a lock that had the name of the railroad on it. First thing I knew, I had a fishing stringer so full of locks I couldn't lift it."

That childhood fascination with old padlocks carried over into his adult life. His collection of all types and styles now numbers nearly 7,000 padlocks, "almost all from the United States" and a library of original catalogues going back to 1855: "every known major lock company's catalogue, more than 300 in all."

The earliest padlocks in the United States date from 1685. They were heart-shaped Pennsylvania Dutch locks of hammered tin. He collects locks from

1685 until just prior to World War II, when mass production of padlocks went into full swing. "I like the antique locks, anyway," he says. But the bulk of his collection comes from the so-called "golden age" of padlocks was between 1860 and 1890, the first patent for a lock was issued in 1839, according to Vaverchak. Newark, New Jersey, during the time of the Civil War, "was the lock capital of the world. There were 66 different lock manufacturers in Newark, alone," he says.

Among the items in his collection are some "early Pennsylvania Dutch screw key locks. Vaverchak has 12 of the locks "which are quite unique, and bear the initials of individual locksmiths who made them."

The basic design of locks hasn't really changed much with the passing centuries, Vaverchak says. "The pin tumbler device, invented by Linus Yale in 1875, was really an offshoot of an Egyptian lock. Actually, the basic design of locks hasn't changed since 2000 B.C."

Vaverchak's collection is neatly placed in drawered cabinets, arranged by company and era. The collection "takes up several rooms in my house," he says. Many of his padlocks have been displayed in various places near his hometown of Pillow, Pennsylvania, 38 miles north of Harrisburg.

A popular new area of lock collecting is "miniature locks. These are especially popular among people who live in apartments. By simply putting a piece of velvet in a display box, you can show off your whole collection in a small space. Polish the locks, put them on little hooks in the case, and you've got quite a collection."

Locks are becoming popular bits of Early Americana, according to Vaverchak. It is "still possible to go out and buy a lock that's 100 or 150 years old for $12 or $15 ," he says. But, in the past 10 years, the "prices of locks have really gone up. "Quite a number of books about locks have been published in the last few years" and that has increased interest and prices, says Vaverchak. Collectors most often seek locks with patent dates on them. The average price is between $5 and $8 for such a lock. All-brass locks go for $20 to $25 and more, he says.

For the beginner, Vaverchak advises: "Pick a particular category as soon as possible." Among the possible categories are door locks, prison locks, and foreign locks, as well as padlocks. "Pick up one of the many books available in whatever category you decide to specialize in." Collecting railroad padlocks, for example, is "a huge field, considering there has been a total of 14,000 railroads in the U.S." He also suggests that novices join either the American Lock Collectors Society (14010 Cardwell, Livonia, MI 48154) or Key Collectors International (PO Box 9397, Phoenix, AZ 85068).

His hobby is more than mere collecting to Vaverchak. "I enjoy researching the history of a particular padlock I have found. I've learned about the ingenious people who thought of the mechanisms; some of them should have been watchmakers, their work was so excellent and finely detailed," he says. "It's quite a challenge to figure out what these old inventors were doing."

Vaverchak is always happy to give appraisal advice on a lock, or simply information on its origins. "If it has something to do with locks, I'm involved somewhere," he says. "I certainly enjoy getting mail." He can be contacted at PO Box 38, Pillow, PA 17080.

STANLEY WILLIS
HANDCUFFS & RESTRAINTS

YOU COULD PROBABLY call Stanley Willis well-restrained — because he has a collection of 330 handcuffs, leg—irons, and other types of physical restraints. He claims his collection is "one of the five largest of its type in the world."

A 37-year-old electrical contractor from Cincinnati, Ohio, Willis first began to collect these items in 1969, when he was intrigued by an old padlock he bought at a flea market. "I couldn't find a locksmith who could cut a key for it," he says. "So, I began playing around with it myself and managed to cut one that worked." Then, he went looking for a set of handcuffs to go with the padlock, and decided "to collect handcuffs, instead, because they were much more fun."

His collection sounds like fun, containing items with names like nippers (which are single-hand handcuffs), twisters (a chain with a handle at each end), thumb cuffs, and the ominous sounding "Oregon boot."

"That was an improvement on the ball and chain," says Willis. It was an 18-pound weight that split in half "like a doughnut" and was placed around the ankle of the prisoner. "You can't very well run with that on one leg," he says. The Oregon boot was patented in 1875.

Another fascinating part of the collection is the McKenzie Mitt. This device, created in 1925, is a pair of sheet metal mittens that "restrain the hands completely," Willis says. But the McKenzie Mitts weren't in use long, "because they worked too well. The guard had to help the mittened prisoner do literally everything." Thus, the mitts are "very scarce now, and a real collector's item."

Most of the articles in Willis' collection of "basically any type of police or prison related restraint" come from the period between 1880 and 1960, though he does have a few items from the 1700s. The bulk of his collection is displayed on a pegboard wall in his basement office and recreation room.

Not surprisingly, Willis has had to do a good bit of research to find out about the history of his collection. He says there is only one book on the subject, "but it's geared to escape artists, and talks more about how to get out of the restraints than about the history of them." Undaunted, Willis researched the patents of these items (all of which were patented, since most of them were mass-produced). He wrote to the companies which were still in business to get information on the history of the restraints they manufactured.

That still wasn't enough, so he read articles and "corresponded with other collectors. I learned a lot, especially history," he says, which adds to his enjoyment of his collection.

Willis builds his collection by visting places like flea markets and gun shows. The better pieces he obtained from "old-time escape artists." He says that "the good quality, older pieces are very hard to find nowadays. About the only way to get them now is to buy out someone else's collection."

What is the value of his collection, as a potential investment? "Like anything, the value is whatever the market will bear," he says. "Antique dealers don't know enough yet to know the value. You almost have to be a collector, because some aren't worth anything, and some are worth a bundle."

The beginning collector should not despair, Willis says. "There are still a lot of pieces that are very inexpensive, but the stuff keeps going up in value." Common handcuffs, like the Peerless, might go for $15 or $20 a pair. He advises the beginner to look around, and "you might turn up something fantastic, at an incredibly low price."

Some people have looked upon Willis's hobby as "kind of kinky. But, most people accept it for what it is, a hobby like any other." Interestingly enough, he says, women are more interested than men in his collection.

"It has never seemed strange to me," he says. "I have always been mechanical and interested in mechanical things. The workmanship and mechanisms on some of the older pieces are fantastic. So is the detailed metal work. We just don't have craftsmen like these today."

Willis would be glad to hear from anyone interested in handcuffs, or other restraints. "I love to correspond with people. I do it all the time," he says. He can be contacted at 6211 Stewart Rd., Cincinnati, OH 45227.

DENVER WRIGHT
BEER CANS

Little DID HE imagine, as he looked at the 12 cans of beer sitting behind his basement bar in Frotenanc, Missouri, that one day he would be the head of an organization devoted to the collectin of beer cans.

But Wright, as founder and president of "The Denver M. Wright, Jr. Foundation," has done much to make beer-can collecting as popular as it is today. He was also a co-founder (and first president) of the Beer Can Collectors of America in 1969, which now boasts over 12,000 members. In addition, he has one of the most unique collections of beer cans in the U.S.

Wright became seriously interested in collecting beer cans in 1965. Until then, he had looked on his little back-of-the-bar collection "as a pleasant conversation piece." But friends and business associates began sending him cans from all around the country, and he began mailing inventory sheets to those contributors, giving them credit for their additions to his collection.

"I was content with the few cans I had, but found that as I began collecting more, it came to be an important part of my life," says Wright.

His collection, consisting of 1,320 different, full cans of beer, has a number of intriguing brands represented. He has, for example, a can of "Soul" beer, which was manufactured by a firm in the L.A. Watts ghetto in the early 1960s.

Wright, the president of a St. Louis advertising specialty distributor, created his "foundation" as somewhat of a lark. The major project of the organization was the publication of *Ye Olde Foundation Herald*, a chatty magazine that Wright put out for several years featuring news and information about the "foundation," as well as profiles of fellow collectors, news of their collections, and other news relating to the hobby.

His journal was not the official publication of the BCCA , but "I featured this organization in the magazine because of my sincere interest in it."

Incidentally, Wright doesn't believe beer cans should be bought or sold, but simply traded among collectors. That is how most people operate, although occasionally there will be some money changing hands (and then its only a matter of 50 cents or so). Wright did most of his collecting "by mail, which was a pleasant way to do it."

What does Wright consider worthy of collecting? Just about any can, of any kind, as long as "at a distance of six or eight feet it is visibly different somehow." And he has sensible advice for would-be beer can collectors: "Be fair in trading, give a little more than you receive."

He also counsels keeping inventory records, displaying one's collection and, finally, "having fun." He suggests joining the Beer Can Collectors of America (747 Merus Ct., Fenton, MO 63026), as it will put the novice in touch with other collectors, providing opportunities for trading and expanding one's collection and connections. The BCCA sponsors an annual "can-vention" (a term he coined) for collectors. A recent convention saw somewhere in the neighborhood of half a million cans on display or available for trading.

Currently, Wright has stopped collecting and is less involved with BCCA. "I had to stop. I ran out of room in the special floor-to-ceiling cabinets I had made." His collection is now housed at his son's home, because there's no room in Wright's condominium for the cans and their display cases. But, he says, this is rather typical of many collectors "who have been in this for 20 years: you love the people in it, and you love the experience, but as for doing it the rest of your life..."

Wright will be happy to advise beer can collectors, who can contact him at 1521 Hedgeford Dr., Chesterfield, MO 63017.

PHILATELY

JOSEPH BALOUGH
PERFINS

WITHIN A GENERAL area of collecting, it's desirable for a collector to develop a specialization in order to enhance both the value of the collection and the collector's enjoyment of its pursuit. Certainly, this is true in stamp collecting. There are increasing numbers of collectors who are specialists, each with their own unique outlook on their hobby.

One of the more unusual areas of philatelic endeavor is the collection of perfins. Joseph Balough, of El Paso, Texas, probably has the largest and most complete collection of U.S. perfins in existence.

Just what is a perfin? Balough says that "perfin" is an acronym meaning "perforated initials" or "perforated insignia." It refers to "a postage stamp perforated on its face with a company's initials or insignia, to prevent the employees from stealing its stamps." Balough says the practice was developed in Great Britain in 1868, and was adopted by some 220 countries, including the United States where it was approved by the U.S. Post Office in 1908. Perfins were widely used in the United States until the early 1930s. "After they came out with the postage meters at about that time, it was much easier to control the use of postage," he says. But perfins are still used today by such institutions as the New York City Board of Education, the County of Los Angeles, and the Chase Manhattan Bank, he says.

According to Balough, there are over 6,000 different perfin patterns from some 5,800 different business concerns in the United States alone. His collection includes some 25,000 worldwide perfins, including a sizeable U.S. collection of 5,750 perfins.

Balough has collected stamps for 46 of his 55 years, specializing for many years in stamps from Germany. By 1963, "I only needed three stamps to complete my collection," he says. "I had to do something to continue my interest." An article in *Linn's Weekly Stamp News* aroused his interest, and he started collecting perfins.

"I'm the type of person who wants to reach the top of a mountain as fast as possible," says Balough. "Perfins seemed to be a facet of collecting that still had room for research," where he could quickly rise to preeminence in the field.

Balough says that numbers as well as designs were used on the stamps. For example, the rarest item in Balough's collection "and one of the scarcest of all perfins" is "U.S. 505, a five-cent blue stamp perforated by the Shellenberg Clothing Company in 1917. What makes the stamp rare is that, at the time, five-cent stamps were red, not blue. This was a printing error."

The retired U.S. Army major, now a sixth-grade teacher, is active in the Perfins Club, a national organization of some 800 perfin collectors founded in 1943.

"Perfin collecting is a good hobby for kids," says Balough. "It's much less expensive than regular stamp collecting, something you can get without cost." He says all but the rarest perfins are traded between collectors, or are sold for paltry sums. The stamps are usually obtained from dealers or collectors circulars, or through stamp auctions, Balough says. Some cost only two or three cents apiece, while a rare French perfin, from the 1930 Paris Exposition, brings as much as $300.

Balough enjoys his hobby because "it's still a challenge. Certain areas of philately have been well gone over and written about. I'd much rather be doing something I can still learn about, and disseminate what I've learned to others."

He is co-author of the *U.S. Perfin Catalogue*, published in 1979, "the most complete book ever written on the subject. It also can be used as an album," he says. The book can be purchased from Balough for $30 in a hardbound edition or for $25 in a looseleaf format.

Beginners in perfin collecting should contact the Perfins Club, c/o Mrs. Dorothy Savage, 10550 Western Ave., Space 94, Stanton, CA 90680, for further information on the club. A stamped, self-addressed envelope should be included with the letter, Balough says.

Balough also will be glad to give information and guidance to perfin collectors, if they write to him at 9108 McFall Dr., El Paso, TX 79925.

TERENCE HINES
STATE REVENUE STAMPS

$\mathbf{O}$NE OF THE MORE interesting and unusual specialties within philately is the collection of state revenue stamps. It's still possible to build an interesting and satisfying revenue stamp collection relatively economically, says Terence Hines, a leading collector since 1967. He is a recognized authority on these fascinating stamps, particularly those issued in his native New England.

According to Hines, a revenue stamp "shows payment of a revenue raising tax." The transfer tax on stocks, and cigarette and liquor taxes are examples of taxes whose payment is shown by affixing a stamp to the item. "A lot of these are like stamps but many are decals or metered imprints," Hines says. The meter-imprinted stamps are heavily counterfeited; so much so, he says, that most metered cigarette tax stamps are forgeries. "If you really want to get technical, an auto license plate can be considered a revenue stamp," he says.

The very first revenue stamps, issued in Delaware in early 1818, were not stamps at all, but embossings on documents. Adhesive stamps, as we know them today, did not make their appearance until the 1860s.

Hines grew up in New Hampshire, a state that has had many different revenue stamps over the years. "I collected regular stamps for several years until I noticed, in the early 1960s, that New Hampshire had decal cigar box stamps. That interested me, and I just branched out from there, starting to collect state revenue stamps."

Right now, few people are interested in this area of philately, according to Hines. But revenue stamp collecting is "becoming more popular as the average collector of other kinds of stamps is being priced out of the market." This spurt in interest "has certainly happened with federal revenue stamps, and spills over more and more into the state collecting. The stamps are hard to come by, for they are often destroyed or thrown away. It's a great challenge to find the rarer stamps. They are difficult to track down, but not too expensive once you do." Building an interesting state revenue stamp collection is "all legwork on the part of the collector," Hines believes.

In his collecting he settled on the states of New Hampshire, Vermont, and Maine. Today, he has between 400 and 500 stamps in his collection, which "for these states, is quite a large number to have found." Often, as in the case of New Hampshire, "the stamps are beautifully engraved." In his collection, Hines says, he has a "fairly complete set of New Hampshire tobacco stamps from 1939, in mint condition."

He wrote a catalogue of the stamps, and found 25 different kinds for Vermont, 250 for New Hampshire (mostly tobacco and fishing and hunting stamps). *State Revenue Stamps of New Hampshire and Vermont*, was published in 1971.

The State Revenue Society is the national organization for collectors. Hines has been involved with it since he first began collecting and is currently the president. There are some 200 members in the United States, he says, who keep in touch through the bi-monthly *State Revenue Newsletter*, which they receive on payment of a $4 per year membership fee. The society is a medium for collectors to exchange old issues of stamps. Trading and selling also goes on at stamp shows, he says.

To start collecting state revenue stamps, Hines suggests the beginner "write to the state you are interested in, and ask if they will sell the stamps to you. Often, they're very unwilling and in some cases, it's illegal to possess mint condition revenue stamps." Hines has gotten around the problem by becoming a licensed cigarette dealer in both Maine and Vermont, so he can buy the stamps as they are issued. "I don't sell cigarettes, " he says, "but I pay two or three dollars per year for a license so I can get the stamps. Many other collectors do this too."

Like any other collectible, the value of these stamps depends "on how many were made, and supply and demand," he says. The average value of the stamps is from 1-cent to $40 depending on the rarity of an issue. "I've never heard of a state revenue stamp selling for much more than $200," he says, adding that this makes collecting the stamps a much more economical hobby than regular philately.

Hines, a psychologist at Cornell Medical College in New York City, finds that "the challenge of collecting something that few other people collect and the difficulty in finding the items" are the exciting aspects of his hobby. In addition, "It's the kind of hobby that it's not necessary to spend a lot of money to avoid having a bad collection."

Hines suggests that revenue stamp collectors (or would-be collectors) contact either the State Revenue Society (c/o Harold Effner Jr., 210 Eastern Wy., Rutherford, NJ 07070) or the American Revenue Association, which concerns itself with U.S. federal and foreign revenue stamps (c/o Bruce Miller, 1010 S. Fifth Ave., Arcadia, CA 91006) for further information.

WILLIAM McCONNELL
ASIAN PHILATELY

WILLIAM McCONNELL has a large collection of Asian stamps — and he never bought any of them! He's now a leading expert on Asian philately, particularly stamps of Japan.

"I have 120 correspondents in Japan, to whom I have been writing for many years," he says, "and I've gotten all of my stamps that way." Through the Japanese Pen Friend Society, the Cover Collector's Circle Club, and the People-to-People program, McConnell has managed to gather an impressive array of stamps, all as gifts from friends he has made through letter-writing.

It is this kind of social contact that makes collecting stamps a meaningful part of McConnell's life. "I don't really do it as much for the stamps," he says, "as I do to maintain communication with people throughout the world, and to maintain some kind of dialogue with them."

Most of McConnell's efforts have been centered on the philately of Japan, although he does collect stamps from other Asian countries such as Thailand, India, Sri Lanka (Ceylon), and Nepal, in addition to having a "worldwide collection" of stamps.

McConnell has long had an interest in the art and culture of Japan. He was a student in the Asian Studies program at the University of California. He studied zen and Japanese art and culture in Japan, and he married a Japanese woman. While he was in college, he was one of the leaders of a successful effort to have the California State Legislature repudiate a World War II-vintage law prohibiting Japanese-Americans from owning property in the state. Thus, it was only natural that an interest in the stamps of Japan, as artifacts of Japanese culture, should have fascinated McConnell.

He has some fabulous stamps in his collection. Among the gems are his Japanese revenue stamps. "These were affixed by the government onto fiscal documents as a means of recording the payment of taxes," he says. The stamps were commonly found on rice bags, for example, or as fiscal stamps on government legal documents.

The fiscal and documentary stamp series features a silkworm design. The one-inch square stamps have calligraphy on them, as well as showing silkworm eggs, in a horseshoe design. "These are very colorful stamps," says McConnell, adding that they had red, blue, black, white and tan colors, and were printed on a special handmade paper. Others of the silkworm series of stamps featured moths in a horseshoe design, with other calligraphy. These were black on white or gray on white, on the same native paper.

"These stamps were created by the same artists who did the famous dragon series of stamps in the 1870s, I'm also fortunate enough to possess some of the dragon stamps," says McConnell. The dragons were the first postage stamps issued in Japan, about 1870. These small, hand-engraved stamps, feature a dragon motif by several artists. "There are secret marks of the artists on the plate," he says. While they were supposed to look alike, "none are actually the same, because of the small differences of each artist."

McConnell has been deeply involved in the work of the Japanese American Society for Philately (JASP). The organization, which has between 350 and 400 members worldwide, is one of several societies in the United States devoted to Japanese philately. McConnell has been editor of the society's bi-monthly magazine *The Postal Bell* since 1967.

"I am lucky to be involved with JASP," says McConnell. "The membership is about 45 percent Americans of Japanese ancestry, and they add so much color and sensitivity to the experience of belonging to the society." The group "tries to make Japanese philately relevant to the culture and heritage of Japan — and to the people of this country. We think we've been pretty successful."

Since 1970, in addition to his chores as the editor of JASP's magazine, McConnell, a financial analyst for Lockheed Corporation finds time to write a monthly column on Asian philately for *The Stamp Collector*, a nationwide publication.

McConnell's advice to the beginner: "just begin. Get involved with writing and stamp collecting — and don't talk too much until you understand the subject." The best way for the novice to learn about Asian philately is through membership in any of several organizations devoted to its study.

"Throughout the United States there are very good Asian stamp societies," says McConnell. "Get into a small society which will tolerate new members." He says that many of the organizations have "become too esoteric instead of relating to people," and make it difficult for the newcomer to become involved.

McConnell doesn't think a major investment is necessary for the beginning stamp collector. Learning what one is interested in is the most important thing. "If you're willing to hang in there, you can do just as well — and get a lot more value out of your hobby — by being in contact with other collectors, both here and in Asia," he says.

The novice must also be careful in purchasing stamps from dealers, says McConnell. "Prior to 1938, there were a great many government authorized forgeries of real stamps, done primarily for the tourist trade." Though the stamps indicate that they are forgeries "by a small chop integrated into the design," only the trained eye of an Asian philately buff could spot the fakes.

Anyone interested in joining JASP should contact the society at PO Box 1049, El Cerrito, CA 94530. McConnell, who will be glad to give information or advice on Asian philatelic topics, can be contacted through PO Box 2730, Santa Clara, CA 95051.

BERNICE MITTOWER
POSTMARKS

Ever been to Tumwater, Washington? Or Sopchoppy, Florida? How about Mauch Chunk, Pennsylvania? Bernice E. Mittower has — and she's never left her house!

Over the last 40 years, Mrs. Mittower has "visited" all these places, and many others, while she was becoming an expert in the interesting philatelic sidelight of postmark collecting. Since 1970, she's also been the curator of a unique museum devoted exclusively to postmarks.

Mrs. Mittower's fondness for postmarks began because "the names of places and the cancellations on letters intrigued me." She tried to interest her stepdaughter in collecting cancels (as postmarks are also called) in the early 1940s, but "wound up doing it myself, because my stepdaughter just wasn't interested."

Today she has a collection of over 10,000 postmarks ("My collection isn't all that great," she says modestly). She specializes in cancellations from Ohio, or postmarks with religious or geological names. "I find that specializing is really the best way to collect," she says, "because there are just so many different postmarks to collect that to try and get them all is impossible."

Besides, she says, "Once you get involved with topicals [postmarks of a specific subject], it's a lot of fun trying to fit postmarks into the categories."

Mrs. Mittower is most excited, however, about the postmark museum of the Postmark Collectors Club. Housed in a small building of its own "that's almost bursting right out the windows" with postmarks, it is a popular attraction at Historic Lyme Village, a reconstructed town in Bellevue, Ohio, about 20 miles from Sandusky.

The club was given what Mrs. Mittower describes as the world's largest collection of postmarks, contained in 575 binders and several hundred pounds of loose materials. This forms the basis for the postmark museum. It represents a lifetime of collecting by a Boston doctor, Howard K. Thompson.

Mrs. Mittower, and eight members of the postmark club who live in the same area, have been hard at work since 1978 remounting, sorting, and cataloguing the massive collection.

The Thompson collection, an estimated one million pieces, features many postmarks from territorial post offices, and some pre-1760 cancels that are worth well over $3,000, Mrs. Mittower says. "It even contains an original Lyme, Ohio, postmark — the only one known to exist," she says.

"It would be nice to live long enough to get it all done," she says wryly, adding that the revamping of the collection should take another year or so of hard work. Still to be done is a complete cataloguing of all the items in the collection.

In addition to the material from Thompson's collection, the Postmark Museum houses many other "funny little oddball things." For example, Mrs. Mittower says, there's a uniform belonging to a Niagara Falls, New York, postman. "That man literally gave us the shirt right off his back," she says.

The museum is open whenever the historic village is open, and Mrs. Mittower always tries to be on hand to greet visitors and talk about the items displayed. The bulk of the museum's materials are not on display, but are reserved for researchers.

"If you want a clean, lightweight, and inexpensive hobby, try postmarks," says Mrs. Mittower. She recommends the beginner specialize in certain topic areas of postmarks, rather than trying to get postmarks from all over.

Active in the Postmark Collectors Club since 1960, Mrs. Mittower feels it is the perfect organization for the novice collector. There are 1,100 members all over the world. "The only continent we haven't covered yet is Antarctica because we haven't found a penguin who collects postmarks." The club offers membership at no charge to veterans and shut-ins, and sends monthly bulletins and extra postmarks for their collections.

To get started in this hobby is quite easy, Mrs. Mittower says. Simply go to post offices and ask them to cancel an envelope for you with their postmark. "If you go into the post office, they can't refuse to give you their local cancel," she says, adding that the club had been influential recently in having postal regulations changed to allow a person to obtain a postmark without mailing a letter.

Then, it's simply a matter of getting in touch with another collector, and offering to swap postmarks. "That's why it's valuable to join our club, so we can help each other."

Mrs. Mittower enjoys collecting postmarks because "I like the variety. I like to be at home, and don't travel much, so my collection lets me travel vicariously."

For information on membership in the Postmark Collectors Club, contact Mrs. Bernice White, 3487 Firstenberger Rd., Marion, OH 43302. Mrs. Mittower will answer questions about the postmark museum or the collecting of postmarks directed to her at RR 2, PO Box 136, Republic, OH 44867.

WILLIAM RAPP
POSTAL HISTORY

IF YOU THINK IT'S expensive today to send a letter, you should have lived in 1825. A letter cost 28 cents to mail, and the tariff increased with the distance the letter had to travel and the number of pages it contained!

Facts like these are the happy rewards of research into postal history. One of the foremost masters of this unique, but rapidly growing, branch of philately is William Rapp, of Crete, Nebraska.

Rapp, the state entomologist of Nebraska, started out, like most postal historians do, collecting stamps. "As I collected," he recalls, "I found myself becoming more and more interested in the locations of various post offices, what their operations were like, and so forth."

As part of his research, Rapp does collect cancellations from post offices, specializing in the "stampless period," prior to 1847 when the government first issued stamps. These cancellations, usually handwritten or rubber stamped onto envelopes, "only come from the early states of the Union, nothing west of the Mississippi," he says.

Interesting as his collection is, it is postal history that intrigues Rapp the most. He specializes in the states of New Jersey, Vermont, and Nebraska, as well as having an interest in railway post offices and rural routes. From his research into Nebraska post offices, Rapp has discovered that there were 5,000 to 6,000 of them during the state's history. "A lot of them were shortlived," he says, "in ranch houses and the like during territorial days."

Nebraska is also fertile ground for studying railway postal routes, he adds, because the state is "crisscrossed with railroads." Many of the Nebraska branch line railroads had only one train a day, all through their existence, Rapp says, and that one train did nothing but carry mail. In fact, he says, the Nebraska branch of the Missouri-Pacific railroad "could successfully operate only because of the mail contracts. When the government took them away, the railroad wanted to go out of business, because the postal revenues always exceeded income from passengers or freight."

Another interesting fact Rapp offers is that small town post office franchises were much sought after. Since most of these operations only netted about $35-$40 per year in stamp revenues, Rapp says it wasn't money that inspired such interest. "These post offices were in general stores," he says, "and the owners thought that if people came to get the mail, they'd probably end up spending money in the store at the same time."

Rapp enjoys his research, but confesses that "the one big thing that hurts is trying to find the material." There is quite a bit written about postal history, though it is spread out all over the country. The researcher has to do a lot of searching to find information. Fortunately, "we have a wonderful interlibrary loan system in this country, so material is available" with relative ease, once the researcher identifies what he is seeking. Much of the material comes from government documents, Rapp says. "Government documents are slow reading and difficult to get through, sometimes," he says. But it's necessary to peruse them, particularly for early postal information. All in all, postal history is "just plain, good old-fashioned history-type research," Rapp thinks.

In 1968, Rapp was one of the founders of a quarterly US postal history journal as an aid to others interested in researching postal history. He is still the editor of *Postal History USA*, which is sent to about 300 people all over the United States. This journal, which runs to about 80 pages over the course of a year, publishes the findings of researchers, handles requests for information, and "just generally keeps postal history buffs in touch with one another."

Postal history "is getting to be a very popular part of philately," says Rapp, adding that his organization is only one of many around the U.S. and in foreign countries, as well. "I'd recommend it as a hobby for anybody," he says. But he suggests the beginner get in touch with the American Philatelic Society first, because that organization frequently publishes articles in its journal about postal history. From there, it's a simple matter of "taking the time to look at what has been and is being published" in the area of interest for the historian. Rapp advises beginners, "You have to have the desire to dig, the curiosity and willingness to do lots of library work."

Through all of this research, Rapp has developed the view that "There have been periods of time when the post office was, at least scandalwise, worse than today. At other times, it has been very innovative." For example, he says, in the period of 1900-20, the United States Post Office " led the world in encouraging private inventors" to create new machinery to modernize postal operations.

Says Rapp, "My hobby is a challenge. There's always something new, and it's relaxing. After having all sorts of problems at work, it's nice to be able to come home and relax and enjoy something."

Rapp will provide further information to anyone interested in postal history, or in the publication *Postal History USA*. He can be contacted at 430 Ivy Ave., Crete, NE 68333.

MARCEL SAGER
ERRORS, FREAKS & ODDITIES

ERRORS, FREAKS, AND oddities are three of Marcel Sager's favorite things. Before anyone gets the wrong idea, these words describe the kinds of stamps Sager collects.

And for one of his relative youth (he's 17), it's even more intriguing that Sager has become an acknowledged expert in the field.

As Sager explains it, "These are stamps with manmade errors" that render them unusual in some way. The stamps usually result from perforating errors or printing mishaps, and derive their value from that fact. Most of the stamps, Sager says, are immediately destroyed once the error is discovered, so the value is in finding a stamp that hasn't been caught by the post office of the country that made it.

Surprisingly, Sager says, it is possible to find these stamps readily. "You find a lot of them," he says. "Sometimes there will be a little perforation missing on the stamps, or there will be a slight color shift." Any of these mistakes mean the stamp is ripe for collection by Sager or a fellow EFO enthusiast.

Sager has been collecting stamps since 1970. He specializes in United States and Canadian stamps, and began looking out for EFOs in 1976. "I have a good general collection of stamps," he says, "but the EFOs are really the most interesting to me, because I enjoy trying to find them."

The most famous example of an EFO is the 1918 U.S. 24-cent air mail stamp. This stamp, with an upside down biplane in the center, is one of the collectors' dream stamps. If one could be purchased, Sager says, it would be worth at least $130,000. "It's every EFO collector's dream to own one," he says. "Of course, the cost makes it impossible."

Within his own collection, Sager has several interesting examples of EFO stamps. He has a "very early " George Washington three-cent stamp, where half the stamp shows the selvage (the outside straight edge) of the next stamp in the middle of it.

He also has a 1960 three-cent stamp with former UN Secretary General Dag Hammarskjold's picture on it. When this stamp was first put on the market, Sager says, the Post Office Department (as it was then called) noticed that the colors of the stamp were inverted. Before they could correct the mistake, a few sheets of the stamps made their way into local post offices, where they were promptly snapped up by collectors. The U.S. Post Office reprinted the stamps in the correct colors.

In addition to his collecting activity (and attending Queens College, where he majors in accounting), Sager has organized fellow EFO enthusiasts into a national organization, the EFO Society. The group, which Sager says now has over 100 members, was founded in 1978. Most of the activities of the society are conducted through its newsletter, which comes out bimonthly, its 18 pages crammed full of information on EFOs, news on new stamps, and advertisements from members about stamps for sale or wanted.

Sager says that finding EFO stamps is not as difficult as the novice collector might believe. "Just keep going to your local post office," he says. "A surprising number of EFOs will turn up." He also recommends the beginner join the EFO Society. "This way you will be in touch with other collectors, and you can learn something about EFO collecting," he says. "And there isn't much written about it anywhere other than our newsletter."

As for stamp collecting in general, Sager finds it a particularly interesting and satisfying hobby, one that most people could enjoy. "It's very educational," he says. "You can learn almost anything from stamps."

To obtain more information about EFOs or the EFO Society, Sager says to send a business-sized, stamped, self-addressed envelope to the society's secretary, John Hotchner, P. O. Box 1125, Falls Church, VA 22041.

HARRY THORSEN
SCOUTING STAMPS & MEMORABILIA

HARRY THORSEN IS a good scout. He has been associated with the Boy Scout movement for over 55 years, as a Scout, as a local leader in the suburban Chicago area, and as a national Scout executive. And he has the "largest collection of Scouting stamps and memorabilia outside of the National Scout Museum."

"I started when I was 12 years old," the retired printing company executive who lives in Sarasota, Florida, says, "and I never got out of it."

Thorsen is the leading collector of Scouting memorabilia (which, incidentally, includes items from The Girl Scouts, as well), publishing the only newsletter for collectors since 1966. He founded the Scouts on Stamps Society, an international organization of stamp collectors that boasts 1,500 members in 42 countries.

Surprisingly, perhaps, Thorsen says that the majority of Scouting memorabilia and stamp collectors are adults. "The prices have just been soaring," he says, "and it costs too much for the kids to participate."

For example, original *Boy Scout Handbooks*, from 1910, are selling for $75 to $150, typical, Thorsen says, of the prices items from Scouting's early days (1911-20) are fetching.

Collecting Scouting memorabilia is interesting, says Thorsen, because there are so many things to collect. For example, the most popular item with collectors is the embroidered merit badges which Scouts earn for their participation in various activities. There have been 5,000 different badges over the years. Another popular area of collecting, says Thorsen, is Scout coins and medallions. These have been made in many of the countries in the world that sanction Scouting. Among other items collectors are interested in are neckerchiefs, Scout toys and games, sheet music, and calendars.

"We're in a terrific period of nostalgia," says Thorsen. Scouting was 70 years old in 1980, and 40 million people in the United States alone have been Scouts so far, he adds. That, in turn, leads to a lot of material being available to the collector.

Thorsen's collection is so extensive that he has converted his two-car garage into a paneled museum room for his collection. The most outstanding item in his collection, Thorsen feels, is an original, 1910 uniform of the Boy Scouts of America. This is thought to be the only one still in existence, he says. It came from an attic in Vermont in 1977. "The little boy who owned it back in 1910 had only worn it once or twice, before he died," says Thorsen. It was neatly folded in a box, perfectly preserved, and almost like new, when the boy's sister, now an elderly woman, sold it to Thorsen.

Turning to the area of stamps, Thorsen says that some 1,300 different Scout stamps have been issued throughout the world. Here, again, he says, the field is rich for the collector.

His personal collection, in 38 albums, covers the full range of varieties of stamps that could be collected. He is particularly proud of a rare 1900 stamp bearing the likeness of Sir Robert Baden-Powell, the founder of Scouting. This stamp, issued during the Boer War for local use in South Africa, honored Baden-Powell for his role in the Siege of Mafeking.

Contemporary Scout stamps also hold great interest for Thorsen. A recent set by the government of Liberia utilized the artwork of Norman Rockwell in "a beautiful set of 50 stamps, the biggest set of Scout stamps ever issued. Liberia really scooped the U.S. by issuing those stamps," Thorsen says.

While some people associate Scouting with a sort of by-gone Rockwell-esque view of American boyhood, Thorsen is nonetheless enthusiastic about the movement. "We believe it's a character building organization, operated by benevolent people who care about what's happening in the community." Of course, for the youngsters involved, Thorsen says "the big attraction is the opportunity for camping, not getting one's character improved."

Thorsen feels his collecting has been of great help in advancing the cause of

Scouting: "I use this to sell the ideas and value of the program, as well as to explain the history of where we came from."

Thorsen advises anyone interested in collecting Scouting memorabilia or stamps to specialize. "That's an important characteristic of a collector," he says. "They usually concentrate on one or two areas. Don't try collecting everything — it's just too expensive."

He also urges memorabilia buffs or stamp enthusiasts to subscribe to his newsletters (there's also one for the Scouts on Stamps group), which contain advertisements from other collectors of what they have to sell, or want to buy or trade for, along with a lot of valuable information on the hobby.

Thorsen can be reached at 7305 Bounty Dr., Sarasota, FL 33581.

MARTIN WILSON
PLATE PRINTING NUMBER STAMPS

A UNIQUE SLANT on stamp collecting has been achieved by Martin Wilson, who collects only those stamps with the "plate printing number" on them. This number, containing as many as six digits, is assigned to each plate made to print stamps. It appears in the selvage area of one of the stamps in each sheet, Wilson explains.

Even collecting this limited sort of stamp, Wilson has managed to acquire "a few thousand," with more coming all the time, as the U.S. Postal Service continues to print new stamps.

Wilson's interest in plate printing number stamps stems from his service in the U.S. Army during World War II. He was stationed in the Philippines in 1944, when the Philippine stamps were overprinted "VICTORY." Since he was already interested in stamp collecting, he offered to trade those Philippine stamps for American issues.

He then put an advertisement in a stamp journal, soliciting stamps to trade for the Phillippine issues. The plate printing number on many of the U.S. stamps fascinated him, and he decided he would start collecting only those stamps.

His collection today is exclusively of United States issues. The oldest stamp he has is plate number 97. "This would put its date soon after 1897," he says, adding that the date can be determined by consulting postal records.

Wilson collects only individual stamps bearing the number. Other people, he says, collect whole blocks of stamps (called "panes") or try to find the same number in stamps printed in the four corners of a sheet of stamps. "But all this is really not necessary," he says. "I'm just going after one stamp bearing one plate number, and trying to get as many different plate numbers as I can. Besides, it makes it a lot easier to store the stamps by just collecting singles."

He says that the plate number is put on the stamp "each time a plate is engraved; it's the Postal Service's way of keeping track of the plates." He estimates that roughly one-tenth of all the stamps produced by the postal service have these numbers on them. Over the years, the postal service has issued some 1,800 different stamps, says Wilson, so the potential number of stamps for collecting is astronomical.

The plate printing numbers also indicate the number of colors used in the stamp. Each plate for each color is assigned a number, which finds its way onto the stamps, as well, Wilson says. Currently, the postal service is using six digits in plate numbers.

In 1974, Wilson organized a club for fellow collectors of these special stamps. The American Plate Number Single Society now has 135 members, mostly in the United States, though there are several in Canada and other foreign countries. Wilson also edits and publishes the organization's bi-monthly newsletter *Plate Numbers*. This publication is the primary medium for the organization's communication, and is an important part of the group's activities.

"We run auctions through *Plate Numbers*," he says. "Members send in their duplicate stamps, I make up a list and circulate it, and other members bid on them. We have exchanges for both mint condition and used stamps, too."

The idea in collecting plate-printing-number stamps, Wilson feels, is to "go for completeness." He is more interested in the earliness of the numbers on the stamps than the design of the stamps themselves. Sometimes, however, the stamps are rare in their own right, and having the plate printing number on them makes them even more so, he says.

The values of these stamps vary widely, says Wilson. "The average price at auction is around one dollar," he says, "but if you have a rare stamp, like a Graf Zeppelin stamp, the value could rise to several thousand dollars."

Stamps are obtained, Wilson says, by purchasing or trading with other collectors. Also, it's possible to go to the Post Office and ask to purchase stamps with the plate printing number on them. "They might give you some trouble, but generally they'll let you purchase the plate printing number stamp," he says.

Collecting in such a specialized area of philately "makes more sense," Wilson says. "When I was a kid and was collecting stamps, I didn't know any better and tried to collect everything." It's much better, he thinks to "work on getting as complete a collection as possible, but in a specifically defined area. Collecting two or three countries, even, is better than trying to collect everything from the whole world."

Lately, Wilson has branched out into another specialized philatelic topic. He has begun collecting government-imprinted and precancelled envelopes. At the moment, he has about 150 of the government-imprinted envelopes and some 1,500 precancelled issues.

His enthusiasm has led to the creation of another club, this one called The Government-Imprinted Penalty Statement and Precancelled Envelope Collectors Club. Since it began in early 1980, the club has already gained 35 members.

His collecting and the organization and operation of his two philatelic specialty clubs are very important to Wilson. "I've been disabled since 1955, after having polio," he says, "and this thing has really kept me going, so that I haven't sat back feeling sorry for myself."

Wilson urges anyone interested in collecting plate printing number stamps, or the government-imprinted and precancelled envelopes to join the organizations. "This way you can make contact with fellow collectors, and learn from them," he says. Membership in The American Plate Number Single Society costs $5 for one year plus $1 in "mint condition, plate number stamps." Membership in the other group is $1.25 per year. Both organizations, and Wilson, can be contacted at 10926 Annette Ave., Tampa, FL 33612.

NUMISMATICS

LARRY ADAMS
BANK CHECKS

W HEN SOMEONE ASKS Larry Adams to "check it out," he really can.

The 31-year-old document examiner from Boone, Ia. has one of the largest collections of bank checks in the USA. In 1969, he founded (with fellow-collectors Richard Flaig and Jack Weaver), the Check Collectors Round Table (CCRT), a nationwide organization of fellow enthusiasts in check collecting and banking history.

Adams had once collected stamps and coins, but in 1964 he became interested in paper money and checks. He soon switched his allegiance totally to checks, because "a lot of banks never issued currency, and I wanted to collect something from every bank." He has over 50,000 checks in his collection, which he keeps in "drawers, envelopes, and albums. I just don't have time to arrange them all."

It is his special interest in the history of banking in his native state that is the primary motivation behind his collection. In his own town, Boone, for example, there have been some 17 banks over the years. In the whole state of Iowa in 1922 there were over 2,000 banks. He hopes to have in his collection one day checks and other documents from all the banks, past and present, in Iowa.

Among the most interesting checks in Adams' collection are those that come from banks with unusual names. He has checks from The Bullfrog Bank & Trust, The Rabbit Foot Mining Co., The Dr. Jackpot Mining Co., The Bimetallic Bank, The All Night and Day Bank, The National Shoe and Leather Bank, The Snowshoe Bank (of Snowshoe, Pa.), and The First National Bank of Intercourse (Intercourse, Pa.).

Researching the history of the bank, or the history of the person who wrote the check, really intrigues Adams. "You can always do a little research, and the possilities are endless. A lot of us who collect the checks know more about the banks than the people who worked in them did."

Adams also collects bank drafts, stock and bond certificates, and other fiscal documents. He even has a collection of old bank pens, paper samples, lithography stones, and check protectors.

A favorite item is a particularly rare lithography stone from F.W. Fitch, a dandruff remedy company that started in Boone. The stone was used to print letterheads and checks, and is made of heavy limestone, three to four inches thick, with "beautiful hand-cut artwork."

Adams is membership secretary of the CCRT, which has a roster of more than 400 people. Among the other specialties represented in the CCRT are autograph collecting, and revenue stamp collecting.

One of the CCRT's most important services to its members is the publication of a quarterly newsletter, "The Check List". Included in this paper (which runs about 50 or 60 pages) are articles, photographs and other data on all phases of banking history and check collecting. In addition, the CCRT has also published *The Handbook of Check Collecting*, which Adams recommends for the beginner and more experienced collector alike.

Adams' lively interest in local history has extended far beyond his bank document and check collecting hobby. He has been a leader in the Boone County Historical Society since its founding 11 years ago, and was instrumental in the effort to preserve Mamie Eisenhower's birthplace. He now serves as a trustee and historian-curator of the birthplace.

For someone interested in beginning a check or bank document collection, Adams recommends joining an organization such as the CCRT or the Society of Paper Money Collectors (of which he is vice-president). He also advises the beginner to attend shows such as the International Paper Money Show (sponsored by the Memphis Coin Club in 1980), which is an excellent opportunity to meet other collectors.

Adams will be happy to assist novice collectors if they will write to him at 969 Park Cir., Boone, IA 50036.

JOHN COFFEE
TRANSPORT TOKENS

WHEN I WAS A KID living in Washington, D.C.," John Coffee recalls, "I liked to ride streetcars. Once, a conductor gave me an out-of-town token, so I began collecting them, the same way people collect stamps or coins." Today, Coffee has over 10,000 of the tokens, from all over the world.

The 50-year-old Unitarian clergyman and professor of history at Boston's Emerson College (where he's currently busy writing the history of the school) edits a monthly newslettter, *The Fare Box*, that goes to 750 fellow collectors all over the U.S. and in 20 countries. He began editing it while a student at Yale University in 1949, and has been doing so ever since.

Tokens were (and still are) used for tollroads, bridges, horsecars, trolleys, subways, cable cars, and even on a sleigh ride at a California ski resort. There are still many opportunities for collectors to begin or add to their collections with relative ease.

Coffee has gone all over the country "to the most God-awful places some-times to track down these tokens. There's just no place I haven't been looking for these things."

His travels led him once to a small Texas town, the site of a former horse-drawn hack line. For $55 he had bought, by mail, the entire collection of those tokens owned by a 90-year-old woman, Miss Baker. A correspondence ensued, and finally, when he went to visit the elderly woman,"I found out she was the wealthiest woman in town. When I got to the station, I was met by a welcom-ing committee, wined and dined, and treated like a celebrity."

Coffee is hard-pressed to name his favorite token, since he owns so many. Among the most valuable and unusual he has collected is an 1862 Chestnut & Walnut railroad passenger token from Philadelphia, with Ben Franklin's pic-ture on it. There are only two of these known to exist, and he estimates its worth at $750-$1,000.

Like other collectors, Coffee would like to get his hands on a token for the Gibbs U.S. Mail Stage Ferry from New Jersey to New York in the late 1830s. Only two are known to exist. They are worth about $1500 apiece.

In addition to his work with *The Fare Box*, Coffee has also authored several books on tokens. Besides two small books, *Real Estate Tokens* and *Car Wash Tokens*, he was the editor and publisher of a 975-page comprehensive cata-logue, listing all known transportation tokens ever used in the U.S. and Cana-da. It is now in its third edition, (published 1970, with a 1978 supplement) and lists some 10,000 varieties of tokens.

For the novice vecturist (as transit token collectors are more properly called), Coffee suggests visiting transit companies and asking to buy out-of-town tok-ens collected through their fare boxes. Often, they will sell them to the collec-tor for the regular fare. New collectors should also join the American Vecturist Society and read *The Fare Box*. Both will put novices in contact with others in the field, and will give the new collector an idea of what kind of items are available in the field.

Coffee will be happy to counsel and advise the transit token collector. He can be reached at PO Box 1204, Boston, MA 02104.

MILTON & VIRGINIA DENNIS
WOODEN MONEY

FORTUNATELY, MILTON and Vir-ginia Dennis never believed the aphorist who advised, "Don't take any wooden nickels." The Torrance, California couple, in 20 years, has amassed over 58,000 pieces of wooden money.

How did the Dennises begin collecting wooden money? As Milton explains, "Like most people, I started out collecting coins, tokens, and medals. But when prices went out of my range, I turned to wooden money." That was in 1960, and since that time, Milton has collected "probably the most complete collection of official U.S. issues in the world."

Wooden money began, says Dennis, in Tenino, Washington, in 1931. "When the banks there went under, the townspeople came up with a monetary program, making square pieces of money out of veneer in 25-cent, 50-cent and $1 denominations." These pieces were circulated in the town, and were as good as money from 1931 to 1933, when the banks recovered.

The custom of issuing wooden money spread elsewhere during those years, Dennis says. Since 1933, though, "they've mostly been issued for celebrations." The pieces actually have a value, usually with a redemption date printed on them, after which they become souvenirs.

Among the highlights of the Dennis collection: one of the original 25-cent pieces from Tenino. "Only 40 of them were made," he says, "as sort of a trial balloon." The first 40 are highly sought after, as they "had nothing printed on their reverse; the later Tenino issues had either a picture of Washington or Lincoln."

Another of the prizes of Dennis's collection is a complete set of 11 denominations, in two issues, from North Bend, Oregon in 1933. "These were round, made of maplewood," says Dennis. There are only five complete sets, and his set is worth $1,000.

"The early pieces are tough to get," says Dennis. "You have to get them from other collectors or someone who has them salted away." He says that they are "very brittle and break easily," so care is necessary in handling them. "It's a challenge to try to get the old ones,"says Dennis.

"I like collecting," Dennis says. "Everyone should have some hobby, for the day when they will grow old and want something to keep them occupied. I have collected lots of things, but had more enjoyment out of wooden money than anything I've tried."

Not to be outdone, Virginia began to share her husband's interest in wooden money in 1969. "My husband was interested in wood, so since we do things as a family, I decided I should do something along the same line," she says. She, however, specializes in the wooden chips that the 700-restaurant Sambo Coffee shop chain issued for a free cup of coffee, from 1957 until 1977, when the company discontinued the program.

"As the program grew, the chips changed," says Mrs. Dennis. "The first type had a picture of a pancake on the reverse, then a restaurant, and finally a cup." Each restaurant had its own address printed on the chip it gave out. The hardest of the Sambo coffee chips to find, she says, are the pancakes. Unfortunately, the supply of coffee chips is also limited. "When Sambo decided to discontinue the program, " she says, "they had a bonfire with the extra chips in their warehouse."

The chips can be purchased for 25 cents and more, she says. For example, the first chip produced sells for $35. The most sought after chips, according to Mrs. Dennis, are those issued during the Bicentennial.

"It's a challenge, really, trying to get one from each location," she says. "When Sambo discontinued the program, I kind of lost interest. But when someone sends me a chip I don't have, I get excited all over again." She estimates she has close to 8,000 pieces in her collection, "though I've never really counted it."

Both Mr. and Mrs. Dennis are active in local, regional, and international wooden money clubs. Milton was a founder of the Torrance Coin Club in 1961, and a founder and the first president of the California Wooden Money Association (CWMA) in 1969. In 1977-78, he was the president of the International Organization of Wooden Money Collectors (IOWMC). His wife, who held various offices in the Torrance and California Wooden Money groups, is currently the editor of *Wood Winds,* CWMA's monthly publication, and also editor of *Bunyan's Chips,* the international group's monthly newsletter.

Somehow, the Dennises have also found time to write books on their hobby. Both of them were contributors to the 6th and 7th editions of *The Guide Book of Wooden Money,* and Dennis co-wrote the supplement to the guide book in 1972. On her own, Mrs. Dennis has written *A Check List for Sambo Coffee Chips,* which is a guide to appearance and price of all the chips known.

Virginia Dennis advises beginning collectors to "Decide what category you wish to pursue and stick with it." Milton Dennis agrees, adding "Don't buy someone's junk." He also recommends novice wooden money collectors join IOWMC: contact N. R. Mack, PO Box 395, Goose Creek, SC 29445, enclosing a stamped, self-addressed envelope for reply.

The Dennises will be happy to advise novice wooden money collectors. Write them at 18814 Florwood Ave., Torrance, CA 90504.

DAVID HENDIN
COINS OF THE BIBLE

IF YOU ASK, David Hendin can show you one of the "30 pieces of silver" Judas received to betray Jesus Christ. Or the "tribute penny" or the "widow's mite" also from the *Bible.*

Of course, he probably doesn't own the actual coins referred to in the *Bible,* but Hendin has amassed an unusual collection of 600 coins from ancient days in the Holy Land, and has become one of the world's leading experts on them in the process.

That's quite an accomplishment for a 34-year-old newspaper features syndicate editor from New York City, who started out with an active dislike of coins.

Hendin's father was a collector of Biblical coins. "He was one of those people who collected things," says Hendin. "I always thought he was slightly eccentric." His father tried to get him interested in collecting the coins, but to no avail.

Hendin went to Israel in 1967, shortly after the Six Day War. "While I was there, I told my father I would try to pick up some coins for his collection. I figured there'd be a lot of them over there since that's where they came from." One day in Jerusalem, Hendin "visited two or three coin stores and got hooked." During the rest of his stay in Israel, "one or two days a week would be spent haunting the antique bazaars" for new pieces to collect. "I learned from Arabs, Jews, and Christians alike about the coins," he says.

Back in the United States, Hendin's interest in the coins subsided somewhat until 1972. When he sold his first freelance writing,"I sent $20 or $30 from the advance check to Israel for some coins, and got hooked all over again."

Today, Hendin is the leading U.S. expert on the ancient Biblical coins, a feat he modestly says "is not so difficult because few others care" about these coins in this country.

Hendin finds collecting the ancient coins educational. In addition to learning the history of the Holy Land and its many civilizations, Hendin asks, "How many people around can read Nabatean?," referring to an ancient language in which he has a working knowledge as a result of the research he does for his coin collecting.

"Through these coins, one can trace the history of Judaism and the rise of Christianity, and even confirm many accounts of ancient history, both from the *Bible* and as quoted by ancient historians," says Hendin.

According to Hendin, "The earliest known mention of money in the *Bible* is in the Old Testament story of Abraham," where it refers to the patriarch's purchase of a burial site for "400 shekels of silver, current money with the merchant."

The "shekel" referred to is not a coin. "It's a weight, since coins as we know them were not used over a wide area until after 600 B.C., well past most of the events of the Old Testament," he says.

The first coins to circulate in ancient Israel came from Athens, Macedon, Thasos, and other Greek cities, says Hendin. "Today it is believed that the first coins struck independently by a Jewish king" were issued by Alexander Jannaeus (103-76 B.C.). Hendin says these "are probably the most common of the ancient Jewish coins." They have designs of anchors, stars, cornucopias, flowers, and palm branches on them. "These agricultural and maritime symbols appear frequently on the coins of the ancient Jews because of the biblical edict against the use of 'graven images.'"

The tribute penny is commonly thought to be the "denarius, a silver penny from the reign of Tiberius, which depicts his mother Livia on the reverse," says Hendin. Another frequently mentioned coin, the widow's mite, was "a small bronze coin of the Maccabeean kings" or possibly the small coins of Herod the Great, Herod Archelaus, or one of the procurators of Israel.

The shekel, in Jesus' time, was actually the silver shekel of Tyre, "thought to be the type of coin used to pay Judas for betraying Jesus," says Hendin. These coins were also used for the annual temple tribute, which each Jew was required to pay. Because these coins were of "uniformly good weight and silver quality," he says, it was decided they would be accepted for the payment.

Incidentally, says Hendin, the purpose of "moneychangers in the temple was to convert other bronze or silver coins into the shekels to pay the annual temple tribute."

One problem in collecting these coins is that "there are some fakes. Anything collectible is liable to be faked," he says, "but coins are fairly easy to spot, if you know what to look for."

The most commonly faked coin, says Hendin, is the shekel. "The forgeries, called 'false shekels,' were made in Europe in the 17th, 18th, and 19th centuries. These shekels have a chalice with flame on the front, with the rod of Aaron on the other side, and three pomegranates on a branch." The writing on the shekels is "modern Hebrew," says Hendin. "The fascinating thing is that these were made by people who never saw the originals."

Hendin has written two books on the collecting of ancient coins: *Guide to Ancient Jewish Coins* (Attic Books, 1976) and *Collecting Coins* (Signet, 1978). He is also a columnist for *The Shekel*, the journal of the American-Israel Numismatic Association. In addition, he has been the consultant in numismatics to New York's Jewish Museum since 1979.

When the New York City department store Bloomingdale's had a celebration honoring Israel's 30th year as a nation in 1979, Hendin organized a special exhibit of coins of the *Bible*."The truth is, coins can be boring," Hendin says frankly. When he sets up an exhibit of coins, he says, "it's always a challenge to make it interesting."

Hendin advises beginning coin collectors to read books and visit museum collections to gain a background in the subject. "To learn about ancient coins, one must know the history behind them, and handle them," he says. "One cannot become an expert without both." In addition, "You have to be able to read the rudiments of many ancient languages," Hendin believes, to get the full benefit from studying the coins. It is difficult to learn much about the coins without some knowledge of the languages.

But the coins still intrigue him, Hendin says, "because they are one of the few remaining artifacts of ancient civilization. Through coins, you can tell a lot about the civilizations they came from."

Hendin has had the most success in locating the coins on regular trips to Israel. "It's almost like going hunting. When I go to Israel, I head for the countryside, the backwoods, and the bazaars, in search of coins." Of course, the cost of coin hunting is on the increase. What he could buy in 1967 for 25 cents is now only available for $40.

Hendin keeps his collection in a safe-deposit box, and "I don't get to look at it very often." He says collecting the ancient coins is "fun and frustrating," but what he collects is "not unattractive and is a nice investment."

Hendin will be happy to advise collectors of ancient and Biblical coins. He can be reached at PO Box 661, Bardonia, NY 10954.

WENDELL MORNINGSTAR
WOODEN NICKELS

WHEN WENDELL Morningstar discovered there was such a thing as a wooden nickel in 1958, he never dreamed that someday he would own thousands of them, and in the process of collecting them, become one of the country's leading experts in the study of wooden money. As he tells it, his interest began quite simply.

"In 1958, Delaware County, Ohio, was having its sesquicentennial celebration," Morningstar recalls. "It was announced that wooden nickels would be distributed through the banks. They would be worth five cents and could be spent as real money during the celebration or could be kept for souvenirs." That intrigued him, and when he went around to other towns in his area to help in promoting the Delaware County sesquicentennial, he found that a lot of other communities had wooden money, too, for their own celebrations or to commemorate special events.

"Mansfield, Ohio, had one; Westerville had two," he says. "So, I began to wonder just how many there were." After placing a story in Coin World magazine, "I got a few names, traded with those collectors, and shortly I had several hundred tokens."

His collection kept growing until "at one time, I had close to 18,000" pieces of wooden money. Since then, Morningstar has dispersed much of his collection to other collectors, preferring instead to concentrate on obtaining Ohio wooden money and more unusual pieces.

Morningstar is particularly proud of the oldest pieces of wooden money in his collection. He has a wooden copy of a medallion commemorating the Dominion Exhibition in Montreal, Quebec, in September of 1880. There are only seven of these wooden pieces known to exist, he says. The medallion is made of black walnut, and features a view of the Crystal Palace (the main exhibition hall) on the front, and a beaver with two crossed maple branches on the back.

Wooden money was designed to be sold as souvenirs of particular events, festivals, and celebrations, according to Morningstar. It would only have a monetary value during the event, when it would be "sold to people as souvenirs. If it wasn't cashed in, then the organizers of the event would have made some money."

Like many kinds of collectibles, wooden money has widely varying values, Morningstar says. Issues from 1939 to 1954 are available for between $8 and $10, while round tokens from 1954 on can cost 50 cents to $20 each.

Morningstar has also become a leader of other wooden money collectors, through the two organizations he founded. The International Organization of Wooden Money Collectors (founded 1964, has 400 members) and Dedicated Wooden Money Collectors (founded 1976, has 300 members) were formed "to advance knowledge of official wooden money along educational, historical, and scientific lines." Morningstar has edited *Timberlines*, the monthly newsletter of Dedicated Wooden Money Collectors since the organization's inception.

Both organizations, and Morningstar, are interested in helping the novice wooden money collector become established. Potential collectors should contact Morningstar, who will "explain the club and send them an application." Once the collector joins the club (membership is $5 per year), he will get some wooden money to start his collection with. "A lot of the members have sent in a number of pieces that we use to give to new members to give them an idea of what to collect," he says.

And he urges collectors to "keep to official issues. There is nothing more disconcerting than for a beginner to buy private issues (like advertising tokens from companies) and find out they have no value for wooden money collectors."

As a dedicated collector, Morningstar is also a careful purchaser of new wooden money for his collection. "I'd like to educate the collectors about legitimate and illegitimate issues of wooden money, " he says, "to be able to stop the printing of fakes, unless they are marked as such."

Morningstar has found his collection of wooden money to be a rewarding experience. "When I went to school, I didn't know a lot about history and geography. Now, when I get a piece of wood, I go right to the map. I've learned more than I got out of any books in school."

Morningstar, Dedicated Wooden Money Collectors, and the International Organization of Wooden Money Collectors can all be contacted at 5575 State Route 257, Radnor, OH 43066.

LEE NOTT
COLORADO MERCHANT TOKENS

MERCHANT AND TRADE tokens are good for a penny, a nickel, a loaf of bread, a drink. They are a means of advertising and a way for the shop owner to get more capital," says Lee Nott.

Collecting these fascinating coin-like objects is a growing specialty within numismatics. Nott, after 13 years of collecting, has become the leading expert in the merchant and trade tokens of the state of Colorado.

Nott collects Colorado merchant tokens because, when he got his start in the field in 1967, he was living in Colorado. "I was already a coin collector," he says. "Then I saw a display of merchant tokens, along with the photographs of the towns they came from. I thought it was an interesting hobby, relating coin collecting with history. It seemed more fascinating to collect a bit of history than just a coin."

In any case, "I had gotten to the place where the next coin would be more expensive than I wanted to go, so I was looking for a new specialty within numismatics."

Today, Nott has over 1,500 tokens in his collection, which he says is only medium-sized. "I enjoy tokens from towns no longer on the map," he says. He conducts research to "try to find out all I can about the town, through photographs and other historical materials."

The bulk of his collection, made up of metal and a few cardboard merchant tokens, covers the period from the 1880s to the 1940s, with the greatest number representing the saloon years of the turn of the century.

Among his favorite tokens is one from Durango, Colorado. It is a silver-dollar-sized aluminum piece. On the reverse, is a picture of a "smelter and a deer, two symbols of the area. It's kind of pretty," says Nott.

In addition to his collecting activities, Nott has written the first catalogue of Colorado tokens. His book, called simply *Colorado Merchant Tokens*, was written with another collector, Jim Wright. Published by Edwards Brothers in 1977, the book is still available, either in hardcover or in a special looseleaf format to allow insertion of updating supplements. The first such supplement was published in 1979, Nott says.

Believe it or not, "so far, we've accounted for 4,000 Colorado merchant tokens, and probably at least that many are still out there." But, Nott says, Colorado was "not the most prolific state in the issuance of these. In Iowa, for example, we know of 10,000 issues." Other states rich in merchant tokens are California, Indiana, Ohio, and Illinois. The Northeastern states and New Mexico and Arizona had the fewest.

The best way to begin collecting merchant tokens is to decide on a specialty, Nott says. Then, join the Merchant Token Collectors Association (METCA) and read their publications to become familiar with the field. Though some tokens are still available for as little as 50 cents apiece, the average price a collector pays is $10-$25 for the older issues. The tokens, he says, can be found at flea markets, garage sales, or coin shows. "When you join METCA, you'll receive a list of members to correspond and trade with. Much of the collecting is done on a trading basis." Nott is enthusiastic about collecting Colorado tokens. "Very honestly, it's been an opportunity to learn a lot more about the state. I've also enjoyed the friendship and correspondence with other people."

To join METCA, write to 1416 Third Ave., Seattle, WA 98101. Nott, a career Air Force officer at Scott Air Force Base near St. Louis, can be contacted through his permanent mailing address, Route 2, Box 274, Colebrook, NH 03576.

JERRY RILLAHAN
STOCK CERTIFICATES

HE PROBABLY HAS stock in more companies than many tycoons. Unfortunately, it's all worthless paper from defunct corporations. But these stock certificates have a definite value for Jerry Rillahan, a leading collector of stock certificates "used, unused, or cancelled."

Rillahan, 62, of Worland, Wyoming, has been selling stamps by mail for about 40 years. About 1965, "I had a letter from a fellow who had 500,000 stock certificates with revenue stamps on the back. I decided to purchase them to get the stamps, and wound up discovering that the stock certificates were interesting in their own right, and quite collectible."

Though Rillahan has only around 300 stock certificates in his personal collection, he estimates he has had 3 or 4 million pass through his hands since that first batch. "I try to keep only the most interesting certificates," he says, "and sell off any duplicates." Surprisingly, most of Rillahan's best customers for the old certificates are Europeans. "They buy them mainly for their historical value and because of the quality of the engraving," he says."Most all of these certificates are in color and make nice decorations as well as being interesting bits of history. The artwork is generally excellent."

Most of the stock certificates pertain to railroads, oil wells, mining companies, and other businesses in the West. The initial stock certificates Rillahan obtained were from the North Butte (Montana) Mining Company, founded in 1905. "It was very profitable until 1917, when there was a disastrous fire in the mine, which killed 175 men," Rillahan says. After the fire, there were so many lawsuits that the company eventually was taken over by Anaconda and vanished by 1928. The company's stock certificate, created by American Engraving, a leading engraver, features "an underground mining scene" Rillahan says, and is typical of most old stock certificates in the excellent quality of the engraving.

Rillahan feels that people like collecting stock certificates because "they take pride in owning them, and feeling like they are part of the business world. Also, a lot of them are interested in business history, and the certificates provide valuable information."

There's also the appeal of stock certificates as antiques, Rillahan says. He estimates that there are anywhere from 7,000 to 10,000 people collecting such certificates in the United States.

While many old stock certificates have little monetary value, he says, some can be quite expensive. "For example, if you have a stock certificate for the Wells-Fargo Company, signed by both Wells and Fargo, it's worth about $700," he says, but the usual price for a stock certificate is between 50 cents and $4. Again, the primary value results from the quality of the engraving.

Rillahan says he was the first person to start selling old stock certificates, but now several other dealers around the country do the same. He suggests that beginners either contact a dealer, or look for the certificates on their own in flea markets, antique stores, and used book stores. Sometimes, it's even possible to get them directly from the company or its successor, he says.

In his personal collection, Rillahan is particularly fond of his Ringling Brothers stock certificate, and "an original *Playboy* certificate, which has a nude woman pictured on it."

Rillahan will be glad to offer advice or provide information on stock certificates to the novice collector. He may be contacted at PO Box 427, Worland, WY 82401.

EDWARD ROCHETTE
JFK NUMISMATICS

AMONG THE MANY commemorations of the presidency of John F. Kennedy, coins and medals have been particularly popular.

Edward Rochette, of Colorado Springs, Colorado, probably has the largest collection of JFK numismatics, over 1,200 pieces, that he says "is destined for the Kennedy Library someday."

Rochette began collecting Kennedy-related coins and medals before the tragic events in Dallas. In 1958, while working in Kennedy's second senatorial campaign, Rochette collected campaign buttons. In 1960, when Kennedy was running for the presidency, "there were a number of medallions and tokens issued, both before and after the election," which he says formed the basis of his present collection. "I have some very unusual pieces," says Rochette. "It has been a lot of fun collecting them."

For instance, The French Mint produced a memorial medal to Kennedy in 1964, in a limited, numbered edition of 200. Jacqueline Kennedy received number one; Rochette has number two. "They took the same design and produced another medal on the 50th anniversary of Kennedy's birth," says Rochette. "This time, I got number one of 200, and Jackie got number two."

An Italian medal, made in 1964 for an Italian museum, was produced from a wax casting. Rochette was able to secure an extra copy of the wax casting from the sculptor who made it. "Flattered that I wanted a casting of the medal he had created, the sculptor asked for my picture, which I gave to him, " Rochette says. "A short time later, there was an exhibition by the sculptor of medallions of three famous Americans: John F. Kennedy, Lyndon B. Johnson, and Edward Rochette. I wonder what American tourists who saw *that* thought," he laughs.

Another of Rochette's favorite items is a token produced in the Phillippines. "This was just a cheap thing that came in the wrapper with a candy bar," he says, "but it was unique in that it featured Jackie Kennedy's portrait and claimed that she was the new President of the United States."

Some of the items Rochette has collected are satiric in nature. During the 1960 campaign, there was a token which, "ironically, had a redemption date of 1963 printed on it." It represented itself to be from "'The Catholic States of America,' and was good for 'one confession.'"

"I don't want to say I have everything in my collection, because some one-of-a-kind items are impossible to get, but I would say I have 99.9 percent of all the JFK-related coins, medals, and tokens, " Rochette says.

Rochette has written *Medallic Portraits of JFK*, (Krause Publishing, 1966), which points out that many of the medals associated with Kennedy did not appear as the result of his assassination.

For example, there is the United States Kennedy "appreciation medal," of which 300 were made, that Kennedy presented as a memento to foreign dignitaries here and abroad, according to Rochette. There was also a medal struck on behalf of the Democratic National Committee in honor of the Inauguration. "The money raised by selling the medal was used to underwrite the cost of the Inaugural Balls in 1961," he says.

Of course, the most common commemoration of Kennedy was on coins. Practically every Western nation issued some form of Kennedy medal or coin, the most widely known being the U.S. Kennedy half dollar. When it first appeared in 1964, it was made of silver ("if silver is selling for $40 per ounce, there's about $15 worth of silver in a 1964 half-dollar," he says), and was widely hoarded by both collectors and people "who just wanted a remembrance." From 1965 to 1969, the coin was 40 percent silver, and now the JFK half-dollar is nickel-clad copper, like dimes and quarters.

Rochette came to coin collecting at a tender age. His grandfather had a restaurant, and used to let him go through the coins. Today, Rochette is executive vice-president of the American Numismatic Association, and thus, professionally "involved in many tangents of the hobby." He also has a collection, of tokens and substitute forms of money dating from the Revolutionary War period to the present."In a way, some of them are really early political cartoons," he says.

For example, he has a token made during the Bank of the United States controversy, that portrays then-President Andrew Jackson as a jackass. This portrait of Jackson as an ass is thought to have been the inspiration for cartoonist Thomas Nast's portrayal of the Democratic Party as a donkey some years later.

"I was, and am, more interested in the history coins relate than in the mere collecting," he says, adding that he will often sell or trade a piece once he has thoroughly studied it.

To the novice numismatist, Rochette says, "I never advise anyone to collect for investment alone. I really believe that if you are collecting, it should be for knowledge and enjoyment. I think you lose a lot by investment-oriented collecting." He also suggests the beginner start small, restricting collecting to a specialized area.

He will gladly give further information on his collection or provide answers to queries of a numismatic nature. He can be contacted at the American Numismatic Assoc., PO Box 2366, Colorado Springs, CO 80901.

FRED SCHWAN
MILITARY MONEY OF WORLD WAR II

ONE OF THE UNIQUE AREAS of numismatics is the collection of paper money. Particularly fascinating are the military and emergency issues of currency by various governments during World War II.

Fred Schwan is one of the leading collectors of this special money, and he has co-written the first comprehensive book for collectors in the field.

Schwan, 33, a career Army officer currently stationed overseas, began collecting coins in 1959. "All the kids in the neighborhood were collecting pennies in those blue penny holders," he says. "My younger brother started me out. I just never quit."

Schwan stuck with coins all through college and during his service in the Vietnam conflict. When he got back to the United States, "I was looking for a hobby in which I could make a contribution, where not much research had been done. "Actually, I was getting a little bit bored doing what everyone else was doing."

What he discovered, after exploring the collection of paper currency in general and finding it too vast a subject, was military money. He received some samples from a friend, and began reading and studying everything he could get his hands on. He began collecting diligently, as well.

Military money, according to Schwan, is currency issued by the government of a country for use either by the military within its own system, or for the general population of an occupied country to aid in the stabilization of that country's economy during the occupation. In addition, there are so-called "emergency issues," like the 1943 U.S. pennies, which were made from steel rather than copper to conserve metal.

"World War II was an economic war as much as anything else," Schwan says. "It had untold economic repercussions. In almost every country of the world, currency changed in ways both drastic and subtle."

"My collection has been called the best collection in the world of military and emergency issues of World War II," he says. "It's the most complete, at least, with quite a few unique items, and a number of 'discovery' pieces, items that resulted in more of the same thing being found."

Though he has only 2,000 items in his collection, they were all chosen with special care, he says. Among his most interesting pieces is a U.S. military pay certificate, series 541, a $5 bill used from 1958 to 1961 by U.S. forces overseas. The pay certificate, which is not U.S. currency, but could have been redeemed for U.S. currency by a military person, was first purchased by a collector for $5.10; at the time Schwan bought it from him, its value was listed in one catalogue at $12.50.

"I had to drive 400 miles to get the bill," he remembers. "I took one look at it, and gave the fellow $750 for it." Today, the bill is worth $3,000 because it is "a pristine, uncirculated bill of which only about 100 are known to exist."

Research plays an important role in Schwan's collection. Often, a piece of money will inspire him to dig into its background. For example, he has a piece of currency for an Army barter store in Frankfurt, Germany. This bill was only good in that particular store, he says. The bill is signed by a lieutenant who was in charge of the store. Schwan, intrigued by this, decided to try to find the lieutenant, and learn more about the currency system in his store. Through a friend, Schwan located the man, now a retired colonel, and flew across the country to interview him, adding some valuable information to his research into military paper currency.

"You research this money mostly by correlating unrelated sources. You start by finding a piece of money and saying 'What's the story behind this?,'" he says. His search for the story has led him all over the country, and he has made some interesting discoveries along the way. He even found some valuable military currency hidden away in the Eisenhower Library, money the library didn't even know it possessed.

Though there are probably only a "few hundred people who specialize in this area of collecting in the world," says Schwan, "much of this money is collected by thousands more." The generalists, or the collectors of specific countries, will frequently have military issue in their collections.

But the people who collect military money exclusively are a close fraternity, according to Schwan. He occasionally publishes price lists and sends them to his fellow-collectors. "The lists serve as sort of a newsletter," he says.

With Joseph Boling, Schwan wrote *World War II Military Currency*, "the first comprehensive book on all issues of military money," with history, price guide, and illustrations. The book, published in 1978, quickly became the standard collectors' reference and was "widely acclaimed," Schwan says.

Schwan is a staunch advocate of numismatics as a hobby. "You can have a good time and make money, too," he says. "As opposed to investing in stock, when you invest in coins or paper money, you have something to look at and enjoy, as well as value."

What fascinates Schwan about World War II paper money is what it represents: "an extraordinary period of history. World War II was incredibly interesting. There was so much human drama and sacrifice. This money was there, it was a part of the whole story."

Schwan will gladly give information and advice. His address is care of BNR Press, 132 E. 2nd St., Port Clinton, OH 43452. His book can also be obtained by sending a check for $19.50 to the same address.

WARD SMITH
CHINESE CURRENCY

WITH ALL THE INTEREST in China these days, Ward Smith's collection of Chinese banknotes has taken on additional importance.

Smith, 62, a freelance writer and editor from California, who spent more than 20 years living in China, Taiwan, and Hong Kong, has co-written the standard collector's reference volume on Chinese banknotes. He is also one of the world's leading collectors of Chinese currency.

"I had been a desultory coin collector" prior to 1944, says Smith, in describing how he became involved in the collection of Chinese currency. While serving in the armed forces, Smith was in Kunming, China, when he was stung in a currency exchange transaction. He lost $2.50, but he ended up with "some handsome notes from the Provisional Bank of Yunan that were worth only half of their face value." He kept the notes, in the vain hope he would someday run across the person who had cheated him. In the meantime, he decided he liked their looks, and began collecting others like them.

Banknotes first appeared in China at least 1,200 years ago, and that's probably a conservative figure, says Smith. His collection dates from the first Ming Dynasty around 1375 A.D. to the present.

"The Chinese have an enormous variety of banknotes," says Smith, and the whole monetary system is "extremely complex. Really there is no system, though everything is supposedly based on a copper coin called 'cash.' Each little area had its own little system." Banks and other establishments issued their own currency. Chinese banknotes were mostly in denominations of "strings of cash," according to Smith. "A bunch of notes would be placed on a string, the ideal amount being 1,000 per string, and that would represent 1,000 cash." Sounds simple enough; but what complicated the process was that each area had its own standard of what was considered a string. "Thus, a string might be worth 1200 cash in Manchuria, and 600 or 850 cash in the Yangtze region," he says.

Understandably, because of its great value, and the tremendous difficulty of replacement, Smith is reluctant to discuss his collection in specific detail or give any personal information that might inspire criminal activities.

He is the author (with Dr. Brian Matravers) of *Chinese Banknotes*. This book, now the standard reference for Chinese currency collectors the world over, contains material on at least 1,800 issuing agencies and the currency they made. Smith is in the process of preparing an updated edition, which will include the currency from another 500 to 600 issuing agencies he has managed to uncover.

Like most kinds of collecting, Chinese currency has undergone an explosive growth in value. It is one of the fastest growing areas of numismatics. "Back in the happy days when I was collecting, you'd spend a couple of bucks and think that was a lot," he remembers. Recently, he ordered an 1860 Peking banknote for $52 from a dealer, and got a note back saying that his letter was the fourth bid received for the Peking currency. "At this point, everything I want costs $300 or $400, and I just can't pay that kind of money," says Smith.

Smith says he is kept very busy by his writing activities. Since the "last of the old-time Chinese banknote experts" died a couple of years ago, Smith has become the reigning expert in the field. "A lot of the queries he might have gotten seem to filter through to me."

"My collecting zeal has diminished considerably, in light of the expense, in favor of research." Chinese banknote collecting "has gone mad. It's really too expensive to start out in today. "I would advise any beginner to try something else."

In addition, says Smith, it's pretty difficult to advance from beginner status in the hobby without being able to read Chinese "or working like the devil to overcome the disadvantage." Smith managed, because he reads Chinese and Japanese "well enough to get by."

It's somewhat ironic that Smith feels that "one of the worst inventions mankind ever perpetrated on himself were banknotes. In China, they were just a continuous disaster." Banknotes "are no goddamned good. Why I want to collect something so pernicious, I don't know," says Smith.

Smith sees parallels between the days in 1948 when it used to cost "3 or 4 million for breakfast in China" and today. He predicts the copper penny will disappear in 1980 and "the nickel won't last much longer."

"It's an interesting thing, not a cheerful thing. With Chinese banknotes, I can take a somewhat more detached view."

Smith will answer queries, addressed to him at PO Box 259, Menlo Park, CA 94025.

TERRY TRANTOW
LUMBER COMPANY TOKENS

$\mathbf{T}$HE FAMOUS SONG says it all: "...I owe my soul to the company store..." This phrase frequently had as poignant a meaning for workers in the lumber mills of the United States as it did for the coal miners the folksong was sung about.

Often, instead of money, the lumber companies used metal, brass, or aluminum tokens in their company stores. "An employee could get an advance, in tokens, and it was deducted from his monthly salary," says Terry Trantow. "The token could only be used at the company store, so the company was actually making money on the deal."

Trantow is one of the most knowledgeable people in the country about this very specialized area of coin collecting — "exonumia," which he describes as "collecting coin-like items, not coins of the realm." Within exonumia, he has specialized even further, collecting the tokens issued by lumber companies in the Pacific Northwest, as well as the rest of the country.

A forest engineer and land surveyor who lives in Binger, Washington, Trantow began collecting the tokens almost by accident. "I used to collect coins. But I was getting discouraged because of the high prices." In 1964, he switched to collecting "Oregon commemorative medals, then Oregon tokens, then Oregon lumber tokens. Since I'm a history buff, I like to research the stories behind each of the tokens I collect."

Trantow has traced about 1,500 lumber companies all over the United States, and he has a collection of 10,000 tokens from them, including about 2,000 used by Oregon lumber companies. Generally speaking, they date from the 1880s to the 1930s, with the age depending on the part of the country they come from. Trantow says the development of the tokens followed the development of the industry.

"They're scarce, simply because of supply and demand," says Trantow of the tokens. "In the Great Lakes states, for instance, the lumber industry was going downhill at the time tokens were most commonly used, so the tokens from that area are few in number and more valuable." Tokens from Wisconsin and Michigan, "when they do turn up, are earlier and rarer than any we have in the Pacific Northwest," says Trantow.

In his collection, for example, he has a "shingle check" issued by the Muskegon (Michigan) Shingle and Lumber Company in the late 1880s. "This was good for 1,000 boardfeet in trade." What this signified, Trantow says, was that the worker got credit in the company store equivalent to the value attached to producing 1,000 boardfeet of shingles. "There are only a half-dozen of these tokens known to exist," says Trantow.

Trantow wrote *Lumber Company Store Tokens*, published in 1979. "It catalogued and described all the known tokens that have been issued," he says.

About 1,200 companies are represented. Since the book came out, he has found out about 300 more companies. "These things keep turning up," he says.

Collecting the lumber tokens has "helped me greatly in my study of lumber company history. There are no books listing the mills in existence in the Pacific Northwest," he says. Because many of them changed hands a number of times, it probably wouldn't be possible to put such a book together. "The mills may exist under a different name," he says, "and tracing the ownership gets difficult, but the existence of the tokens is proof, at least, that such a company existed, and gives me further evidence to use in tracing down the company's history."

Tokens are fairly easy to come by and relatively inexpensive, he says, in spite of their scarcity. "When the company quit using the tokens, or went out of business, the tokens were destroyed. As a result, not too many survived. But for every 20 issues of which only a few tokens are available, there is a hoard of one issue still in existence," he says.

Trantow encourages new collectors. "The tokens show up in junk boxes at antique shops or flea markets all the time." A dedicated lumber token hunter can also "use a metal detector at the site of an old lumber mill," he says. In addition, there are mail auctions conducted between collectors and dealers, but Trantow suggests the novice stay away from those. "The prices are just exorbitant."

Lumber token collecting, and all the researching that goes along with it, is enjoyable to Trantow. "From the standpoint of digging into facts and finding out where mills were located, I think that's the most enjoyable part of the hobby," he says.

Organizations that can provide useful information for the beginning collector include the Token and Medal Society (611 Oakwood Wy., El Cajon, CA 92021), Merchant Token Collectors Association (752 N. 74th St., Seattle, WA 98103) and National Scrip Collector's Association, (PO Box 29, Fayetteville, WV 25840).

Trantow will be happy to give information to beginners if they write to him at PO Box 287, Binger, WA 98605.

HARRY WIGINGTON

OBSOLETE PAPER MONEY

$\mathbf{Y}$OU COULDN'T TEMPT Harry Wigington with a crisp, new $50 bill. But show him a worn-out $1 bill from a long-defunct bank, and his eyes will light up like a child's.

Wigington, 44, is a collector of obsolete U.S. currency from the 19th century. The older the bill, the more he's interested in it. He specializes in collecting notes printed by the American Bank Note Company, the major supplier of currency from 1857 to the late 1870s, and the banknotes and scrip made by the Pennsylvania General Bank Note Company, another important manufacturer.

"They're a little bit more ornate, colorful, and the style is sharper," says

Wigington, explaining why he collects bills from American Bank Note over others. "I just like looking at them. It's the same feeling as looking at a Rembrandt portrait."

He was a coin collector back in 1960, when a friend "showed me some obsolete bank notes. I was instantly intrigued. I just traded in my coin collection and started collecting paper money."

It wasn't until 1862 that a unified national currency was issued, under the provisions of the National Currency Act, says Wigington. "Before that time, every piece of money came from private or state banks. The money was printed to circulate within a certain general locale. Its value for redemption depended on the solvency of the bank, its reputation, and how good the assets were."

Wigington says that the most reliable currency was thought to emanate from state banks. "These banks were financially more sound than the private banks," he says. Private banks, in fact, were often fly-by-night affairs, frequently operated by con artists who coerced leading citizens into putting their money and reputations behind a "bank," and the conman absconded with the funds, leaving the backers with a pile of worthless banknotes in the hands of their irate customers.

All the banknotes had ratings "like bonds do today," says Wigington. The merchants and bankers exchanges "used lists showing the solvency of a bank, what notes were good, and what were counterfeit." Also, he says, the notes of "some banks were worth more than others. Many bank notes were commonly discounted outside of their area, but the banks with the best reputations for solvency were redeemable at full face value anywhere." According to Wigington, "These notes were good as gold, better than our bills today."

The obsolete currency of this era was "larger in size than our contemporary bills, and much more elaborately executed. Each note was engraved with a vignette from the locale in which it was issued. For example, many of the notes from the East have shipbuildings scenes. The South is represented by many farming scenes. In Pennsylvania, labor and industrial scenes predominate." It was not at all unusual, he says, "for the portraits of prominent local citizens, the signers of the Declaration of Independence, Roman emperors, or prominent figures in art and literature to be depicted on the banknotes."

Says Wigington, "With the passing years, the banknotes were made more intricate and progressive in their design to prevent counterfeiting." In the early days of paper money, it was easily duplicated. The invention in the 1820s of the "Perkins plate," a series of fancy designs laid down in strips, with the denomination of the bill appearing many times in the background, changed the course of banknote engraving.

"Each banknote manufacturer then developed their own style of 'Perkins plate' to prevent forgeries. To the collector, these styles are easily distinguishable. It's possible to identify the banknote manufacturer, the engraver, and whether or not the bill is counterfeit" just by studying the note.

Among the 1,000 notes in Wigington's collection are ones that were stolen from a Lawrence, Kansas, bank during the famous Quantrill Raid in 1863. In addition, he has some notes from Leavenworth prison, and from the Clark-Gruber banknote manufacturing concern that later became the basis for the Denver Mint.

Starting a collection of banknotes is not terribly difficult, according to Wigington. "There are plenty of dealers and the notes have to be searched out, but they are fairly accessible. The average price for a note is in the range of $3 to $10, though the prices rise steadily from that point. The super-rarities (usually notes with an historical, as well as a collectible, value) go for as much as $2,000."

Wigington enjoys his collection principally because of the beauty of the notes. "But I also like to do research. Collecting bills is different from collecting coins. With coins, you know how many were made. It's cut and dried, so to speak. With this paper money, on the other hand, no one really knows how much was made and how much still remains. You are always finding new issues, and the history of many of these banknotes is still unknown. I enjoy tracking down the banks and the engravers.'"

A good organization for novice collectors to join is the Society for Paper Money Collectors, he says. Wigington can be contacted for further information at PO Box 4082, Harrisburg, PA 17111.

CIVIL WAR

TIMOTHY BURGESS
CONFEDERATE ARMY

THE SUFFERING OF the Confederate Army in the Civil War hasn't been as well-documented and isn't as well-known as that of the Union Army. The reason for this has to do with the availability of the records, and until Timothy Burgess came along, no one apparently thought the problem important enough to pursue.

Burgess, of Hendersonville, Tennessee, wants to make sure the individuals of the Confederate Army, their brave deeds and noble sacrifices, don't get lost in the maelstrom of history. He's been doing extensive and ground-breaking research into the organization of the Confederate Army, with some outstanding results.

Burgess was a sophomore in high school in 1967 when "I had to do a report on the Confederate Army, and the more I dug into it, the more interesting it became," he says. For the next 12 years, Burgess researched the army and compiled "a systematic outline of Confederate Army data for all major battles of the Civil War," says Burgess. The listing includes the organizations of the troops, the commanders of each unit and whether they were casualties, battle flags, how the organization was structured for each battle, a list of captured Union and Confederate soldiers and officers, and a list of all Confederate generals, noting whether killed, wounded, or captured.

Burgess says researching all of these details has frequently proven difficult. "Most of the records of the Confederate Army are incorrect, since a lot were made up from memory after the war. I've found a lot of discrepancies." In addition to perusing the entire 132-volume official *Record of the War of Rebellion*, published by the U.S. government, Burgess has relied on other old records, autobiographies and books by participants, regimental histories, and information available from cemeteries. "You pick up bits and pieces here and there," he says."It's like a giant jigsaw puzzle."

Burgess has discovered that the "casualty rates for Confederate commanders were much higher than for their Union counterparts." Not only was the Union Army larger than the Confederate Army, but during the period from 1864 to 1865, the South was losing more men and "couldn't rely on conscriptions or volunteers any longer. The soldiers were becoming a little shy, due to the heavy casualties, so the commanders had to egg them on more by leading the charges." Thus, says Burgess, more of the Confederate command personnel were killed or wounded.

Burgess, who works for the State of Tennessee's supply department, estimates he spends three to four hours a night on his research and writing. He also researches in the libraries of the State of Tennessee, the Tennessee State Archives, and the municipal library in Hendersonville, and obtains additional material via the interlibrary loan system.

Burgess's massive research into the organization of the Confederate Army is just about completed. "I think I've found most of what can be found," he says. The research, in chart form, is being compiled for "other Civil War buffs to use in their research so they no longer have to rely on outdated information about Confederate troop activity."

Burgess has spent all this time compiling the information, because he feels "the public needs to have a better understanding of how bloody war can be. To read casualty figures is one thing, but to see names with 'killed' written beside them, page after page, might lead people to draw some stronger conclusions."

Burgess doesn't know what his next research project will be. "It's hard to say. I've never looked past this one. I've enjoyed doing it so much." He thinks he might like to try his hand at compiling information on Confederate Amry pensions. Believe it or not, he says, "There's still one Confederate soldier's widow getting a pension check."

"I wish I knew why this project has been so absorbing for me all these years," says Burgess. "I don't really know. Part of it is the sacrifice these men made; they gave up an arm, a leg, a life for something they believed in. What's heart-rending is that buried somewhere is someone who might have been one of the great composers of all time, or a great scientist, but he never got the chance."

Burgess will answer queries about the Confederate Army directed to him at 121 Fresh Run Dr., Hendersonville, TN 37075.

WILLIAM FRASSANITO
CIVIL WAR PHOTOGRAPHS

THROUGH THE WORK of Alexander Gardner, Timothy O'Sullivan, James Gibson, and many other pioneers of the infant art of photography, the War Between the States became the first war in history to be recorded extensively on film.

As reflections of history and an absorbing source of information about the lives of the individuals caught up in the tumultuous events, Civil War photographs fascinate William Frassanito. So much so, that the Gettysburg, Pennsylvania, man has become an expert in the photographs of that era, and a leading author on the subject.

Frassanito, 34, discovered his interest in the Civil War when he was nine years old. "That was in 1955, and *Life* magazine put out an article, with many pictures, on the approach of the centennial of the Civil War," he recalls. "I read the article, and something just clicked."

The photographs in the article were what interested young Frassanito the most, so he began collecting books full of them. Then, in 1962, as he was developing more knowledge about the Civil War and its photographic history, "I began to notice some curious inconsistencies in the traditional captions of a number of famous views," he says.

For example, in a series of dramatic "death studies" from the Battle of Gettysburg, "there was one distinctive body shown that had its leg up in the air," he says. "It was identified as a dead Confederate soldier's leg." Later on, in the same book, it was identified as the leg of a Union soldier, in a slightly different view of the same scene. "No one apparently realized the bodies were the same," Frassanito says. This was the beginning of his research efforts, which led, eventually, to the publication of two well-received books on Civil War photographic history.

Though he has collected some photographs himself, most of his research has been done on photographs available from the Library of Congress, the Army War College, and the National Archives. "The Civil War was photographed by hundreds of photographers, and there are probably a million pictures," he says.

The ongoing process of researching Civil War photographs is a complex one, says Frassanito. Since he was involved with military intelligence during his service in the U.S. Army, he is especially fond "of doing detective work" to find out the truth behind the photographs.

Frassanito's specialty is documentation of historical scenes from major battles. In doing his research, it is necessary to "find out what the photographer said about his own work." That necessitates finding the original caption, and then reconstructing from there.

To really do an accurate job on the documentation of the photographs, says Frassanito, it is necessary to "become intimately familiar with the battle and with every photograph taken of it." He studies the battle terrain, both as it was during the war and as it is today, and also researches such seemingly tiny details as when the dead bodies were buried and exactly where they were located before burial.

Most Civil War photographs "were taken after the fact. The photographers would hear about a battle, throw their equipment into a wagon, and head out to the field to photograph" after it was over. It wasn't until Antietam that "photographers were there before the bodies were buried." Alexander Gardner, in fact, made a series of photographs of the dead on the battlefield of Antietam "which attracted more attention than almost any other photographic image of the war." From then on, says Frassanito, "the drive was on for photographic immediacy." The faster the photographer got to the battle, the better. In 1864, near the war's end, Timothy O'Sullivan began traveling to the front with the Union Army. He was the first photographer to do so, according to Frassanito.

Another intriguing aspect of Frassanito's photographic sleuthing has been in determining the identities of soldiers captured in the "death study" shots that many photographers took. He managed, through careful research, to "start coming up with names of soldiers portrayed in these death studies." He has a dozen identified so far, the youngest just 12 years old. "The whole idea is to get to know the men if possible," he says.

For Frassanito, "the value of these pictures is that they are my link with the past. Ultimately, I make the photographs come alive. It enhances the relevancy of the past for the present."

Frassanito's book *Gettysburg: A Journey Through Time* (Scribner's, 1975) was a Book-of-the-Month Club selection, and won the Photographic History Society of New York Distinguished Achievement Award in 1976. His other volume, *Antietam: The Photographic Legacy of America's Bloodiest Day* (Scribner's, 1978) similarly chronicles that epic battle. These books use the photographs of the era to carefully reconstruct the battles, with emphasis on the correctness and precison of the identification of events portrayed by the photos.

Frassanito invites questions, which can be directed to him at 333 Baltimore St., Gettysburg, PA 17325.

CHARLES KLEIN
BATTLE REENACTMENTS

HE FOUGHT IN MORE than 70 Civil War battles with Company A of the Fourth Virginia Volunteer Infantry ("the Stonewall Brigade") and other military units, and lived to tell the tale.

Charles Klein wasn't alive during the actual War Between the States, but he's one of a unique group of Civil War history buffs who believe just reading about the battles isn't enough. They reenact them, complete with uniforms, equipment, and weapons that are authentic to the last detail.

How did a 36-year-old steel construction worker become involved in fighting the Civil War all over again? Says Klein, "At the age of five or six, I became fascinated with the woodcut drawings in an old history book about the Civil War." As he grew up, he read about and studied the Civil War, with particular emphasis on the leaders, strategy, and logistics of the battles.

Klein's interest in the Civil War was focused by the centennial commemorations of the 1960s. "I always enjoyed the history," he says, "but when they started doing battles again, that caught my eye." When he got out of the U.S. Army in 1967, he went to Gettysburg to see a re-creation of the battle there. He talked with some of the people involved, and soon found himself back in the "army."

He founded Company A, a Confederate unit, in 1971, and commanded it until 1979, when he switched to two other battle reenactment groups: the 5th New York Infantry (the famed "Zouave" regiment of the Union Army), and the 4th North Carolina Infantry of the Confederate Army. "When I first started out, I was just interested in reenactment from the Confederate side, but now I'm doing both," he says.

Since he first started, Klein estimates he's been in 70 battles. The most exciting, he says, was the three-day Gettysburg reenactment that was part of the 1976 U.S. Bicentennial celebration. "It was the biggest one ever held," he says, adding that more than 2,500 men took part.

A master calendar of battles to be fought is made up each winter, since the reenactment season runs from April to October, says Klein. All the units involved make plans for what battles they will participate in during the coming year.

Civil War battle reenactments "began as a commemoration of a battle at its exact location, usually sponsored by a community organization." Now, says Klein, these reenactments don't necessarily take place on the actual battle sites, but are done as attractions for town celebrations, state fairs, and the like.

Klein has seen a change in the way reenactments are done since he's joined the organization. "Years ago, they were not as authentic as they are now. People just put on any uniform, took a gun and went out and shot at each other." Now, each reeanctment is painstakingly planned to be as exact a replica of the engagement as possible.

"A military reenactment is somewhat like a staged play," says Klein, "only on a full-scale outdoor stage." The underlying purpose of the reenactment is "not an inhibited desire to 'play war,' as some uninformed person might think." Rather, it is a desire to "provide an intimate, in-depth experience in history" by accurately portraying the events and people of a particular time. Not only in appearance is this authenticity important. There is thorough study of the battle plans, and every effort is made to repeat exactly the course of the battle. The fighting of the battles is choreographed carefully, Klein says, "even to the point that certain people play casualities and lie down dead for the duration of the battle; other people act as the wounded who need to be attended to, and so on."

All of this precision enables the public "when looking at a reenactment, to see not only the individual soldiers; it also gives them a chance to see traditional warfare at close range." The spectators at the events often visit the soldiers' camps, which are laid out according to 1860s military standards.

There's a growing trend to increased authenticity and more of a 'living history' type of approach by many units," says Klein. The buffs not only re-create a specific engagement, they live the life of the soldiers, drilling, eating the food of the time, and enduring many of the hardships. To have this sort of accuracy, "everyone involved must be his own researcher and designer."

"Some of the men are striving to go a step further in authenticity," he says. "Instead of lecturing the tourists who visit the camp site, the 'soldiers' take on the personality of a character from the Civil War, either real or invented, and talk to the visitors as that person would." These so-called "first-person impressions" are gaining popularity among the battle reenactors.

Naturally, "no one living today can duplicate what happened over 100 years ago," but battle buffs like to get as close as possible, Klein says. Thus, a cottage industry has sprung up to reproduce authentic weapons, uniforms, and other military equipment. "The people who make this stuff do a lot of research, and try to duplicate the items exactly," says Klein.

Why do Klein and his fellows go to all this elaborate preparation? The average history buff simply reads about what has happened. "Enthusiasts like us want to take our reading one step farther." Klein says. The Civil War "seems to have captured the American imagination as the most fascinating aspect of our military history. The ideals the people fought for are ones we can identify with today. That's especailly true in the South, where they haven't gotten over the war yet."

Klein can be contacted at RD 1, Box 233A, Aspers, PA 17304.

PAUL LOANE
GAR UNIFORMS & EQUIPMENT

Even AS A 10-YEAR OLD, Paul Loane was a Civil War buff. He was hooked at that early age by finding a Civil War musket in the closet of his family's summer house near Mt. Holly, New Jersey.

Today, Loane, 32, is a collector of items relating to the Civil War, particularly the uniforms, equipment, and personal effects of the soldiers of the Grand Army of the Republic.

Loane has turned a room in his Merchantville, New Jersey, home into a completely burglar-alarmed museum, where he displays his 800-item collection.

His assemblage of Union Army uniforms is one which Loane is especially proud of. Fifteen of the 17 different uniforms used by various branches of the army (he's only missing the Veteran Reserve Corps coat and the Cavalry officer's frock coat) are on display in his museum room.

Loane's collection of Civil War headgear, "which is considered to be one of the finest in private hands," is another interesting aspect of his hobby. "While there was essentially only one type of soldier's hat," he says, "they tended to be very individual, like the soldiers who wore them. For example, one soldier scratched his name on the visor and poked holes in the top for ventilation (the hats were notoriously hot, says Loane). Another even used a patented venting device similar to that on a pot-bellied stove, that would open and shut with a little lever, allowing air to enter the top of the hat. All in all, Loane says, "I have 20 good specimens" of these special and highly original hats.

By far the most intriguing items in Loane's collection are personal effects of soldiers. Loane has a series of letters from a Civil War Marine, Daniel Boyce, who ran away from his Philadelphia home in February of 1861 at the age of 17. The letters, written mainly to his younger brother, detail his progress through the war, until his death in 1862 from typhoid fever. The letters describe Boyce's attendance at the burning of the Norfolk Navy Yard and his service on a ship that was part of the Atlantic Ocean blockade. Loane even has letters from Boyce's captain and the ship's chaplain, saying that the Marine had died.

Another fascinating documentary item concerns Private Samuel Walcott of Salisbury, Connecticut. Loane has correspondence between Walcott and his parents. This young man, who enlisted in the 7th Connecticut Infantry in October of 1861, "was quite a Yankee trader," according to Loane. Several of his letters ask his farmer parents "to box, and send down to him by steamer, apples, corn, pies, and other foodstuffs from the farm, which he sold to his buddies in camp." Included in this package of 35 letters, two photographs, his writing kit, bayonet and scabbard, and personal diary, is a touching letter from his mother, begging him not to reenlist, since his brother had been killed in 1862. Walcott did re-enlist, and died August 16, 1864 at Deep Run, Virginia.

Loane is particularly interested in collecting these personal effects of soldiers. "There are people who collect things that have value, but no true personality. But I feel there are things that may have little monetary importance that are much more worthy of collecting."

Collecting military antiques "really makes history come alive," he says. And it's enjoyable to research the belongings of a specific person, for "you get a very interesting, personal look at the soldier of the time." These personal effects are, "literally, the stuff history is made of," says Loane.

Collecting Civil War artifacts "is more expensive than it was 20 years ago, when I started, but it's still possible. You just have to be a patient person. You can't simply go out with a bankroll and expect to have a great collection instantly."

It has gotten to the point, "what with the expense and rarity," that the day of the generalized Civil War collector is pretty much over; now, people are concentrating more and more on specific aspects," says Loane.

Loane has derived much satisfaction from his collection of Civil War items. "I feel good that I am able to preserve things that otherwise would not be appreciated, things that are part of a very important time in our nation's history." He adds that "all collectors are nothing but caretakers. When I'm gone, my collection will be passed on to others who will care for it."

Loane will gladly answer questions about Civil War military uniforms and equipment, addressed to him at 223 Victoria St., Merchantville, NJ 08109.

RICHARD MUDD
LINCOLN ASSASSINATION

On JULY 26, 1979, after more than 114 years, Dr. Samuel Mudd was at least partially exonerated of charges that he had participated in the conspiracy to assassinate Abraham Lincoln.

Mudd, the Maryland doctor who set the broken leg of assassain John Wilkes Booth, was convicted in 1865 of conspiring to kill the President, and spent four years in Ft. Jefferson prison in the Florida Keys, before he was pardoned by President Andrew Johnson.

Although the July 26th telegram from President Jimmy Carter to Mudd's grandson, Richard Mudd, expressed Carter's personal opinion that Samuel Mudd was innocent, it stopped short of official exoneration.

Richard Mudd, a retired physician for Chevrolet, says that he was somewhat satisfied by the Carter telegram. "I guess it's the best I'm going to get," he says. "I had hoped for the last 60 years to get Dr. Mudd legally exonerated, but the Department of Justice, Library of Congress, and the President's attorneys said it would not be legal for the President to declare him exonerated. Apparently, you can't exonerate a person after he's dead."

The lifelong interest in clearing his grandfather, whose conviction and imprisonment "ruined the family and left a lot of bitterness," has resulted in Mudd becoming an expert on the Lincoln assassination, particularly John Wilkes Booth and the role of the so-called conspirators in the murder. He has "over 1.5 million pieces of paper" relating to the assassination and its aftermath, which may make him the most prolific collector of Lincoln assassination material in the United States.

"I have practically all the information available on all the persons involved in the Lincoln assassination," says Mudd, "including not just the eight conspirators who were actually tried, but all people suspected, as well."

Among the aspects of the assassination in which Mudd is an expert are Mary Surratt, (the female "head" of the conspirators); Ft. Jefferson, (where Dr. Mudd was imprisoned); Ford's Theater (where the assassination took place) and the escape and 12-day flight of John Wilkes Booth.

Mudd's famous grandfather was, he says, an innocent victim of circumstance. Indeed, Samuel Mudd's conviction, by a military commission, was the result of largely circumstantial evidence. "It is true that my grandfather had met Booth on two separate occasions, prior to Lincoln's assassination," says Mudd. The two men met for the first time when Booth bought a horse in Mudd's neighborhood, and a second time on Pennsylvania Avenue on Christmas Eve, 1864, where Dr. Mudd had gone to purchase a stole for his wife. On that occasion, Mudd and Booth had a drink together, and that meeting was later used by the government as an indication that the two men had discussed the assassination.

Actually, his grandfather only became involved, Mudd says, "because when Booth was fleeing Washington, he just knew where there was a doctor."

The arrest, conviction, and imprisonment of Dr. Mudd had a ruinous effect on his family. The Mudds were a "semi-aristocratic, Catholic family who had lived (and still do) on the same property since 1675" in southern Maryland.

Dr. Mudd, educated at Georgetown University and the University of Maryland, "had a nice country practice, a farm, four children, and was a very respected member of the community," his grandson says. He lost everything by his imprisonment, and his family had to depend on the kindness of relatives. When Dr. Mudd returned to Maryland in 1869, he was "heavily in debt, his reputation, health, strength — and hair — were gone." He died of pneumonia at 49, a tragic victim of circumstance.

Mudd feels that his grandfather was treated so severely by the government not only because of his acquaintanceship with Booth, but largely because "there was a great anti-southern Maryland feeling in the government" caused by that area having been full of Confederate sympathizers during the Civil War. "They suspected everybody around there" of disloyalty, Mudd says.

Unfortunately, when Dr. Mudd was arrested, all of his personal belongings were confiscated. So, the family doesn't own any of his medical instruments or other objects today. "Supposedly, they're all stored in the Union Station in Washington, D.C.," says Mudd. "He never got anything back, and neither will we." He adds that the items are probably lost by now, anyway.

The family doesn't even have Dr. Mudd's original letters anymore. They were stolen from the house of Mudd's aunt in 1911, not, however, before many of them had been published in a book, *The Life of Dr. Samuel Mudd*.

For the beginner in genealogical research or research into the Lincoln assassination, Mudd has words of caution.

"Lincoln, his assassination, and related subjects are all lifetime and expensive hobbies. Don't start unless you know how time-consuming and extensive the study and research are."

Though he retired from Chevrolet in 1966, Mudd has been busy. Not only does the 79-year-old doctor lecture on the Lincoln assassination two or three times a month all over the U.S., but he plays handball three times per week.

Mudd will be glad to give further information on Dr. Mudd or the Lincoln assassination. He may be contacted at 1001 Hoyt Ave., Saginaw, MI 48607.

SEWARD OSBORNE
20TH N.Y. STATE MILITIA

THE 20TH NEW YORK State Militia is the oldest continuously existing military organization in the state of New York (and one of the three oldest in the United States). It dates from 1658, when it was founded in Kingston, New York. Today, it's known as the 156th Field Artillery of the New York National Guard.

In many ways, the glory days of the 20th New York ocurred during the Civil War. From the time it entered the conflict on April 18, 1861, until it was mustered out on July 29, 1866, the militia distinguished itself on the field of battle — and suffered appalling casualties.

The 20th New York might have faded into history, its brave soldiers forgotten, were it not for the efforts of Seward Osborne of Olivebridge, New York. Osborne, himself a disabled veteran of the Vietnam War, has been interested in Civil War history for 20 of his 34 years. "My father had a large part in sparking my interest," says Osborne, "He was interested in history, though not particularly in military history, but he encouraged my involvement." Osborne had a number of ancestors who served in the Civil War, and his interest "mushroomed into a way of life, not a passing hobby."

Since the 20th N.Y. State Militia originated near his home, it was natural that Osborne should concentrate his intensive research efforts on that group, which he feels, like "Civil War history in general, is sadly being neglected in history."

New York State, the largest in the Union at the time of the Civil War, sent the most men into battle.

The 20th New York, says Osborne, was "a very hard fighting regiment, which distinguished itself on the battlefields of Second Manassas, Antietam, and Gettysburg," with major casualties. The regiment suffred 50 percent casualties at Manassas, 34 percent at Antietam, and over 60 percent during the three-day Gettysburg fight. The regiment played a major role in breaking the famed Pickett's Charge on the third day of Gettysburg (which Osborne terms "one of the greatest events in military history").

Though the 20th New York was an important part of that battle, Osborne says, "they've been all but denied credit" for their efforts. Thus, in 1978 Osborne was prompted to begin lobbying with the Gettysburg National Battlefield Park superintendent and the National Park Service in Washington, to have a monument erected to honor the 20th New York on the battlefield.

Even though it had been "government policy for over 60 years that no more monuments were to be erected at Gettysburg," Osborne succeeded in convincing the government to erect one honoring the 20th New York. It was dedicated in 1980 and Osborne feels it is his most important achievement of his years of research.

Research is Osborne's abiding passion. "I'm at it night and day," he says. He does most of it by mail, corresponding with the government and other scholars and experts in Civil War history. He has also managed to visit most of the major battlefields of the war. A great deal of his material comes from his collection of over 3,000 original documents relating to the 20th New York. Many of these documents are unpublished, and unavailable elsewhere.

Osborne has built an addition onto his home to house "what West Point considers a very nice collection" of military uniforms, hats, flags and other items relating to the Civil War and the 20th New York State Militia.

About his work, Osborne reflects,"It's ironic that people have very little interest in what their forefathers went through. The individual soldier has been all but ignored. History has covered him over with the shadows of the big names. I'm doing something about it." He feels that his writing, researching and lecturing about the 20th New York has helped fill an important gap in our understanding.

"I'm a law-abiding, peaceful person, and believe strongly in God, and I really feel this is my niche in life. It's right for me...How many people are there today — or ever — who do something they really want to, who fulfill any committment, or see any goals reached? I have."

Osborne will gladly provide information on the 20th New York State Militia. He can be contacted at Route 2, Olivebridge, NY 12461.

LLOYD OSTENDORF
ABRAHAM LINCOLN PHOTOGRAPHS

THE FIRST U.S. PRESIDENT to be photographed extensively was Abraham Lincoln. His craggy, plain, but arresting face is a brooding reminder of the tumultuous years of the Civil War, perhaps the darkest period in American history.

"I've been fascinated since boyhood with the unusual face of Lincoln," says Lloyd Ostendorf. "The rugged individualism in evidence in the nobly balanced features appeals to my artistic taste."

As a youngster, Ostendorf used to put a picture of Lincoln on his bedroom wall on the President's birthday. Today, he owns the world's largest private collection of photographs of the 16th President.

The freelance artist from Dayton, Ohio, looks upon Lincoln's countenance as a supreme artistic achievement. "I always felt God never created another face like that," he says. "I don't expect ever to see a face like it." For artists trying to draw or sculpt it, however, Lincoln's face has frequently been "a downfall, because there is such a difference in angles; not many people have that kind of balanced imbalance about their features."

In addition to the many photographs of Lincoln in his collection, Ostendorf also owns a number of engravings, negatives, and other pieces of art relating to Lincoln as well. One of his most highly prized posessions isn't a Lincoln photograph at all. It is a life mask of the President done by sculptor Clark Mills two months before Lincoln's assassination. Ostendorf has the second of the plaster impressions made from the original mold. "I particularly like this life mask because it is the closest you can get to what Lincoln actually looked like: every pore, every pockmark, every wrinkle shows clearly."

The first impression from the mold, which is now housed in the Smithsonian Institution, is not as clear, Ostendorf says. He obtained his plaster cast from the family of John Hay. Hay was Lincoln's confidant and personal secretary.

Ostendorf is also particularly proud of the six autographed Lincoln photographs he has in his collection, one ("which is very rare") from his pre-Presidential sojourn in Springfield, Illinois. There are only about 75-100 signed Lincoln photographs known to exist, he says.

The first photograph of Lincoln is thought to have been taken in 1846, in Springfield. From that time, until shortly before his death, the President was a fairly frequent visitor to photographic studios.

Though he was terribly occupied with the burdens of the Presidency, Lincoln had "little outside recreation; he didn't run around making speeches like the President does today, and he didn't take vacations," Ostendorf says. About his only relaxation was an occasional trip to the theater, and visits with friends to swap stories. The trips to photographers, then, were probably looked upon as diversions in the often oppressive routine of his office.

"Actually, he really didn't participate in that many sittings," says Ostendorf, noting that a fairly large number of photographs were taken each time Lincoln visited a photographer's studio. According to Ostendorf, there are 125 known separate poses of Lincoln that appear in photographs.

Contrary to popular belief, "Lincoln was not the most photographed man of his time," says Ostendorf. He cites General U.S. Grant, Mark Twain, and even Lincoln's assassain, John Wilkes Booth, as being far more image-conscious, and therefore, more frequently photographed than the President. "There were a number of famous people who weren't camera-shy in those days," he says.

Another familiar misconception people have about Lincoln photographs, Ostendorf says, is that they were all done by Matthew Brady. While it is true that the renowned photographer did take a few pictures of Lincoln himself, it is also true that he was going blind during Lincoln's term of office, and frequently had other photographers doing his work, under the umbrella title "Matthew Brady and Company."

Actually, the most prolific Lincoln photographer was Alexander Gardner. From 1863, until Lincoln's death, "in the truest sense, Gardner was Lincoln's cameraman, because of the number of pictures and the variety of poses. He's head and shoulders above Brady," says Ostendorf.

Naturally, because Lincoln "isn't sitting for portraits anymore" the original photographs are extremely valuable, says Ostendorf, who keeps all of his in a bank vault, and only displays reproductions. "The prices are really getting out of sight, just like gold."

He says that a photo that could be bought for $15 to $50 when he started collecting in 1935, now brings $1,000 or more. Recently, a photograph sold at Hamilton Galleries, a New York auction house, for $4,000.

"Anybody with money can be a collector," Ostendorf says. Pictures of Lincoln, while relatively scarce, are still occasionally available through auctions or at the selling-off of other collections.

Then, too, some people go into their attic, find an old photograph that "looks a little like Lincoln, and think they've made a great discovery," says Ostendorf. While someone might tell these people the photo they have is a genuine Lincoln portrait, it has been Ostendorf's experience that none of the so-called discoveries have been Lincoln. "I think the majority of the photographs that still exist have already been found," he says.

Utilizing his collection, Ostendorf has been able to illustrate most of the books on Abraham Lincoln that have come out in the last 10 years. In addition, he has published several books on his own, most notably *Lincoln in Photographs: An Album of Every Known Pose*, on which he collaborated with Charles Hamilton. This book, published in 1963, is considered "the most complete, definitive work" on Lincoln photography.

Ostendorf will gladly give information on Abraham Lincoln in photographs, and will provide free appraisals of suspected Lincln photos. He can be contacted at 225 Lookout Dr., Dayton, OH 45419.

JERRY RUSSELL

BATTLEFIELD PRESERVATION

JERRY RUSSELL IS A talented organizer. He's the founder of a major Civil War buff group, Civil War Round Table Associates, tying together all the Civil War Round Table study groups in the United States, and he is also a leading force in the preservation of the battlefields of the war.

He has been at the forefront of some of the major battles of the 1970s — to keep the Civil War battlefields as safe as possible from encroaching civilization. And he's had a good deal of success.

Russell, 46, of Little Rock, Arkansas, always had a fondness for history, particularly that of the Civil War. After many years of study, he decided in 1964 to publish a newsletter which he sent to other Civil War buffs. That newsletter grew into *The Civil War Round Table Digest*, the journal of Civil War Round Table Associates.

Though continuing research into the history of the War Between the States interests Russell (he also founded the Confederate History Institute in 1979, a group of buffs interested in scholarship on all aspects of the Confederacy), his greatest expertise lies in the preservation of battlefields.

He cut his teeth in the preservationist movement a few years ago when the U. S. Government erected a 300-foot high observation tower at Gettysburg.

Though protests against this "Tinkertoy in the sky" were unsuccessful, it whetted Russell's appetite for further forays in defense of authenticity.

He is an important worker in the effort to have the U.S. Congress pass legislation to add some 1,700 historic acres to the Manassas National Park, site of an important Civil War battle. "The measure has passed the House in three sessions," says Russell, "but it keeps getting bottled up in the Senate because a single group of local people are opposed to taking that land off the tax rolls." U. S. Sen. John Warner (R-Va.) has introduced a bill calling for an additional 700 acres of Manassass to be set aside, but Russell, and his fellow buffs, are hoping the House version, for the full 1,700 acres, will prevail.

Enlisting the aid of local Civil War Round Table chapters, Russell also participated in the successful scuttling of the Marriott Great America amusement park adjacent to Manassas. "The battlefield would have suffered greatly from an invasion of tourists, and the traffic, sewage and water systems would have been strained beyond belief," he says. The group successfully blocked the building of a highway interchange in the proposed park's location. They also scored a success by blocking a 1979 Environmental Protection Agency approval of a sewage plant in The Town Grottoes, Virginia, on the Point Republic battlefield.

Among the other preservation projects Russell and his group are supporting is the restoration of the famed Cyclorama in Atlanta, Georgia. This huge painting, depicting the Burning of Atlanta during the Civil War "is deteriorating and the city won't do anything about it," says Russell. Another Georgia preservation project is near the Chicamaugua battlefield, where the state is trying to widen the highway through the battlefield.

"We're not only involved in battlefield preservation," says Russell. For example, at Grant's Tomb in New York City, an artist was commissioned to "paint surrounding benches with an expressionistic design, which is totally out of character with the shrine. We're trying to get the benches changed."

In Philadelphia, the building housing the tomb of Gen. William Hancock Scott is in a cemetery in a tough neighborhood; it was broken into and vandalized., "With our help," says Russell, local Sons of Union Veterans raised $5,000 to fix it up.

The list goes on, with many other places deserving support for their preservation. "More attention needs to be paid to these historic places," he says. "If you don't have any pride in your country or in your past, you are not going to have hope for the future." Merely reading about the Civil War (or any historic event) isn't worth much unless you can actually visit the place, Russell thinks. "If we keep letting them put up hamburger joints, and freeways, and so forth in these places, it's no longer going to be possible to get a firsthand feel of history. After all, you can put a 'theme park' anywhere — you can't put the site of a historic event where it didn't happen."

Russell will gladly give further information on the work of Civil War Round Table Associates, or other matters pertaining to Civil War site preservation. He can be contacted at PO Box 7388, Little Rock, AR 72217.

JOSEPH RZOTKIEWICZ
GETTYSBURG

THE BATTLE OF GETTYSBURG on July 1-3, 1863, was one of the most bloody and decisive of the Civil War. But for Joseph Rzotkiewicz, the most fascinating aspect of the battle is what effect it had on the town of Gettysburg and its citizens, past and present.

Rzotkiewicz's interest in Gettysburg had its genesis in a college anthropology project. While a student at Temple University in 1972, Rzotkiewicz came to Gettysburg to do an anthropological study of business and housing trends in the Pennsylvania community.

"I liked the town, the people, and the history," he says. When he began doing background research for his study, he became intrigued by the question of "what happens to a quiet, small town when 250,000 soldiers come to do battle."

Since then, Rzotkiewicz has been deeply involved in studying the town and the battle which had a devastating effect on it.

The Battle of Gettysburg is probably the most written-about encounter of the Civil War, Rzotkiewicz says. The town was chosen as the site of the battle because it was a road center and both sides saw it as important. Strangely enough, on the first day of the conflict, the Confederates were attacking from the North, the Union Army defending from the South.

"The true story has not been told. As historians, we can only piece together what happened," Rzotkiewicz says. "There have to be 250,000 stories of Gettysburg." More and more information is turning up all the time, he says, to aid in researchers' understanding. "We have the benefit of hindsight. Fortunately, a lot of the veterans of the battle wrote down their reminiscences."

But for Rzotkiewicz, the most burning research issue is the effect the battle had on the town. For a long time, he says, it was thought that no one from the town had fought in the famous encounter. Then it was discovered that a man named John Burns had participated in the battle, as a civilian, and that, in fact Company K of the First Pennsylvania Reserves (made up largely of men from Gettysburg and its environs) had also fought there. When the battle was over, many of the men went home to the town to check on their families.

"Gettysburg was invaded many times over," Rzotkiewicz said. "Many people came to the town after the fighting, looking for their relatives, sweethearts, husbands or brothers. And the people of the town were stuck with dealing with the bodies of the dead soldiers."

"The battle was three days long," says Rzotkiewicz, "and it has been fought every year since." Gettysburg is still used by the U.S. Military Academy at West Point as a teaching example in battle strategy, he adds. It is notable for its troop movement and position, the strategy of each side, and the personalities involved.

In doing his research, Rzotkiewicz has not been troubled by a shortage of material. "Basically, it has all been written. Now it's time to start putting the pieces of the puzzle together."

He has been using this approach in the study of the 26th Pennsylvania Militia, which was Gettysburg's first defense against the Confederates. A small skirmish took place on June 23,1863, in which the 26th Pennsylvania barely escaped capture, according to Rzotkiewicz. Even so, some 200-300 soldiers died.

Gettysburg also was the base for a band of independent scouts, who were very important in the Union strategy of the battle, Rzotkiewicz believes. "Today we have mass communications. Back then, there was poor communication, so the scouts were necessary to help inform the Union leadership of the Confederates's whereabouts." Through the efforts of the "Independent Adams City Scouts," the Union army knew a lot about Rebel movements before the battle took place.

Rzotkiewicz, who belongs to several historical societies and military history groups, has also been elected to the Company of Military Historians, an organization of professional historians. "I was voted in unanimously, and it is a great honor because it is a very selective and knowledgeable group."

His advice to the novice historian: "I feel the best thing to do is really specialize." He also recommends that novices join a Civil War Round Table, of which there are many located around the country, to develop contacts with other people interested in the study of the Civil War.

The Civil War is an interesting period for study, Rzotkiewicz feels, because "here was a war where brother was against brother. It was a violent war, but many gentlemanly acts occurred." For example,. during the nightly breaks in the battle of Gettysburg, Union soldiers would go out onto the battlefield and bring water to wounded soldiers, Union and Confederate alike.

Rzotkiewicz sees a parallel between the Civil War and the upheavals in America in the 1960s, one hundred years later. "We almost ended up in the 1960s with the actual brother against brother fighting we had during the Civil War."

STAN SCHIRMACHER

SERVICE RECORDS

WHEN SHERMAN MARCHED to the sea by way of Atlanta in 1864, Christian R. Mittelstadt was leading the way, as a drummer and flag bearer. After the epic battle, Mittelstadt was marched off to Averysboro, North Carolina, where he was wounded in the heel and sent back to Dodge County, Wisconsin, to recuperate. His entire Civil War service lasted less than six months.

That any of these details (and the records of them) still survive more than

100 years later, is in large part due to the initiative of Mittelstadt's grandson, Stan Schirmacher.

A retired shop teacher who lives in Tempe, Arizona, Schirmacher founded the Sons of Sherman's March to the Sea in 1966. This national group of Civil War buffs has made it its business to uncover and preserve the service records of Civil War soldiers in both the Union and Confederate armies.

Why was Schirmacher interested in looking for his grandfather's (and other people's relatives') service records? "Living in Wisconsin as a person with German ancestry during the World War," he says. "It finally dawned on me that I had an American background better than a lot of the people who were prejudiced against me." Thus began his efforts to find out more about his grandfather's service in the Civil War.

The going was rough, because Schirmacher had no artifacts or other information from his grandfather that might provide a clue to the man's Civil War experiences. Then, Schirmacher discovered that the National Archives in Washington, D. C., maintains the service records of Civil War veterans and the veterans of most other wars.

He wrote to the archives, and received, in return for a small copying fee, photostatic copies of his grandfather's Civil War service file. In those copies, he discovered the facts about Mittelstadt's participation in the famous March to the Sea.

"Other people might want to know how to do this,'"thought Schirmacher. So, he founded his organization.

Today, the Sons of Sherman's March to the Sea has some 350 members scattered all over the country. "Basically, we do nothing," says Schirmacher. "There are no meetings. We're just a 'show and tell' outfit." There is a lot of correspondence among the members, discussing finds they have made in the records and supplying information to others on Civil War soldiers.

Incidentally, the term "service records" refers to the military's files on the whereabouts and assignments of people in the service. Such information as rank, assigned unit, wounds, date of discharge, etc. are given in the records, Schirmacher says.

Locating service records for a Civil War veteran is a relatively easy matter, says Schirmacher. In addition to the National Archives, it is a good idea to check with the historical society of the state in which the veteran lived. Records for Confederate Army soldiers are, of course, more difficult to come by, Schirmacher says. In that instance, the researcher is probably better advised to get in touch first with the state historical society, as many of the records were never moved to the National Archives.

Schirmacher's wife's grandfather was in the Civil War as a Confederate soldier. When he was researching that man, Schirmacher discovered, through a number of pages supplied by the Texas Historical Society, that the grandfather was a surgeon with the Texas Cavalry and that he had been in charge of military hospitals in New Orleans.

Another rich source of information for the person intent on finding a Civil War ancestor's records are the pension records. Schirmacher used this approach and got 21 papers from the State of Texas confirming the information about his wife's grandfather.

Schirmacher sees his organization providing a much-needed service for people whose ancestors were involved in the Civil War. "A lot of people want to find their roots, and we try to help them out, because they just don't know how to do it." Thus, Schirmacher and his fellow members operate as a clearinghouse of information and advice for people all over the nation.

According to Schirmacher, another important function of Sons of Sherman's March to the Sea is to supply replicas of medals, guns, and other Civil War artifacts to people with a Civil War heritage but no memorabilia to go with it. "People like to have something they can touch," he says, even though it may not be the actual medal or weapon owned by their ancestor. Schirmacher, who spends at least an hour a day on his interest, says he really likes the human aspect of his work. "I like helping people,"he says. "They're always so pleased to know about their ancestors."

The National Archives, says Schirmacher, will undertake a search for a long-lost Civil War veteran's service record if they are provided with (at the least) a name and a state of residence at the supposed time of service. Archives personnel will search the records, Schirmacher says, and send copies of whatever information and documents can be found, charging the questioner three dollars for the service. If, as a result of the search, the archives is not able to find anything, there is no charge. State historical societies usually charge ten cents per page for making copies.

Contact Schirmacher, or the Sons of Sherman's March to the Sea, at 1725 Farmer Ave., Tempe, AZ 85281. For a $2.50 "lifetime" membership fee, Sons of Sherman's March of the Sea will send a member a certificate, a wallet-sized card, and a photo of General Sherman himself.

JOHN WALTER

REGIMENTAL HISTORIES

JOHN WALTER ESTIMATES that the North and South had a total of 8,000 military units in the Civil War. At any rate, he's sure of 7,500 of those regiments, for he's researched and written their histories.

"I'd guess there are another 500 or so," he says, "but they were so obscure, so short-lived, that we may never unearth the facts about them."

Walter's interest in the Civil War "came about through a general interest in history, as well as encouragement from my father, who was a Civil War buff."

In 1958, he read a book that "detailed the operations of the 15th Arkansas Infantry at the Siege of Vicksburg, and also at the Siege of Point Hudson." Since both events occurred simultaneously, he says, "I wondered how the same unit could be in two places at once." He decided to do some research. "What I discovered was that there were not only two, but three regiments, all called the

'15th Arkansas Infantry,'" he says. The reason for the three identically designated regiments was typical of many of the duplications Walter later uncovered.

"When a man organized a regiment, he might have liked the idea of calling
it 'the 15th Arkansas Regiment,' and he would send in that designation to the
adjutant general in Richmond, Virginia." Even though there might be one or
two other regiments already claiming the same name by the time the later
regiment's paperwork arrived in Richmond, "it took forever to get the bookkeeping problem ironed out, so, the regiments kept the numbers but added the
name of their originators." Thus, the three Arkansas regiments are properly
called Gee's, Johnson's, and Claybourne's 15th Arkansas Regiments. Slightly
less confusing, perhaps, but Walter says it still leads to all sorts of research
problems in compiling the regiments' histories, because most of the time writers or other record-keepers left off the name designation.

Continuing his research, Walter decided to try to find out how many other
times this duplication of names occurred. "One thing led to another" and
before he knew it, he was deeply involved in a research project that had never
been attempted before in the annals of Civil War history.

Walter maintains a card file of his research for ease in finding the history of
a particular regiment. Included in the information Walter obtains for each unit
are date and place of formation, records of various engagements, the name of
the commanding officer, and the fate of the unit (surrendered, captured,
disbanded, etc.). In addition, for Union units, Walter also tries to list the site of
the unit's discharge and the number of casualties sustained.

He has had the most difficulty obtaining information on the Confederate
Army. "A lot of Southern information was destroyed in the burning of
Richmond," he says, "and Southern bookkeeping just was not as thorough as
Northern. The casualty figures either weren't kept up or were destroyed."

One of Walter's particularly notable achievements has been in developing
the history of the First South Carolina Artillery (later the First South Carolina
Infantry), which was the major Confederate unit at the opening battle of the
war at Fort Sumter. The museum at Fort Sumter "heard about my research, so
they asked me for a history of the First South Carolina, to use as the basis for
reconstructing the unit for their 'living history' program," he says.

What Walter discovered was that the First South Carolina had been raised
before the hostilities began, and was made up of men from every state of the
Confederacy. In addition, Walter researched some of the individuals involved
in the unit.

"What started as a spare time hobby is now a full-time project at home,"
says Walter. He sells the regimental histories to "Civil War history buffs, and
other people, mainly those who are interested in finding out about their
ancestors." He charges $7.50 for a regimental history.

For the novice researcher of Civil War history, Walter advises reading everything possible in the subject. "I am a nearly daily visitor to the New York
Public Library," he says. "Historical research is time-consuming and you have

to be willing to dedicate at least 15 years to it before all your research starts to pay off."

Walter says the most interesting aspect of his research is "all the unanswered questions which I enjoy trying to find answers to."

Walter can be contacted at 79-13 67th Dr., Middle Village, NY 11379, for further information or for the purchase of a regimental history.

MILITARIA

NEAL CROWLEY
TOY SOLDIERS

NEAL CROWLEY IS A MAN with his own private army — some 5,000 men strong.

Crowley, 48, from Pacific Palisades, California, had toy soldiers when he was a youngster. When his family broke up their household in 1966, his toys resurfaced, still in their original box. Since that time, Crowley has been deeply involved in expanding his collection and restoring the figurines.

"Toy soldiers have passed into history along with most of the other hand-crafted goods that were once plentiful. It is the joy of being able to repair and restore them that turns me on,"says Crowley. "This requires research, and trial-and-error attempts to make molds of the missing parts."

He did a lot of traveling in connection with his job for 18 years, and visited secondhand stores and flea markets wherever he went to find broken toy soldiers to be repaired.

Crowley specializes in collecting "composition" toy soldiers from two German concerns, made between the turn of the century and 1958."Composition" is a combination of sawdust and casein glue, over a metal frame, similar in texture to papier-mache. It is more durable than papier-mache, however, because it resists moisture.

Roughly half his collection is of these figures, made by the firms Elastolin and Lineol. In addition, he collects and restores metal soldiers made in Great Britain by the Wm. Britains Co., from 1893-1966. Crowley says that toy soldiers were made in the U.S. from roughly 1928-40, "perfect little Art Deco pieces that were quite charming" but they never really competed effectively with the British and German figures.

The high peak of production for the composition soldiers was in the 1930s. "Most collectors cherish these and want them in mint condition," Crowley says. "I like to retrieve ones that are crippled and fix them up."

His most unusual pieces, Crowley says, are also the most mysterious. So far, he hasn't been able to find out where they were made, when, or by whom. They must have been made prior to 1918, because they are of Germany's Kaiser Wilhelm, Emperor Franz Joseph of Austria, and King Victor Emanuel of Italy, and "these people fell from favor" at the end of World War I. The figures, nearly 5 inches tall (most toy soldiers are only about 2 inches tall) are so well-sculpted they can stand on their feet without a base. They would make "hefty but handsome toys for a child," Crowley said, but they cannot be identified because they don't have a base that the manufacturer could put its marking on.

The restoration process is all handwork. Crowley uses sculptors' and dentists' tools to achieve the greatest precision possible. He uses a mixture of epoxy and other materials, then recasts each part. To do this accurately, he has to find one perfect figure, so he can use the various parts to make castings from. It takes about 1 hour per figure, with painting time, but he does 10 or 15 pieces at one time.

The soldiers, in a variety of conditions, are still fairly plentiful, particularly the British ones. At its peak, the Britains concern was producing 1 million figures per week. The German soldiers, not as plentiful, still can be found in parts of the country that have large German populations such as Milwaukee, St. Louis, and the Chicago area.

Anyone, Crowley is convinced, can learn how to restore the soldiers. There are over 150 books on the subject, and "it is easy to learn." The cost for the soldiers, varies widely. "If you go for the banged-up ones," 50 cents or $1 per soldier is not uncommon. Mint condition soldiers, in their original boxes, "go for astronomical prices," Crowley says, citing the Britains "medal" set. It was only made for one year, and only a few sets are known to exist, bringing the value to $4,000.

Crowley will counsel toy soldier collectors/restorers, on request. Contact him at PO Box 784, Pacific Palisades, CA 90272.

CRAIG HERBERT
WORLD WAR I BALLOONING

A LITTLE KNOWN fact about World War I is that hundreds of balloons were used for observation purposes by the Allies. Strung from the English Channel almost to Switzerland, the balloons provided vital information on German troop movements.

Craig Herbert, 80, of Lafayette Hill, Pennsylvania, remembers those days pretty well. He was a member of the Second Balloon Company of the U. S. Army, and he's devoted considerable time to making sure other people don't forget the role of balloons in the Great War. In 1932, he founded the National Association of American Observation Balloon Corps Veterans (NAAOBCV), which has held an annual meeting of the balloon veterans ever since.

"There are still about 600 of us left," Herbert says."But they're going pretty fast. Most of the members are around 85, and many can no longer get around." But Herbert plans to keep holding the reunions as long as people are still able to show up.

Herbert was only 16 when he joined the U.S. Army, and 17 when he shipped out with the Second Balloon Company. "We were the first U.S. air service unit of any kind" on the scene in France, he says.

His company spent an astounding 244 days at the front, without relief, the longest, he says, of any unit in the war. "Actually, it was 251 days, but we spent the first seven days lying around in pup tents" preparing to move to the front lines.

The Second Balloon Company was involved in most of the major battles of World War I, including the Second Battle of the Marne, the Chateau-Thierry drive, St.-Mihiel, and, finally, the Meuse-Argonne Woods campaign. After that, the company spent six months in Germany, before returning to the United States.

Herbert, who was "a second class private — about the lowest rank you can get," worked as an airplane spotter.

"In those days," he recalls, "we could tell by their shape whether the airplanes were ours or theirs. It's not like today, where they all look alike."

According to Herbert, the hydrogen-filled balloons, 92 feet long and 32 feet in diameter "were attached to the ground by a 4,100-foot cable, and were raised and lowered, depending on what kind of observation was needed." During "quiet" periods on the battlefield, two men went up in the balloons at a time. During battles, only one man was in the basket, so that he could more easily evacuate if the balloon were hit by enemy fire.

"The balloons were located with the artillery," says Herbert, near the six-inch howitzers. They were used both to regulate the artillery fire and provide reconnaissance information.

Herbert's most pungent memories are of life on the front, which was far from pleasant. "We had no bathing facilities, so we had to take sponge baths. We never got to take our uniforms off." In addition, the company "spent five months sleeping in the mud," was stricken by dysentery and "cooties," and was "gassed quite often, which kept a lot of the company on the sick list."

After the war, Herbert sponsored annual reunions of the Second Balloon Company members. In 1931, "we met jointly with another company in Detroit, and all got along so well" that he decided to start a reunion organization for everyone who had served in the Balloon Corps.

Herbert sees the NAAOBCV as a necessary organization to keep the public informed about the important role played by the Balloon Corps in World War I. "I got tired of people saying, 'What's that? Never heard of it,' when I told them what unit I'd served in during the War.

"I think the NAAOBCV's importance is that it is a unique organization," says Herbert, explaining why he continues with it after so many years. "There wasn't anything like the Balloon Corps before or since, in any war."

In addition to the social and historical aspects, the NAAOBCV also sponsors a magazine for its members. Called *Haul Down and Ease Off* after a familiar command to the balloonists, the magazine has been edited and published by Herbert for 48 years.

In 1979, Herbert was instrumental in having an observation balloon put on display at the U.S. Air Force Museum at Wright-Patterson Air Force Base in Dayton, Ohio. "It's the only one left in the world," says Herbert. It took three years of correspondence, and the cooperation of the British Army (who owned it) to get the balloon to the United States. The balloon at the Air Force Museum "looks quite huge hanging up there; it's very impressive," says Herbert.

The balloon, which was actually of World War II vintage, but of the same design as the World War I models, was in need of repairs before it could be hung at the museum. "Even if there were any World War I balloons left," Herbert says, "they would be far too deteriorated to put on display."

Most of the balloons used in World War I were bought by a man named Richard Walters, says Herbert. He used them for exhibition flights at state fairs and the like, featuring the destruction of the balloon at the end of the act. Thus, none of them survived.

Herbert, through his work with the NAAOBCV, is the leading historian of World War I ballooning. Much of his expertise came to him through copies of the official U.S. Army records of the Balloon Corps.

The originals of these records, including company histories, and technical data were all destroyed in a fire at Bolling Field near Washington, D. C., in the mid-1920s. Thus, Herbert's "copies" have become the "originals." They've provided information for government and researchers alike, and now are deposited in the Air Force Museum's archives.

Herbert will gladly answer questions about World War I ballooning, or NAAOBCV. He can be contacted at 634 Wagner Rd., Lafayette Hill, PA 19444.

VINCENT KEHOE
18TH CENTURY BRITISH ARMY

AMONG THE MOST exciting events of America's Bicentennial celebration were reenactments of several battles of the American Revolution. All up and down the Eastern seaboard, communities and groups of individuals banded together to recreate everything from skirmishes to full-scale engagements.

In the forefront of much of the activity, though assuming a somewhat different perspective than most of the participants, was Vincent Kehoe, who was the leader of the American contingent of the Tenth Royal Lincolnshire Regiment of Foot, a re-creation of a British Army unit that participated in the Revolutionary War.

Kehoe, 59, of Chelmsford, Massachusetts, fell into his military leadership role by accident. "I was a freelance photographer working on an assignment for Time-Life and had gone to Concord, Massachusetts, in 1967 to take photos of a reenactment of the Battle of Concord Bridge," Kehoe recalls. "I found that the British side was not particularly suitable to photograph because the people recreating the troops were so ragtag and bobtail in their appearance."

He pointed this fact out to the organizers of the event, at a meeting of the press after the reenactment, "but it didn't make an impression." His interest was piqued, and in 1968, decided to reconstruct a proper British regiment. In 1970, his group was granted permission by the Tenth Foot Royal Lincolnshire Regimental Association in England to call itself the American Contingent of the group.

From 1970 to 1975, Kehoe and approximately 150 other people rehearsed for the Bicentennial battles in which they would be involved, and prepared the uniforms and equipment they needed to appear as authentic as possible on the battlefield.

Kehoe did much of the necessary research to authenticate the regiment's uniforms and equipment and traveled to England frequently during the five years of preparations.

"We wanted to be able to recreate as closely as possible the 18th century regiment's appearance, using 20th century materials," Kehoe says. Utilizing wool, linen, and leather ("we avoided polyester scrupulously"), Kehoe's regiment was "able to recreate physically quite closely the look of the 10th Regiment of Foot in Revolutionary times."

The careful attention to detail in uniform also paid off in other ways. "It really helped everyone develop the attitude of a soldier of the time," Kehoe says. "It created a very strong *esprit de corps.*"

Kehoe and his regiment participated in several important battles, the same ones the original regiment had been involved in during the Revolution. Among them, the battles of Lexington and Concord, Bunker Hill, and Long Island could not be fought on the actual battle sites, given urban growth. When it came to the New Jersey battles (Trenton, Princeton, Monmouth), Kehoe says the reenactments took place on the real battlefields.

The attention to detail at most of these battles was "pretty good, and they went very well," according to Kehoe. At the recreation of the Battle of Monmouth more than 4,000 men participated.

The reenactments continued until 1978, when the regiment commemorated the bicentennial of the original group's return to England "and ceased all field operations. Now, the regiment is known as the 10th Foot Regimental Association of America, an association of a mainly social nature, part of the larger association of regimental veterans in Britain."

Kehoe is particularly proud of the record of his regiment in the reenactments. Not only did they manage to get through the battles without any of their number actually being injured, but the regiment was the Guard of Honor in Boston during the visit of Queen Elizabeth II on July 11, 1976. Later that year, Kehoe says, the regiment journeyed to England, where they appeared at the reunion of the regiment in Lincoln, and went on to London to appear in several royal festivals.

The authenticity of his regiment is the source of Kehoe's greatest satisfaction. "Every town in New England had a Minuteman group during the Bicentennial," Kehoe says, "but frankly, we were interested in having a more military group than the sort of 'chowder and marching society' that most places ended up with.

"When you're doing a sort of play — which these reenactments really were — unless both sides are authentic, you don't really have a good show," he says.

During his research into the regiment's history, Kehoe managed to collect a great many artifacts. Some of them have now been sold, but many were donated to the regimental association's museum in England.

Kehoe continues to be interested in the role of the British Army in the American Revolution, and has written several books on various aspects of the period, including *We Were There — April 19, 1775.* This two-volume work (one volume on American, the other on British, troops) "is the first published complete collection of all the diaries, depositions, accounts and letters of both sides from participants and witnesses of the Battle of Lexington and Concord," says Kehoe.

"My participation in the regiment opened a new area of social contact for me," Kehoe says. "It isn't every type of group that gives you a chance to command a guard of honor for the Queen of England. We really developed a great deal of camaraderie that we would not have met with otherwise."

Kehoe will be glad to give further information on the regiment, the battle reenactments, or the role of the British Army in the American Revolution. He can be contacted at 235 Old Westford Rd., Chelmsford, MA 01824.

ROBERT KLINGER
MILITARIA RESTORATION

WHEN HE WAS ABOUT 12 years old, Robert Klinger had an experience which determined the course of his life.

One day, while playing around the site of Ft. Lincoln in northeast Washington, D.C., which was "one of the fringe forts used to defend the city during the Civil War," he made a fascinating discovery.

"I was running along near the B&O railroad tracks, when I stumbled over something. It was the butt of a pistol, with the muzzle down in the dirt," he says. The gun was "very rusty, full of roots and soil," but he pried it out of the ground. It was, he later discovered, an 1860 Colt Army revolver.

After he had cleaned it up, he "loaded it with black powder, pounded in some lead, and managed somehow not to hurt myself" when he fired it.

Klinger has come a long way from that first restoration job on the Colt revolver. Today, he is an exhibits specialist in restoration and conservation of military artifacts for the Smithsonian Institution in Washington.

"I've been with the Smithsonian for 25 years," he says, "and I've worked on all kinds of different things pertaining to history and technology: from steam engines to watches to farm implements. You name it, we do it."

His favorite items, however, have to do with militaria — the uniforms and equipment used by the armed forces. For example, Klinger had to recreate missing buttons for a uniform which belonged to George Washington in the Smithsonian's collection. "It is thought to be the one he wore when he resigned his commission," says Klinger, "and over the years, a dozen buttons had disappeared." It was his job to painstakingly reproduce the buttons from the same materials they were originally made of. "Now, you can't tell them from the originals, except, of course, the replicas have the date they were made imprinted on them," he says.

Another interesting project Klinger has been involved with is building a replica of the machine for which Abraham Lincoln received his only patent. It was a device that was supposed to lift barges over shoals between canals. It had pontoons, says Klinger, "but was impractical, because you never could have made anything big enough in the late 1840s to lift a barge — loaded or empty."

There's an important distinction to be made between "conservation" and "restoration," according to Klinger. Most of his work with the Smithsonian (and outside) involves restoration, that is "putting a piece back in the condition it was when it was used, or maybe in new condition," he says.

On the other hand, conservation is "taking a specimen, in some state of deterioration, and attempting to do something to stop the deterioration," he says.

Klinger is a prolific author of articles for historical society magazines and scholarly journals. His book on American Revolutionary dress, *Sketch Book '76* featured patterns and photographs of the uniforms and equipment of that era, and was published for the Bicentennial in 1976. Another book, the *Distaff Sketch Book*, about women's clothing of the same period, was published in 1970. Klinger did all of the research and artwork for the books himself.

Though he is mostly self-taught, Klinger says, "I learned a lot from my dad, who was a cabinet maker, and worked at the White House and the Lee Mansion. Most of it I just picked up on my own."

Klinger thinks "I should have been born 200 years ago. I don't feel much for computers, stampers, and automatic machinery." That's why he enjoys restoration.

"Of course, most of the reason I like it is the history; but I have a love for the handwork and craftsmanship of a couple of hundred years ago."

He advises that anyone thinking of doing restoration work "should have some natural ability, and should take the time to seek out how to do it right. Don't jump in without finding out how to do what you want. You could ruin a piece very easily."

He suggests a novice check with a major museum or art gallery in his hometown for advice, before undertaking a restoration. "If they can't help you, at least they will aim you in the right direction," he says.

Klinger will be glad to counsel beginners and answer questions about restoration. He can be contacted in care of the Smithsonian Institution, Washington, D. C. 20002.

RICHARD MUNDSCHENK
IMPERIAL GERMAN MILITARY ARTIFACTS

"THOUGH COLLECTING MILITARY material might lead some people to say I'm glorifying war," says Richard Mundschenk, "I feel it serves better to remind us of the soldiers' sacrifices, and to what lengths men will go to defend their beliefs. I think that the soldier must have the greatest desire for peace, for he must pay the highest price for it."

Munsdchenk, 32, a collector of militaria from boyhood, has a special interest in the military of Imperial Germany and Austria-Hungary from 1870 to 1918. His interest led him to his career as an associate editor for R.J. Bender, a San Jose, California, military book publishing firm.

Mundschenk began collecting military items when he was 13, after a childhood interest in toy soldiers that "just sort of stuck." He found a shop in his hometown that sold military souvenirs and "I thought the spike helmets of the

Imperial army were neat looking," so he bought one for his very own and his collection was born.

Mundschenk's collection is housed in his home. Along with his extensive research library ("I've always considered reference books very important," he says), he has a dozen fully outfitted mannequins, wearing Imperial German and Austro-Hungarian uniforms. Among the uniforms are those of a naval officer, a Prussian general, an infantry man, and cavalry. Mundschenk has about 100 uniforms in all, 100 service caps, 40 to 50 swords, "a whole case of spiked helmets," and many other items of military memorabilia. "I enjoyed the idea of discovering forgotten and highly interesting material," he says.

One of his prize posessions is a regimental standard for the Prussian 39th Infantry Regiment, complete with battle streamers and flag pole tops. This flag, measuring 3/4-feet square, is a real find, says Mundschenk. Because the regimental standards led the front lines into battle, not many survived World War I.

Mundschenk obtained the flag from a U.S. veteran of World War II, who had picked it up in Germany. He answered an ad of Mundschenk's in a collectors' magazine, and Mundschenk went to the man's home to look it over. "He had kept it folded in a trunk all these years, so it was well-preserved." "When he pulled it out, and showed it to me, I nearly fell out of my chair." The flag, which Mundschenk describes as "a fantastic piece of embroidery," features the Prussian eagle in the center, surrounded by other decorations and the words "Pro Gloria Patria."

Though the flag is valuable because it is so rare, Mundschenk says it would be difficult to put a price on it. As in so many areas of collecting, the worth of an item depends on how much someone is willing to offer. Besides, says Mundschenk, the value of these items really isn't all that important to him. "I tend to appreciate them for their historic value more than their monetary worth," he says.

Mundschenk says that the collecting of Imperial German militaria is "a fast growing hobby." He has been involved with The Imperial German Military Collectors Association, for several years. This international club, with some 2,000 members in the United States and abroad, publishes a newsletter *Kaiserzeit* ("The Imperial Time"), and sponsors meetings and other activities.

Someday, Mundschenk would like to found a military museum dedicated to the preservation of the military history of Imperial Germany, Austria-Hungary, and the U.S. armed forces. This museum would feature the "actual materials worn by the military of these countries, a sort of living history display for students, veterans, and the general public." He thinks such a museum would fill an important function,"as something that would remind people of both the glory of the past and the necessity of not forgetting the past, but learning from it, for the future."

Mundschenk's own heritage has influenced his interest in military artifacts. His great-grandfather was a Prussian grenadier, and Mundschenk grew up around some of his memorabilia. In addition, Mundschenk feels that, in previous eras, the military was "a class of people rather than a war machine. It was a way of life. Just because you wore a uniform in those days it didn't mean you were an aggressor."

According to Mundschenk, the lot of the beginning collector of militaria is a pretty happy one. "You can find something relating to this subject simply by going to antique shops." At one time, he says, Imperial German items were very expensive, but in recent years the market has been rather glutted.

Metro-Goldwyn-Mayer studios "sold off this stuff by the ton" a few years ago, a leftover of the great days of the costume pictures. All the items they had were authentic, Mundschenk says, because "after World War I, who needed Imperial German uniforms?"

There is still a lot of the material in Germany, as well, says Mundschenk, although the prices are going up there because the Germans "are realizing more and more that this is their heritage."

Mundschenk feels that if a person has an interest in militaria, it is better to specialize in one or a few areas; collecting and researching everything would be impossible. He also advises that "those who are just beginning in the hobby try to stay within their financial means, and not become obsessed with the idea of collecting. Too many people do, and it can be destructive to their personal lives."

He also feels that it is "important to share knowledge with others: give some guidance to a beginner, help him along, and don't take advantage of him, because what you show to others will always come back to you in the long run."

Mundschenk suggests anyone interested in the subject join the Imperial German Military Collectors Association or contact it for further information. Write to Eric Johansson, PO Box 12122, Kansas City, KS 66112.

GEORGE WOODBRIDGE
U.S. MILITARY CLOTHING

HARD AS IT MIGHT be to believe, the soldiers who fought for the Colonies in the American Revolution were not as badly off as a lot of history books report — at least, not in terms of having adequate clothing.

That is the contention of George Woodbridge, a Brooklyn, New York, illustrator and historical researcher, who says that the 18th century American soldier "was not as bad off as he was painted. There was a real shortage of the regimental long coats the men wore, but I'm having great difficulty trying to discover information about that problem."

Woodbridge is doing this research for a book on Revolutionary War clothing, as part of his hobby of studying U.S. military clothing and equipment from the Revolution to the Civil War.

He chose this particular era of military history, Woodbridge says, "because there's so little known about the Revolutionary War aspect, and the Civil War is close enough to our era for us to relate to."

Woodbridge has been interested in military clothing and equipment most of his life. He became a serious student of it when he began to make drawings of military uniforms "and realized there wasn't enough material available" to be sure he was drawing them accurately and completely.

His research has been a matter of gathering information from widely scattered sources. "Research of this kind is accomplished with long hours in museums, historical societies, and state and U.S. government archives," he says. Surprisingly, his research has taken him to Europe, "where there's a great deal of information about American military clothing available."

Collecting the actual uniforms and equipment "is also a good avenue in this kind of research, and I've used that," says Woodbridge. However, "collecting is very expensive. As a result, I own no original 18th century clothing," although he does have "a very limited number " of items from the 19th century and beyond.

Primarily, Woodbridge has acquired documents and photographs or drawings of specimens. "I'm gathering enormous amounts of material, most of which is probably of questionable value," he says.

That may be, but along the way, Woodbridge has uncovered some interesting facts about military uniforms, in general, and U.S. armed services clothing, in particular.

Military attire has "changed for the better" over the years, Woodbridge believes. "Up to the turn of the century, most armies wore what was, in effect, a dress uniform. What became slowly and painfully obvious was that these uniforms were not only uncomfortable, but also could be dangerous."

He says, "There certainly were incidents in battle where similarity in clothing lead to confusion and attacks on the wrong people." In the American Revolution it "happened more than once," because, at certain times, both the British and the Americans were wearing red uniforms and one side or the other mistakenly fired on its own troops.

"It is said that 'The Germans made uniforms to look good, the British made them for comfort, and the Americans made them for fighting,'" says Woodbridge.

Woodbridge has participated in several reenactments of Revolutionary War battles, and feels they are an important aid to understanding history. "I think the benefit lies in the sense these people give of what the actual battle looked like. It's as much a show as a re-creation of history. People today are not necessarily deeply interested — and needn't be — in these battles." But, through watching the re-creations, they can get an idea of the attitudes of the people, "where the people were coming from and where they thought they were going."

Woodbridge recommends that anyone interested in military uniforms or military history become involved with one or more of the many special interest groups dealing with military topics. "Join an existing organization of this sort (they're all over the country) or your local historical society. You'll develop valuable contacts with people more knowledgeable than yourself and you'll learn a great deal. It will make your researching task a lot easier."

Woodbridge will be glad to answer questions on U.S. military uniforms and equipment, particularly from the time of the American Revolution through the Civil War. He can be contacted at 5818 Fourth Ave., Brooklyn, NY 11220.

VEHICLES

NOLAND ADAMS
CORVETTE RESTORATION

FEW CARS HAVE EXCITED as much consumer interest as the Corvette. A status symbol since the first one rolled off the Chevrolet line in 1953, the fiberglass-bodied, sporty 'Vette has been the dream car of a couple of generations of drivers.

For many, the thrill of driving a Corvette isn't enough; their enjoyment has been heightened by the restoration of the cars to their original condition.

Noland Adams of Albany, California, is just such a Corvette enthusiast. Adams, a 47-year-old industrial instrument technician for a pharmaceutical manufacturer, may know more about the early years of the Corvette than anybody. With information gleaned from the vast (and frequently difficult to trace) files of General Motors and Chevrolet in Detroit, he wrote a book about the subject, containing a wealth of technical information not previously available to the Corvette restorer.

Adams' own Corvette adventure began rather routinely, in 1955, when he impulsively purchased a used car dealer's 1954 'Vette. Adams had just been discharged from the armed forces, and "I hadn't even seen a Corvette up close yet." It was love at first sight. Even though Adams totaled that car a few months later, he promptly replaced it with a 1953 Corvette, and in 1957 bought another one. Adams sold both in 1959 when his oldest daughter, Kim, was born. The cars "seemed a bit of a luxury" once he had a family.

Corvettes disappeared from Noland Adams' life until 1968, when he repurchased his 1953 Corvette from the man he had sold it to. It needed a lot of work — and a lot of expensive parts — to restore it to its original condition. "I realized I wasn't going to be able to put a lot of new parts on it because of the expense and availability," Adams said. "So, I began looking around at parts that guys were reproducing." And that was how Adams got involved in Corvette parts reproduction.

While trying to verify the originality of the parts for his Corvette, Adams did considerable research and thoroughly explored the burgeoning field of parts reproduction. The going was often tough because technical information from Chevrolet and General Motors was lacking. Corvette restorers like to re-do their cars as accurately as possible, Adams says, but "GM wasn't being helpful, mainly because they aren't too interested in anything but selling new cars." The information Adams and his fellow Corvette buffs needed was in the archives, but "the company just didn't care. And no one really knew where or what to look for."

Help was on the way, a lot sooner than Adams had expected. After he had written a strong criticisim of one Corvette book, he was approached by *Automobile Quarterly* and asked if he could do better. "I said yes," and he was on his way. The magazine helped him gain access to the hitherto unexplored territory of the Chevrolet archives in Detriot.

"I was the first 'outsider' allowed in the files," Adams said. What he found was a veritable treasure trove of pictures, diagrams and literature on Corvettes from all eras scattered through a mountain of files. After three years of research, he unearthed enough information to compile *The Complete Corvette Restoration and Judging Guide*, which covers the 1953-62 models.

The book, published in 1979, contains much of the previously unavailable reference material that is so important for proper restoration. A second book, on Corvettes from 1963-67, is in the planning stages.

Given the popularity of the Corvette as a sports car, and as a car for people interested in restoration, "it's getting hard to find a completely unrestored car today," says Adams. The 1954-62 models, currently the most popular for restoration, can run anywhere from $6,000 to $8,000, even in unrestored condition.

Among the models most sought after by collectors is the 1953. Worth some $30,000 today, there were only 300 of them made. So far, Adams says, 200 of the cars have been located. "That's an incredible survival rate." Other much-searched for Corvettes are the 1955 and 1957 models. The latter had a fuel-injection system.

Adams is hard-pressed to describe why the cars are so popular. "You get as many answers as Corvette owners," he says. Corvettes are "adequate cars for all purposes. It's a fun car. You can have a great day driving one—if you can afford the gas."

For anyone thinking of entering the complex world of Corvette restoration, Adams has sound advice: "Don't modify an original Corvette and don't try to restore a modified Corvette. We're interested in correct restoration," says Adams of his Crovette buff cronies. "Over-restoration is just as incorrect as not restoring the car at all."

Since the highest value car is the one in original condition, it makes sense to "get the parts rebuilt, making sure the original tags or casting numbers are not removed." If you own a modified 'Vette, Adams recommends keeping it modified and building it into a "dependable, sharp-looking street machine," as restoring it to its original condition is prohibitively time-consuming and expensive. If one must own an original Corvette, Adams advises looking for an old, shabby, but complete original car to start with.

Adams recommends that Corvette restorers get in touch with the National Corvette Restorer's Society, PO Box 81663, Lincoln, Neb. 68501 for advice, assistance and information. His book, retailing at $70, can be obtained from *Automobile Quarterly*, 221 Nassau St., Princeton, NJ 08544. Adams can be contacted at 715 Talbot Ave., Albany, CA 94706.

BILL BARTH
MODEL T RESTORATION

It CHANGED THE FACE of American transportation forever. Henry Ford's success with the first mass-produced (and, thus, affordable) automobile revolutionized our way of life. Ford's Model T became the most famous car of all time, setting the pace for the exciting future of motorcars.

For Bill Barth, of Troy, Michigan, the exciting days of the Model T live on right in his own backyard, where he has collected and restored some notable examples of Henry's work. In the process, Barth has become a frequently consulted authority on the restoration and history of the Model T.

The 37-year-old industrial education teacher has "always been interested in cars and engines and making them run." In fact, when he was a youngster, he used a Model A for "commercial fishing in the winter, because it was light on the ice."

In 1971, when he found a 1926 four-door Model T sedan all in pieces, "I jumped at the chance to try a restoration." Since then, Barth has restored several Model Ts of various styles for himself, and has helped friends restore others.

Three of his cars — a 1911 Model T touring car, a 1915 Model T touring car, and a 1915 Model T Detroit body speedster — have won best of show awards in major shows put on by such major organizations as the Canadian National Exhibition, the Veteran Motor Car Club of America, and the Antique Automobile Club of America.

Unlike most restorers, Barth really starts from the ground up on his cars. He prefers to purchase the so-called "basket cases." "Almost every one I buy is in pieces," he says, "because the previous owner lost interest after discovering the expense and time involved in the restoration; the whole project just overwhelmed them. I can tell if the car has all the parts, and it's a lot less expensive to buy them this way."

Altogether, Barth has seven cars "in various stages of restoration." Included in his collection: a 1911 Model T touring car which his wife restored and drives; a 1915 Model T speedster; a 1925 Model T one-ton truck; a 1915 Model T center-door, stainless steel model; a 1908 Model T touring car; a 1912 "pie wagon" delivery car; and a 1915 express-body Ford.

Barth declines to discuss the value of the cars he owns and restores. "As soon as you mention money, everyone gets goofy," he says. It's a fact, "the collector who wants a perfect car will pay a lot more than someone who wants a car just to drive around in."

"I don't like to get involved in setting prices," he declares. "Often it creates misconceptions, and leads people to think these cars are worth a fortune." Some cars are worth a good deal of money, Barth says, but others are real dogs, and the unsuspecting amateur, who doesn't know the market well enough, is likely to get stung.

In addition to the expense of purchasing a car, Barth says a great expenditure of time is necessary to do a proper restoration. "There's painting, bodywork, and so forth. " It takes the average person three to six years to restore a Model T, he adds, "and in six years, you can get pretty disinterested."

"I think you will find that the entire family is involved with most restorations," he says. "It's really a family hobby."

Barth counsels the would-be Model T restorer to "buy a complete car that is running, so that you can drive it and enjoy it for awhile." The major purpose of owning and restoring an antique car is "to have fun," Barth believes. So, after you've had a chance to enjoy driving the car around, "maybe you'll want to try to restore it — or another one."

Barth is active in Model T Ford Club International (PO Box 915, Elgin, IL 60120), a nationwide group of fellow Model T buffs. Participating in the group is an important part of the enjoyment of his hobby. "You meet a lot of interesting people. With 99 percent of the people I know through the hobby, I don't even know what they do for a living. But it doesn't matter, everyone is on the same level."

Activities sponsored by the Model T Ford Club International include races, touring, and other opportunities to get together to swap parts and advice. Many of the members participate in the annual Glidden Tour, which has been running since the early 1900s. Originally an opportunity "to test and promote cars," according to Barth, it has now become more of an entertainment, with car buffs gathering at different points in the country "to try to retrace a lot of the old tours." In 1984, Glidden participants will make a cross-country tour from Maine to Seattle, Washington, commemorating Henry Ford's similar trek in 1909.

Barth is extraordinarily dedicated to his hobby. "When I get home at 3:30 p.m., I generally go right to my workshop and stay there until midnight. Weekends, I put in 14-18 hours in the shop per day. I enjoy working on a car as much as most people do driving."

Barth will be glad to advise beginners or answer questions about the Model T. He can be reached at 1590 Rockfield, Troy, MI 48098.

DONALD BOUGHER
PONTIAC-OAKLAND AUTOMOBILES

FOR THE AUTMOBILE restorer, one of the most frustrating experiences can be attempting to find accurate, precise data on the construction of a particular model. Donald Bougher, of Dayton, Oregon, experienced that difficulty in 1967. To solve it, he made himself an expert on all makes and models of Pontiac and Oakland automobiles.

When Bougher purchased his 1926 Pontiac, he discovered that "not even the factory had much information on early Pontiacs," so he had to turn to alternate sources. In particular, he looked up other Pontiac buffs and traded information with them. Through this effort, "a core of interest was developed," he says, and in 1972 he founded the Pontiac-Oakland Club International, Inc. (POCI). The club now has over 3,200 members, in 22 countries. And Bougher has become so well-versed on Pontiacs that now even the factory looks to him for information.

Bougher had been in the old car hobby for six years, mainly with Dodges, when he obtained his first Pontiac in 1967. It was a 1926 model, in practically mint condition with only 27,000 miles on it. The car had been in storage in a garage for many years. "All it needed to be perfect was a new radiator shell, the original having been rusted away by water left in the radiator over the years," says Bougher.

While Bougher "knew a lot of parts researchers, and did a lot of advertising, nobody could come up with a radiator shell for me." Then he advertised that he would print a roster of Pontiac owners if they would send him their names, "thinking that I might be able to find the part that way." He heard from 99 Pontiac owners in one year.

Pontiacs and Oaklands came into being in 1907. That's when the Pontiac Buggy Company "decided to build an automobile. They didn't want people mixing up the buggymaking and automaking operations," says Bougher, "so they named the auto division Oakland, after the Michigan county in which the firm was located." When Oakland was bought by General Motors in 1909, GM kept the name until 1926, when the first car with the name Pontiac was introduced.

According to Bougher, the Oakland "was never really a very good automobile. They were never able to get the right amount of power to go with the chassis. It either was underpowered, or used too much fuel or used too much oil. Plus, it was overpriced for its time."

The Pontiac, on the other hand, "was an immediate hit." It was less expensive (the 1926 Pontiac sold for $825, compared to the Oakland's $1,500 to $2,000), and it was a six-cylinder car while the Chevrolets and Fords of the day were only four-cylinder. Within four years, the Pontiac had "larger sales than Oakland had in its entire history."

Bougher's inventory of Pontiacs "is low at the moment, because I sold my collection in 1979 to finance the purchase of the farm in Oregon that I now live on." Right now he has only a 1954 Pontiac station wagon, which he is in the process of restoring. He's had a number of the cars over the years, his favorites being those from 1940 ("because they're very beautiful") and 1954, which was the "last of the straight-eight Pontiacs, with four-speed hydromatic transmission. It had the nicest looking trim of any of the cars."

Pontiacs are highly desirable collector's items, he says. But, surprisingly perhaps, it's not the cars from the 1920s and 1930s that are attracting the most collectors. "The Pontiacs of the early 1960s are the hottest thing now," he says, crediting this interest to the fact that "people who were in high school at that time now are at a point in life where they have enough time and money to pursue a hobby. So, because of nostalgia, they think of the cars they dreamed about owning when they were high school kids."

Why are Pontiacs so popular? "Pontiac enthusiasts like to think they're more reliable then other makes. Pontiac had a reputation for being a reliable family car, 'built to last 100,000 miles' as the slogan went. And they did!"

In the mid-1950s, Bucky Knudson, Pontiac's president, "wanted to change the car's image. They dropped the Indian logo, and worked toward creating a fast, stylish image for the car," he says. Pontiacs in the 1960s were popular racing cars. "It was the rebirth of the marque," says Bougher. "Now they're known as performance automobiles. The popularity of the car in the 1960s was more along the line of performance."

A beginner can purchase a 1960-67 Pontiac for a few hundred dollars, but "restoration gets expensive." Bougher estimates that it costs another $3,000 or $4,000 to restore the car. The early Pontiacs "are hard to find, and they're mostly in private collections, and they sell for a good amount of money, as much as $2,000 unrestored. If you do the restoration work yourself, you can save about half the cost of having it professionally done," he says.

Bougher's advice to the novice vintage car owner: "Don't spend any money until you have looked around. A lot of mistakes can be made by novices. Join a club that caters to the make. Read publications to see where the action is and decide what your pocketbook can afford."

He feels that "lesser known makes are just as much fun to work with and drive" and probably less expensive than the more popular collector's items. He thinks Chrysler products, and early American Motors cars are particularly ripe for collecting.

Bougher suggests that a Pontiac or Oakland buff join his society. For a $15 annual membership fee, members receive an annual roster and the monthly newsletter of 20 to 24 pages by first class mail. In addition, members will have the opportunity to consult with the club's "technical advisors, who are expert in certain Pontiac model years," and they also can consult the club's extensive library of Pontiac-Oakland literature and information, which is housed in Marissa, Illinois.

Bougher is willing to give advice, counsel, and direction to fellow Pontiac or Oakland fanciers. He can be contacted at PO Box 612 Escondido, CA 92025.

KEN BROCK
GYROCOPTERS

EVER SINCE ICARUS'S wings melted on the way to the sun, man has been fascinated with flying. With the advent of the airplane in the early years of this century, and its perfection through each succeeding decade, the pioneering spirit has largely left conventional aviation. So it is that one-person flight has become the newest frontier; hence, the popularity of soaring, hang-gliding and, perhaps the most exciting of all, the gyrocopter.

What is a gyrocopter? According to Ken Brock, a 47-year-old gyrocopter builder and flyer from Stanton, California, it's "a little like a flying lawn chair."

Actually, it's a small, 250-pound, single-person aircraft, with a rotor on the top, like a helicopter. Unlike the helicopter, however, the rotor is not powered by an engine. The plane's engine operates a propellor to create forward motion, while the rotor spins freely to provide lift for the stubby-winged craft.

Brock, who long was interested in flying, discovered gyrocopters in 1957, when a friend let him take a ride. It was love at first flight, and he has been flying and building them ever since.

Without a doubt, Brock's most exciting achievement was a June, 1971 trip he made, flying his gyrocopter from Long Beach to Kitty Hawk, North Carolina. "It took 10 days to make the trip," Brock says, "and it was just a great way to see this country." He flew in "pretty much of a straight line" from Southern California to the East Coast, stopping 44 times along the way.

The gyrocopter, flying at a few hundred feet, was powered with a 90 horsepower, two-cycle McCullogh engine, and had a top speed of 90-95 miles per hour, according to Brock. Generally, however, he cruised along at 70 or 75 miles per hour, and over some fairly rough terrain, including the Rocky Mountains. With a distance of 75 to 100 miles between landings, Brock says he was able to see a lot of the United States during his journey, which went "very smoothly all the way through."

According to Brock, the gyrocopter was invented in 1924 in Spain by Juan de la Cierva. The craft was very popular in the early 1930s ("even Amelia Earhart piloted one"), and there was even a mail service that was operated with gyrocopters. The vehicle went out of fashion in the late '30s, "overshadowed," Brock says, "by the development of the helicopter. The government was more interested in promoting that."

Today, however, Brock says the gyrocopter is "one of the most popular recreational vehicles around," particularly in California, although "they spring up all over the place. They operate all over the world."

Brock's company, Ken Brock Manufacturing, has been building gyrocopters and making kits for do-it-yourselfers for several years. Brock says that the average cost of a gyrocopter is $6,000 to $6,500, but that it could be less or more, depending on what kinds of options are included.

It's quite easy to learn how to operate a gyrocopter, Brock says. It is a licensed aircraft and pilots need a license to fly it. It can be flown anywhere a regular airplane can be flown. And, says Brock, it's relatively safe, even safer than a private plane.

Might not the skies of America become overcrowded with these machines, if they are so comparatively easy to own and operate? Brock doesn't think so. "Contrary to what you may have heard, there are no 'crowded skies,'" he says. "Unlike automobiles, motorcycles, bicycles, and so on, all on one level on land, we have hundreds of levels in the air." If he follows the regulations and stays at designated levels, Brock says, the gyrocopter pilot will have no problems with traffic.

Brock is president of the International Popular Rotorcraft Association, founded in 1963, the organization for amateur flyers of gyrocopters. Among the activities of the 2,500-member group are flying meets, which feature contests in precision take-off, spot landing, and something Brock calls a "bomb drop," throwing items from the 'copters onto a target on the ground.

"I really enjoy flying a gyrocopter," says Brock. "Everybody likes something different, and probably thinks what the other person does is strange. But flying is just a lot of fun."

Brock advises anyone interested in gyrocopters to take lessons from an experienced gyrocopter pilot or flight instructor, before attempting a flight on your own. "Be sure to read up on all the technical data you can get your hands on, too," he says. Since both the craft and the pilot have to be licensed, Brock adds, the novice must learn and obey all regulations.

To learn more about gyrocopters, contact Brock at 11852 Western Ave., Stanton, CA 90680.

BRUCE COMSTOCK
HOT AIR BALLOONS

PHILEAS FOGG TRIED it in *Around the World in 80 Days*. In the 1960s, The Fifth Dimension singing group was urging us to go "up, up, and away in a beautiful balloon." And Bruce Comstock says, "I think it's beautiful to go riding high in the sky."

The hot air balloon, that wonderfully quaint and exciting mode of transportation, has captured the imagination and enthusiasm of people the world over. Comstock, a record-setting balloonist from Ann Arbor, Michigan, has made hot air balloons his major interest in life.

One fall day in 1967, Comstock "saw a balloon when I was mowing my lawn. I was surprised, because I didn't know they were still flying, but there it was, just flying by, slowly, gently, and elegantly." He followed the balloon to its landing point. "I felt like I had found my place in life. I knew I had to fly balloons."

Though Comstock was "sold on it from the beginning," it wasn't until 1970, after he had finished graduate school at the University of Michigan, that he began actively to pursue his interest. He took 14 hours of flight lessons, including 10 balloon flights, from two balloonists who lived about an hour away from his home. "I would get up in the wee hours of the morning to drive to their place to learn," he says. When he got his license, he was the 50th person to become a hot air pilot in the United States.

After Comstock made his first solo flight, he and his wife decided to purchase their own balloon. "We wanted to get deeply involved in the sport," he says. For $5,400, they bought a 56,000 cubic-foot balloon (about 50 feet in diameter and 70 feet high when inflated), with a carrying capacity of two or three people. The Comstocks are now on their 10th balloon, the fifth largest balloon in the world. It's a 210,000 cubic-foot model that can lift some 4,200 pounds off the ground with ease.

Comstock admits it costs roughly $40 per hour to operate a balloon. "It's not just a sport for wealthy people, but it is expensive," he says.

Comstock says technology has eliminated the need for the sandbags and ballast that were common characteristics of the balloon in the early days. Instead, there's a furnace (with the heating power of 100 home furnaces) which heats the air and blows it through a hole in the mouth of the balloon. By regulating the heat of the air inside the balloon, it is possible to make the balloon ascend or descend at will. Though many modern balloons have fiberglass or aluminum baskets for the passengers, Comstock says there has been a resurgence of the use of the traditional wicker baskets which, besides being esthetically more pleasing, "are lightweight and absorb shock."

Though there are at least 3,000 licensed balloon pilots today, when Comstock first began flying, "I got an awful lot of funny looks from my friends when I told them what I was going to do. It was certainly not considered normal." Fortunately, he says, "I got into ballooning early and have been able to grow with the sport as it gained popularity in the U.S." Nowadays, he says, with the increased interest in ballooning and greater publicity about balloons, "most people see it as something a reasonable person might do for entertainment."

Ballooning "is and isn't hard to learn," says Comstock. "Balloons are deceptively simple things, with only two or three controls. But, like figure skating, it looks a lot simpler than it is."

Naturally, as with anything "that takes you up in the air, there's the potential for getting hurt." In 1979, for instance, eight people died in ballooning accidents. Comstock plans no such fate for himself. "I'm a big chicken, really, and I approach balloon flying that way. I think it makes me a much more careful pilot, so ballooning is safe for me." Balloons themselves are "very well-designed devices; the only way to get hurt is by doing foolish things."

His training, confidence and skilled piloting have paid off. He is the four-time (and current) U. S. National Hot Air Balloon Champion, the only person to have ever won the honor more than once. His efforts have also been recognized with the Montgolfier Diploma from France's Federation Aeronautique Internationale, the highest award a balloonist can receive.

Comstock is also involved professionally with balloons. After working 40 hours a week in a job in data processing, "the rest of my time is taken up with ballooning as the U.S. sales representative for Cameron Balloons of England." Ballooning "is my life. I really feel at home in my little wicker basket above the clouds. When I say I go to work to rest, I'm saying it only half in jest,"says Comstock.

Comstock will be happy to provide advice for novice balloonists, who can contact him at Cameron Balloons, U.S., 3600 Elizabeth Rd., Ann Arbor, MI 48103.

JAMES DWORSCHACK
NASH AUTOMOBILES

ONE OF THE EARLIEST and cleverest of the American "economy" cars was the Nash. Even though they haven't been made since 1957, James Dworschack is doing all he can to make sure the Nash is not forgotten.

Dworschack says he's "always been interested in mechanical things and history." These two interests found a meeting ground in the collection and restoration of Nashes.

The Nash, Dworschack says, was an influential force in automotive development, right from its beginnings in 1918. "It was always a unique car," he says. "Nash pioneered the economy field, and created many features which the auto industry adopted as standard later on." For instance, Nash's Metropolitan was capable of giving 35 miles per gallon in the 1920s. Perhaps the most important Nash innovation that the other automakers copied in time was "unit construction, the body and the frame being all one piece."

"The Nash was always a lot of car for its size," says Dworschack. "That's something that the industry has had to become more cognizant of in their production of cars today."

Dworschack obtained his first Nash, a 1948 model, in 1969. Today, he has 18 Nashes in running condition, and another 20 which he uses for "parts cars." He keeps them all on his family's farm near Clinton, Iowa, and drives one of them, a 1946 Nash Ambassador, every day. He is especially proud of his collection of early Nashes, which includes a 1918 touring car ("the first model made"), a 1926 coupe, and a 1929 roadster with a rumble seat. Currently, he is restoring the 1926 coupe. The bulk of his collection, though, concentrates on post-World War II models.

"Some of my cars are in good, original condition," he says. "Some have had some work done on them, and some still need a lot of work. With 18 cars, you can see I have plenty to keep me busy."

Even though Dworschack has been busy restoring and driving his Nashes, he is also organizing other Nash fans. In 1970, he founded the Nash Car Club of America, the first organization for Nash collectors, and he still leads the 1,400-member group. "There wasn't a club for them at the time," he says. "I didn't think when I first started that it would grow to be such a large organization. I thought I could just get some people together, get the group going, and step out. But it didn't work that way." The club has a bi-monthly publication, *Nash Times*, and a bi-monthly classified ad sheet for "members to advertise parts or cars to sell or trade." He feels the Nash Car Club of America provides a valuable service for Nash buffs. "The purpose is really fellowship, and providing aid in restoring cars."

Although Nashes have not been made for over 20 years (the firm combined with Hudson to create American Motors), "there are still a fair number of the cars around, of all vintages. Obviously, the most available are those from the early 1950s," Dworschack says. "You can still buy an unrestored car from the 1950s for anywhere from $25 to $500, depending on its condition. When you talk about the older cars, though, you can go anywhere from $500 to $10,000. I've heard of a restored car selling for $20,000." He admits that finding parts to restore the cars is sometimes difficult. "There's no doubt that parts are getting a lot harder to find," he says.

Of his hobby, Dworschack says, "I really like working on the cars. And I like to drive mine a lot. They're fun." He says he puts 500 to 1,000 miles per year on some of his cars, driving them around and taking them to car shows.

The beginning Nash connoisseur should join the Nash Car Club of America,

Dworschack says, because it is an excellent source of information, as well as being the best way to find cars and parts to restore them with. The annual membership fee is $10, and includes the club's publications.

Dworschack, and the Nash Car Club of America, can both be contacted at Rte. 1, Box 253, Clinton, IA 52732.

WARWICK EASTWOOD
HORSELESS CARRIAGES

SPACECRAFT ARE HIS specialty at California's Jet Propulsion Lab during the day, but Warwick Eastwood's evenings and weekends are devoted to horseless carriages, those first primitive motorized vehicles from the "brass and gas era before 1915" that changed the course of transportation forever.

As Eastwood recalls, "A friend from Los Angeles gave me a ride in his 1911 Cadillac one day in 1940. I liked it a lot." In 1942 Eastwood was able to purchase his first horseless carriage.

It was a 1913 Ford roadster, "in need of a complete restoration job," says Eastwood. "I'd acquired it from the original family that owned it. The restoration took a couple of years, and a couple thousand hours of labor, but I restored it all by myself."

Over the years, Eastwood has had about 40 early cars. Currently, he owns five horseless carriages. Three are 1910 Stevens-Duryea touring cars (two four-cylinder models, one six-cylinder model) "that cruise along at 50 miles per hour," he says. The other two are two-cylinder Buicks of 1905 and 1910 vintage.

The first U.S. auto was built by brothers Charles and Frank Duryea in 1893, Eastwood says. In 1901, Frank Duryea went to the Stevens Arms & Tool Company in Springfield, Massachusetts, where he built automobiles until 1915, when he sold his business to Westinghouse.

The Stevens-Duryea "was an expensive, but well-engineered, quality car," says Eastwood. "They had a good metal department, so they built lightweight, strong cars. The engines, transmissions, clutches, bodies, even the fenders, were all aluminum." This was a first, according to Eastwood, and only recently "has Detroit 'discovered' aluminum all over again."

Thus, the Stevens-Duryea cars Eastwood owns are valuable reminders of the heyday of America's first important automaker and innovator. In 1910, you could buy five Fords for the price of one Stevens, Eastwood says. "It was the Cadillac of its time."

Eastwood is a past-president and a continually active member in the Horseless Carriage Club of America, an organization for horseless carriage fanatics that was founded in 1937. There are some 8,000 members scattered all over the world. One of the chief advantages to the club is the assistance it provides in the mechanical rebuilding of the members' vehicles.

"Through the club's publication, you can run ads for missing parts," he says. "When you find a member who has the part you want in his car, it's possible to duplicate that part for your car." Eastwood and his fellow horseless carriage buffs "try to rebuild as nearly to the original as possible, so it's important to find the right parts."

It is still possible to obtain a car of pre-1915 vintage to restore, but it will cost a lot. "Unfortunately, the prices keep going up," Eastwood says. "When I first became interested in horseless carriages, you could buy a real nice one for $500; now they're getting $10,000 for some of them." Coupling an initially high purchase price with a restoration time of 3,000 hours ("to get a top restoration job"), means that horseless carriages are not a hobby for the penny-pincher.

Eastwood recommends the Horseless Carriage Club as the best source for a car at a fair price. By making contacts with the members, it is possible to find cars for sale. Eastwood's "best advice to the novice is to find a car before someone else has reworked it, because if they did, they probably did a rotten job, and you'll have to do it over."

He thinks this is an ideal hobby "because the average American loves autos, and rebuilding an old one is quite a challenge. Through a period of restoration, be it 1, 5, or 10 years, you can learn a lot. That's why I love to rebuild them and love to drive them.

"Actually, for me, it's a family hobby," he says. "We all go out in the old cars. Sometimes we crank them all up and go riding. Each of my son-in-laws drives a car and we have a big time."

Eastwood is glad to answer questions about horseless carriages and will provide information to beginners. He can be contacted at 3565 New Haven Rd., Pasadena, CA 91107.

WALTER GOSDEN
AUTOMOTIVE HISTORY

THE LAND YACHTS of a past era can't be forgotten. They were rolling sculpture."

Walter Gosden is an eloquent spokesman for the grand and glorious history of the automobile. And, at 31, the Floral Park, New York, artist and writer has become an impressive expert on the history of America's automotive industry.

It all began for Gosden in 1965. That's when he bought a 1931 Plymouth to restore. "I wasn't satisfied just to own and use it," says Gosden. "I wanted to find out why someone would make something like this." His interest in automotive history resulted "from curiosity, more than anything else."

Since that time, Gosden has done a lot of research into the history of American automobiles and has concentrated his efforts mainly on the history of automobile companies in New York State, as well as road races and "those off-beat companies who custom-built cars" for the very wealthy in the 1920s and 1930s.

His special interest is the Franklin Motor Car Co., which from 1902 to 1934 produced a series of luxury cars in Syracuse, New York. The cars were luxurious by anybody's standards. In those days, when a new Ford could be had for $450, the Franklin's cheapest model was $1,800 — enough to buy a small house.

The luxury of the Franklin, with its "burl walnut and real leather interior and bronze fittings was beyond comprehension." The Franklin "wasn't flashy, but elegant and well-made," Gosden says, adding that the V-12 car weighed 4,500 to 5,000 pounds, and was 132 to 136 inches long. "I stand six feet tall, and I can stand next to a Franklin and feel like a midget," Gosden says. "They were the pioneers in the use of lightweight aluminum in the bodies of the cars." The Franklin was "the favorite of aviators, because the engines were so similar to airplanes. They ran much hotter and burned fuel more efficiently" than did other cars of their era.

Custom-built classic cars also interest Gosden. There were actually companies in New York (and elsewhere) which would make a car to order, to the tune of $5,000-$20,000, an incredible sum in those days.

Gosden says the likes of Al Jolson, Gary Cooper, and assorted Astors and Vanderbilts tooled around town in autos with snakeskin or needlepoint upholstery, mother of pearl and rosewood interiors, and bone window cranks.

"You could design your own car. The car makers would use a chassis from a Lincoln, and build the car from scratch. It took four or five months to build the body and handpaint the car." While the cost might not seem much now, remember, Gosden says, "gasoline was only 18 cents a gallon then."

The interconnections in the auto industry also fascinate Gosden. "Nobody worked for one company," he says, "especially in those early days. One guy might have bounced around to 10 or 12 different companies," so it's interesting to track him through his professional career, and determine the effect he had on the auto industry.

Gosden is the director and editor of the Society of Automotive Historians, a group of some 500 auto history buffs from across the nation. The group issues both a newsletter, *Society of Automotive Historians Newsletter*, and a journal, *Automotive History Review*.

Gosden hasn't contented himself merely with delving into the history of automobiles. He owns five classic cars himself: a 1917 Vim half-ton pickup, a 1931 Franklin Victoria (one of a kind, built for the New York Auto Show that year, he says), a 1941 Packard station wagon, and two Cadillacs — a 1953 hardtop and a 1969 convertible.

To the novice car restorer, he offers this suggestion: "Do your homework. Join a club, buy books, and talk to people before you buy a car. Spend about a year studying before buying the car. You can get burned pretty badly if you are ill-informed."

The coming thing, for auto collectors, is going to be "the big muscle cars, like the GTOs, of the late 1960s," says Gosden. "The survival rate of cars from the 1950s and 1960s is pretty slim because of the rust problem." While the mechanisms of the cars are all right, the bodies are shot. Therefore, scarcity will give these cars a great deal of value.

For Gosden, "it's the people that make the hobby" of automotive history. "They're the greatest around. They can be anybody from a surgeon to a truck driver, but we're all on an equal basis when we talk cars."

Gosden will gladly provide information on the Automotive History Society, or will answer questions about auto history. He can be contacted at 197 Mayfair Ave., Floral Park, NY 11001.

GLENN HANSEN
BMW 700 AUTOS

ONE GOOD CAR LED TO another for Glenn Hansen. While he was having his BMW 2002 sports car serviced in Madrid, Spain, in 1969, he happened on the BMW 700, the car on which today he is expert.

Hansen was an American serviceman, and had "fallen in love" with his BMW 2002 after a test drive. When he went to pick the car up from the BMW dealer in Madrid after its first servicing, "I noticed that, in the corner of the workshop, on a workbench, a mechanic was revving up a motor. This attracted my interest." When he found out about the car the motor went with, Hansen decided he had to own one.

The BMW 700, manufactured from 1960 to 1965, "was the final step in the evolution of the micro-car in Germany that had begun in the late 1950s, when everyone could afford a car, but not too much of one." The car, which resembles a present-day BMW Alpine, was "sleek and low-slung, and built for good gas mileage." The car's 2-cylinder, air-cooled engine was a direct copy from BMW's famous motorcycles, and it got 35-40 miles per gallon.

Hansen wanted to buy a 700 while he was still in Europe, "but I couldn't afford to do it and keep the 2002, too, which I was using for road racing." When he returned to the U.S. in 1971, he bought his first 700 from two college students for $50. "They were having trouble with the car and couldn't get it to run," he says. He discovered that "they had put the clutch plate in backward, so the clutch wouldn't disengage" and when he fixed that, "I started it up and drove it home," much to the former owners' dismay.

"My expertise is in bringing 700s back to life," says Hansen, who owns six of the cars today. He has two 1964 models he hopes to completely restore, in addition to a 1964 Luxus sedan, and 1960, 1961, and 1962 models that he "cannibalizes" for parts. He obtained the 1960 car "for five dollars. I was driving by and saw it in the front yard of a house. I asked the owner what he wanted for it, and he said a six-pack of beer. Well, I didn't have time to go to the liquor store," so he wrote the man a check for $5 and took the car.

The reason Hansen has so many "parts cars" is that "you can't get parts for 700s anymore. When someone needs something, there's a lot of exchanging back and forth among the owners of the cars. If you can sell it out of your car, you do. I would rather just get my money back and have another guy have a car that runs. I look on this as a hobby, not as an investment, anyway," he says. There is still one company in West Germany that stocks parts, and it has even reproduced some of the rubber parts, Hansen says, but getting delivery is difficult and time-consuming.

When BMW North America was getting rid of its inventory of BMW 700 parts several years ago, Leif Anderberg, representing the BMW Registry (the national organization for BMW enthusiasts), tried to work out an arrangement to purchase the parts in the group's name, says Hansen. "But it was determined that it was illegal for anyone but an authorized dealer to sell the parts, so Leif couldn't buy them. Now, we don't even know where the parts are."

According to Hansen, "There are more BMW 700s around than you might believe. I'm always surprised to find them." He says many of them "are just sitting in somebody's backyard, usually not in running condition. Often, they'll belong to someone who was an enthusiast at one time, but lost interest." The best places to locate the cars, he says, seem to be in Pennsylvania, California, and South Carolina.

When Hansen drives one of his 700s to auto fanciers' meetings, "everyone is always enthusiastic, and they wonder why they quit making the car." He says that the BMW 700 line was "sacrificed to produce the BMW 1600 and 2002, the larger cars that later saved BMW financially." But, says Hansen, there has been renewed interest in the 700, given its economical use of gasoline, so "there's talk that BMW might bring them out again. They're such well-engineered cars that it's really a joy to drive one."

Hansen advises BMW 700 restorers to "be willing to give the car plenty of attention to detail in restoration. In return, you'll have a lot of excitement in driving."

BMW 700 buffs, or anyone interested in any of BMW's automobiles, should get in touch with the BMW Registry, 15931 Carrara St., Hacienda Heights, CA 91745.

JOHN HOSCHEK
BUSES

USUALLY, WE DON'T think of buses as an interesting subject for photographs. They're a utilitarian means of transportation for daily commuting or for making trips to places where more rapid forms of transit may not go.

But John Hoschek of Trenton, New Jersey, thinks differently. He's very fond of buses. Over the last 33 years, he has collected over 90,000 photographs and negatives of them from all around the country.

The 47-year-old county government administrator of Gloucester County, New Jersey, has been interested in this humble form of transportation ever since his youth.

"In my younger days," Hoschek says," I had friends in the bus business" in New Jersey. He became interested in collecting photographs relating to the Public Service Corporation, the forerunner of today's Transport of New Jersey busline.

Hoscheck has accumulated his collection of photographs in many ways: he took some himself, traded with other collectors, and got pictures directly from buslines across the country. Some of his photographs "go way back into the 1910s," he says. In addition to his collection of pictures, he has also amassed some 500 model and toy buses, several of which are valued at over $100. "They range from small die-cast models to a 3-foot long replica of a 1954 Greyhound Scenicrusier," he says.

Hoschek is prominent among motor bus buffs. He was a founder of the Motor Bus Society in 1948, and holds the only life membership in the 2,000-member organization.

From 1969 to 1974 Hoschek worked for the New Jersey Department of Transportation. In cooperation with Morris County, New Jersey officials, he worked on a project that won him the Commuter Man of Year award in 1972.

Hoschek describes his fascination with collecting photographs of buses as "almost the same" as that of the railroad or auto buff. "It's really twofold: you meet a lot of nice people in the transportation field" and "it's the same love of machinery that makes somebody go out and spend a lot of time restoring an old car. Transportation has to be in your blood."

Hoschek once even owned his own bus. It was a 1931 Greyhound, which he partially restored, but had to sell some 20 years ago when he went into the Army. Currently, he and a friend are restoring a 1952 model, built by The Beaver Manufacturing Co. of Beaver Falls, Pa. The bus, which they found in a truck yard, is considered unusual, Hoschek says, "because Beaver was a relatively unknown company. In fact, the bus was the last one delivered to New Jersey before the company went out of business."

The information he has gathered in pursuing this hobby has helped him professionally, Hoschek says. With the current energy crisis, "many government agencies are now trying to go back in time to look at the historical aspects" of transport, while developing new transportation programs. They often contact Hoschek for information.

For the novice bus buff, Hoscheck recommends contacting the Motor Bus Society, 4 Tall Trees Rd., New Rochelle, NY 10802. The organizaton's publications will be of help. In addition, joining the group will put beginners in touch with experienced members.

Within motor bus buffdom there is a great variety of collectors, says Hoschek. "Not everyone collects just photographs. Some collect tickets and transfers, others the cap badges the drivers wore." A potential bus buff should "define what he is really interested in and work from there."

Hoscheck has much advice for beginners in the field of motor bus research and collecting. The beginner must often do research "in public facilities. The administrators can't or won't be bothered with researchers, so their first line of defense is that the material doesn't exist. Don't take no for an answer — ferret the information out. But be professional in your approach. What turns off sources faster than anything is a slovenly person who asks for the moon."

He cautions beginners not to expect a free ride from other buffs in the field, even though "buffs generally will willingly share information with others who have also done research. Everybody's collection and knowledge benefits".

"It's not too hard for us to help collectors get started,"he says. The members of the society have, over the years "squirreled away" some extra copies of materials, which they are able to use on occasion to help a collector get started.

Hoschek is interested in trading information with motor bus or public transportation buffs and will advise beginners. He can be contacted at 14 Shelton Ave., Trenton, NJ 08618.

RICHARD KNUDSON
MG SPORTS CARS

ONE OF THE MOST persistently fascinating cars to the American sports car buff is the MG. The product of many decades of designing and racing, this car is unique in the annals of automotive history.

Like many another brand of auto, the MG has its fans and collectors. Chief among them in the United States is Richard Knudson, a professor of English at the State University of New York in Oneonta, who not only collects and restores the cars himself, but has founded a unique group dedicated to keeping track of the many thousands of MGs that began pouring into the country from England in 1947.

"What we're talking about here are the vintage MGs, the cars made between 1923 and 1955, the traditional 'square-riggers' with the big square radiators," says Knudson.

Knudson's love affair with the MG began, like that of many others in the U.S., by "seeing and having a ride in one in the early 1950s. I had gone through the hot-rod stage, and was interested in another challenge." He found it in the MG.

He was a Fulbright fellow in Belgium in 1962 when he bought his first vintage MG. It was a 1948 MG-TC with "big 19-inch wire wheels, long sweep fenders, two seats, and was drivable," he says. He managed to get it back to the United States for $450: $300 to purchase the car, $150 for shipping.

Knudson drove the car daily for 10 years, and still owns it. He apparently got a pretty good deal on it, too, because even though "all sorts of figures are bandied about, British Leyland (the current maker of the MG) has put its worth at $17,000," he says.

Knudson now owns four other MGs: two 1948 TCs, a 1933 J-2 and a 1932 J-2 racing special. "That's really all I want right now. I have enough to keep me busy in retirement," he says. He works on restoring the cars by "taking them apart as far as they can come apart, and renovating everything. It's about a five-year process to restore a car."

In fact, Knudson says, "It's a very simple, straightforward car to work on. The availability of spare parts is quite good, and there are even a couple of firms involved in remanufacture of vintage MG parts." One possible difficulty for the restorer lies in the body of the car. "A lot of people don't know, but under the metal skin of the body is a frame made of English ash wood," he says. The wood does have a tendency to rot, so "sometimes you have to be a pretty good cabinetmaker to restore an MG."

Not only has Knudson collected the real thing, but he has well over 400 miniature toy MGs, too. They've come from all over the world, and date from the early 1930s to the present. A particularly interesting item is a cigarette lighter, modeled after a "Magic Midget" MG.

This is unusual, Knudson says, because it is the only one known to exist. "It apparently was a prototype of some kind, because it's only seen on a desk in a photograph of Cecil Kimber, the head of MG, taken in 1933. I'm almost sure it is the same one."

According to Knudson, the T series of MGs was the most popular of the cars produced between 1936 and 1955, and today they are the most collectible. Recognizing that fact, Knudson was a founder in 1964 of the International MG-T Register. "We established the Register to cater to the TA, TB, TC, TD, and TF cars, since there was no other organization that was handling them. It was just one of those uncanny things of being in the right place at the right time."

Today, the group has grown to 6,000 members worldwide. It has sponsored two large and very successful meets, and publishes "a good magazine," *The Sacred Octagon*, six times per year.

The popularity of the T series MGs was responsible "for a turnaround in the whole American car market," Knudson says. The MG's so-called "innovations" such as two-seater cars, with gear shift on the floor, gave inspiration to the makers of the "muscle cars of the 1960s."

With all of the fun Knudson has had with the International MG-T Register, and with restoring his own cars, he's found time to write six books on various aspects of the MG. The most important, *MG: The Sports Car America Loved First* (Motor Cars Unlimited, 1975), was the first U.S. history of the cars. "There were several histories written by the English, but they had very little to say about the MG in this country. Since we were MG's biggest customer, and if it wasn't for U.S. purchases they would have gone down the tubes long ago, I thought it was important to have a book about the car's history in the U.S.A.," says Knudson.

Knudson feels that, "like any hobby you keep at for a period of time, the focus on the hobby itself becomes almost secondary to the people you come in contact with. You end up being associated with people who feel the same way about things. I have friends from all over the world, thanks to the MG."

But it is the MG, after all, that is the focus of his hobby, and he is equally enthusiastic about the car. "For me, one of the appeals is that they have a very colorful history, a tradition of gentlemanly racing. And they're typically British — very traditional; that's a large part of their charm."

Knudson will gladly answer questions about MGs, or the International MG-T Register, directed to him at Drawer 220, Oneonta, NY 13820.

RUTH LANDESMAN
HOUSEBOATS

WHEN THE LAST of our children left the fold in 1969," says Ruth Landesman, "my husband and I opted for a new lifestyle, one which would be simpler, yet provocative."

It certainly was. Mrs. Landesman and her husband, William, found their new lifestyle as year-round residents aboard a houseboat on a tributary of the Hudson River. Though Mrs. Landesman's husband died in 1977, and she doesn't live on the houseboat anymore, she is an expert on living aboard ship in northern climates.

"We had a very large property in Woodstock, New York, and we decided we were too encumbered by possessions that were too important to us," she recalls. "We decided to simplify our existence."

The Landesmans settled on a houseboat because "my husband wanted a sailboat, and a sailboat just wasn't a practical option, at least as far as I was concerned. I wanted a house. So, we compromised on a houseboat."

They ordered the boat from a Tennessee firm, it was delivered to Brooklyn, and they sailed it up the Hudson River to its permanent mooring near Kingston, N.Y. They called the 43-foot boat "The Boarding House." "It was really quite spacious," she says.

She and her husband redesigned the interior of the boat. Instead of sleeping 10, as originally constructed, they altered it to sleep six in comfortable staterooms below the deck, in the pilot house, and at the stern. "We had a fireplace, electricity, a piano, all the creature comforts," she says.

Living aboard a houseboat is very economical, says Mrs. Landesman. "There were no property taxes to pay, and our utilities were extremely low. Our docking fee started out to be $50 per month, including utilities. By the time we left in 1977, it was up to $90 a month."

"I thought that it would take a lot of getting used to, but it didn't, because it was moveable," Mrs. Landesman says. "When we wanted to go anywhere, except in the winter, of course, we could take our house with us."

"We had some very severe winters," she says. "There often was ice four feet thick. The first year, we had 120 feet of snow." But the whole experience of living on a houseboat was "absolutely marvelous. We were the only people north of New York City living on a boat on the Hudson. We were all alone at our marina, which was glorious," she says.

If her husband hadn't died in 1977, Mrs. Landesman says, "we would have kept on living on the boat forever. But it was just too difficult for a woman living alone."

Landesman wrote about her experiences aboard the boat in a monthly column in the national magazine *Houseboating*. She wrote the column for six years, and that "brought people from all over the world to visit us, from as far as India and Australia. We made many, many friends.

"It was a wonderful shot in the arm. For people approaching retirement age, but not yet ready to retire, they can have the best of both worlds. Their expenses are smaller, and they can use their money for more interesting things than a house and property. With a houseboat, you're quite free of responsibility, and yet you have a good way of life."

People are sometimes afraid to make such a radical change in their lifestyle, but they shouldn't be, she thinks. "This is a wonderful thing to do. Our children were very much against it. They thought we were crazy when we sold the house and moved onto the boat. But within a couple of months, they were coming over, and bringing their friends, for visits."

She will gladly give information, offer advice, and provide encouragement for anyone contemplating life aboard a houseboat. She can be reached at 3081 Plaza Blanca, Santa Fe, NM 87501.

DAVE NEWELL
CORVAIRS

THE CORVAIR was one of the first so-called "economy" American automobiles. Its initial popularity, however, could not withstand the double death blows of Ralph Nader's *Unsafe at Any Speed* and price competition from Ford's Mustang. So, production ceased in 1969, just ten years after Chevrolet introduced it.

Now, these small cars are collectors items for many people. And there is certainly no more enthusiastic a Corvair advocate than Dave Newell, a 28-year-old General Motors parts manager from Hayward, California.

The Corvair's decline, according to Newell, "was more a matter of cost, and the fact that the car couldn't compete effectively with the Ford Mustang in terms of cost and available options" than a result of Nader's investigation, but he doesn't deny the Nader report pronounced the sentence on an already terminal product.

Newell "learned to drive my dad's 1961 Corvair when I was nine, and I've been into Corvairs ever since. It's something emotional you can't get away from."

Newell claims to own "the premier collection of Corvair literature." In 1970, he discovered the Corvair Society of America. "I'd always collected literature and now had people to share it with. My interest skyrocketed from there." He was member number 32 in the group, which today boasts 7,200 members nationwide. He was one of the directors for six years, and was president of the club from 1972 to 1974.

In 1967, Newell bought his first Corvair, a 1962 Monza station wagon, a rare model. This car was made for only one year, and "I knew when I looked for it that it was one of the rarest," he says. "I combed the entire San Francisco Bay area. It took months, but I finally found one on a used car lot. It was in excellent condition, as Corvairs go," so he didn't have to do much work on it. He purchased the car for $700. When he sold it in 1977, it was worth $2,500.

It was restored so well, Newell says, that he won second place in the Corvair Society's national convention competition in 1970. The man who bought the car from Newell in 1977, won best in show at a 1978 Corvair convention with it.

Right now, Newell has two Corvairs: a 1965 Monza, the top of the line for the cars; and a 1964 Greenbrier, which Newell describes as "a combination station wagon and small bus."

To Newell, however, owning Corvairs "is just a small part of my interest." His two-bedroom apartment has been "set up like a museum," he says. "There are Corvair posters on the walls, models everywhere, a 1966 display engine that really works, training films, filmed commercials, neon signs, all the promotional literature issued — just thousands and thousands of items. Actually, it's pretty weird."

Newell often shows his collection to people who are interested in Corvair history. The most popular attraction is the display engine from the 1966 model. "People really like it," he says. "It's a cutaway so you can look inside and see all the moving parts. Not only that, it runs." According to Newell, "I have every reason to believe my collection of Corvair memorabilia is the largest in existence," noting that he has absorbed the complete collections of two other buffs into his.

The Corvair is important to U.S. auto history, Newell feels, "because it was one of the Big Three's attempts to stem the tide of imports in the early 1960s." There were 1,786,243 Corvairs made over the decade of the brand's existence, says Newell. While Newell admits that the Corvair had its problems, "the car can be considered a success in the sense for which it was originally intended: it was important for Chevrolet to keep dominating Ford in sales, and they did it with this little car." Of course, the cost of lawsuits later on probably insured that the Corvair was not a financial success, but Newell feels the car's real strong points came in the esthetics.

"It inspired such emotional enthusiasm," he says. "The Corvair's style has never been exceeded to this day." Its unique design, with the body crease line running around the car "was blatantly copied in Europe." The car had "a very sensual, low-slung design, compared to the choppy, angular Mustang. Its appearance inspired a tremendous reaction."

Most of the Corvairs "that still exist are out here in the West," he says, citing the fact that cars tend to last longer in drier areas. "The bodies just rust out with excessive salt and moisture conditions," he says.

The biggest problem in owning a Corvair today, Newell says, is "finding the parts." For example, on the 1965-69 models, "There are no shock absorbers available anymore. You have to get parts from other members of the Corvair Society and sometimes you have to wait a long time."

Since "word has gotten around that they're collector's items," Newell thinks the novice Corvair purchaser today can expect to pay $500 to $2,500 for a car, depending on its condition. "There's not really a set value," he says. "It's just what the owner thinks he can get, and what the buyer can be conned into paying."

His advice is to "buy the best original, unrestored car/you can find. Otherwise, you'll probably spend at least as much in restoration costs as you would save by getting a cheap one in bad condition."

Newell encourages beginning Corvair buffs to meet other Corvair fanciers by joining the Corvair Society (PO Box 2488, Pensacola, FL 32503). "If it hadn't been for the Corvair Society giving me an outlet to share my enthusiasm, I wouldn't have done all that I've done in the field," he says.

He will also be happy to advise novice Corvair owners, and can provide information on the history of the Corvair. Contact him at 1481 Hamrick Ln., Hayward, CA 94544.

PERRY PIPER
EDSELS

THE GREATEST SOOTHSAYER of them all would never have dared to predict that 12 years ago the greatest automotive flop of all time would have risen from the ashes of obscurity and be one of the most desired collector's cars in the world," says Perry Piper.

The flop Piper refers to is Ford's Edsel, a grand experiment that didn't come off, much to the corporate embarrassment of the automaker. "It was introduced on September 2, 1957, as a 1958 model, and died an ignominious death on November 18, 1959," Piper says. Over those three model years (1958-60), only 110,600 of the cars were manufactured. Ford had projected production of 200,000 cars per year when the Edsel was introduced. Today, the Edsel has a new lease on life, as a collector's item.

Piper first bought an Edsel in 1959. "I had been traveling as a salesman for some years, and always had a Packard," he says. "When it came time for me to trade in my Packard, I found out I couldn't get anything for it." Packards were no longer made, and the car had no trade-in value. So, he thought, "I'll buy a car that won't go out of date before I have to buy a new one." He drove his new Edsel with delight until 1961, when after 100,000 miles, it was time for a new car. Of course, the Edsel wasn't being made anymore — and his car again had no trade-in value.

Today, Piper's Edsel collection contains 15 of the cars, representing all body styles of the three model years

Piper has been a leader in the movement to preserve and restore these cars. In 1962 he founded the Edsel Car Club. "It struggled along for about five years, with not much increase in membership," he says. Then, in 1967, a California man, named Edsel Henry Ford ("No relation to the automaker," Piper swears) asked for a charter to start a West Coast chapter of the club. "Well, with a name like that associated with the club, it took off like wildfire," says Piper. Instead of granting Ford the charter, the two men joined forces and created The Edsel Owners Club in 1968. Today there are some 2,000 members, all over the world.

"We're primarily a history group interested in preserving and restoring the cars," says Piper, who also edits and publishes *Big E*, the organization's quarterly slick paper magazine. The group has a monthly *Green Line* newsletter, as well, and meets in annual convention.

Why was the Edsel such a bomb? It's a bit complicated, says Piper.

"The Edsel was no 'Edsel,'" says Piper, "Edsel became the byword for commercial failure, but actually it was something of a success." Ford Motor Company, for example, got to write-off some $278 million in losses, and gained five years of valuable research time to build the Mustang and the Falcon, "Ford's most successful cars of all time," which used the same tooling as the Edsel had.

But the major reason for Edsel's demise, Piper thinks, was "lack of dealer and employee loyalty. Ford wanted dealers to handle Edsels exclusively, and when there was a delay in production in the beginning, there was nothing for these dealers to do: no cars to sell or service." In addition, Piper says, there is evidence of sabotage on the Ford assembly line. "A lot of dogs were made. Parts were deliberately misinstalled and there were numerous problems with the labor force."

Several other factors also contributed to the debacle. After a big publicity build-up for the "new" car, the Edsel was disappointingly similar to other cars on the market. Nevertheless, it was priced slightly higher than comparable models. Carrying these handicaps, it had to enter competition during the economic recession of 1958-59.

Piper and his fellow Edsel enthusiasts are happy with their cars today, however. "The quality of driving in an Edsel is excellent," he says. "It drives and rides better than any car ever built. It was constructed with the comfort of the operator in mind."

There is "very little difficulty in the restoration and maintenance of an Edsel, as compared to other vintage cars," says Piper. Though parts availability can be a problem, "as some of the parts were built strictly for the Edsel," it's not insurmountable. "You can either find new old stock or cannibalize another car." The cars are also fairly plentiful. "You can buy an Edsel for most any price in any condition," Piper says. It is possible to buy a "restorable, running Edsel for $1,200 and up."

Piper says the best way to get an Edsel is to join The Edsel Owners Club. For a $10 annual membership fee, the novice will get extensive information on the car, Piper says, and have the opportunity to correspond with other buffs who are more experienced in the restoration of the cars.

He enjoys driving his Edsels around. "You get a lot of attention when you drive an Edsel," he says. "People know what you're driving, it's an easily recognizable car, not like most of the cars made today."

Even though Piper has abandoned the life of a travelling salesman to "nursemaid a bunch of old cows" on his West Liberty, Illinois, spread, "If I were back on the road, I'd drive an Edsel. In fact, when I was still selling, I was known as 'the Edsel salesman.' There's a certain amount of prestige attached to that."

Piper will gladly give further information on the Edsel or the club to persons writing to him at West Liberty, IL 62475.

DON RICARDO
VINTAGE AUTOS

VINTAGE AUTOS, motorcycle racing, and setting records are all as familiar to Don Ricardo as the records he's made as an orchestra leader.

Ricardo, 72, has had a varied and interesting life, combining success in the entertainment business with success in the equally exciting world of auto collecting and racing.

The leader of his own orchestra for NBC and Paramount Pictures (among others) since 1930, Ricardo has an impressive record as an auto restorer and racer, including setting a world speed record for E-class stock cars at the Bonneville Salt Flats in 1967. "I went 154 miles per hour in a 300-SL Mercedes gull-wing car," he says, "and I held onto that record for nine years."

"It was quite a thrill to set that record," says Ricardo. Though he was inexperienced at racing the grueling course at Bonneville, he was an experienced drag racer, having competed in the 1955, 1956, and 1957 Winter Nationals at Pomona, California, and many other races.

Setting his record was not without hazard, however, Ricardo says. During trial-runs at Bonneville, he had persistent problems with his throttle, and once, "while I was going 150 miles per hour, the gull-wing door on my car flew open, and lifted the whole lefthand side of the car off the ground." Fortunately, Ricardo maintained control of the car, but missed setting the record that day.

"Bonneville, itself, you can't possibly describe," says Ricardo. In the week of the Bonneville Nationals, some 10,000 people congregate in that desolate spot. "They leave their cars and other stuff there all night," he says, "with just one guard to patrol. But there is a 12-foot-wide-by-21-foot-deep ditch all around the car park. Someone would have to jump it if they wanted to get in there."

Ricardo's been around fast vehicles most of his life. He started out at 17 racing "dirt bike" motorcycles. Then he got a Model T which he hopped up and raced. "I just continued on through a standard route of MGs, Jupiters, and Jaguars." He bought his first gull-wing Mercedes (he now owns six of them) in 1955, and the car has won 28 best in show awards, and 125 other trophies, since he's had it.

Today, when he's not touring with his orchestra, or supplying music for the film industry, Ricardo puts his effort into readying his car for an assault on the current world's record of 164 miles per hour. Since he lost the speed record in 1976, he's tried five times, unsuccessfully, to regain it. Right now, he's working in his home machine shop with a new engine, new exhaust system, and some other improvements that he hopes will enable him to capture the record once more, in the fall of 1980.He also finds time to maintain his collection of 24 vintage automobiles of all types.Besides the six Mercedes gull wing cars he owns (all vintage 1955-57), he has three Mercedes 300-SL roadsters, two 1928 Mercedes SSK two-seater racing roadsters, a 1935 Mercedes 500-K that belonged to Nazi Heinrich Himmler's family, a Mercedes 300-D limousine, a 1967 275 GTB-4 Ferrari, a 1964 Avanti, a 1970 Gianinni (one of a kind, he says), two BMWs, a 1956 Thunderbird, a 1915 Model T depot truck, along with a Cadillac El Dorado, VW squareback, a four-cylinder Volvo, and a 1967 Checker station wagon that he uses to tow his racing cars.

He keeps 17 of the cars in a specially-built showroom attached to his 14-room house. "I like having them displayed," he says, "and, fortunately, my wife Esther is very much interested, too."

Racing is Ricardo's real passion, however. "It's a challenge to your ability. It's macho or fun or something to see if you can do it." Ricardo scoffs at the notion he might be too old for such demanding racing. "At the sports car races and drags you see a lot of old cats," he says. "At Bonneville, there are guys older than I am who compete." He doesn't worry about danger, either. "It's good clean fun. You don't have time to get scared. You have to train your reflexes."

Ricardo is always glad to answer inquiries addressed to him at 64 Hillside Terr., Pasadena, CA 91105.

WALLY SCOTT
SOARING

WALLY SCOTT AND FLYING have been a twosome for years — ever since he got his pilot's license at the age of 18. These days, however, Scott's flying is oriented toward swiftly and silently gliding across the landscape, soaring motorless in a sailplane.

Scott has taken to soaring in a big way. He's a national and international distance champion at flying sailplanes cross-country.

The 56-year-old theater owner/manager from Odessa, Texas, made his first sailplane flight at the invitation of a friend in 1961. "It was 'love at first flight,'" Scott recalls. Not long after, he bought his first glider, and "my new hobby was born, at the expense of boating, skiing, hunting, and archery."

As a natural outgrowth of his participation in soaring, Scott became involved with cross-country distance sailplaning. There are three rankings that each sailplane pilot tries to achieve, based on various distances flown, he says, and it was in the course of trying to obtain the badges for the three rankings that he fell in love with cross-country soaring.

The lowest rank, the Silver C, is awarded for a flight of 31 miles across country; the middle rank, the Gold C, is for a 187-mile cross-country flight; the Diamond C is earned after a flight of 312 miles. "In obtaining these badges, I got to like distance flying, " he says, "and I've been doing it ever since."

Scott's accomplishments have soared. He has held four world distance records, six national and class records, and is the only person in the history of the sport to hold three world distance records simultaneously.

The first world distance record Scott achieved came in 1964, when he flew 520 miles from his home in Texas to Goodland, Kansas. But it was in 1970 that Scott's record-breaking ways made the soaring world sit up and take notice.

Three distance records are possible on the world level, Scott says. They include a "free distance record," meaning the pilot goes as far as he can on one flight; the "distance to goal record" is achieved by the pilot who flies to a specific place; and the "distance to goal and return record" is won by the pilot who flies the farthest distance to a specific goal and then back to his homebase, all in one continuous flight.

Scott, in 1970, set each of those records at 720 miles, 605 miles, and 550 miles, respectively, for a performance unparalelled in the sport of gliding.

The sailplane Scott flew to a national distance record in 1976 hangs today in the National Air and Space Museum at the Smithsonian Institution in Washington, D. C.

According to Scott, the popularity of soaring is growing at a remarkable rate. "When I got into it in 1961, there were about 8,000 people doing it around the country," he says. "Today, it's close to 30,000." He adds that soaring is "much more popular in Europe than it is here."

Naturally, a lot of people think flying along in a motorless plane is kind of crazy — to say nothing of dangerous. But Scott tends to minimize the dangers of soaring.

"Sure, there's an attrition rate of maybe 10 or 12 fatal accidents a year," he says. "But I think soaring is safer than flying a small plane, providing you learn proper flying and emergency procedures." Scott has logged some 3,500 hours of flight time, and flown over 120,000 cross-country miles, with no accidents, "but a few close calls," he says.

What turns on Scott the most about soaring is "the freedom involved. You see so many different things when you go up, things you don't see from the ground." Scott finds soaring competition to be particularly meaningful. "You're always competing against yourself, trying to learn by experience and trying to achieve the ultimate."

Scott would like someday to be the first to fly a sailplane for a straight distance record exceeding 1,000 miles. "It would be nice to win an international event," he says (having placed sixth and ninth in the only two he's entered),"but the distance record pursuit holds priority."

For the novice sailplaner, Scott advises, "Receive good instruction from reliable schools. Read books on the subject and contact other people involved in the sport for questions and answers."

He also advises, "Leave the nest and go cross-country as soon as you are adept. Learn your ship and equipment, and know your capabilities. It may take years, but it will be worth it."

Scott is willing to advise beginners in soaring. He can be contacted at 1304 Parker Dr., Odessa, TX 79761.

BOB SMILEY
JAGUAR XK SERIES

BOB SMILEY IS the only man on his block with five Jaguars — of the mechanical, not animal, variety. Smiley is a fancier of one of the world's most exciting sports cars.

A 45-year-old high school English teacher from Northport, New York, Smiley has been romancing the Jaguar (particularly the XK series, made between 1948 and 1961) since the 1950s, when they first began appearing in his hometown. His father, who was also a fan of fine cars, influenced young Smiley's taste, and at age 19 he bought his first Jag "sight unseen." It was a Marque IV "saloon" sedan of pre-World War II vintage and, says Smiley, "I couldn't afford it." Now, these many years later, "the magic of the marque still holds." So much so that he owns five of the XK series cars, which he has restored.

He has also built up an impressive record in racing the cars. The XK series of Jaguar, in the 120, 140 and 150 models of coupes and roasters, were "very desirable, tremendous performance cars," that were popular in the 1950s for racing. To that end, Smiley has been participating in Sports Car Club of America races with a 25-year-old XK 140 that "has never finished worse than third. This Jaguar is a potent car."

The car, a veteran of 17 years of racing under two previous owners, has been a surprise to Smiley's fellow racers. "When you show up with a 25-year-old car, people think you have to be a little crazy." But they laugh out of the other side of their mouths once the car hits the race course.

Because of his interest in racing, Smiley restores his Jags for performance. "The Jaguar represents grace and speed," he says, in commenting on the type of performance he is looking for in the car. "I'm trying to revive the racing feeling."

With his many years of experience in the restoration of the cars, Smiley is a rich source of advice for the novice. He urges purchasing the best possible car available, "even if it means waiting and saving money. Ultimately, it saves time, money and aggravation." He has seen too many people get stuck with cars which really weren't good values, because they didn't want to take the extra time to save enough money for a really good used car.

"The result of waiting," says Smiley, "is usually a better restoration and a better investment." So, he advises, "do it right, even if it is more expensive. In the long run you will not be sorry."

Shortcuts such as substituting vinyl for leather in the interior "is a mistake, not only from an investment standpoint, because the car won't be an original restoration."

And the investment potential is high. With cars that are used strictly for their parts going for $5,000 these days, it is not unusual for a fully restored Jaguar XK to be worth between $20,000 and $25,000, according to Smiley.

The essence of restoring a Jaguar XK, Smiley feels, is taking time, varying the work on different tasks "so you won't get in a rut."

"A really great part of the fun of owning a Jaguar is the actual restoration work itself, " he says. "You don't usually realize this at the time, however, because of the enormous amount of work and the great number of aggravations involved."

With all of the work and expense, along with the pressures of the racing life, it's ironic that Smiley terms his hobby "a tremendous way to relax." But, after a day of working with high school kids, "I just like to put a wrench to things."

The appeal of the Jaguar for Smiley is that "you can take something that isn't anything and put it back to where it once was." He is justifiably proud of his work. "As I drive the car, I can see all the parts moving in the motor, and I know that I put them there.

"It's a bit of an ego thing, too. I want to show people what I can do."

Smiley is frequently called upon for advice and assistance in the restoration and care of the Jaguar XK Series, and is glad to help out any way he can. He can be reached in care of Jaguar-Rover-Triumph, Inc., 600 Willow Tree Rd., Leonia, NJ 07605.

KENNETH SODERBECK
FIRE TRUCK RESTORATION

SIRENS BLARE, bells clang, and everyone stops to watch the big red fire engine dashing by. To Kenneth Soderbeck this clamor is music to the ears. He's translated this fondness into an absorbing special interest: the restoration of fire trucks and other fire vehicles.

Soderbeck developed his interest in fire trucks as part of his antique collecting. "My wife and I collected antiques in general, and decided to specialize in fire department items because I was a volunteer fireman." In 1968, Soderbeck bought his first fire truck. It was a 1923 American La France 600-gallon pumper, 22 feet long and weighing about five tons. He purchased it from a private collector in Angola, Indiana.

"After I got it, I discovered I was going to have to restore it," he says. "Fortunately, it was in fairly good condition," and he had the advice and help of the American La France company and fellow fire truck buffs in his area. The whole job took about six years, and his fire engine is now in a museum.

Today, Soderbeck still has three fire trucks in his backyard — but they're all unrestored. "They're going to stay that way for another eight or nine years," he says. "There are a lot of other people's trucks ahead of them."

Soderbeck developed so much expertise in the restoration of fire equipment over the years that in 1976 he began restoring other people's equiipment too. Now, it's a profitable sideline business, with "some part-time guys who are interested and one of my daughters, who helps on the upholstery." Operations are conducted in a 40-by-40 foot garage, and an additional 10-by-20 foot painting area on Soderbeck's Jackson, Michigan, property.

Since opening up his shop, he's restored seven fire vehicles. "Some were real basket cases that needed a lot of work. Others were just cosmetic jobs," he says. But restoration of a fire truck is expensive. While an unrestored vehicle can cost anywhere from $1,000 to $4,000, Soderbeck says a restoration from the frame up could cost as much as $10,000.

"There are so many variables in the trucks," he says. "Most of them were custom-built to the whims of the fire departments. I've learned one thing in this business and that's never to say, 'American La France never built a truck like that,' because sure enough, I'll turn around and there'll be one."

Restoring fire vehicles differs from working on automobiles, Soderbeck says, because fire equipment "was built to do a job, and to last a long time — built heavier with a little more care" than the average automobile.

"One of my beefs with fire vehicle restorers is that, like a lot of auto restorers, they tend to over-restore their trucks," he says. He prefers to retain a more authentic, rugged appearance in the equipment.

The national organization of fire truck buffs goes by the name of The Society for the Preservation and Appreciation of Antique Motorized Fire Apparatus (or, more often, the jawbreaking acronym SPAAMFA). Soderbeck says this organization, with close to 2,000 members all over the country, is a great way for novices to learn the craft and to communicate with other fire apparatus fanatics. SPAAMFA is also a good source for finding out where to buy old fire trucks. Their quarterly publication *Engine Engine* has a wealth of this kind of information, says Soderbeck.

For information on fire truck restoration, or SPAAMFA, contact Soderbeck at 749 E. South St., Jackson, MI 49203.

HORACE SOWLES
HORSE-DRAWN VEHICLES

EVEN THOUGH HORACE Sowles is an automobile dealer, he doesn't flinch when someone shouts, "Get a horse." He's got a intriguing collection of horse-drawn vehicles that could make even the most confirmed auto buff long for the good old days!

Sowles, who lives in Portland, Maine, is an ardent advocate of horse-drawn vehicles. He has between 300 and 400 of them in his collection of "all kinds of two- and four-wheeled and sleigh vehicles, everything from gigs to stagecoaches, just about every kind ever made," he says.

He keeps all of these conveyances on his Skyline Farm, 75 acres outside Portland, where he's creating a museum of horse-drawn vehicles. They're kept in a number of small, specially constructed buildings, including a very special 1850 stable.

"This is an actual stable I bought out in South Portland," he says. "It has beautiful hardware and paneling, an elevator to move horses, coachman's quarters, a harness room, and so forth." He had it cut into eight pieces and moved from its original site to the farm.

Horses, carriages, and Sowles have been a natural trio for most of his life. Growing up in Brookline, Massachusetts, Sowles' family had horses and horse-drawn vehicles, and "I have been working with horses ever since I was a child." It was just a small step to the vast collection he has accumulated throughout his life.

Among the many fascinating and historic pieces in Sowles' collection is a sleigh that was owned by John Quincy Adams, the sixth President of the United States. It's an 1820 Albany Cutter sleigh, "which came down through the Adams family, and is still in its original, unrestored condition," says Sowles. He thinks that the Adamses used the sleigh when they were living in Quincy, Massachusetts.

Although he claims that "they're all my favorites," another piece he is especially fond of is is an original Abbot and Downing 12-passenger stagecoach. This coach, built about 1850, was sold to the Atlantic House, a hostelry in Kennebunkport, Maine. "It was used to bring guests to the hotel from the main town," says Sowles.

Sowles' collection of horsedrawn vehicles isn't just for looking at. He has horses, and, when the mood strikes him or "if somebody comes over and wants to go out," he'll hook up a pair of horses to a phaeton, a gig, a runabout, or some other sporty vehicle, and take off over the backroads of Portland. "It's fun to drive them," he says. "I guess I'm just a buggy nut."

He is the executive vice-president and secretary-treasurer of the Carriage Association of America, an organization founded in 1959 for horse-drawn vehicle buffs. The organization, which has some 2,500 members scattered about the country, publishes a quarterly journal and sponsors an annual convention and competition in a different "horsey" location each year.

Even though there are "more horses in the U.S. now than at the turn of the century, and people find them a pleasure and a sport," Sowles doesn't foresee a return to the days when "horsepower" meant something with four feet.

"Having a horse and carriage isn't like having a car," he says. "You can't just go out and turn on the ignition and take off. There's a lot of work involved. It was a very difficult life, and we couldn't possibly do it."

It's not as difficult as one might think to find horse-drawn vehicles to collect, Sowles says. There are carriage auctions all over the country these days, and the buyer can pay anywhere from $200 to $60,000 depending on the type of vehicle and its rarity.

"If you buy an old vehicle, you'll have to restore it a lot, and it can be very expensive," he says. The restorer has to have the professional help of a wheelwright and a metal shop, for example, to do the proper job of restoration. "There is an art in carriages, " says Sowles, in explaining his fondness for his hobby. "The craftsmanship, design, paint-job, upholstery, all combine to make real artistry in construction." There is so much work to be done in restoration, that "when you see a nice carriage all done up properly, it's a work of art."

Sowles will gladly answer questions about horse-drawn vehicles or the Carriage Association of America. He can be reached at PO Box 3788, Portland, ME 04102.

JIM SYKES
NSU AUTOS

THEY'RE VERY NIMBLE, corner sharply, and love to climb hills." That's how Jim Sykes describes the NSU, an obscure German car that from 1956 to 1972 was one of the most experimental cars on the road, creating some of the innovations that automakers use today.

"Much of the reason NSUs were obscure was that there were never very many of them on the road," Sykes says. "The company did a lousy job of selling them; they were more interested in the technical aspects."

Indeed, it is the advanced technology that made the NSU such a memorable car. They were small sedans, designed to have "low air-drag aerodynamics," with air-cooled Wankel (rotary) rear engines, and front wheel drive.

How did a copy editor for the *Seattle Times* become a self-proclaimed "fanatic" on a car made in Neckarsulm, Germany? Sykes explains it this way. In 1970, a close friend who was an auto enthusiast bought an NSU. "I was really impressed," says Sykes. "I liked the curved design, and it was obvious that the maker had put a lot more work into it than most other cars got." Also, the NSU was "a lot of car for $2,500 or $3,500. By jove, they were about three times the automobile the VW was — there was so much more room; and they were better than the Japanese imports, too."

Sykes was hooked, and in 1971 he purchased his first NSU. He's had 15 since.

"I've seen close to 2,150 NSU cars," he says, "and no two are identical." He estimates there are probably about 3,500 of the vehicles in the United States.

He claims to have the largest collection west of Illinois, at present, with six of the cars in his garage, driveway, and another garage he rents from a neighbor. The centerpiece of his collection is the "very sophisticated, very sexy" RO80, the NSU top-of-the-line car. As far as he knows, he's the only person who has two of these models.

The NSU didn't catch on in the United States. "Most people were discouraged because of the difficulty of obtaining parts. They wanted mass-produced cars that were easily fixed," he says.

Sykes has partially solved the parts problem; in 1976, and again in 1978, he bought out the entire parts inventories of two NSU dealerships. He has been able to swap and sell parts to other NSU collectors, mainly through NSU-USA, the national organization of the hobby.

One of the innovations that NSU brought to the U.S. automotive industry was the Wankel engine. Unfortunately, it didn't catch on any better than the cars did. Sykes feels "it was marketed too quickly by Mazda and tooling up was a problem." Actually, however, the dual demands for air pollution control and increased gas mileage were "extensive challenges" that the engine could not meet, he says.

Sykes plans to keep driving his NSU. He likes them because they have "unsophisticated air pollution control devices," so they get really good gas mileage." Also, since he has managed to become an expert in the care and restoration of the cars, "I'm not at the mercy of auto repair shops or mechanics."

"I've just heard too many horror stories and don't want to be at someone else's mercy," he says. "And when I think how dirty I've gotten in trying to do everything over the years..." Still, certain technical aspects of the NSU elude his expertise. "I'm not a real authority on the gear boxes, for example."

Sykes recommends that anyone who is interested in NSU autos contact NSU-USA, 20477 Nolina Ct., Johnstown, CO 80534. He'll also be glad to give advice or information to potential (or confirmed) NSU fans. Send a stamped, self-addressed envelope to him at 717 N. 68th St., Seattle, WA 98103.

JOHN THOMAS

HUDSON MOTOR CAR COMPANY

WHEN HIS HEALTH forced John Thomas to retire in 1972, he "needed something to keep me both physically and mentally active." Hudson Motor cars were a natural choice, for he had helped a friend restore one. But, he soon discovered that it wasn't the restoration of the cars, but their history, which most fascinated him.

In fact, Thomas has become the leading expert on the history of the Hudson Motor Car Company, its affiliates, and subsidiaries.

"In 1941, I'd helped restore a 1914 Hudson that belonged to a friend of mine," he says. Later, he bought a 1930 Hudson touring car and, still later, a 1929 Essex. Both cars are still awaiting final restoration, because Thomas has been too busy researching the history of the Hudson Motor Car Company.

Actually, it was in trying to find original factory information to help him restore his Hudson, that Thomas first became aware of the fact that the history of the company was being slighted. From that beginning, "and a lot of correspondence, I can tell you," Thomas gathered data about the company and the automobiles it made from any place he could find it.

Tracing the actual history of the company proved to be very difficult. Time obscures a lot of things, and Thomas had to do extensive research to uncover the facts of the company's creation and existence.

He began by looking up the officers of the company. He knew that three of them, Roy Chapman, Howard Coffin, and Roscoe B. Jackson, were graduates of the University of Michigan at Ann Arbor. Thomas paid a visit to the university, where he found that Chapman had studied law, Coffin went to night school ("he worked by day designing one of the first automobiles ever driven on the streets of Detroit," says Thomas), and Jackson was "such a brain at engineering that when he graduated, they made him assistant dean of the engineering college."

These three men joined the firm of Thomas Detroit ("which for some reason was actually based in Buffalo, New York," says Thomas), a company that also made automobiles, in 1908. In 1909, they obtained financing from J.L. Hudson to start their own automaking concern. "In the northern plant shack of Thomas Detroit, they assembled 1,100 little roadsters, which were the first 'Hudsons,'" Thomas says.

In 1910, joining with several other men, they finally formed a completely independent company, called Hudson Terraplane Motor Car Company. For the next 47 years, they made Hudsons. The cars had "three-speed transmissions, and were extremely powerful and cheap compared to other cars."

These cars, at least partially, live on today in the American Motors "Hornet." Hudson and Nash merged in 1953, to form American Motors. They shared the same assembly line until 1957, when both names were dropped, and the Rambler took over as the premier car of the American Motors line.

Through his research, Thomas was fascinated to discover "a spiderweb of people in one company that worked in another company. They all backed one another." A major partner in the Hudson enterprise was Hugh Chalmers, who later started Chrysler Corporation. "Half of all the major automakers can trace their roots right here to Buffalo," says Thomas. "These men had such guts. They were going absolutely against the odds all the time."

Having pretty much covered the historical aspects of the Hudson Motor Car Company, Thomas has turned his attention of late to the technical side. Working with other interested members of the Hudson-Essex Terraplane Club, the leading collectors' organization, Thomas is attempting to gather technical data about the firm's automobiles for use by restorers.

Why has Thomas found his work so satisfying? "Maybe I'm just history-minded. I love the challenge of doing reserach. There was nothing written on Hudson before I started. Now, there's *The Hudson — The Postwar Years*, among other books." He is proud of the fact that he has provided source material for a number of researchers and writers on the Hudson.

Thomas will be glad to answer any Hudson related questions — and he'd really like to receive any information anyone might have about the company and its products. He can be contacted at 268 Heath St., Buffalo, NY 14214.

JOHN VOELCKER
MORRIS MINOR AUTOS

IT'S A SMALL British auto which looks rather like a pregnant VW Beetle," John Voelcker laughs when he's asked to describe a Morris Minor. These fascinating little cars were the rage of Britain from 1948 to 1971 when the company was swallowed up by the giant British Leyland conglomerate.

Voelcker has spent most of his life around the cars. "I was born in England," he says, "and we brought a Morris Minor wood-bodied station wagon with us when we came to America when I was four." The Voelcker family settled in Rochester, N.Y., and that plucky Morris Minor "is still running today," Voelcker says. "I literally grew up in that car."

"When I was about 15 years old, I was messing around with it and thought, 'Gee, this is neat. I wonder if anyone else has a car like this?'" Well, Voelcker discovered another Morris Minor buff in Connecticut, Hank Pinckney, and together they started the Morris Minor Registry, a club for Morris Minor enthusiasts. In 1977, after Voelcker had moved to California to attend Stanford University, he ran across another Morris buff, Rick Feibusch. Feibusch was the head of another club for Morris nuts, The Morris Owners Association of California. Voelcker and Feibusch decided to join forces and create one Morris Minor organization.

"We've done a pretty good job," says Voelcker, noting that the Morris Minor Registry has slightly more than 800 members, in 48 states, four Canadian provinces, and seven foreign countries. One of the major purposes of the Morris Minor Registry is to list all existing Morrises by serial number, with details on car and owner. "So far, we have about 1,500 listed, so you can see we have quite a ways to go," says Voelcker. Interestingly enough, says Voelcker, "the distribution of Morrises is not at all even. Between 1948 and 1967, there were some 56,000 Morris Minors imported from England. I haven't the vaguest idea how many have survived to this day, probably around 10,000 to 15,000. Most of those can be found in the Pacific Northwest or California."

There are six different Morris body styles. The most common is the two-door sedan, but there are also a four-door sedan ("very rare"), a convertible, the Traveler "woodie" station wagon, a panel van, and a pick-up truck. The most valuable of these, according to Voelcker, are the Travelers ("due to their wood sides and leather interiors") and the panel van ("its small but roomy, a neat little truck").

Voelcker owns three Morris Minors himself. Two, a 1961 Traveler and a 1967 two-door sedan, are back home in Rochester. The other, a 1967 two-door sedan, is Voelcker's "everyday car. It was totalled three times before I bought it, but it was running when I purchased it, and I've had quite a bit of work done on it."

For the beginning auto buff, Morris Minors are "superb cars because they are extremely simple to restore," says Voelcker. "You can see every piece of the engine when you open the hood; all the parts are clearly visible and easy to get to. It's just a straightforward, simple, easy-to-understand vehicle."

What the beginner might have difficulty with is finding a Morris Minor in the first place. "Availability depends a lot on where you live," he says. "It's easy to find one in the San Francisco Bay area, but on the East Coast there are almost none left." He blames the salt and chemicals used on snowy roads for the demise of the cars in the East.

Additionally, "it's an extremely volatile market. The prices have shot up because of the economy value of the car: they get 35 miles to a gallon." A good, running Minor, not restored, can be obtained for $1,000 to $1,500; a restored car might go for up to $4,500, says Voelcker, emphasizing that "these are the roughest of estimates."

"The Morris is a remarkable car," says Voelcker. "The fact that 30 years after it was introduced it is still used by many people for reliable transport — and is not a pampered antique — is fantastic."

Explaining the satisfaction derived from his work with the Morris Minor Registry and participating in the Morris Minor hobby in general, Voelcker says, "I never had any idea it would grow to this. The response has been just marvelous. Basically, it's fun."

The 21-year-old industrial engineering student recommends anyone interested in the cars join the Morris Minor Registry (or the Morris Owners Association, if they live in California). For a $10 annual fee, the member will get 12 issues of the *Morris Minor News*, which Voelcker edits, a packet containing membership roster and available parts list, "and a lot of personal advice from members, if that's desired." The Morris Minor Registry (and Voelcker) can be contacted at PO Box 6848, Stanford, CA 94305; the address for the Morris Owners Association of California (with the same membership benefits) is 2311 30th Ave., San Francisco, CA 94116.

PEOPLE

JACK BALES
HORATIO ALGER

HE WAS THE MOST popular author in the U.S. in the final 30 years of the 19th century, and his novels inspired several generations of youngsters to overcome their humble origins with hard work and perserverance. His name was Horatio Alger — and Jack Bales is one of his most appreciative 20th-century readers.

Bales, 28, has been an Alger fan since he was 15, when he found a book by the author tucked away in his Milwaukee, Wisconsin, home. "I had heard of Alger as the 'rags to riches' writer, so I gave the book a try," he says. He liked what he read, and decided to collect as many books by and about the author that he could. "I think of myself as kind of a Horatio Alger hero, anyway," he says. "I'm one of nine children, and I had to put myself through college and graduate school"

Today, Bales's collection of Horatio Alger books contains editions of most of the 120 different titles Alger wrote. "I don't have as many first editions as I would like," says Bales, but he is certain he has an outstanding representation of most of the writing of the author. The Alger books were also translated into other languages ("it's hard to say how many"), and Bales has a goodly number of those, as well. His total collection consists of about 200 volumes.

In addition, Bales has one original Alger letter, and "a really rare letter from his father to the Unitarian Church, in 1825, withdrawing from membership." Bales obtained this letter from a boy in Massachusetts (Alger's home state), who had found it in a junk pile, wrapped in an old newspaper.

Alger began the series of novels about plucky lads in 1867, with a serialized version of *Ragged Dick*, which appeared in *Student and Schoolmate*, a popular children's magazine. Alger was prolific and churned out three or four books a year for his fans. When he died in 1899, he left 11 manuscripts behind, all of which were published posthumously.

Contrary to popular belief, it was not Alger's intention to push the philosophy "any poor boy can pull himself up by his bootstraps," Bales says. Rather, he was simply "writing didactic, moral tales for children, with such themes as be kind to your mother and work hard. Alger didn't intend to become the myth-maker of success. He just wanted to write good literature for children."

Not everyone thought Alger's writing was good, however, Bales says. In 1879, for example, the august *Library Journal* published "a scathing attack on

Alger, saying his books were too sensational, unrealistic, and painted a picture of America that was not feasible." In 1907, the Worcester, Massachusetts, public library, near Alger's hometown, banned his books.

Bales is active in the Horatio Alger Society, a nationwide organization of 235 Alger enthusiasts. The group was founded in 1961, Bales says, by a publishing executive and a retired postal worker "who thought Alger's ideals should not die." Basically, Bales says, the organization is a group of book collectors, who meet in annual convention to discuss Alger-related topics.

Bales is the editor of the society's monthly publication, a newsletter entitled *Newsboy*, named for the sort of lad most often featured in Alger's sagas.

For the potential Alger book collector, Bales, a college reference librarian in Illinois, suggests searching used book stores, flea markets, and antique stores. "You never know where the books are going to turn up," he says. Also, novice Alger buffs should join the Horatio Alger Society. Contact Carl Hartmann, 4907 Allison Dr., Lansing, MI 48910, for further information.

For Bales, Alger's writing "is what the great American dream is all about. I really do think it's true. I'm a firm believer in it. I think hard work has a lot to do with success."

It is Bales' goal to someday write the "definitive" biography of Horatio Alger. The one biography that is most often quoted in other writings about Alger is a hoax, Bales discovered. It was written in 1928 by the distinguished magazine publisher Herbert R. Mays. He wrote it as a satire of the type of biographies that were appearing at the time, and included a lot of sensational "facts" about Alger.

For some reason, Bales says, the book was reviewed with praise, and "everybody believed it was legitimate. Mays didn't want to offend anyone," Bales says, so he "let the hoax ride for nearly 50 years." The Mays biography has since been quoted in all the scholarship about Alger as an authoritative source.

Bales and Mays became friends, and finally, in 1976, Bales broke the story in *Newsboy*, causing a sensation among Alger scholars.

Bales will also answer questions, addressed to him at 1214 W. College Ave., Jacksonville, IL 62650.

TYRA BERRY
HANK WILLIAMS

To MANY IN POST WAR America, country and western music meant Hank Williams. A singer and guitarist, Williams came to prominence with such songs as "Your Cheatin' Heart" and "Cold, Cold Heart" in the late 1940s and early 1950s. Unfortunately, Williams died at the age of 29, burned out on alcohol and pills, with the career that had shown such promise in ruins.

Despite his brief stardom, Williams created music that mightily influenced many of today's country and western music performers, and made Williams himself a cult superstar — his records could still climb to the top of the charts over 25 years after his death.

But, to Tyra Berry, who became fascinated with his music at an early age, Williams is more than just a posthumous success. Fourteen years ago, Berry began researching Hank Williams's life and work, becoming perhaps the most authoritative source of information on Williams.

"What makes my interest in Hank so fascinating to some people," says Berry, "is that he died on January 1, 1953, almost two years before I was born."

Berry, a 25-year-old truck driver from Oneonta, Alabama (a town 30 miles north of Williams's birthplace in Georgiana, Alabama), first became familiar with Williams through some old 78-rpm records his father had. Among them were Williams's hits "Cold, Cold Heart" and "Dear John." Then, too, a friend of Berry's "had a bunch of Hank's records and he used to play them all the time. In fact, that's about all he did."

Besides, says Berry, "Here in Alabama you hear a lot of stories about Hank" since he is one of the state's most famous native sons. Through his appreciation of Williams's music, Berry became first a fan, then a collector and researcher.

Among the more than 250 photographs in Berry's collection, there is one especially rare color photo of Williams. Berry, who says the collection "may already be the largest of its kind in the world," has that distinction as his goal.

Berry hasn't relied on printed source materials alone, in his search for information about Williams. "I've gotten to know all of Hank's people, and a lot of his friends and foes," he says. "They've helped me tremendously."

Though Williams was a brilliant songwriter and performer, Berry says, his behavior, as the years went on, became increasingly difficult for friends, business associates, and loved ones to handle. He had a stormy eight-year marriage to an ambitious singer named Audrey Mae Sheppard. It ended in bitterness and divorce, but during their marriage, Williams wrote his most famous songs. With his tendency to be a "loner," Berry says, Williams had a hard time coping with his problems, and those around him couldn't pierce his shell to offer help.

Berry admits that, at times, "it has been very difficult to find material. People just don't want to respond. They have very bad recollections of Hank when he was alive, and it has taken considerable time for many of them to think favorably of him again." But Berry was able to obtain information about Williams by befriending those close to him. "I got pretty well-known because I hung around and pestered people to death," he says.

Berry personally interviewed many of Williams's family and friends, including his son, Hank, Jr., (now a well-known performer), and his cousins, Taft and Erline Skipper, all of whom have provided Berry with "an insight into Hank's character, what kind of person he was, what caused him to drink, and what caused his downfall at the age of 29, a time when a man's usually just getting started."

What does Berry think caused Williams' problems, and his untimely death? "He got too much too quickly for a country boy like he was," says Berry, explaining that the semiliterate Williams came from a poor family and had dropped out of high school to pursue his musical career. Success, it seems "came too fast for him and he wasn't ready for it." In addition, Berry blames Williams's "basic ability to be a loner...and his marriage to Audrey" as two powerful forces in his decline.

Realizing that searching out accurate information about Hank Williams or, for that matter, any famous person, can be a time-consuming, thankless and difficult job, Berry has some advice for beginners. "Don't give up, be sincere, listen and study the music to get a feel for the person, and read everything you can about him." Then, and only then, he stresses, does "the real research begin."

Berry advises researchers always to be cognizant of the reliability of sources, and check and double-check any information received for accuracy. He favors going directly to sources, however.

"Start writing and calling to get in touch with the people and places that were important to the subject's life," he says. "Be persistent, and don't be afraid to ask questions, and you'll often get good results."

Berry is willing to assist those interested in Hank Williams, or in the general area of researching a performer's life and work. He may be contacted at 713 Magnolia Ave. S., Oneonta, AL 35121.

SAMUEL BURR
AARON BURR

ONE OF THE MOST controversial political figures in Federalist America was Col. Aaron Burr. Most often remembered for his famous duel with Alexander Hamilton, whom he killed in the confrontation, Burr has typically been portrayed as a womanizer, rogue, and traitor. That picture, according to Samuel Burr of Linden, Virginia, is false.

The 83-year-old president general of the Aaron Burr Association has devoted much of his life to trying to correct the historical myths about his famous ancestor, whom he feels has been "misunderstood by the American public and misrepresented by his enemies."

Ever since he was an eighth grader, Dr. Burr has fought the controversy that surrounds his famous ancestor. His "spinster school teacher got up in front of the class one day and made an utter tirade — just put her heart and soul into it — about some man named Aaron Burr who had tried to cheat Jefferson out of the presidency, tear the United States apart, and didn't believe in God. The 30 kids in the class glared at me and would have nothing to do with me for several days."

When he mentioned this to his father, Dr. Burr says, his father simply told him: "That's what a lot of people believe. It isn't true, but we have to put up with it." Well, Dr. Burr wasn't about to do anything of the kind; he began then and there to research the life and times of his famous relative.

In 1946, he (along with two other Burrs and their wives) founded the Aaron Burr Association which has been dedicated to supporting historical research and accurate presentations of the "real" facts about Aaron Burr and his role in history. Many of the group's findings are published in its quarterly magazine, *Chronicle of the Aaron Burr Association*, which Dr. Burr edits, publishes, and mails to nearly 1,000 subscribers.

Dr. Burr is not sure exactly how he is related to Aaron. "Our immigrant ancestors Jehue [Aaron's ancestor, arrived in U.S. 1631] and Henry [Dr. Burr's ancestor, arrived in U.S. 1688] were probably cousins, but I've never been able to verify the connection."

"Aaron Burr had political enemies," Burr says. One of them, Governor George Clinton of New York, appointed Burr Attorney General of the state. "We think he did that to remove Aaron from the political scene, to keep him from being competition."

It was after 1800 that the controversy surrounding Burr intensified, when Clinton's nephew, DeWitt Clinton, became another powerful enemy. Young Clinton "misrepresented Aaron's motives, saying that he was selfish and would change his political position as the tide ran. This simply was not true," Dr. Burr says.

Burr's two greatest enemies, however, were Hamilton and Thomas Jefferson. Dr. Burr feels that Hamilton, illegitimate, under-educated, and unsure of himself, saw in Aaron "a well-born, polished, and highly educated man and was jealous."

"Hamilton did everything possible to ruin Aaron's reputation from the financial, political and social points of view. He just couldn't get along with Burr," though they were allied on many occasions and worked together, Dr. Burr says.

For Jefferson, Dr. Burr has even harsher words: "Jefferson accepted Burr's help in the election of 1800, but he didn't like being indebted to him. And he didn't relish any competition. So, he determined that Aaron should be destroyed." Aaron Burr had been elected vice-president, but he had no powers to grant patronage. Jefferson undercut Burr's power base by appointing cronies of DeWitt Clinton and New York Governor Livingston to office, instead of Burr's supporters.

"It was a perfidious, despicable way to treat Aaron," Dr. Burr says, "but Jefferson was determined that only a Virginian could be President. Any one of these men would be formidable enough enemies, but with all of them against him, Aaron never had a chance."

Dr. Burr is bitter about the way in which history writers have traditionally handled the story of his relative. "What the hacks wrote became accepted as true," he says. "These slanted, biased people made Jefferson a demi-god and Burr a devil. That's not the way history ought to be written," Dr. Burr says. "I think people are starting to wake up to the fact that there is a lot of distortion in American history."

Gore Vidal's recent book *Burr* was helpful, Dr. Burr feels, in giving the public an alternative, more accurate view of Aaron Burr. Though he thinks "there are two or three things included, like Aaron having an affair with his daughter, which was utterly false, Vidal has done a lot of good" with his novel.

Dr. Burr once had extensive files of research materials, Burr family memorabilia, and many papers belonging to the Aaron Burr Association stored in his home. One winter evening in 1978, the entire house burned to the ground, and all of his belongings were destroyed. Even worse, Alice, his wife of 53 years perished in the fire and Dr. Burr was severely injured.

"It was a horrible, unspeakable experience," he says, "but it taught me to live not in terms of age, but in terms of projects." So he has been busy ever since, building a new house, refurnishing it, and taking up the work of the Aaron Burr Association with renewed vigor.

The satisfactions of his sometimes lonely quest for the truth have been considerable. "The extensive correspondence which I have maintained over the years has put me in contact with at least 1,000 nice people." He's only had two "abusive" letters (one man challenged him to a duel) since 1946, out of the several thousand he has received. But there are other, deeper satisfactions, too.

"I've learned a whole lot about a certain period of history. Everybody ought to have some kind of field to be an expert in, and I get great satisfaction from having picked this period, particularly with an important man at the center of it."

Dr. Burr is modest about his accomplishments, saying, "I'm not in this for financial gain. I feel I have done something for the Burr family which certainly should have been done by somebody. I was the one who came along and did it."

Dr. Burr will gladly answer queries or provide further information on the Aaron Burr Association. His address is TremonT, Inca Rd., Linden, VA 22642.

SANDOR BURSTEIN
LEWIS CARROLL

SANDOR BURSTEIN CAN date the beginning of his love for Lewis Carroll's "Alice" books. "It began with a kindergarten teacher who played the White Rabbit in a semi-professional production. Some of the love for the teacher was immediately transferred to the Wonderland world."

Today, the 55-year-old internist from San Francisco, California, still lives in the Wonderland of Charles L. Dodgson (Carroll's real name), through his collection of books and other memorabilia relating to the author, and particularly his books *Alice in Wonderland* (1865) and *Through the Looking Glass* (1871).

Burstein became a serious collector of Carroll books and related materials about 12 years ago. He had written parodies in a Lewis Carroll vein while a college student, and retained much of his affection for the two "Alice books" over the years. But while attending a medical conference in Portugal in 1968, he made "my first serious purchase, an edition of *Alice in Wonderland* in Portuguese." *Alice in Wonderland*, Burstein says, has been translated into 30 languages. Today, he has editions in some 20 languages, and he is still looking for the remaining books to complete his collection.

Carroll was a prolific author. Not only did he write the "Alice" books, and other fantasy material such as *The Hunting of the Snark*, but within his 180 known works are books of philosophy, mathematics and logic. In fact, one of Carroll's books on symbolic logic, somewhat re-edited, has been reissued, and is an influential book in the field, Burstein says. Burstein has collected first, and other, editions of these books, as well.

With his books, Burstein's collection includes over 850 items relating to Carroll, including books about Carroll, pictures, T-shirts, and the like. Perhaps his most unusual item is Carroll's personal cribbage board, which Burstein purchased several years ago. Burstein has branched out into collecting these non-book items because "while the books get scarcer, the ephemera are more common."

Cost is another factor. The first edition of *Alice in Wonderland* (of which there are only 19 known to currently exist) would fetch about $150,000. Burstein doesn't have a first edition *Alice*, but "I held one once."

With his son, Mark, Burstein founded the West Coast chapter of the Lewis Carroll Society of North America in 1979. This organization is composed of some 375 Carroll buffs from the U.S. and Canada. The two chapters, east and west coast, feature frequent meetings, and publish a newsletter which is a good source for finding out about material available to be collected.

The beginning Alice fan needs to "haunt bookshops" to find copies of books in various editions, Burstein says. "Go back frequently and make your wishes known to the dealers." He also recommends joining the Lewis Carroll Society of North America (617 Rockford Rd., Silver Spring, MD 20902).

Burstein will be glad to counsel Lewis Caroll buffs. Contact him at 2233 Post Street, San Francisco, CA 94115.

MARIO DI GIOVANNI
CHRISTOPHER COLUMBUS

Christopher COLUMBUS DID more to direct the course of history than any individual since Augustus Caesar," Mario DiGiovanni believes. He speaks with the authority of an expert on the life and times of the great explorer.

Over the last 30 years, DiGiovanni, 68, a Pacific Palisades, California, scientist and inventor, has done extensive research, writing, and lecturing on Columbus, his contemporaries and his times.

It was DiGiovanni's scientific research in instrumentation for navigation that first led him to study Columbus. "Naturally, because of my professional interest, I researched early navigators and the type of instrumentation they used. Actually, they didn't use much, but I became fascinated by the courage and stamina of the people."

Columbus was an important part of the research because "he could unerringly navigate anywhere. Wherever he wanted to go, he could hit it right on the button. He never lost a ship," says DiGiovanni. This so intrigued him, that DiGiovanni began to follow his trips, and he even went to Spain and Italy to study Columbus.

"I became a nut," says DiGiovanni. "I researched everything ever written about Columbus."

Through his research, DiGiovanni feels he has been able to uncover some important misrepresentations and distortions of facts about Columbus.

"One of the biggest misconceptions is that Columbus never explored continental America," he says. On his third voyage to the New World, in August of 1498, Columbus set foot on present-day Panama and Venezuela. "That was even before John Cabot was supposed to have discovered Labrador," DiGiovanni says.

"A lot of people don't know that Columbus actually left people in the New World," on the north shore of present-day Haiti, when he set out to return to Spain early in 1493. When he returned in November of that year, DiGiovanni says, he came with "a whole fleet" and some 1200 people, who started a settlement in what's now known as the Dominican Republic.

Incidentally, says DiGiovanni, "Columbus didn't do it all alone. He had a lot of help from his brothers, Diego and Bartolomeo. It was a real family effort."

Columbus, (whom DiGiovanni describes as "a tall, magnificent person" with blue eyes and red hair) and Spain's Queen Isabella (his major benefactor) "had a mutual attraction to each other, but their relationship remained platonic." DiGiovanni speculates that they liked each other because "they were so similar in age (both were born in 1451), appearance (Isabella also had reddish hair), and both were extremely devout Catholics."

In fact, DiGiovanni says, Columbus is sometimes cited as a racist for his support of the Spanish effort to expel the Jews from Spain, at about the time of his voyages to the New World. But, says DiGiovanni, people who advance that view "fail to recognize that they are judging him on today's standards. Much of what we abhor today was a way of life then."

DiGiovanni has found no shortage of material in his research into Columbus's life. Among the most influential items are Washington Irving's biography of Columbus, which DiGiovanni says "has a tremendous bibliography." He found that many of the documents in Italy about Columbus "are completely wrong in their dates, and what they say happened." He has also heavily utilized material written by the noted American historian Samuel Eliot Morison.

"Unfortunately," says DiGiovanni, "my occupation has prevented me from doing the work of a scholar" on Columbus. Thus, he has concentrated mainly on trying to compare the information and viewpoints of others, rather than doing original research.

DiGiovanni has been lecturing across the country since 1946. As an active participant in (and former national president of) Unico International, an Italian-American service club, it is DiGiovanni's purpose in his speeches "to enrich America with Italian culture, and to foster interest in our heritage." In his speeches, he concerns himself with Columbus, and other Italian notables such as Galileo and Verrazzano, emphasizing their positive contributions to world culture.

The World Book Encyclopedia had the explorer Verrazzano, who discovered New York harbor, "listed as a pirate. But that just wasn't true," says DiGiovanni. He was successful in having the encyclopedia change its listing.

DiGiovanni speaks familiarly of Columbus, as he would of a close friend. The explorer has been so fascinating to DiGiovanni over the years because of "his qualities. The guy had so much courage. All of us daydream about wanting to accomplish something great. Here was a man who did it. He dreamed of something equivalent to going to the moon in our own time, and he put his dream to the test."

According to DiGiovanni, that feat is all the more amazing because Columbus "was not even equipped to do what he did. Most of his schooling came after the age of 25; fortunately, he married into a family of navigators and learned that skill. He was the classic 'late bloomer.'"

DiGiovanni, who "likes to straighten people out" about Columbus, welcomes correspondence. He can be contacted at 15400 Albright Street, Pacific Palisades, CA 90272.

JOHN GABLE
THEODORE ROOSEVELT

A BOYHOOD VISIT to the home of Theodore Roosevelt at Sagamore Hill, Long Island, sparked an interest for John Gable that led to a lifetime of study about the 26th President, and an interesting career as director of an organization devoted to historical research and preservation of sites associated with Roosevelt..

"Though I started out being interested in TR for the usual heroic Rough Rider exploits, as I got older I began to appreciate him for his political and intellectual viewpoints and attainments," says Gable. Most intriguing about Roosevelt, to Gable, "was his sense of who he was, combined with his almost infallible sense of timing." TR knew, for example, "just when he could and could not get a bill through Congress. He never recommended a bill that failed. If he thought it wasn't going to have a chance, he would never directly propose the legislation," says Gable.

A particular example of Roosevelt's activities in that regard occurred with the Federal Trade Commission, which came into existence in 1915. According to Gable, Roosevelt "wanted to create the commission as far back as 1902, but no bill was ever introduced, though he hinted it would be a good idea. He just knew it couldn't happen at that particular time."

Gable attributes TR's strength of character and perceptivity to his childhood. Theodore was asthmatic as a boy and went to great lengths to build up his strength. "During this process he got to know himself both physically and mentally. He was very much the self-made man. Because TR didn't go to school until he went to Harvard, he spent a great deal of his youth alone."

The outside world was "strange to the President," Gable thinks, particularly "interaction with people. It was practically impossible for him not to charm all sorts and conditions of men in his later life, but in his youth, he had great difficulty doing so."

Gable, 36, has been the executive director since 1974 of the 700-member Theodore Roosevelt Association (TRA) based in Oyster Bay, New York. He describes the TRA as "a general historical society and public service organization interested in all sites and historic places of TR's life." It was founded within a week after Roosevelt's death in 1919. Public subscription to finance the association's activities raised $2 million initially, "which we've spent many times over." The association's quarterly *TRA Journal*, begun in 1975, is mailed to all members.

The organization, of which Gable is only the third executive director, has been intimately involved with the preservation of sites relating to TR. "We owned his birthplace in New York City, and his home in Sagamore Hill." They were donated by the TRA to the National Park Service. Also, says Gable, "there's a huge endowment" that has kept the organization functioning since its inception. The association is also actively working on preserving the inaugural site in Buffalo, the Roosevelt ranch in Roswell, North Dakota, and his mother's family home in Georgia. They also maintain TR's grave and a memorial bird sanctuary in Oyster Bay.

"Most importantly, the TRA gives information to authors and others interested in getting the true facts about the life of Roosevelt," says Gable. Gable himself frequently lectures and writes about Roosevelt.

According to Gable, Roosevelt buffs fall into several categories. Some collect political items, such as campaign buttons, others collect books and pictures, and some simply visit TR sites and attend the activities sponsored by the society. A great many, however, "do all of those things. Interest is clearly on the upswing."

Gable keeps "a very limited personal collection of TR materials," he says. Most of the items he collects concern the ill-fated "Bull Moose Party," which TR organized for an independent Progressive campaign for the presidency in 1912. "My favorite is a badly discolored badge that says 'Roosevelt-Washington Party' on it." In 1912, the Commonwealth of Pennsylvania couldn't list the name "Bull Moose" or any other name associated with Roosevelt on the ballot because the political bosses had already registered all possible party names they could think of when TR bolted the Republican party, says Gable. So, "The Roosevelt-Washington Party came into being, and Pennsylvania was the only eastern state Theodore carried in the election."

In collecting items relating to TR, Gable says, "the prices are out of proportion to the supply." The President's signature, for example, "is not rare. He signed hundreds of thousands of letters in his lifetime. But a Roosevelt signature is hard to get, for some reason, and often costs from $35 to $40."

Gable believes TR's philosophy of "popular government combined with rights and responsibilities," along with his stand on environmental issues, are the most appealing things about Roosevelt today.

Gable will answer questions about the life and times of Theodore Roosevelt or about the TRA written to him in care of the Theodore Roosevelt Association, PO Box 720, Oyster Bay, NY 11771.

PEARL HODGES
ROSE O'NEILL & KEWPIES

In 1909, AN ADVERTISING artist named Rose O'Neill had a dream. From that dream, she created Kewpies.

Kewpies, for anyone who hasn't heard of or seen one sometime in the last 70 years, are roly-poly elfin babies, with topknots of hair and tiny blue wings.

O'Neill's dream soon became a thriving industry, with countless "Kewpie pages" of drawings and poetry appearing in such major magazines as *Good Housekeeping*, *Ladies Home Journal*, and *Women's Home Companion*. In 1913 came the first Kewpie doll, the chubby-cheeked rascal that charmed children for generations. O'Neill lived much of her life in Branson, Missouri, where she had a large estate, Bonniebrook, the site today of Kewpiesta, an annual April festival commemorating her creations.

That there is a Kewpiesta at all, or even that many people remember Rose O'Neill today, is largely due to the efforts of a Branson artist, Pearl Hodges. In 1967, Mrs. Hodges founded the International Rose O'Neill Club, which grew from an initial membership of 50 to nearly 1,000 from all over the U.S., and from Canada, Norway, India, and Japan, dedicated to perserving the memory of Rose O'Neill and the artwork she left behind.

Mrs. Hodges became interested in Rose and her Kewpies in 1961, while working as a tour guide at the Shepherd of the Hills Farm, west of the Ozark mountain town. "I was originally from Branson," she says."My husband and I began working at the museum. As part of my job as a tour guide, I told people about Rose O'Neill and showed them some of the things the museum had on display. And I got to thinking, why don't they honor this lady like they do the other famous people from the area."

"I wanted to recognize her contribution to the arts," Mrs. Hodges says. Not only did O'Neill draw the Kewpie pages, but she wrote poetry, short stories, and music, as well. She created Kewpies, Mrs. Hodges says, "to do good in an amusing way".

The major collectible for Kewpie enthusiasts, of course, is the Kewpie doll, which has appeared in many forms since in 1913. The original Kewpie dolls were bisque and imported from Germany. Today, Kewpies are made from soft plastic by a New York toy manufacturer.

Why has the Kewpie and the philosophy of Rose O'Neill remained so popular over the last seven decades? "They have a very happy smile and create an atmosphere of love and good feeling, and I think people are impressed by this." says Mrs. Hodges. Kewpies are "slanted to children, but I think the grandmas like them too," she adds, in explaining the diversity in the Rose O'Neill Club's membership.

Kewpiesta is held in Branson "when the dogwood and wildflowers, which Rose O'Neill loved, bloom in profusion." Between 200 and 300 men, women, and children gather for the three-day celebration, bringing their latest acquisitions of Rose O'Neill memorabilia, getting together for banquets, entertainment and the opportunity of comparing notes with fellow enthusiasts.

Mrs. Hodges is glad to provide information about the International Rose O'Neill Club or Kewpies. (A club membership is $3 for the year, sent to the club at PO Box 668, Branson, MO 65616.) Mrs. Hodges can be contacted at Star Route 3, Box 45, Branson, MO 65616.

WILLIAM HOGARTH
RICHARD III

SHAKESPEARE DESCRIBED HIM as "that abortive rooting hog...that poisonous hunchbacked toad...that bottled spider." For the last five centuries, he's been credited with the dastardly murder of his two nephews, who were potential claimants to the throne of England. But William Hogarth thinks Richard III, King of England from 1483 until his death at the Battle of Bosworth Field in 1485, was the victim of a vicious smear campaign by his Tudor rivals.

Hogarth, a 54-year-old professor of art at the C.W. Post Center of Long Island University, isn't alone. He has more than 600 fellow members of the Richard III Society behind him. This group, the offshoot of the Fellowship of the White Boar in England (founded 1924), has dedicated itself to the restoration of Richard's memory as an intelligent, progressive, and noble king and to erasing his bad reputation.

Ever since he read Shakespeare's powerful drama *Richard III* and saw a performance of it at age 12, Hogarth has suspected something was rotten in the characterization of Richard as a deformed and brutal villain. He began to research the historical background of the period, especially the War of the Roses, and came to the conclusion that Richard wasn't as bad as he was cracked up to be. Another source of inspiration was Josephine Tey's masterful novel, *The Daughter of Time*, which discussed the Richard III enigma as if it were a modern detective story. Hogarth joined the Richard III Society in 1966. Currently, he is the vice-chairman of the group, and the editor of its newsletter.

Richard III received bad press all through English history, according to Hogarth. It wasn't improved until the Victorian historian James Gairdner "did much to resuscitate Richard's reputation" in a controversial biography he wrote in 1878. Says Hogarth, "present-day historians have come up with a more benign view of Richard's reign."

It is Hogarth's view (shared by many members of the society) that "had he lived, Richard would have been a brilliant king." He introduced many innovations in his brief term of office, says Hogarth. The society is preparing an account of his reign, using original documents, that "will go an awfully long way" in proving that he was an important and tragically misunderstood king.

The greatest mystery of the Richard III story is, of course, the murder of the little princes, the potential heirs to the throne. In the official version (promulgated, Hogarth says, by Richard's Tudor enemies) he was seen as "the arch-villain, the wicked uncle"who assassinated the boys. What is far more likely, Hogarth feels, is that either misguided supporters of Richard in his fight to gain the throne or enemies seeking to discredit him, were the ones who murdered the two boys. Of course, "once possession of the crown was in sight, Richard really wanted it, and he was terrified of a regency." However, says Hogarth, "it is impossible to clear him on the basis of known documentation." There is no documentary evidence, either, of his supposed deformity.

Why does Hogarth find Richard's tragic story so fascinating? "It was the first great political lie. What is the statute of limitations on a lie?"

Hogarth's concern with something that happened so long ago "offers its own satisfaction. Should new and conclusive evidence turn up, it will be gratifying. Also, I love the anecdotage, and I have strong interest in the theatrical side."

The society is deeply involved in plans for the quincentenary of Richard's reign. They plan special activities, and are actively campaigning for a construction of a memorial to the king in Leicester, England. Every year they put a memorial announcement in the *New York Times* obituary section, commemorating his death.

It is interesting to note, says Hogarth, that many members of the Richard III society are professionals in the field of criminal justice, including judges, lawyers, and the like. The group is also heavily peopled, obviously, with librarians, educators and actors.

The society's primary interest in scholarship has led them to establish a graduate fellowship. The first one was awarded in 1979, and the winner is studying in England.

Hogarth invites interested persons to join the Richard III Society. Contact him at P. O. Box 217, Sea Cliff, NY 11579.

LOUDILLA, LORETTA & KAY JOHNSON
LORETTA LYNN &
COUNTRY MUSIC FAN CLUBS

COUNTRY MUSIC is a family affair for the Johnsons. The three Wild Horse, Colorado, sisters, Loudilla, Loretta, and Kay, have made quite a name for themselves in the worldwide country music scene. Life on an 8,000-acre wheat and Black Angus cattle ranch some 150 miles southeast of Denver has taken on a decidedly Nashville flavor for "the Johnson Girls," thanks to their dedication to country music.

It began back in 1961, when they fell in love with "Honky Tonk Girl," the first recording by a little-known country singer, recorded on the obscure Canadian Zero label. The Johnsons first heard Loretta Lynn's records first over Colorado Springs radio station KPIK, and they thought "she was just about the greatest thing since amplified guitars," says Loudilla Johnson, who is the family spokeswoman.

"We grew up in Oklahoma and Texas," says Miss Johnson, "so country was all we heard. When we moved to Colorado, we started attending the country music concerts put on by KPIK." The Johnsons got to be well-known around KPIK, and their first venture into country music fandom was working with country and western singer George Jones on his fan club. After hearing the Lynn recording, they met with Jones in Colorado Springs, "and he said he knew Loretta and she'd be thrilled to get a letter from us," Miss Johnson says. "She had no money and, with her husband, was literally living out of the back of their car."

Loretta Johnson was picked to write the letter ("she thought it was fun writing to someone else named Loretta," Miss Johnson laughs), and eventually, they got to meet her in person.

They arranged an engagement for her at the Four Seasons Club, a country and western music nightspot in the Denver suburb of Aurora. "Loretta came out on the Greyhound bus from Nashville," says Miss Johnson. "And she outdrew anybody they'd ever had there, including Patsy Cline, who was a superstar at the time."

The Johnsons promptly adopted Mrs. Lynn, taught her how to use makeup, helped her with her performance, and then and there decided that she ought to be a star. Since then they've been her number one fans, and are the founders and co-presidents of her international fan club.

"I don't know what it was about her that we liked so much right away," says Miss Johnson, "but everywhere we'd go, we'd say 'You don't have Loretta Lynn's record on the jukebox,' and they'd say, 'Who?'. Then we'd just look at them like they ought to be ashamed for not knowing who Loretta Lynn was. We got her on quite a few jukeboxes that way." From then on "we all teamed up and did a lot of things, just sort of struck out on our own. It's amazing now that they didn't laugh us out of the business."

Miss Johnson says, "When we met Loretta it was never like meeting a stranger. We kept all of her letters. Mooney Lynn, her husband, had made some stationery with her picture in the corner, and whenever we needed a picture in those early days, we would cut a picture off one of her letters. So now, we have a whole stack of letters with holes in them," she laughs.

Today, the Loretta Lynn International Fan Club has 3,000 members all over the world. And the Johnson gals are lively promoters of Mrs. Lynn, with a monthly, slickly published newsletter, a magazine, and a booming business in Loretta Lynn souvenirs. All of their work is done without pay.

The Johnson Girls (as they're commonly known in the country music world, though they're all in their 30s) wouldn't have gotten into the fanclub business at all without their father's help. "He bought us about $1,000 worth of equipment, but he told us we'd have to make ends meet ourselves. So, we sell a lot of things, and Loretta gives us money, buys pictures, and so forth. It funds itself," says Miss Johnson.

Even though the Johnsons freely admit they have never had any training in management, business, writing, or public relations, they've built an astounding empire. In addition to their work with the Loretta Lynn International Fan

Club, the Johnsons founded "the biggest little news sheet in country music" (as it says on the masthead), *Tri-Son News*, in 1963. The newsletter (the name stands for "Three Johnsons") was begun to counteract what the Johnsons felt was the image of fan clubs "as a bunch of screaming maniacs that weren't respected by the disc jockeys" and thus weren't of much use in getting their favorite artists any air time. "We thought we were pretty clever with this newsletter, disguising that we were fans." By the time anyone found out they were, *Tri-Son News* was already a success: it goes to some 1,200 dj's and others in the industry each month, filling them in on the latest news of country and western musicians.

"I think they didn't know what fan clubs were all about. I've met thousands of fans, and there are about as many squirrels in the industry as there are among the fans. Most of them are hardworking, plain people," she says. Members of the Loretta Lynn club, for instance, have occupations as diverse as a priest, a penitentiary warden, and an attorney.

Perhaps the Johnsons' most important accomplishment, however, is the International Fan Club Organization (IFCO). They started it, at Loretta Lynn's suggestion, in 1965, "because so many country music fans wanted to know how to start clubs for their artists," says Miss Johnson. Since that time it has grown to 200 member fan clubs, and has become an important voice in the country music movement.

"Country music has come a long way just in the time we've been associated with it," says Miss Johnson. "People used to hide and listen to it. Now they're open about it."

"Our involvement in country music started as a hobby, but the hobby has become a business almost," she says. "We've had offers to do similar things for money," but the Johnson girls have always turned them down, choosing instead their life on the ranch and the relative freedom it gives them to pursue their main interest.

"We enjoy all the people and the responsibility. There is a sense of acomplishment about doing things for people," she says. "It's not like we're doing it for nothing, even though we aren't getting paid. There are other satisfactions."

The Johnsons, and their various enterprises, can be contacted at PO Box 177, Wild Horse, CO 80862.

JOHN McCABE
LAUREL & HARDY

THE RIB-TICKLING antics of Stanley Laurel and Oliver Hardy have filled theaters with smiles, chuckles, and belly-laughs for over 50 years, ever since they first teamed up in a 1926 silent film, *Slipping Wives*. Far from being the fumbling buffoons they so effectively portrayed, Laurel and Hardy were sensitive, intellgient, creative men, who made film history.

The lives of Laurel and Hardy, and their contributions to the art of film, have interested John McCabe for many years. The 60-year-old professor at Lake Superior State College in Sault Ste. Marie, Michigan, is the leading authority on Laurel and Hardy, has written several popular books on their lives and work, and is the founder of a worldwide organization of their fans.

McCabe's involvement with Laurel and Hardy began when he was a youngster. He was a child actor then (he still appears in local productions) and "really enjoyed their films." But his serious interest was sparked in 1954, when he met Laurel in person.

"I was in England working on my doctorate, when I went backstage at a music hall where Laurel and Hardy were appearing and introduced myself to Stan Laurel." Finding Laurel "a charming, loving man," McCabe formed a friendship with the actor that lasted until Laurel's death in 1973.

"Laurel's whole world was laughter," says McCabe fondly. "He was the most genial of men. He took the place of the father I had lost at a very early age."

McCabe says that Laurel and Hardy "were both simple men, in the best sense of the word." Oliver "Babe" Hardy was "much devoted to the country club life. He was a fine dancer, an expert card player and golfer, and he loved people," says McCabe. "At the end of a day of work, he'd most often be found at the Lakeside Country Club" pursuing one of those interests.

Laurel, on the other hand, "was just the opposite. Work was his hobby. He'd put in eight or more hours in front of the cameras, and then spend as much time thinking up gags and bits of business," says McCabe. Laurel was "the creative half of the duo" and all of the bits in their films were "either created by Stan or sifted through his fine comedic mind."

Laurel and Hardy made 105 films, many of which have gone on to become classics. Laurel, who was Charlie Chaplin's understudy in the Karno vaudeville troupe, went with Chaplin to Mack Sennett's studio. "He was very successful, and made his first film in 1916," says McCabe. In 1926, Laurel and Hardy were introduced to each other, by film director Leo McCarey. They formed a partnership that made the Hal Roach studios one of the greatest in Hollywood's golden era.

McCabe wrote his first book on the duo, *Mr. Laurel and Mr. Hardy*, in 1961. His second book on the team, *The Comedy World of Stan Laurel*, was published in 1975, after the actor's death, because "it says some things Stan's modesty wouldn't permit to be said while he was living." A third, highly technical book, *Laurel and Hardy: The Films*, was published in 1977.

In addition to writing about his favorites, McCabe was also a founder, in 1963, of the Sons of the Desert, a group of some 4,000 Laurel and Hardy buffs from around the world. The organization was named after the 1933 film of the same title. McCabe says, "Some people think that is their best film. I would simply say there are none superior to it."

If McCabe had to pick favorites, he would choose *Two Tars* (1928), *Big Business* (1929), *The Perfect Day* (1929), *The Music Box* (1932), *Sons of the Desert* (1933), *Way Out West* (1936), and *The Swiss Miss* (1938). McCabe credits the pair's enduring popularity to the "high strain of sheer and loving English nonsense" that pervades their films. "They were extremely human in their characterizations," he says. "They represented innocence and were very much like children who haven't grown up to know how to double deal and lie."

"Life's little troubles writ large" was the essential ingredient in their films, says McCabe. For most of us, if we opened the cupboard door, some little thing might fall out. "If Stan and Ollie opened the cupboard, a 50-pound sack of flour would fall on their heads."

In their later years, Mr. Laurel and Mr. Hardy had a series of artistic disappointments. Their last film together was a disaster called *Atoll K*, made in 1950, but never released. "They were supposed to have total creative control," says McCabe, "but the director of the film, which was being made in France, was a hack who didn't speak English, and they couldn't communicate effectively with him." Laurel became ill during the filming. "It was one of their worst films, really wretched," says McCabe.

Hardy made a film without Laurel, *The Fighting Kentuckian*, when Laurel was ill. The film starred John Wayne and was a limited success, with Hardy playing a character role rather than his usual comedic persona, says McCabe. Hardy died in 1957, before the pair could reunite with Hal Roach's studio to make more films.

McCabe's interest in Laurel and Hardy "has been a professional one, bolstered by my deep friendship with the charming and lovable Laurel."

McCabe has also become somewhat of an expert on two other great showmen, George M. Cohan and James Cagney. In fact, he was Cagney's "creative consultant" on the star's autobiography.

People interested in Laurel and Hardy who are "unseriously disposed to celebrate that interest," says McCabe, should join the Sons of the Desert. Contact Dr. Roger Gordon, 2230 Country Club Dr., Huntingdon Valley, PA 19006 for further information.

McCabe can be contacted at PO Box 363, Mackinac Is., MI 49757.

SUE McCASLAND
ELVIS PRESLEY

AUGUST 16, 1977: A DAY that will live long in the memories of many people. It was on that day Elvis Presley died.

But if Sue McCasland, from San Jose, California, has anything to say about it, Elvis will live on long past his demise. For Miss McCasland is one of Presley's number one fans.

"I've been a fan forever and ever it seems," she says. "The very first time I heard him, I was just in sixth grade." As she grew up, Miss McCasland bought Presley's records and attended all of his films. She began to go to Presley's concerts in the 1970s, and, as time went on, "I realized I couldn't just sit far from the stage any longer; I had to get nearer to him."

So, beginning with a 1972 concert by Presley in Oakland, California, "I followed him wherever he went, when I could, always sitting in the front row of seats." Miss McCasland traveled to see her idol all over the South. "It was just something I wanted and needed to do." Before Presley died, Miss McCasland had seen him perform over 100 times.

"I was lucky enough to have him look at me in recognition with a smile" on several occasions, she remembers.

Miss McCasland collects Presley memorabilia. In addition to owning all the albums and single records he made, "even the bootlegs," she has a huge collection of photographs, many of which she took herself during Presley performances. "I've provided pictures for several books on Elvis, too," she says.

Miss McCasland's most cherished items are "13 scarves that Elvis wore. He used to throw them, drenched with sweat, to the audience, but he always handed them to me." Once, he gave her a guitar pick, because he recongized her as a faithful fan. In addition, she has a "red rose from his casket," which she is preserving.

Miss McCasland, a remedial math and language teacher, is active in the San Jose Elvis Presley Fan Club. In 1977, when the president of the club retired, she was elected to the post. Since then, she has tripled the membership and donated over $6,000 to charity from the club coffers. The club has some 300 members all over the United States, but it's basically a local club, part of the "thousands of clubs" for Presley fans worldwide, she says.

The focus of much of the fan group's work centers on charity. "Elvis was an extremely generous man," she says. "Much of what he did, we may never find out about. He gave his money freely and he gave freely of himself to his fans." So, her club makes charitable contributions to Muscular Dystrophy, the San Jose Children's Center, and the Elvis Presley Foundation in Tupelo, Mississippi.

The charitable work of the Elvis Presley clubs nationwide has been astounding, she says. The foundation began in 1977 after his death, and was devoted for two years "to building a chapel that Elvis had wanted for his fans at his birthplace. It took two years, but the chapel was built in 1979, all with $150,000 in donations from fans."

Miss McCasland's club raised nearly $3,000 on its own for the chapel fund. "We have lots of little events to raise money," she says, "but our major effort is an Elvis Day festival once a year." During the festival, there's live entertainment, and dealers in Elvis mementos sell their wares, all the proceeds going to the club's fund-raising efforts.

Appreciating Elvis is easy "for those people who have seen him live. You get caught up in the charisma. We all have the same feeling," says Miss McCasland. "No matter what he sang, it always seemed like you were the only one he sang to."

Says Miss McCasland, "What impresses me most is that someone that famous, that rich could remember me, and the other fans, who put him where he was. He never forgot us."

Miss McCasland will be glad to give information on the Elvis Presley Fan Club, or on "the King" himself, to anyone writing her at PO Box 6581, San Jose, CA 95150.

CHRISTE MC MENOMY
DOROTHY L. SAYERS

THE WRITINGS OF DOROTHY
Leigh Sayers, British mystery author and Christian apologist, have been of
great interest for many years. While Sayers is probably best-known to the
general public as the author of the Lord Peter Wimsey series of novels, Christe
McMenomy of Los Angeles says there's much more to the mysterious author
than mystery stories.

Miss McMenomy has made it her business to know about Dorothy Sayers.
She's been studying Sayers' works extensively for the last several years, and she
edits and publishes a magazine about the author who, she says,"had a profound impact on my life."

Miss McMenomy was interested in reading books by J.R.R. Tolkien, Charles
Williams and C.S. Lewis before she tackled Sayers, as a student at Scripps
College. "The first Sayers book I read was *Five Red Herrings*, a Lord Peter
mystery," she says. "I didn't know until later that that was one of the worst
ones."

Apparently, Miss McMenomy found that first book fascinating, because she
continued reading works by Sayers. In addition to the Lord Peter books (eleven
novels and three collections of short stories), Sayers also wrote several plays,
and translated Dante's *Divine Comedy* and *The Song of Roland*. But it was
Sayers's philosophical writings that most excited Miss McMenomy.

"I was right in the middle of a theological crisis of my own," she says,
explaining that she found Sayers's book *The Mind of the Maker* an important
help in the resolution of her conflicts.

The Mind of the Maker discusses "how man imitates God in creation," says
Miss McMenomy. "It is Sayers's point that the created thing becomes independent of the artist, separate of the artist, an event unto itself."

She also cites Sayers's work *The Man Born to be King*, a collection of 12
radio plays that "was impressive in its portrayal of Jesus Christ as an historic,
human figure."

Miss McMenomy could also credit Sayers with helping persuade her to
change her major in graduate school. She's working on her doctorate in the
history of science, having switched to history from astrophysics after reading
Sayers's novel *Gaudy Night*.

"*Gaudy Night* is the story of a woman who goes back to her college for a
reunion, " says Miss McMenomy. "She is a writer, wondering if she is doing
the right thing by being a writer. At the reunion, she runs into people all
doing things they think they ought to do, but aren't good at."

Says Miss McMenomy, "The point Sayers is making in the book is that you
have to be true to the thing that is most important to you and you have to be
good at it." This made her realize, she says, that"I was a much better historian
than mathematician," and so she changed her grad school program to the
history of science from astrophysics.

Many of Miss McMenomy's writings about Sayers find their way into the magazine she edits, *The Sayers Review*, a thrice-yearly publication that she publishes from her home. She began the magazine in 1976, when she decided to create a newsletter for "the people I knew across the country who were interested in Sayers."

Today, that newsletter is a 35-page magazine, sent to 60 subscribers all around the world. The magazine features scholarly essays on Dorothy L. Sayers, some of which have been reprinted in other journals. "The magazine is a forum for people to try out their articles in," Miss McMenomy says.

"The definitive biography of Sayers has yet to be written," McMenomy feels. There are two biographies, *Maker and Craftsman*, by Alzina S. Dale, and *Such a Strange Lady*, by Janet Hitchman. Both present somewhat different views of Sayers, but Miss McMenomy says neither of them are definitive because "no one has had access to Sayers's personal papers, which are in the custody of her son." Supposedly, Miss McMenomy says, a writer is now working on a biography, using those hitherto unavailable papers.

Sayers does "appear to have been pretty strange," Miss McMenomy says. She dressed "in mannish clothes, was very precise, and didn't pull punches in her speech; yet, she could also be very sensitive. But, when friends of hers were asked 'What do you remember most?' the phrase 'She was such a strange lady' inevitably were the first words they said." Apparently, Miss McMenomy says, "There was some difference between what she did and what she wrote."

Miss McMenomy will be glad to hear from anyone interested in Sayers, or who would like to subscribe to *The Sayers Review* ($5 for a year's subscription). She can be reached at 3138 Sawtelle Blvd. Apt.4, Los Angeles, CA 90066.

DONALD REED
DRACULA

H E'S COME IN a number of guises, from bat, wolf, and demon to Bela Lugosi, Christopher Lee, George Hamilton, and Frank Langella. His name has struck fear into Eastern European hearts for centuries. He's based on a real character in Rumanian history. He is the count of darkness: Dracula.

Perhaps the most knowledgeable American expert on Dracula, in truth and fiction, is Los Angeles law librarian Donald Reed. He's the founder of the Count Dracula Society, the only organization devoted exclusively to the study and appreciation of the bloodthirsty count. Since its start in 1962, the society has grown to more than 500 members, including such Dracula-related notables as actors Christopher Lee and George Hamilton, and scholars Radu Florescu and Raymond McNally.

Transylvania's favorite native son has fascinated Reed most of his life. "I really can't recall how I first became interested. I suppose it was through seeing the films of Bela Lugosi, and then reading Bram Stoker's book." He got the idea for the Count Dracula Society around 1960 ("nobody else was doing it"), because he felt the great films and books on Dracula deserved recognition, but it wasn't until a couple of years later he was able to get it off the ground.

Since Reed is a self-confessed lover of films and literature, of which "Dracula has been a marvelous part," it's only fitting that the society should present awards annually to honor achievements involving Dracula in literature or the arts. Count Dracula Society awards (one-foot tall porcelain statues of Count Dracula) have gone to such notables as Christopher Lee, Bela Lugosi, Darren McGavin, and George Hamilton (honored in 1979 for his portrayal of Dracula in the spoof *Love at First Bite*, a sleeper film that earned back many times its production costs).

Though Reed admits "it's been a hard struggle," Count Dracula seems to have come into his own as a popular cultural figure. "People are always interested in the romantic, mysterious, and the supernatural," he says, in explaining the Count's attraction. "He's a symbol of immortality. Besides, people prefer to be entertained rather than taught, and the Dracula films and books are entertaining."

Stoker's *Dracula* was the "last of the great Gothic romances," says Reed. Written in 1899, it appeared at the end "of an age of reason, in which religion had declined, " says Reed. "The Gothic novel appeared to be calling people back to spiritual matters; there was a great deal of spiritual strength to be found in the book."

It is, of course, through films, that most of Dracula's popularity has been achieved. "Bela Lugosi was my favorite, because he was the first one I saw. Lugosi *was* Dracula to me. He wasn't the Dracula of the book. Christopher Lee is closer to the book's conception." Reed feels that Lee "lent dignity to the role of Dracula, and helped raise the level of his portrayal in film."

Reed has also been interested in collecting items related to the Count. "I have an extensive collection of several hundred items," he says. One of his favorites is a 1930 film lobby card, featuring an 11-by-14 inch color photograph of Bela Lugosi. The card, he adds, is worth $500.

Since 1973, however, "90 percent of my time" has been taken up with the Academy of Science Fiction, Fantasy and Horror Films. Reed founded this group of 3,000 people (most of them associated with the film industry) to pay special attention to films of the science fiction, fantasy and horror genres. The group gives awards annually for oustanding achievements in production of these films on a nationally syndicated 90-minute television show each spring.

For Reed, working with both groups is a labor of love. "These are my children," he says. "I've never gotten any financial reward for my work, except for a $400 speaker's fee from the University of Southern California for a half-hour speech on Dracula. That made me feel good, that so august a body as USC would pay me for a speech on Dracula."

Reed welcomes new members either to the Count Dracula Society or the Academy of Science Fiction, Fantasy and Horror Films. He, and the organizations, can be reached at 334 W. 54th St., Los Angeles, CA 90037.

JULIAN WOLFFE
SHERLOCK HOLMES

PERHAPS THE MOST enduring and popular of fictional detectives is the intrepid English sleuth, Sherlock Holmes. Aided by his constant companion, Dr. Watson, and armed with his infallible nose for clues, Holmes has delighted generations of mystery fans.

In the vanguard of the Holmes cult are the Baker Street Irregulars, a group of Holmes admirers from all over the world, led by Julian Wolffe, himself an accomplished and fascinating man.

Wolffe, a retired physician who lives in New York City, has been one of Sherlock Holmes' staunchest fans for decades. "I was mildly interested in him when I was a schoolboy," he recalls. "It wasn't until 1930 when the first omnibus of Holmes stories was published that my interest really caught on." He specialized in drawing maps (cartography being another of Wolffe's hobbies) based on events in Sherlock Holmes' career. His maps were brought to the attention of Edgar Smith and Christopher Morley, the two leading lights of the Baker Street Irregulars in 1941, and Wolffe has been dedicated to the organization ever since.

To Wolffe, the outstanding characteristic of the Holmes stories is "the quality of the writing. The stories had nothing complicated about them like modern mystery stories." The characterizations present "a very well-drawn picture of life. It seems to be a nicer, easier time — at least to those of us looking back at it."

"Real Holmes addicts like the stories because they give a picture of a life that isn't their own," says Wolffe. "We like all the little details. The fact that they are good detective stories is secondary."

But detective stories they are, 60 of them in all, representing the most popular work of their author, A. Conan Doyle. "Even though that's what made him all his money, Doyle never liked the Sherlock Holmes stories," says Wolffe. "He felt it made the public neglect his other books." Doyle's other works include two historical novels, *The White Company* and *Sir Nigel.* "In the latter part of his life, Doyle was interested in spiritualism and wrote extensively about it, but we pay no attention to that."

Wolffe is particularly interested in "trying to identify the characters in the stories with real people." For instance, the "Illustrious Client," in the story of the same name, is thought to be King Edward VII of England while he was still Prince of Wales, Wolffe says. Wolffe compiled a book, *The Practical Handbook of Sherlockian Heraldry*, about these characters and the real people they supposedly represent, along with heraldic emblems and information about the families.

Wolffe is "trying to collect all the items written about Sherlock Holmes over the years. Lately, there have been more than ever, so it's getting out of hand." While he never "went in for collecting first editions, I have managed to collect many books, in various languages, of the Holmes stories." Since he lives in apartment, where space is limited, "I've had to curtail my collecting activity, or there would be no room for me." Wolffe says of his fellow Irregulars, "We are the most assiduous collectors in the world."

Wolffe is the Commissionaire (President) of The Irregulars, which he says "is a very informal organization" that was founded in 1934 by Morley as a literary society devoted to the study of the Holmes stories. *The Baker Street Journal,* published under the auspicies of Fordham University Press, brings some 2,000 subscribers monthly news about Sherlock Holmes and the doings of the many "scion" societies (local chapters) of the Irregulars around the world.

The major activity of the Irregulars, aside from the *Journal,* is their annual dinner on January 6, the date Morley decided was Holmes's birthday. This celebration honors Holmes in toasts, speeches, and the reading of research papers, and attendance is "limited to Investitured Irregulars, who have received the Irregular Shilling for service and demonstrated interest over a period of years." Also by tradition, the dinner is "stag," says Wolffe. In addition, the Irregulars sponsor an annual horserace, the Silver Blaze Handicap, run at Aqueduct some time in September.

Sherlock Holmes is remembered by most people from the popular Basil Rathbone films of the 1930s and 1940s. "Very few of the films are true to the stories, but most of them are quite enjoyable," says Wolfe, adding that Rathbone "was the best Sherlock Holmes ever."

The sleuth's popularity shows no sign of diminishing. Doyle tried to kill the hero off in the 1894 story "The Final Problem," but the outrage of his fans forced the author to resurrect Holmes and continue with his exploits in further stories. What's more, "new writings by Dr. Watson are turning up all the time these days," says Wolffe. One gratifying note about all this popularity, from Wolffe's view, is that it means "the Baker Street Irregulars organizaton isn't going to die, even though a lot of the old timers are gone already."

Wolffe will be glad to answer questions about Holmes or the Baker Street Irregulars, adding,"You can't make my mail much heavier than it already is." He can be contacted at 33 Riverside Dr., Apt. 14C, New York, NY 10023.

HISTORY

ROBERT ALOTTA
PHILADELPHIA HISTORY

WHEN ROBERT ALOTTA was a schoolboy, he hated history. "I did anything I could to avoid taking the subject," he said.

But today, at age 43, history is the abiding interest in his life. Alotta has become an expert on the history of the Philadelphia area, particularly Old Fort Mifflin, an important Revolutionary War landmark.

Now the director of public information for Philadephia's Housing Authority, Alotta's interest in history developed when he started working for The Philadelphia Inquirer in 1959. "I became a bore on the subject of how history should be presented," Alotta said. Finally, in 1962, "I was told to put my money where my mouth was." He began writing vignettes of little-known episodes in Philadelphia history for the paper.

As his interest grew and his vignettes became full-scale magazine articles, Alotta became involved in the restoration of Old Fort Mifflin. He was instrumental in developing a living history program for young people and a military re-enactment group, while continuing to write on the subject. "As a result," he said, "I became a recognized historical authority on the fortification."

Alotta's specialty is digging out obscure incidents from history and writing about them. One such incident, the execution under strange circumstances of a Pennsylvania-Dutch soldier in the Union Army during the Civil War, became a critically acclaimed book, *Stop the Evil*, which was published in 1978.

"My main goal is to write history in an easy-to-understand manner and make it more comprehensible to students," Alotta says. He writes a weekly column on local history for *The Philadelphia Daily News*, and has published many pamphlets and books.

Alotta is encouraging to beginners. "I wish that more young people would begin to research the history of their nation or their community. It is only by studying the past that we will be able to avoid future errors." But he cautions that before one can become a true historian, "not one who has read just the 'right' books," the individual must be willing to delve into original documents, diaries and old newspapers, "and throw away many preconceived notions. From my standpoint," he says, "my mind wasn't cluttered with the erudite opinions of those who rewrote the statements of others. I was able to discover the past by studying firsthand accounts, judging them and then presenting them for the reader's decision."

His writing style has been compared to novelization, but with the all-important difference that "my statements are backed up with fact."

Alotta is willing to counsel novice history writers, and will gladly offer advice or information. He can be contacted at 315 S. 12th St., Philadelphia, PA 19107.

JOHN BAEDER
DINERS

THEIR NAMES TELL only part of the story: Curley's, Stella's , Alice and the Hat, the Tick Tock, the Day and Night — diners all, and all a chunk of Americana that's as familiar (and as taken for granted) as apple pie, the Fourth of July, or baseball.

But, for John Baeder diners are more than the soon-to-be-forgotten curios of the days before fast food joints and urban decay. "I am moved by them," he says. "They're the equivalent in our society of the temples of ancient civilizations."

To put it simply: Baeder loves diners, and he's been preserving them in a unique way: by painting their portraits, an artistic interest that began as a hobby and has become a full-time occupation.

Baeder, 41, of New York City, traces his love back to his Southern childhood. He spent some of his happiest hours chomping on "drippy hamburgers" and chocolate cream pie at the Majestic Diner in his native Atlanta. It was there, for the first time, that he observed and began to appreciate the charm of the diner: its food, its decor, its ambience, the customers. Even "the choreography of the short-order cook" took on meaning.

It was this love affair with the Majestic, Baeder thinks, that led him in 1968 to begin collecting postcards of diners, gas stations, tourist cabins, and other gems of roadside architecture. "I became fascinated with the postcards," he says, and he studied them in minute detail. "After a while, I determined to paint them." His first thought was to "do a painting of the postcard, and then photographically reduce the painting back down to a postcard size."

He also began "going out every weekend taking photographs" to supply new subjects for his paintings, which after a period of recreating in postcard size, he decided to increase the size to 8-by-10-inches.

"Most of the pictures I took were of diners, and I found that I was loving them more and more." Baeder quit his job as an art director at a New York advertising agency in 1972 and turned to painting full time. By the end of 1973, he was painting diners exclusively.

His paintings have sold in New York art galleries for as much as $10,000. *Diners*, a book containing reproductions of 105 of his paintings, as well as a commentary on his development as an artist and diner fanatic, was published by Harry Abrams, Inc., in 1978. "Writing the book got me more involved in the whole concept of diners," says Baeder. "It led to a deep kind of passion."

When he's researching diners, he feels "like an archaeologist on a dig. It's the whole nature of the work, really the best part; coming back and doing the painting is almost secondary."

Diners originated in 1872, Baeder says. A man from Providence, Rhode Island, Walter Scott, started serving food from a converted horse-drawn freight wagon. This innovation, called the "lunch wagon," was refined along the way, and eventually included the use of old trolley cars instead of wagons, until Charlie Gemme, head of The Worcester Lunch Car Company for 55 years, created the "classic" diner, which resembled a railroad dining car. Of the 12 major diner maufacturers, only five are still in existence. "But," says Baeder, "they no longer manufacture the quintessential diners that my pictures portray."

Queried as to the popularity of his diner paintings, Baeder says, "I can't keep the gallery supplied with enough art to sell. There's a great deal of interest, apparently." Baeder has branched out from only painting diners to doing etchings and bronze sculptures of them, as well.

Another Baeder project in the works is a book entitled *Gas, Food and Lodging*, which Baeder describes as "a trip around the country by postcards." It's a serious study of diners, gas stations, and tourist cabins, and other pieces of roadside architecture as portrayed on picture postcards, which Baeder sees as "important bits of folk art."

Baeder, who "likes to let the diners find me," urges anyone who knows of a diner to write to him and let him know about it. His address is PO Box 5174, FDR Station, New York, NY 10022.

JESS BARROW
NAVAL AVIATION

AVIATION HAS BEEN in Jess Barrow's blood ever since he took his first plane ride at age 10. By the time he was 16, he was working at the old Stickney Airport in Toledo, Ohio. He sold tickets, washed airplanes, and did other odd jobs, in exchange for flying lessons.

Today, aviation is still in the forefront of the 61-year-old engineer's life, for he has become a leading authority on the history of the U. S. Navy, Marine Corps, and Coast Guard adventures in flight.

In addition to his youthful interest in flying, Barrow served as an engineering officer in Naval Intelligence in the Pacific in World War II, compiling flight and performance data on enemy aircraft. After the war, he had a chance to exercise his commercial pilot's license when he worked as chief pilot for a carburetor manufacturing firm.

But it has been the history of aviation that has captured Barrow's most profound interest over the years. "I became a history buff in high school," he says, "and started dabbling with aviation history then." He received encouragement from his parents and his grandfather "who were also interested in history and passed their enthusiasm on to me."

Over the years, Barrow has specialized in Navy, Marine, and Coast Guard aviation from 1918-41. Lately, however, the focus of much of Barrow's enthusiasm and research has been on the Fighting Squadron Nine, a special Marine Corps flying unit. This famous exhibition unit, about which surprisingly little has been written, Barrow says, represented the major attempt by the Marine Corps in the years prior to World War II to obtain funding from the Congress to develop their aviation program. The squadron was formed in 1925, and continued until 1965, when it was disbanded.

According to Barrow, Fighting Squadron Nine was just another fighter group until the early 1930s, when the Marine Corps "decided to take their case for an aviation program to the public." So, the full squadron of 18 planes became, like today's "Blue Angels," a crack exhibition flying unit that performed at air shows and other public events all over the country.

In its heyday, in the 1930s, the squadron included such pilots as "Pappy" Boyington, "Sandy" Sanderson, Roy Geiger, "Rusty" Rowell, and "Tex" Rogers. Flying Boeing F4BF single-seat biplanes, Fighting Squadron Nine made a name for itself in aviation, and eventually, helped the Marine Corps obtain the financing needed for an all-out aviation program, Barrow says.

The most interesting aspect of this research, he says, is how the squadron was promoted and "how the Marines, in order to get aviators, trained a lot of their own men." That was, strictly speaking, illegal at the time, since they had no official training program, Barrow says.

Nonetheless, the Marines trained pilots at their base at Quantico, Virginia, until Congress finally approved their aviation program. An interesting sidelight, Barrow says, was his discovery in the early 1930s the Marine Corps graduated two fully-qualified pilots who had only the rank of private. This, of course, is unusual because pilots were (and still are) traditionally officers. Barrow says he was never able to find an official explanation of why this happened and "I'll be darned if I have any idea. I've never heard of that before or since."

Over the 10 years that Barrow spent researching Fighting Squadron Nine, he unearthed enough material for two books. One, on the squadron, was published in 1980 by Tab Books.

In addition, Barrow has one of the top three collections of Navy, Marine, and Coast Guard aviation photographs in existence. He has some 15,000 negatives and pictures of all kinds, as well as a comprehensive library of aviation history publications and other items of military memorabilia.

Barrow feels that the time to dig out information is growing short. It is essential, he says, that more people become involved in the study and chronicling of recent events. Now is the time to record aviation history by "talking with the old-timers. They are the ones that made the history. And it is important we do it soon — our early pioneers are passing away fast."

"I just love to do it," he says. "Like a college professor, I do my research for the prestige or the good, not money. If I did it for money, I'd starve to death."

"To the novice aviation historian," Barrow advises, "First define the areas of aviation history that interest you most—then pursue them with vigor." A good place for the early aviation historian to begin his research, says Barrow, is with the National Archives in Washington, D.C. Visiting aviation museums around the country and subscribing to the many aviation history periodicals are also helpful.

Barrow will be glad to assist any would-be aviation historians, particularly those interested in naval aviation, in getting started. Contact him at 24313 Hanover St., Dearborn Heights, MI 48125.

FRED & BETTY BEALS
OLD BUILDINGS & BRIDGES

SINCE 1968, FRED and Betty Beals have visited over 600 covered bridges and 300 mills in 40 states and Canada. Their objective: preservation.

The Beals, from Mishawaka, Indiana, have become experts in the old mills and covered bridges that dot the North American continent. And they are active in several movements to preserve the buildings.

Fred, a production electrician at Wheelabrator-Frye, Inc., has been the assistant editor of *Old Mill News* since 1977. This monthly publication of the Society for the Preservation of Old Mills, has been at the forefront of the preservation movement.

How did the Beals come to be interested in old mills and covered bridges? "About 1968," says Beals, "a foreman at the plant, who was an artist, was always talking about visiting an old mill in central Indiana that had a covered bridge near it. He finally talked us into coming down there over Thanksgiving weekend to see it.

"We couldn't imagine what anybody could see in an old mill and a covered bridge, but we went along, anyway. Well, once we saw the mill and the bridge, we knew."

Since then, the Beals have visited numerous mills and covered bridges to study their architecture, and to photograph them. "We have about 3,000 photos of mills and covered bridges," he says. Covered bridges and mills were often built together, Beals explains. Usually, the miller would have the covered bridge built to get to and from the mill.

According to Beals, there are only 1,000 to 1,500 mills left standing, and the number of operating mills is far fewer. "The big milling companies have pretty much taken care of that, " he says. Mills are most prevalent in the East and Midwest, with the highest concentration in Pennsylvania and Virginia, Beals says. "Unfortunately, I've never been to Virginia, but I have a list of 350 mills there." He adds that on a recent trip to the West "we found hardly any."

"I belong to eight different societies relating to old mills and covered bridges," says Beals, "and we try to impress on local communities and the owners of these structures the importance of keeping them intact."

Mills are different from bridges, Beals says, because they're all privately owned. "A lot of the buildings haven't been used for 10 to 40 years, and the owners don't have an interest in spending the money to preserve them — and I'm not sure I blame them." Therefore, he feels it's important to have photographic records, at the very least, of what the mill building looks like, inside and out.

As might be expected, the Beals have a favorite mill: Bonneyville, in Bristol, Indiana, owned by a county parks and recreation department. This 1832 flour mill, in a three-level wood frame building, "has been carefully restored so you can understand what the milling business was all about," he says. There's a miller on the premises to provide information, and he grinds "the best buckwheat flour you can imagine." The watermill is powered by "the only horizontal turbine in Indiana," he adds.

The Beals are mainly interested in mills that are powered by water. "Electricity is too modern for us,"says Fred.

The era of the mill extended from the early 1800s until about the turn of the century. "Since then," says Beals, "there haven't been too many of the picturesque type built." With the recent nostalgia craze, some entrepreneurs are building reproductions of old mills as tourist attractions. One such development is at the Squire Boone Cavern, Harrison, Indiana, where a replica of a mill that stood on the site 125 years ago is being built.

The Beals feel it is important to remember that "this era of the 19th century, when so many of these mills were constructed, was a period of genius. The workmanship was something that's just not duplicated today" and it's important to preserve as many examples of their accomplishments as possible.

"The milling industry in this country was really the beginning of the American Industrial Revolution," says Beals. "If a lot of the big conglomerates of today wanted to pinpoint their beginnings, it would be a little wooden shack on a riverbank, with a mill operated by water."

Beals is somewhat optimistic about the return of water as an aid in producing energy. There are many small dams around the country, he says, with enough water power to produce electricity. "In five or ten years, we're going to find an awful lot of electricity generated from dams."

The Beals advise persons interested in either old mills or covered bridges to get in touch with the societies devoted to their preservation: the Society for the Preservation of Old Mills, 232 Roslyn Ave., Glenside, PA 19038; the National Society for the Preservation of Covered Bridges, 17 Beaumont St., Dorchester, MA 02124.

The Beals can be contacted at 123 N. Wenger, Mishawaka, IN 46544.

CUESTA RAY BENBERRY

QUILT HISTORY

QUILTING HAS BEEN an enduring, uniquely American craft throughout our history. For several hundred years, particularly in the mountainous regions of the South, and the rural areas of the Midwest and West, quilts were (and still are) important heirlooms, treasured and passed lovingly from one generation to another as a continual reminder of the heritage of the family.

Cuesta Ray Benberry, like many Americans, has a family tradition that includes quilts. Visits to her mother-in-law in rural western Kentucky ("where quiltmaking is a way of life," she says) in the 1950s sparked her interest in quilts. Her mother-in-law "marked events in our lives with the gift of a hand-made quilt," Mrs. Benberry recalls. "A 'Lone Star' for our wedding, a 'WPA Tulip' for our first anniversary, a 'schoolhouse' quilt for our son's first birthday. So, I felt the need to know something of this subject."

She first studied quilt patterns as a large body of folk designs. Then she began to be interested in the larger topic of quilt history and lore. However, what Mrs. Benberry found in her search for information was that there was a dearth of historical material about the art. Even though quilting in America dates from the Colonial period to the present day, "the majority of the quilt books published have been manuals for quilt construction or pattern books," she says. "So, the field of quilting history is wide open for research and investigation."

She plunged into the study, and soon found her primary interest to be in the relationship between American black women and quiltmaking. It is, says Mrs. Benberry, a long and interesting one. She has been particularly fascinated by the anti-slavery needlework fairs held in the Philadelphia, Pennsylvania area, beginning in 1832. At these fairs, she says, white women and black women got together to make quilts, as well as to display and sell quilts to raise money for the abolitionist cause.

Mrs. Benberry has found "so many fascinating stories" in her research that she is hard-pressed to single one out as most interesting. She does tell of a family from Harper's Ferry, Virginia, who, when the Emancipation Proclamation was issued, freed all their slaves, except for one little orphan girl. This girl was adopted by the family, and they all moved to Kansas (a free state). The family "treated her as a daughter, and when the children grew up, the black daughter made a quilt for her white sister's wedding in 1870." Mrs. Benberry has seen that quilt, a "lone star" design (a single star of Bethlehem on a plain background) and says it's still beautiful, despite its age. "That woman was a magnificent quilter," she adds.

Mrs. Benberry has written many articles for publications in the field. She has had her work published in *Quilter's Journal*, *Quilter's Newsletter*, and *Canada Quilt*. In addition, she researched and wrote about old needlework publications in the newsletter of Pittsburgh's Center for the History of American Needlework. Amidst all of her research and her work as a public school reading specialist, she's found time to lecture on quilt history to groups in the St. Louis area, where she lives. She also participated in a national quilting symposium held in Columbia, Missouri, in 1980, discussing her research on black women and quilts.

Since there is so much about American quilt history that is waiting to be discovered, Mrs. Benberry encourages newcomers to enter the field. She advises novices to first study old quilts in museums and private collections, to gain a basic understanding of the design elements involved. It is important to "have full knowledge of quilt patterns as to date, area of origin, and designer, if possible," she says.

Among her other suggestions: interview aged, life-long quiltmakers, whose fund of knowledge and lore "will prove invaluable"; and investigate periodicals from the 19th and early 20th centuries, "especially farm magazines, which are fruitful sources of quilt information." Frequently, she says, it will be necessary (and desirable) to study as many original documents, such as diaries, bills of sale, etc., as are available.

Mrs. Benberry stands ready to help the novice researcher, and to exchange information with colleagues in the study of this fascinating piece of Americana. She can be contacted at 5150 Terry Ave., St. Louis, MO 63115.

BARBARA BROWN
GENEALOGY

ALEX HALEY'S bestselling *Roots* (and the highly popular TV miniseries) sparked a great deal of interest in searching for one's ancestors. For some people, like Barbara Brown, looking for ancestors has become a full-time pursuit. Mrs. Brown's interest in genealogy is not of such recent vintage, but the public's current thirst for knowledge has helped turn her hobby into a successful career in genealogical research.

She began in 1957, when her mother offered to pay for her application to the Daughters of the American Revolution if she would research her mother's ancestry and "join on her line." Mrs. Brown did that, and while she was at it, looked into her father's family background, too. She made an interesting discovery. "My Dad's ancestry proved to be more illustrious, with two Mayflower lines," she recalls. She became a DAR member, and continued with her research. In 1966, she took a part-time job in the genealogy section of the library in Pueblo, Colorado, where she lived at the time, to "look after books donated by local DARs over the years." This further sparked her interest, and intensified her study.

Mrs. Brown turned to genealogy as a career when she was forced to stop teaching school due to a throat condition which impaired her speech. "I enjoyed the research aspect, and I wanted something to do where I wouldn't have to do a lot of talking," she says. Though she is mostly self-taught ("you really have to learn by experience"), Mrs. Brown did graduate in 1968 from the Genealogical Institute, sponsored by the National Archives, the American University, and the State of Maryland. She also studied in Salt Lake City, Utah, at the World Conference on Records.

While Mrs. Brown "hasn't found any horse-thieves — yet" on her family tree, she has made some gratifying discoveries. "When I was a small child, my great-aunt gave me a sampler that my mother's grandmother had made," Mrs. Brown says. "I have had it ever since, and I wanted to find out more about the grandmother's family." After searching through various records, Mrs. Brown discovered that the family of Pennsylvania Quakers her great-grandmother belonged to was related to the Lippincott publishing family.

Mrs. Brown was able to find original material, in manuscript, that proved the connection. "It's difficult to make it sound as exciting as it was to me," she says, emphasizing that an original manuscript is the most desirable source material for confirming connections, but is often the most difficult to find.

Searching for one's family background can be a lot of fun, Mrs. Brown says. And a lot of work. But Mrs. Brown is enthusiastic about genealogy as a rewarding interest for anyone, young or old. The best way to start, says Mrs. Brown, is to "get all the information you can by yourself from home sources. Write down your relatives, and your spouse's relatives, as far back as possible.

"Then, talk with the oldest people in the family. Have them reminisce." The best way of preserving these conversations is with a tape recorder, because "the way in which the old people express themselves, and their voices, as well as the content of what they are saying, are important."

Once the researcher has exhausted all the living family sources, Mrs. Brown says, the next step is to look in government records, old letters, family Bibles, obituaries, probate records, school records, and so forth.

Surprisingly, Mrs. Brown says, the genealogical researcher may have less difficulty obtaining information from farther back in history. "Much recent history is hard to come by," she says, "because since 1900 many government and other institutional records have not been opened to the public." To help the novice genealogist, Mrs. Brown has prepared a mimeographed list of do's and don'ts, including such helpful hints as "Don't believe everything you see in print. Do believe what can be documented from reliable sources," and "Don't get upset if you find a wormy apple on your family tree. Do have a sense of humor and be willing to accept people for what they are or were."

With an estimated 40.5 million people involved worldwide in some form of family history research, Mrs. Brown says it should not be too difficult to find an experienced genealogist to counsel the beginner. The National Genealogical Society, and other such groups have local branches that researchers can join. "I would certainly advise people to join a local society," Mrs. Brown says. "There are many opportunities for sharing information and learning the science of genealogy."

Genealogy "if it is done properly, should be a scientific undertaking," she says. "You are after information that would stand up in a court of law." Naturally, such unimpeachable facts aren't always possible to obtain, she adds, so the researcher must search for the best, most reliable information possible.

Research, for Mrs. Brown, "is like a detective hunt or trying to put together pieces of a puzzle that sometimes don't fit. Since I'm a precise person, I like the detail it engenders. It's just challenging."

Mrs. Brown is happy to give advice and counsel to genealogists, amateur and professional alike. She may be contacted at 6583 S. Downing St., Littleton, CO 80121.

ELIZABETH BROWNELL
SOUTH ARIZONA HISTORY

WHEN ELIZABETH Brownell moved to Tubac, Arizona, she "thought it would be interesting to know something about the place I lived in."

Her research has led to a fascination with the history not only of Tubac, but of the entire surrounding region, as well as the lawmen and outlaws of the Old West. She has become a valuable resource for other historians of southern Arizona.

Dr. Brownell (she received her doctorate in sociology from Charles University in Prague), 79, has been spending the winter months in Tubac since her retirement from the Department of Defense in 1965. She summers near Jackson Hole, Wyoming, and says she's also become quite an expert in the history of that town and its surrounding Teton County.

"I'm not a professional historian," she says, modestly. Nonetheless, she has managed to compile an astounding 10,000-card file on Southern Arizona history (especially Tubac history), along with files on 2,000 Old West outlaws and 2,000 lawmen.

Her home in Tubac (pronounced "two-bake, meaning place of water or something like that," she says) is just a few yards from the site of the historic presidio built by the Spaniards in 1753 to protect the nearby mission of Father Kino.

"The fascinating thing about Tubac," says Dr. Brownell,"is that it goes back 10,000 or 20,000 years archeologically." She has found pre-historic shards of pottery near her house, as have many other people around town, she says.

The Spaniards came to Tubac in 1691. It was the site of a Jesuit mission until 1767, when "the Jesuits were expelled in favor of the Franciscans," says Dr. Brownell.

"Tubac's chief claim to fame," says Dr. Brownell, "is that it was the starting point, in 1775, of Juan de Anza's famous trek that led to the founding of San Francisco in 1776." In fact, during Bicentennial celebrations, Dr. Brownell was chairman of a group that "rode all across Arizona and up to San Francisco, recreating this epic journey." She didn't go along on that 1975 jaunt, "but it was a great event."

After the departure of de Anza, Tubac had a checkered history. Attacked by the Apaches, it was abandoned by the Spaniards after the Mexican War of Independence in 1821. Tubac, like the rest of Arizona, became part of the United States under the Gadsden Purchase of 1853.

"It was a very exciting place between 1856 and 1861," Dr. Brownell says. The town was growing and prospering. The first newspaper in Arizona was published in Tubac, beginning March 3, 1859, and a man named Charles Poston arrived on the scene to begin exploiting the considerable natural resources of the area.

With the start of the Civil War, Dr. Brownell says, "All military posts were withdrawn, and there was no more protection. Once again, Tubac was abandoned."

Gradual redevelopment started in the 1880s, and today, Tubac is a lively artists colony, with some 200 year-round residents, and an annual two-week festival of the arts that draws thousands of visitors each year.

Dr. Brownell relies heavily on the research facilities of the Arizona State Historical Society and the University of Arizona Library in Tucson, some 40 miles north of Tubac. "It's pretty hard to find just where the archives of Tubac are," she says. Originally, it was part of Pima County, but since 1899 is part of Santa Cruz County. Some of the material inevitably got lost in the shuffle.

Dr. Brownell says she has had to rely a lot on secondary sources (newspaper accounts, other history books) in doing her research, as there isn't a great deal of original material available. She did, however, make an exciting find one day in the Arizona Historical Society's archives.

"It was just luck that I came across it," says Dr. Brownell. What she found was a collection of personal letters written by one John Smith to his brother and sister back in Ohio. Smith, Dr. Brownell discovered, lived in Tubac in the 1870s, where he was "a miner, cattleman, legislator and Indian fighter" among other things. His highly detailed letters of everyday activities "are a wonderfully rich source of original information," says Dr. Brownell.

That's what historic research is all about for Dr. Brownell: searching relentlessly for what she wants and never giving up. She recommends novice historians haunt libraries and historical societies, as well as local government offices, to try to get material. " Even old telephone or city directories can have a lot to tell you."

As a member of a local historical society, Dr. Brownell is also becoming involved in oral history, recording the legends, impressions, and memories of the Mexican families who live in Tubac. "Some of them have been here for five or six generations," she says, "and the old-timers have many wonderful stories to tell."

Dr. Brownell thinks she'd like to write a book on the history of the area. She has "written little articles on the area as background," she says. "I'm very green at it, but starting to become more adept."

Historical research is so satisfying to Dr. Brownell because of the excitement of sleuthing and discovery. "I really love finding clues and trailing them," she says. There's the additional satisfaction "of being able to present a picture of what happened here, to educate the public on the rich heritage of our area."

Dr. Brownell will gladly answer queries, addressed to her at PO Box 1204, Tubac, AZ 85640.

ERRETT CALLAHAN
PRIMITIVE TECHNOLOGY

SOME MIGHT CALL HIM a Stone Age man. Others might think it odd that a white man is teaching Indians how to make primitive tools, weapons, and pots.

But for Errett Callahan, what's called the "primitive technology" of prehistoric Indians in North America, lives on in the skillful work he does as part of a unique restoration project in Virginia.

Callahan's prime interest is "flintknapping," the making of tools using only the methods and materials available to primitive man. After graduating from high school in 1956, he spent the summer working at Yellowstone National Park, surrounded by a bountiful supply of obsidian, elk horn, and other natural material. "I had a lot of time to recycle the glass and obsidian into more useful objects," he says, and he began working the stones into primitive tools.

It was exhausting, time-consuming work. "I broke a lot of stones," he recalls. Flintknapping is a reduction process, the wearing down of one stone with another.

"It's always a challenge," Callahan says, "because there's a possibility you could snap the stone in half. You're matching wits with the stone." Among the tools made through this method were choppers, axes, knives, and arrowpoints.

Interest in primitive technology led Callahan to advanced degrees in anthropology and archeology from Catholic University in Washington, D. C. He taught at Virginia Commonwealth University in Richmond from 1971 to 1977, where many of his courses dealt with the techniques of so-called "primitive technology."

In 1976, Callahan tackled his most challenging project. At the request of the Pamunkey Indian tribe in nearby King William, Virginia, he began planning the reconstruction of "a totally authentic, pre-contact [with white men] Indian village." For Callahan, the project "brought together a lifetime of learning in primitive technology, and paved the way for teaching the same to native Americans and students of material culture on a broad scale."

Construction on the village began in 1977. What Callahan is re-creating is a 16th century community of the Powhatan Indian Confederacy, a highly organized Indian nation that had important influence on white American history, he says. For instance, Captain John Smith was welcomed by Powhatans when he arrived in the New World.

Upon completion, the village will consist of four to six houses, and other buildings, all built with only the tools and materials that would have been available to the Indians of the time. An interesting aspect to the reconstruction project, Callahan says, is that "We're trying to help the Pamunkey people find their natural technological roots." To this end, members of the tribe are learning how to re-create old pottery patterns and make well-made pottery once again. Traditionally, the Pamunkey were noted for their fine pottery, but in the modern era "they were just making tourist stuff," Callahan says.

There are between 800 and 1,000 Pamunkeys around the country, many in Pennsylvania, and about 50 on the reservation where Callahan is working. "The tribe hopes the project will attract young Pamunkey back to the reservation," he says.

Callahan works on the construction of the village primarily by himself, though an archeological assistant and students from Catholic University do assist him on occasion. In addition, "we are booked solid" with stud nt groups who spend weekends visiting the site and offering some help in the work that needs to be done, says Callahan.

He feels the project is important because it emphasizes the carrying capacity of the environment and "man's place in nature. The Pamunkeys were just about an ideal fit with their environment. They were living close to the capacity of the land without destroying it." Perhaps, he says, this is "knowledge we can use somewhere in our contemporary life."

For the person interested in exploring flintknapping and other primitive technologies, Callahan emphasizes that care and accuracy are vital qualities to possess, or success in such an endeavor isn't possible. "Be very sensitive about not disturbing existing archeological sites in any way," he says. "Gather lithic material [stones] from stream beds carefully, and keep records and samples of all areas where you create potential archeological imbalance."

"No matter how proficient you think you've become" at utilizing the techniques of primitive technology, Callahan says, "never attempt to pass off your work as authentic, even in jest. Distorting the archeological record of the Native American is a matter they, and professional archaeologists, take very seriously." Anyway, he adds, "Analysts will be able to tell your work is a fraud."

For further information, Callahan suggests reading *Flintknapper's Exchange*, a publication he co-edits. Subscriptions are $6 for three issues, and may be obtained from 1701 Catron SE, Albuquerque, NM 87123.

Callahan will be happy to answer queries about primitive technology, in general, or the Pamunkey project, in particular. He may be contacted in care of 3412 Plymouth Pl., Lynchburg, VA 24503.

ALEXANDER COOK
GREAT LAKES HISTORY

The MOST THRILLING inland waterways in the world border the United States and Canada: the Great Lakes. Each one — Erie, Michigan, Huron, Superior, and Ontario — possesses a personality all its own, and their development has been an essential ingredient in the development of North America.

Alexander Cook's life has always been tied to the Great Lakes. As a youngster growing up in St. Joseph, Michigan, Cook learned to sail on Lake Michigan. "I became fascinated by ships and the men who captained and sailed them," he says. He had a great deal of contact with the old ship captains who came to St. Joe in their retirement. Also, "whenever we heard the horn of a steamer, we'd run down to the waterfront" to watch, he says. Thus began a lifelong interest which today has brought him recognition as an expert in the history of the Great Lakes.

Though his full-time job is that of a special art teacher for Cleveland's Public Schools, Cook is a freelance artist and writer who is also curator (since 1978) of the Great Lakes Historical Society Museum at Vermilion, Ohio.

Marine art, particularly ship portraiture, is Cook's specialty within Great Lakes history. Like their counterparts on the Eastern seaboard, the Great Lakes ship painters were "itinerant, primitivist artists who made their living doing pictures of vessels for their owners. Not much is known about these artists," Cook says, "because they were considered kind of a shirtsleeve, commercial business, not fine art, but the product they produced was charming."

The leading artists of Great Lakes shipping were probably Vincent D. Nickerson, Charles W. Norton, Howard F. Sprague, and Seth Arca Whipple. The artists were active in the latter part of the 19th century, and covered all the Great Lakes in their works.

Most of the painters, except for Sprague, had no formal art training, Cook says. Nonetheless, the pictures they have created are today "highly collectible" examples of American folk art, coveted by museums and private collectors alike.

According to Cook, Nickerson was probably the most prolific of the artists. "I'm quite fond of his work," he says. "He was a very good 'primitive'-type painter." Many of the paintings by Nickerson and the other artists, which were all done on commission, grace the walls of steamship company offices in Cleveland and other important Great Lakes ports.

The art of the Great Lakes marine artists is scarce," says Cook. "It's very expensive if you can find it. Most pieces are in museums or private collections, and are likely to stay there." Nonetheless, he does own a couple of ship portraits by Great Lakes artists.

A major activity for Cook has been his connection with the Great Lakes Historical Society, and the operation of its museum, 40 miles from Cleveland. Cook became involved in the organization when he helped them do some public relations work in the 1950s. The society, begun in 1944, now has more than 3,000 members all over the Great Lakes region — and beyond. The museum itself has been operating since 1953, and is a unique collection of memorabilia and art relating to shipping and life in the Great Lakes region.

"I'm always available to help the museum," he says. "I wear many hats, and provide whatever talent I have in various areas" to the volunteer position of curator. A business manager operates the museum, which is open mainly during the summer. "I haven't been giving it as much time as I would like to," he says of his museum work. "Maybe one week I'll spend an hour at it, the next week, full-time. I give time as it's needed."

One of Cook's special accomplishments was the creation of a mural for the museum in 1969. The 16-foot-wide by 8-foot-high mural commemorates 100 years of Great Lakes shipping, depicting various vessels that were in use on the Lakes during the period 1869 to 1969.

"Iron ore trade is what really made Great Lakes shipping," says Cook. In 1855, the first load of iron ore was shipped across the lakes on the brigantine schooner *Columbia*. In addition, there was a hefty passenger trade, when the immigrants came from Europe and traveled west before the coming of the railroads.

Why his continued interest in Great Lakes history? Says Cook, "I once told an old captain of my acquaintance that there's only one thing I'm concerned about in the next life. If there are no boats or trains, the next life won't be much fun, and he agreed with me."

Cook feels that there is a "sudden consciousness that something has to be done to preserve this part of our heritage." Thus, there is increased interest in the work of the Great Lakes Historical Society, and other groups. "So much is gone, even in recent years," he says, although there are some of the "old style steamships from 60 or 70 years ago that are still running. Since the Great Lakes are freshwater, the hulls don't corrode."

Cook will be happy to give further information on Great Lakes history, marine art, or the Great Lakes Historical Society. He can be contacted in care of the society, 480 Main St., Vermilion, OH 44089.

ISAAC DAVIS
MAINE TOWN HISTORIES

WHEN ISAAC DAVIS set out to write the history of his hometown, he had no idea he would eventually become an expert on the histories of the other 414 towns in the state of Maine.

Davis is a Gardiner, Maine, high school history teacher and the part-time proprietor, since 1975, of Bunkhouse Books, a seasonal bookstore that specializes in books about Maine, and especially in the town histories its owner loves.

Davis's interest began with his master's thesis. He was a student at the University of Maine in 1961 when he wrote *The History of Solon, Maine*, which was his hometown. "A lot of people read it and asked me why I didn't publish it," he says. He did, and sold some 500 copies in the first year. "I discovered that most people who were buying the book didn't have any direct connection to Solon, they were just interested in the history," he says.

"So I became intrigued with the collectibility of state town histories." He began collecting the classic history volumes of the towns and counties of Maine, and sold them in his bookshop. "I don't keep a personal collection, myself," he says. "I decided when I started that I would sell everything if I had the opportunity." But that fact doesn't keep Davis from being extremely knowledgeable about the books, and the history they record.

Since he began his bookstore, Davis has actively pursued his interest in acquiring town histories, "I've had over 300 Maine town histories come through my shop, and there are only 415 towns in the state," he says.

The oldest history he carries is really a chronicle of the entire state, *Sullivan's History of Maine*, which Davis says was published in 1795. Most of the town histories, however, date from the "late 1800s. The '80s and '90s seemed to be the era when so many of the towns had their histories written."

Davis has obtained his town histories in a variety of ways. "The really good old ones have to be purchased at auctions," he says. He does find them in other old bookstores, and sometimes purchases duplicates from the collections of his customers. "They're much more difficult to find every day," he says, noting that a recent paperback edition of a town history can go for $6 or $7, while an old volume commands as much as $200. Several of the Maine town histories are exceedingly rare, he says, and every collector is on the lookout for those: Bethel, Maine; Mt. Mica, Maine, and *North's History of Augusta, Maine.*

The reason for the rarity, Davis says, is that the town histories were frequently published in such small numbers. "Sometimes they printed 500 copies, but before all the books were distributed, the printer burned down, so there would be actually only 200 or so in circulation. Then, it's even more of a limited edition."

By studying the town histories, as Davis has, it is possible to see a great change in the way these books are written. "It used to be that one person would do all the researching and writing," he says. "Now everything is done by committee: one lady takes care of the churches, one does the schools, and so forth. You're seeing cooperative efforts. But, they might be just as good as the old ones."

Davis is especially drawn to the vintage town histories. His particular favorites are *North's History of Augusta, Maine* or "any of the histories by William Lapham. He did several towns, and the books are well-researched and loaded with information."

"There's an awful lot of family history in most of these stories," says Davis, explaining their appeal to the book-buying public. Increasing interest in finding one's roots has made the Maine town histories (as well as local history books everywhere, Davis says) much sought-after as research tools.

Someday ("it's my first project after retirement"), Davis plans to compile and publish a complete bibliography of all Maine county and town histories, listing the latest selling prices, auction prices, each book's scarcity, and so forth.

For now, Davis is happy to give advice to people interested in collecting Maine town histories, or to advise them on how they might obtain histories in their localites. He can be contacted at Route 5A, Gardiner, ME 04345.

THOMAS DIXON
C&O RAILROAD

FEW AMERICANS can trace their roots back to George Washington — but Chessie can.

Chessie (as the venerable Chesapeake & Ohio Railroad is known to her admirers) does trace her routes to our first President. Many of the railroad's earliest lines follow canals and wagon roads planned by Washington to ease travel between the Atlantic seaboard and the Midwest.

At her peak, Chessie was one of the nation's most active and profitable rail lines, stretching 5,100 miles east-to-west through eight states, the District of Columbia, and Canada. The C&O was a line of crack passenger trains, heavy freight schedules, and enough traditions and characters to fill a railroad history book.

Today, virtually all of the C&O's great trains have vanished into Amtrak anonymity. But one of Chessie's staunchest boosters isn't about to let those wonderful memories fade. Thomas Dixon, president of the Chesapeake & Ohio Historical Society, Inc., leads a group of over 1,000 people from 46 states in an increasingly successful effort to preserve the railroad's history.

In 1966, Dixon, a 32-year-old career Army officer, stationed at Ft. Belvoir,

Virginia, discovered his interest in railroads, and the C&O in particular, while at work on a history of his hometown, Alderson, West Virginia. "Since Alderson is on the C&O tracks," Dixon says, "the history of the railroad was as much a part of the history of the town as anything else. And I became fascinated with it."

Since then, he's traveled over most of the system, riding the last C&O passenger trains before they were discontinued, and has taken thousands of photos of the operations, equipment, buildings and people that make up the railroad.

Dixon started the C&O Historical Society in 1968. One of its chief projects is a monthly journal, that has grown from four mimeographed pages into a publication the size of a weekly newsmagazine (and sometimes as thick), with a glossy photographic cover and plenty of interior artwork enlivening the informative, highly detailed text.

A look at a recent *C&O Historical Newsletter* reveals Dixon's fondness for, and expertise in, his subject. There's a spirited interchange between Dixon and the group's members on all aspects of C&O lore, from tracking down specific pieces of equipment by car number, manufacturer and identifying characteristics, to a long and loving article on the C&O's showpiece passenger train of the 1930s and 1940s, "The George Washington."

Other projects of the society include an annual convention, in a different C&O city each year, and an oral history project, which Dixon is spearheading. "We're attempting to capture on tape the memories of railroaders from the steam age, who are fast dying," taking much of the history of the railroad with them.

Amidst all this activity, Dixon has managed to build up a research library of notes, publications, and memorabilia pertaining to Chessie and her antecedents. As a further aid to understanding and preserving the history of the C&O, Dixon has gathered an impressive collection of "several thousand" photographs and negatives of the C&O from the 1890s to the present.

Dixon finds his work with the society and its members has taught him "a great deal about human nature. There are many trials and tribulations in running an all-volunteer organization, and you get to see all manner of people who become interested, and remain so, or drop out along the way."

The railfan hobby "has perhaps a stronger core of devotees than anything that I have seen or been connected with," says Dixon. He attributes this intense interest ("a passion for many") to the present "nostalgia fad in America and because times are good."

There are all kinds of people in the hobby, says Dixon. "Some come to get away from normal work and life, others come with a mission to dig out and preserve history, or a minute episode in history, for the future."

Dixon is also interested in model railroading, particularly in the creation of model C&O trains and settings. To this end, he writes articles on a regular basis for several railroad hobbyist magazines, and offers model trainmakers actual pictures of C&O equipment from his collection to use as guides in the creation of accurate models.

Dixon urges potential C&O railfans to contact the C&O Historical Society, PO Box 417, Alderson, WV 24910. He can also be reached at that address.

PHILIP GARDNER
CUSTER COUNTY, NEBRASKA, HISTORY

WHEN ANYBODY, ANYWHERE, wants to know something about Custer County, Nebraska, or its county seat, Broken Bow, they get in touch with Philip Gardner. He probably knows more about the area and its people than anybody else. Gardner, a district court deputy clerk and bailiff in Custer County (which is in the geographic center of the state), has assembled over 35,000 biographies and obituaries, covering the entire county's existence from 1877 through 1978.

Gardner began compiling local history over 20 years ago at the inspiration of a next door neighbor who contacted him because he knew of Gardner's affinity for history and genealogy. Gardner traces his awareness of history to his association with his uncle, J.C. Keller. Keller, a life-long resident of the area, kept a diary for some 55 years, which Gardner says is a lively account of not only the "social activities of the time, but also such everyday things as egg prices and happenings in the community."

Working in his spare-time, Gardner combed the local library, perusing the back files of the six newspapers Custer County has had in its 100-year history. From contemporary accounts and obituaries, he was able to compile (and often rewrite into a more readable format) a staggering amount of information. The fruits of his labor now reside in the Broken Bow library, available to anyone interested in the area's history. Not content with merely researching the lives of Custer County residents, Gardner has also compiled a chronology of the county's notable (and not-so-notable) events from 1877 to the present day, resulting in a foot-high pile of typewritten information, which he is still working on.

Gardner tends to be modest about his accomplishments, but does find that the work "sure broadens your overall view of the progress of time and history. I find it very interesting that men can overcome unbelievable obstacles and adversities to improve themselves or their families," Gardner says. His work is really a tribute to "man's ingeniousness."

Among the interesting people Gardner discovered in his research into Custer County, was Morris Ainsley, who lived to be 128 years old, and "was the oldest man in America at that time." Another notable born in Broken Bow was the pioneer photographer Solomon D. Butcher. Butcher's 4,000 to 5,000 pictures of pioneer dwellings, particularly the famous Nebraska sodhouses, of which there were several thousand in the Broken Bow area, "captured the essence of the pioneer days here in the state."

In addition to his exhaustive study of Custer County and the hamlet of Broken Bow (population 4,500), Gardner has also become involved with Nebraska history as well. It took almost four years, but he visited all of the state's 93 counties, taking photographs, and keeping detailed diaries and logs about the geographical and architectural details of the countryside.

Gardner feels the importance of local history and historians cannot be emphasized strongly enough. "We have to become aware that a lot of our heritage is being lost," he says. "It is important to interview our senior citizens before they pass on. And it's important that every community has someone to record its history, and not leave the job just to the editors of the newspaper."

For the novice community historian, his suggestion is to "keep a diary of the tragedies, triumphs, and attainments of your community. Don't edit what you write — record it as it is day-by-day, not neglecting the tragic, bizarre or unbelievable." One must "become a chronicler of the happenings of your time." And it is vitally important to do plenty of research in the local library, which Gardner feels is an excellent source of information about the past life of the community.

Gardner is happy to give advice and counsel, because he is "interested in people and enhancing their efforts in genealogical research and related fields." He only asks that he be reimbursed in advance for postage, copies or other expenses before undertaking any research work. He will also give advice and counsel to novices in the field of local history research. He can be contacted at 705 S. 9th Ave., Broken Bow, NB 68822.

THOMAS HAHN
CANALS

ONE OF THE MOST widely used parks in our nation's capital is the towpath of the old Chesapeake & Ohio Canal. All along its 20-mile route beside the Potomac River, Washingtonians hike, bike, jog, and enjoy nature, in an area that was once slated to be turned into a superhighway.

Thomas Hahn is no stranger to the banks of the C&O Canal. He's been hiking there for over 30 years, long before it became a fashionable pathway.

Hahn discovered the pleasures of walking along canals and towpaths in 1948, when he was first assigned to Washington, D. C. "I started taking hikes along the C&O Canal, and began to realize that canals were nice places." His interest in the preservation of canals took off in the 1950s, thanks to the efforts of Supreme Court Justice William O. Douglas.

In 1954, Douglas challenged an editor of the *Washington Post* to hike the 185 miles from Washington, D.C., to Cumberland, Maryland, along the canal, in order to focus attention on its preservation. "It generated a lot of publicity, and it excited me that someone as important as Douglas would take the time to save this canal from being turned into a highway." The efforts of Douglas and other like-minded people saved the canal and its towpath from obliteration, and the area was finally declared a National Historic Park in 1971. The C&O Canal "was a good candidate for preservation and park status because all the real estate could be picked up intact. Unfortunately, most canal ownership problems are much more complicated," says Hahn.

After all the excitement generated by this project, he began thoroughly exploring and researching the C&O Canal, and started investigating the other canals and towpaths around the nation (and in Great Britain) that were coming under increasing scrutiny by preservationists.

With two friends, Hahn founded the American Canal Society, in 1972. This organization is dedicated to the preservation of canals in the United States, and publishes a quarterly magazine, *American Canals.*

According to Hahn, there are no independently operating canals in existence today in the United States. "Parts of the Erie Canal are connected with the New York State Barge Canal, and there's the Dismal Swamp Canal, which is a part of the coastal waterways system in the Carolinas, and so on," he says, "but canals today are nothing like they were in the 19th century."

At one time, there were 4,200 miles of canals in the United States. "They were concentrated mainly in the East, as well as in Ohio, Indiana, and Illinois," Hahn says, and played a very important part in the transportation history of this country. But, in the 1850s and 1860s, the canals "virtually died out, for many reasons, the chief being the advent of the railroads, which made transportation faster and more reliable."

The preservation of any remaining canals is imperative, says Hahn. "Almost all of them are in need of help or they will completely disappear." One of the projects with which Hahn is closely involved is the preserving of the oldest canal in the U.S: the Potomac Canal. Built in 1785, the canal runs from Washington, D.C., to Great Falls, Virginia. The Potomac Canal, says Hahn, "has the oldest set of locks in the U.S., the building of which was supervised by George Washington."

Between 1977 and 1980, the U.S. Park Service "wanted to abandon the canal completely," says Hahn. Finally, "they agreed to fix the old locks, and got the money to do it. They agreed, as well, to use old stones and other materials to make them as authentic as possible."

That kind of preservation effort is paying off with increasing frequency across the country, says Hahn, and "that's what our organization of over 600 members does best: it stirs up interest in these projects."

Very few of these canals could be rebuilt and rewatered now. Just too much time has gone by. Nonetheless, many canals are still navigable but seldom used by boats. "I have traveled many times to England, and ridden on their wonderful system of canals," he says. "But when English friends come to the U.S. and take a look at the canals here, they always ask, 'Where are the boats?'" Portions of both the C&O Canal and the Illinois-Michigan Canal, for instance, have "long stretches of open water, but no boats." About the only part of canals used today are the towpaths, which serve as hiking, nature, or jogging trails.

Hahn likes canals because "I like to trail out in the country. The towpaths are level and just a great place to walk, observe wildlife, and have a good time enjoying nature."

As an adjunct to his interest in the actual canals, Hahn has become interested in studying the lock structure and the lock houses. I am also very interested in the people who used to work on the canals." Since the C&O Canal was still in limited operation as late as 1924, he has been able to conduct oral history interviews "with some of the boat captains, who are all in their 80s and 90s now." He published some of these interviews in a book, *The C&O Canal Boatmen.* "More should have been done" to record the history of the canals and their workers, he feels.

His research and interviews with canal personnel have led Hahn to conclude that "most of the things you read about canals are rehashes and secondhand literature. In the end, it wasn't at all like what books said it was."

Hahn advises newcomers to canals to get in touch with the American Canal Society, c/o Charles Derr, 117 Main St., Freemansburg, PA 18017. A one-year's membership is $8. Hahn can be contacted for information about canals at PO Box 310, Shepherdstown, WV 25443.

EUGENE HUDDLESTON
RAILROAD PHOTOGRAPHY

A BABY BROWNIE camera for eighth grade graduation in 1944, and a chance look at a copy of a special interest magazine about the same time, opened the door for Eugene Huddleston to a fascinating lifetime hobby: railroad photography.

He grew up in a railroad family (his father was a trainman) in the small town of Russell, Kentucky, where both the Chesapeake & Ohio and the Norfolk & Western had main lines.

"When I was an adolescent," Huddleston remembers, "I was searching for an interest. I had tried airplanes, stamp collecting and building models of battleships and tanks."

One day he was in the grocery store with his father and happened to look at the magazine rack, where he encountered a copy of *Railroad* magazine. The magazine led him to the discovery that "there were people who didn't consider railroading a vocation, but something for spare-time pleasure." Thus, he, too, became a railfan.

Huddleston was guided through much of his early picture-taking by Horace W. Pontin, a Boston photographer who ran the Rail Picture Service. Pontin (who Huddleston describes as "the prime mover in getting recognition for railroad photography") had advertised in the journal of the Brotherhood of Locomotive Engineers for railroad photographs, and young Huddleston answered his ad. "I started taking pictures under his direction, " Huddleston says. " I consider him the father of my railfan photography. He kept the negatives, and sent me back prints."

Through Pontin's shop, many of Huddleston's pictures have ended up in the collections of other buffs, or in the multitude of railroad picture books, usually without his knowledge and without compensation."It didn't occur to me, at the time, that he was reaping a pretty good profit on my labors. For me, it was a labor of love."

When Huddleston was a teenager, he would hop a train or a bus, hitchhike, or borrow the family 1934 Dodge to pursue his railroad photography. But, often, he had trouble getting close to the equipment. This was during World War II and the Korean War, and "if you appeared on railroad property with a camera, they thought you were a spy," he says. He had to do some sneaking around, but the restrictions also got him interested in taking action photographs.

"I have a strong sense of place," he says." Like writers who associate themselves and their feelings with particular places, I associate railroading with small towns and the geography of rural America." Thus, his pictures concentrate on the equipment, in action, in a particular setting.

Though "people in my hometown would hardly have understood why anyone would have this as a hobby, there was a kind of romance about railroading; the railroadman used to be the aristocrat of organized labor."

Most of Huddleston's steam-era pictures were taken with a Crown Graphic press camera. Now that he shoots mostly in color, he uses a Leica M-2. "I still take loads of pictures," he says.

Currently a professor of American thought and language at Michigan State University, the 49-year-old Huddleston has found time to write or contribute to several railfan books. He was the co-author of *C&O Power: Steam and Diesel Locomotives of the Chesapeake & Ohio Railway, 1900-1965*, which is considered to be the definitive book on that subject. His photographs have also appeared in several important books by noted rail historian Don Ball.

One of Huddleston's chief goals is to "accumulate a complete photographic record of the Chesapeake & Ohio Railway as it physically existed at the time of its merger with the Baltimore & Ohio Railroad in 1961." He's also interested in doing a book on railroads and geology, and hopes to put together a pictorial history of the "Pocahontas region carriers, the railroads which carried coal through the Appalachians."

"This hobby is a real relief, "when I get fed up with my job," says Huddleston."Everyone should have a hobby and ride it hard, but not to the exclusion of other responsibilities."

Huddleston advises railroad photographers to "specialize, to film either motive power, rolling stock, structures or track work."

Huddleston will be happy to advise rail photographers. He can be contacted at 3926 Raleigh Dr., Okemos, MI 48864.

EDWARD KAMUDA

THE TITANIC

THE MAGNIFICENT passenger ship Titanic was hailed as "unsinkable" when it was launched in 1921. As every schoolchild knows, that proud boast proved false when the Titanic struck an iceberg in the Atlantic Ocean, and sank on its maiden voyage. More than 1,500 lives were lost. It was the greatest tragedy of peacetime shipping.

A good many of the survivors of that fabled night now are dead, but the memories of this historic event are kept alive, largely through the work of Edward Kamuda and fellow members of the Titanic Historical Society.

Kamuda, a 40-year-old clockmaker from Indian Orchard, Massachusetts, first became interested in the sinking of the Titanic after watching the 1953 20th Century-Fox film of the same name, (featuring Barbara Stanwyck) in his grandfather's movie theater. His interest "just grew" from there, says Kamuda, and in 1957, when he learned there were survivors of the disaster still living, he wrote to each one of them, obtaining their recollections.

In 1962, he founded the Titanic Historical Society. This organization, which now boasts some 1,700 members all over the world (even as far away as Japan), is dedicated to preserving the memory of the Titanic, and researching the events surrounding her tragic demise. In 1973, a 10th anniversary meeting of the society was held in Greenwich, Connecticut. Some 250 members showed up, along with six of the estimated 100 survivors.

One of the organization's major involvements is with the attempts to "raise" the Titanic. According to Kamuda, it would be virtually impossible to physically raise the ship from its 2-mile-deep watery grave. However, with the assistance of a firm called Seaonics, International, and $3 million, the group hopes to find the ship and photograph her. Kamuda says oceanographer Jacques-Yves Cousteau conducted a similar operation and found the Titanic's sister ship, the Britannia, which was torpedoed during World War I and lies at the bottom of the Aegean Sea.

Another important goal of the society, says Kamuda, is to start a museum about the Titanic. There are, surprisingly, a substantial number of artifacts left from the ship. Many were found floating on the surface of the water after the ship's sinking: wood railings, life preservers, pieces of furniture, etc. Other artifacts have simply turned up from unexpected sources. Kamuda himself obtained a life preserver from a New York chiropractor, whose father had been a ship's doctor on the Carpathia, the ship that rescued the survivors of the disaster. Most of the society's collection, says Kamuda, is in bank vaults.

According to Kamuda, there are still some intriguing mysteries about the sinking of the Titanic to be solved. "For instance, what was the mysterious ship that saw the Titanic's signal rockets and then went away, without coming to its aid." It is believed to be the U.S.S. Californian but, says Kamuda "there were other ships known to be in the area that night. Why didn't they come to the rescue?" Someday, Kamuda is confident, an answer will be found, as new information is coming in "all the time."

Did anything positive happen as a result of the Titanic's demise? "Yes, " says Kamuda, "a number of good things. Now there is the International Ice Patrol looking out for icebergs, and lifeboat drills at sea. Ships have been made much safer as a result of this terrible sinking."

Kamuda advises anyone embarking on historical research, or founding a historical society, "just to stick with it and be sincere. Seek out all the information you can."

Kamuda, and the Titanic Historical Society, Inc., can be reached at PO Box 53, Indian Orchard, MA 01151.

RICHARD McCLOSKEY
TRANSOCEAN CRUISES

$\mathbf{B}$RAVING A LONELY trip across an ocean in a small boat is one of the most challenging and exciting experiences a person can undertake. Either as a solo trip, or with two people, such ocean crossings provide some of marine history's most fascinating moments, according to Richard McCloskey, who with over 40 years of research is the leading historian of one- and two-person voyages.

"We're talking about a period from 1857-1957," he says, "from the time of the first documented journey by a single man across the Atlantic Ocean, until 1957, when it was apparent to me that such journeys were becoming entirely too commonplace."

McCloskey, 70, a retired U.S. foreign service officer who lives in Bothell, Washington, also founded The Slocum Society, a worldwide organization that honors and studies the individuals who made those trips.

From his years of research, McCloskey has obtained an accounting of some 125 important voyages of one- or two-person boats between 1857 and 1957. "We are referring to continent-to-continent voyages, over any ocean," he says. "For example, a voyage from California to Hawaii would not qualify. A trip from New York to England would qualify."

McCloskey was a long-time member of Great Britain's geographic historical society, the Hakluyt Society, when he decided in the 1940s "that no one was paying any attention to the explorers who set out in small boats." He spent six months in Europe, going to maritime museums and libraries, "and could discover only one obscure pamphlet," from 1892, that even made any attempt to record the history of these voyages."So I determined to make a record."

The first documented transocean crossing was in 1857, by one C. H. Webb, thought to be an American. "He set out from New York City and sailed to England in 61 days," McCloskey says. His boat, *The Charter Oak*, was approximately 25-feet long and had a 7-foot beam, says McCloskey.

He has prepared a chart of all the voyages he has studied. "There is one point I should make: no other person or organization in the world is doing this. I'm really the expert."

Most of McCloskey's research is conducted by a "vast correspondence" he has with a network of people in shipping centers around the world, who do research on their ports and convey the information to McCloskey. In addition, he has an "immense library of newspaper files, clippings, books, logs of many of the voyages, and photographs," he says. "I've started a serious reference service."

McCloskey got much of his information from the original source, too. "I've obtained the logs of a great many of the ocean voyages," he says, "and I'm old enough to have been able to interview some of the people who actually made the journeys."

When McCloskey first began his research, "many people wanted to make one- and two-person ocean crossings." But they had no place to turn to for information. Now he can advise would-be ocean crossers. "We get letters all the time from people seeking advice." McCloskey is able to give them all the data he has on the particular route they wish to take, since the trip has usually been made before by someone. This information includes such essential items as how much food is needed, how many days the journey will take, what medical supplies are necessary, and so forth.

"People have always been fascinated with the prospect of sailing the world alone," says McCloskey. Most of the attempts have been serious, but a great many of them have been "stunting, not cruising." In the 1880s, for example, it was a fad for British fishermen to try to row across the Atlantic Ocean to America. "Surprisingly, some of them actually made it," he says.

In 1955, McCloskey, eager to encourage the one-person cruising experience, was the founder of the first single-handed transatlantic race, "hoping it would develop interest in the sport." That race is still held annually, but he severed his connection with the event several years ago.

"It has turned out to be a catastrophe," he says. "All the boats are sponsored by firms now, and are as much as 125-feet long. It defeats the entire purpose of one person having an adventure on his own, depending solely on his skill and wit for survival."

Single-person ocean crossings, McCloskey says, are no longer news. "There are so many you just can't keep track. The rate of attempts has quadrupled over the last 30 years, so much so that the news media no longer take much notice of the voyages, thus making it difficult to obtain research materials."

Why has McCloskey pursued his work with such vigor all these years? "It's a matter of curiosity for me," he says. "If somebody doesn't do it, what's going to happen 50 years from now when no one knows about these voyages? It's not a mania with me, just something no one else has done."

McCloskey never made a transocean crossing himself. At one time, he planned to leave from Hong Kong and sail around the world, but was never able to make the trip. "I have made a number of island-to-island cruises, however," he says.

McCloskey, who says he is "delighted to receive sensible queries" on transocean cruising, can be contacted at 9206 N.E. 180th St., Bothell, WA 98011. He can also provide further information about membership in the Slocum Society (which costs $20 per year).

HAROLD MELOY
MAMMOTH CAVE

AT 212 MILES LONG, it's the longest cave in the world, and "there's more history connected with it than any other," according to Harold Meloy, who has studied Mammoth Cave for over 50 years.

Meloy, an attorney in Shelbyville, Indiana, was a 12-year-old tourist in 1925 when he first became fascinated with the huge cavern, which is located about 85 miles southwest of Louisville, Kentucky. Meloy isn't sure what it was that has made him devote so much energy to finding out about the cave's "history, legends, myths and folklore. Maybe it was that different books told different things, and I wondered which was right."

Whatever it was, down through the years, Meloy, and a dedicated group of other Mammoth Cave buffs have "made many facts myth, and taken the myth out of facts" about this intriguing underground world that is a U.S. National Park and has been a favorite tourist attraction for several generations.

Shattering myths about Mammoth Cave seems to be Meloy's specialty. For instance, he discovered that Stephen Bishop, a famous guide in the cave in the early 1800s, didn't die in 1859, as his gravestone marker proclaims. Meloy discovered from old documents Bishop had actually died in 1857. "The reason for the discrepancy, " says Meloy, "is that Bishop's gravestone wasn't put up until 30 years after his death and the lapse of time accounted for the error."

One of the more intriguing myths Meloy had the opportunity to debunk also involved Bishop. It was widely reported (even by the guides in the cave) that Bishop had used a "slender cedar sapling to cross a particularly dangerous pit in the cavern. The pit is 150 feet deep, with sheer walls straight down." Strongly suspecting that wasn't possible, Meloy examined contemporary accounts, and discovered from an old letter that on October 20, 1838, Bishop and a visitor had, in fact, crossed the pit, using a ladder as a bridge. That shattered the legend told for years. "You can imagine I wasn't very popular with the mythmakers for that one."

Often, however, strange stories about Mammoth Cave are based on fact, Meloy says. Indian artifacts dating from 1000 B.C. have been discovered in the cave, as well as seven mummified bodies of Indians. The seven bodies were discovered at different times by various people connected with the cave. Several of the mummies were displayed for many years by the National Park Service, but have been withdrawn from public view, Meloy says.

The two best preserved mummies, named "Little Alice" and "Lost John," have been thoroughly studied by scientists, Meloy says. Carbon-14 dating methods determined they were from about 100 A.D.

Another compelling fact about Mammoth Cave, Meloy says, is that it was used as the very first hospital for tuberculosis sufferers in the United States. "As early as 1820, a doctor living in the vicinity urged the state of Kentucky to buy the cave and turn it into a hospital," he says. But it wasn't until Dr. John Croghan appeared on the scene in the 1840s, and purchased the property, that the hospital became a reality. According to Meloy, it was thought that the saltpeter present in the cave, as well as the constant 54-degree temperature was conducive to curing TB. There were 12 or 13 patients in the hospital from 1842 until it closed in the spring of 1843, when it was decided keeping patients in the cave had no therapeutic value. Ironically, says Meloy, Dr. Croghan himself succumbed to TB, in Louisville in 1849.

Meloy has written several books and articles on the cave and its traditions and lore. Among them: *Mummies of Mammoth Cave* (1968) and "The Pursuit of Health in Mammoth Cave," which Meloy co-wrote with Dr. Stanley Sides in the *Bulletin of the History of Medicine.*

There is an organization for people who, like Meloy, are interested in the history of caves. The American Spelean Historical Association, of which Meloy was a founding member in 1968, is dedicated to historic research of United States caves. "About a third of the members are interested specifically in Mammoth Cave," Meloy says.

Meloy enjoys his research, and looks upon it as an interesting hobby that performs a public service. "I suppose the reason I enjoy this hobby is the opportunity it provides to uncover facts — and myths — and convey them to others. What, after all, makes a person choose a particular hobby? Simply that it interests him and gives him enjoyment."

Meloy will gladly answer questions, accompanied by a stamped, self-addressed envelope for reply, addressed to him at PO Box 454, Shelbyville, IN 46176.

IRENE ODORIZZI
SLOVENIAN IMMIGRANTS

NESTLED IN THE northwest corner of present-day Yugoslavia, surrounded by Hungary, Austria, Italy, and Croatia, is a 7,819 sq. mile-land of mountains, woods, and broad fertile valleys. It is called Slovenia, and though the area is part of Yugoslavia, a hearty spirit of independence survives in its people — a spirit that has traveled all the way to America.

Beginning in the 1880s, and continuing until 1920, large groups of Slovenians left their native land for the similar countryside of the Midwest and Far West of the United States. Today, the more than 500,000 people of Slovenian background are thoroughly Americanized, though there are those who still remember — and revere — the heritage of their forefathers.

One such person is Irene Odorizzi, a Slovenian born in Joliet, Illinois. She has become the historian of her people's migration to America and of the life they left behind. Much of the research she has done over the last several years resulted in a book *Footsteps Through Time*, a collection of individual histories of some of the Slovenian immigrants who came to the United States.

The Slovenians were a highly cultured people, Mrs. Odorizzi says. "At one time, right around 1900, there were more books read per capita in Slovenia than anywhere else in Eastern Europe." Despite their cultural achievement (much of which was derived from Slovenia's close association with Austria, she adds), "conditions were very poor for most of the people. Many of the peasants just weren't able to eke out a living on the land."

Thus, when North and South American "industrialists and plant owners came over to recruit workers for their factories, people were enticed by their promises of high wages and improved living conditions," says Mrs. Odorizzi. "They left, not because they disliked their country, but they thought they could make so much more money elsewhere. A number of people also feared a war was brewing in the area, and wanted to escape that "possibility."

When they came to the United States, the Slovenians settled primarily in the

Midwest and in Colorado, California, New York, Pennsylvania, Maryland, and West Virginia. They were chiefly involved in industry and mining, though a number owned their own small businesses, worked on the railroads or on farms, Mrs. Odorizzi says.

In doing her research, she says, "I've noticed that so many of the second and third generation have moved around. The Slovenian community is not as tightly knit now. Slovenians can be found in all states now, not just in the enclaves they were in before."

Mrs. Odorizzi, an English and theater instructor in a Reston, Virginia, high school, was inspired to begin her research when "I began to realize that many of the immigrant people I knew were dying off, and traditional events remembered from my childhood weren't happening anymore. I started to think, 'Nothing has been done to tell about this group; they're too modest to acknowledge anything noteworthy in what they've done.' Maybe putting things down now will be important 100 or 200 years hence."

As part of her master's thesis at Catholic University in Washington, D. C., Mrs. Odorizzi began an oral history project on the Slovenian immigration. "A lot of the people who had immigrated to the United States were still living, " she says, "so I decided it would be good not only to write down their recollections, but videotape them as well."

Armed with a videotape outfit borrowed from school and tapes she purchsed herself, Mrs. Odorizzi proceeded to interview people, most of them in their 80s and 90s "and even one lady who was 102!"

These interviews resulted in a unique visual record, and in the book *Footsteps in Time*, which was privately published for the Slovenian Women's Union, the leading heritage group of Slovenians in this country.

While doing her research, Mrs. Odorizzi discovered that there are some prominent Slovenians in the mainstream of American life (Sen. Frank Lausche of Ohio, for example), and many Slovenians have become successful in private business. "The ordinary people go often unnoticed by history. But it's more important that they were a certain kind of people, than what they did in life."

The Slovenians "came to contribute something to this country: their high standards, their character, their perseverance," says Mrs. Odorizzi. "That had something do with the American spirit. We often overlook what America is: all these small people who make it great." Many of the immigrants "did the very hardest work in the sweating steel mills and factories. Even though we know all of this existed, we just take it for granted," she says."

Mrs. Odorizzi is actively involved with the 10,000-member Slovenian Women's Union, and serves as the group's heritage director. The group hopes to establish a Slovenian heritage museum in Joliet, Illinois.

All of the work and research has been worth it for Mrs. Odorizzi. "I've truly enjoyed meeting all these people individually. Their determination, strength of character, and the way they didn't want anything for nothing, are characteristics I am impressed with."

Mrs. Odorizzi can be reached for further information on Slovenian immigrants or guidance in similar projects for other groups by writing her in care of the Slovenian Women's Union, 431 N. Chicago St., Joliet, IL 60432.

CHUCK PARSONS
TEXAS OUTLAWS & LAWMEN

THE OUTLAWS who roamed the Wild West are some of the most engaging characters in American history. Their nemeses, the noble sheriffs and marshals who pursued them over sagebrush, desert, and mountains are equally fascinating.

When Chuck Parsons thinks of the good guys and the bad guys, he thinks of Texas. He's an expert on the hardy ruffians who made the Lone Star State the exciting place it was in the good old days between 1860 and 1900.

Parsons, a high school principal from Hutchinson, Minnesota, has been a specialist in the history of these wild and wooly characters ever since he was a youngster. "In ninth or tenth grade I read a book by the great Western author Ed Bartholomew, called *Kill or Be Killed*. The main character was a Texas outlaw, and I was impressed. That's the reason I concentrated on that area," he says.

In his study of Texas in those rough 40 years that were the heyday of the Old West, Parsons has made some interesting discoveries. Along the way, he's written many articles, two books, and pursued a particular interest in the outlaw John Wesley Hardin.

"Mainly, my expertise is in Texas figures who one way or another crossed the path of Hardin," says Parsons, explaining the focus of his research. Hardin is "credited with being the most notorious Texas gunfighter," he says. Beginning in 1868, when he killed a former slave during the "Reconstruction period of Yankee law in Texas," Hardin killed (by his own admission) "40 men in personal combat" before his death in 1895.

"He may have stretched the truth a bit, but I'm inclined to believe him," says Parsons. "After all, he had a bounty of $4,000 on his head, which at that time was a heck of a lot of money."

Lawmen pursued Hardin all over the country and finally captured him in Florida in 1877. Even that event is surrounded by controversy. According to Parsons, "The history books usually give the credit for his capture to John Armstrong of the Texas Rangers, but "I did a lot of research, utilizing original source materials — like letters and news reports of the time — and came to the conclusion that a Florida sheriff, Hutchinson, should get the credit." The hapless Hutchinson also missed out on the $4,000 reward.

Much of the information Parsons has obtained on Hardin comes from the gunfighter's autobiography, published posthumously by his children in 1896. Parsons has nine copies of the first edition of the book, along with a couple of Hardin's business cards, which are very rare. "Hardin became a lawyer while he was in jail, and after he got out, practiced law for awhile, so he had these cards made up," says Parsons.

Parsons has immortalized Hardin in a book *The Capture of John Wesley Hardin* (Creative Publishing Co., 1978). He says of his subject, "He never has been as popular as Billy the Kid or Jesse James. I guess he didn't have the right press agent."

In addition to his extensive research into Hardin and associates, Parsons has also found time to study the Texas Rangers thoroughly. He found them to be "not quite like the Lone Ranger, but they basically believed in law and order, and enforced them as best they could." Though the Rangers are best known for their pursuit of outlaws, Parsons says, most of their work was protecting Texans from Indian attacks. "Generally speaking, they were a credit to the force. It was dangerous work for which they were only paid $40 a month," he says. Parsons estimates that between 5 and 10 percent of the Texas Rangers lost their lives in the line of duty.

In his research, Parsons has "uncovered unpublished photos of men closely associated with some of the famous outlaws." For example, he has found a picture of Philip Coe, a gambler who "was the last man to die courtesy of Wild Bill Hickock."

Parsons is the president of the National Association for Outlaw and Lawman History, the leading interest group in the field. He's also been active in The Westerners, another nationwide group that is devoted to studying the many aspects of Wild West history "in a very scholarly fashion."

"I generally spend about five percent of my time during the school year doing research or working in some other way on the hobby. In the summer, however, I forget about my job completely."

For the novice researcher into outlaws and lawmen (or, in fact, any aspect of Western history), Parsons advises joining The Westerners (their local chapters, called "corrals" are in many cities and states) and the National Association of Outlaw and Lawman History (229 Merrill Library UMC 30, Utah State University, Logan, UT 84322).

Any researcher faces the problem of finding reliable sources. Parsons suggests Western history buffs consult the three bibliographies by Raymond F. Adams, the most respected authority on books of Western history. *Six-Guns and Saddle Leather* and volumes one and two of *Burrs Under the Saddle* are musts for the beginner, says Parsons.

Parsons, too, will be glad to provide further information on Hardin, or any aspect of Texas outlaw and lawman history. He can be contacted either at his home (530 Larson, Hutchinson, MN 55350) or his office (229 Lake St., Silver Lake, MN 55381).

MICHAEL PENDER
WORLD'S FAIRS

THE 1939 WORLD'S Fair, held in New York City, was one of the most memorable events of the Depression-weary 1930s. Young Michael Pender was so dazzled by the splendor of the fair that he's since made a fascinating hobby out of world's fairs. He even had a role in the planning and management of the subsequent world's fair in New York, 25 years later.

Today, Pender, the commissioner of public works for Nassau County on Long Island, is a leading collector of world's fair memorabilia and an expert in the history of world's fairs. In addition, he was the director of state exhibits for the 1964-65 New York World's Fair, working under the legendary Robert Moses.

"I got my start in collecting fair memorabilia at the 1939 fair," Pender says. Among the now-valuable items he collected were a Heinz pickle pin, a General Motors "I Have Seen the Future" button, and some souvenir spoons. Pender estimates he has 500 different items (and a lot of duplicates) in his collection today. Since he has attended every world's fair held in his lifetime from 1939, he collected items at all of them, in addition to gathering a great many from the 1964-65 New York fair.

Among the unique items in his collection: Pender has one of the maps from the 1964-65 fair that were posted in phone booths at the fairgrounds. Other New York World's Fair items that Pender is fond of are several replicas of the Unisphere, the focal point of the fair, as well as replicas of the buildings on the fairgrounds. Also, he has an unusual cigarette lighter from the 1962 Seattle fair. It's a foot-high replica of the Space Needle.

A particularly important part of Pender's collection, which includes many books, pamphlets and other documents about world's fairs and their history, is a collection of souvenir spoons starting from the 1893 Columbian Exposition in Chicago right through to the present day.

Pender says his "personal involvement with the 'state day' activities, in which the governors of all 50 states participated" was the aspect of his work with the 1964-65 fair that pleased him most. What was his favorite exhibit? "I think it was the General Motors pavilion. I spent many happy hours going through it."

World's fairs aren't a 20th century invention, Pender says. The first one, "the grandfather of world's fairs," was the 1851 London Exhibition. The first fair in the United States was in New York in 1853, but it wasn't until the Centennial Exhibition in Philadelphia in 1876 that world's fairs came into their own.

"World's fairs began primarily as opportunities for merchants and manufacturers to show off their wares," says Pender. "Later, they became vehicles for states or countries to advertise their tourist and cultural aspects." Essentially, however, they have "always remained trade shows."

Among the most popular fairs have been the Columbian Exposition in Chicago in 1893 which introduced the ferris wheel to the public, the 1939 fair in New York, and the 1962 Seattle fair. But, in Pender's opinion, Montreal's "Expo '67" was probably the most popular, at least in terms of attendance.

"World's fairs usually lose money in themselves," he says, "but they are a favorable influence on the municipalities surrounding them, bringing in additional tax revenues and an increase in local business."

In 1968, Pender, along with other world's fair buffs, founded the World's Fair Collector's Society. He served as president of the organization until 1977. Now, he is the editor of its bi-monthly newsletter *Fair News*, which is sent to the organization's 250 members all over the United States.

The World's Fair Collector's Society was formed, Pender says, "to preserve the memory of world's fairs, as well as the relics, and to do research into the effects the fairs have on human life." To those ends, the society has established a small research library (currently located in Pender's Garden City, New York, home) "which we hope will be a part of a permanent library and museum" in the future.

Pender advises the beginning collector of world's fair memorabilia can start a collection with relative ease today, even though there haven't been any world's fairs since Expo '67. "If the collector wants a general collection, there is plenty of material available, at reasonable prices. If he wants to specialize, it gets expensive," Pender says.

On a recent trip to Seattle, Pender stopped off to pay a nostalgic visit to the Space Needle. "I was absolutely shocked to see they were still selling souvenirs from the 1962 fair there," he says. "They must be loaded down with them."

Collecting world's fair memorabilia and becoming an expert in the fairs has been a great source of satisfaction for Pender. "I think it's like any collecting hobby," he says. "You have the opportunity to get to know about regions of the world and countries you wouldn't normally have the chance to see. It gives you the chance to expand your horizons."

Pender says it is of special concern to him that the "true facts about the fairs are maintained. If somebody comes along and says, 'Such and such a fair was lousy' I want to be able to refute that." Pender sees his hobby and his association with the society as prime ways of keeping the public informed.

Pender advises the novice fair buff to join the World's Fair Collector's Society. Pender and the Society can be reached at 148 Poplar St., Garden City, NY 11530. He would appreciate it if correspondents would send a stamped, self-addressed envelope with their letters.

EVERETT POWERS
OLD MILLS

F ROM THE BEGINNING of our history, water-powered mills played a vital role in the commercial development of the United States. Whether they ground grain into flour or made tools or textiles, mills could be found by rivers and streams in many a town, large and small.

With the coming of the machine age, "down by the old mill stream" became a nostalgic refrain. Since they weren't used anymore, many of the old mills were torn down or fell into disrepair. If it were not for the efforts of Everett Powers, and the 1,200 members of the Society for the Preservation of Old Mills, which he founded in 1971, many of these wonderful buildings would be lost forever, torn down, forgotten, mouldering into oblivion.

Powers, now retired, spent over 50 years as a salesman, traveling the countryside. "I saw the deterioration of the old mills around the country," he says, "and thought something should be done about it." Aside from their interesting architecture, Powers says he was attracted to the mills because " they are operated by a different kind of mechanism than we usually see today. We don't have many water wheels or water turbines in operation, except in these old mills."

Though many of the members of the society are interested in textile mills, saw mills, iron forges, and the like, Powers and the majority of his membership are most interested in the preservation and historical documentation of grist mills. "There are so many of these left," says Powers, "around 200 or 300, that it seems a shame to let them go into disrepair."

While Powers and his group "have not done much in the way of restoring as a group," they have provided the impetus and the expertise for local community efforts. "We try to get people in various localities where there are old mills to form local organizations to preserve or restore them," he says. So far, he says, the society's efforts have inspired roughly a dozen local preservation projects. "In the last few years, there has definitely been an increased awareness of the value of these old mills to history." In fact, he says, many governmental bodies and local historical societies are getting into the act.

"In Montgomery County, Pennsylvania, where I live," he says, "the county has bought a mill and is fixing it up. The State of Pennsylvania has purchased two mills nearby, and in Bucks County, another couple of mills are being restored." This kind of perservation is becoming common in other areas of the country, as well, he says.

Though Powers estimates that he has visited probably 100 mills, and has a picture postcard and photographic collection of many more, his chief interest these days is in writing about old mills. He edits and publishes *Old Mill News*, a quarterly magazine, which he founded in 1972. The magazine, which is the official publication of the society, is a lively 20 pages per issue of "news of old mills, and what's happening with their preservation." The magazine's most important features, says Powers, are the articles, heavily illustrated, that tell the histories of old mills from all over the country. He estimates that about 500 old mills have been given the *Old Mill News* publicity treatment since the magazine's inception.

The interest in old mills has had another important development, says Powers. "Old mills have carried the government now into small-scale hydro-power, encouraging the use of small dams to produce energy." With an estimated 50,000 small dams unused around the country, Powers sees a great potential for electricity produced by energy-saving water power.

"The Department of Energy has a program now for encouraging small hydro-power operations," he says, "but, like most government things, they aren't moving very fast with it. He says that the New England states, the Pacific Northwest, and Alaska are the areas that can primarily benefit from this resurgence of water power. "Wherever there are mountains, there's a great deal of excess water power," Powers says, and with the right equipment, this water power can be harnessed successfully to produce electricity. "The Society for the Preservation of Old Mills is very interested in furthering the development of water power, " he adds. "We think it really makes sense in light of our energy problems. We have to use what we've got."

"I have found my work with the society very interesting," Powers says. "The best part of it, for me, is the opportunity to correspond with and meet a great many very well-versed people."

Powers suggests that anyone who is interested in the preservation of old mills who knows of a mill in their town or surrounding area they want to help save, should contact him at 232 Roslyn Ave., Glenside, PA 19038.

PHILIP RASCH
LINCOLN COUNTY, NEW MEXICO

DURING THE TURBULENT period from 1877 to 1885, Lincoln County, New Mexico, was the scene of important moments in the history of the Old West. Especially noted for the range wars that spawned the famous outlaw, Billy the Kid, Lincoln County is rich in the wildest of western history.

For nearly 40 years, Philip Rasch, a retired Navy officer from San Pedro, California, has been studying the events in Lincoln County during this hectic period, with particular attention to the Lincoln County War of 1878-82, and the rise and fall of the outlaw Billy the Kid.

"While I was serving on patrol duty during World War II in the Pacific, I read Walter Noble Burns' book *The Saga of Billy the Kid*, and was fascinated by the story it told." On his return to the States after the war, Rasch decided to take a trip to see the locale of the book. "I discovered that this supposedly factual book was the wildest of fiction," he says. "So I decided to start doing my own research to see what the facts were."

Over the years, Rasch has made some discoveries that have effectively corrected the misconceptions he feels authors like Burns (and even some historians) have purveyed about Lincoln County.

Located in south-central New Mexico, Lincoln County "was the size of four or five small Eastern states" when New Mexico was still a territory. The cattle industry was thriving on what appeared to be limitless open land, and fortunes could be made by those strong and ruthless enough to grab the opportunity.

"The Lincoln County War, which was the episode that made Billy the Kid a household name," says Rasch, was the outgrowth of a feud between the L. G. Murphy Company and another group backed by John Chisum. The war was fought "for economic control of the county." Billy, who's real name is believed to be William Bonney, was a ranchhand for John Henry Tunstall, one of the first victims of the Lincoln County War.

Tunstall was murdered by a posse sent to foreclose on his ranch, which had been mortgaged to a Chisum-controlled bank. Billy, who was present when Tunstall was gunned down, "set out to avenge his boss's death," says Rasch. Legend claims that Billy killed "21 men by the time he was 21," but Rasch thinks the figure is greatly exaggerated. It is known that he killed at least six people, directly as a result of the Lincoln County War, which went on for four years after Tunstall's death.

Aside from determining that Billy's real name was William Bonney, Rasch says that he also discovered many gaps in the outlaw's life which are still unexplained. "We know that for a period of his life he was in Indianapolis, Indiana, and also in Wichita, Kansas. Then he disappears for a time and turns up in Santa Fe, New Mexico. We don't know where he was born. There's just no record of his origins."

The traditional story has it that Billy was born in New York City, Rasch says, but "in 1880 he told the census-taker that he was born in Missouri. Of course, that could have been something the census-taker made up, as they often did in those days, just to complete their forms." It's possible, says Rasch, "we may not be looking in the right place to find out about Billy."

In his quest for information on Billy, Rasch has managed to track down the descendants of some of his associates and contemporaries. He found the niece and nephew of William Antrim, Billy's stepfather, in Paso Robles, New Mexico, and they were able to give him some information and hints for research. He also got in touch with "the daughters of one of the participants, just after they burned a trunkful of documents relating to the Lincoln County War," he says.

He enjoys his historical research because "it's like reading a detective story, but more fun. I feel I have added a bit to history and there's a certain fascination in tracking people down."

It was a "very exciting time in our country's history," says Rasch, "a time which is not too far removed from our own. Through my work, I have met the children of seven of the prominent figures involved in the troubles in Lincoln County, and heard firsthand what most people only read about in the often fictionalized, inaccurate accounts of those days."

Rasch admits that the history of Lincoln County is somewhat confused, mainly because information is sparse. "We don't know a whole lot about the people involved. They moved around so much. Unless someone was publicly killed, there are virtually no records on them, and even those are none too good," he says. "I think we've gone about as far as we're going to go. Nobody can unravel the truth."

For the researcher who might want to explore any aspect of Wild West history, says Rasch, it's important "to familiarize yourself with the work done already. Throw away Walter Burns, Stewart Lake, and the others and take a look at the documented work done by serious researchers." He adds that the National Association for Outlaw and Lawman History, and The Westerners, are "two fine, serious historical study groups that can provide much information on Western history."

All's quiet on the Lincoln County front today, says Rasch, adding that it has been divided into four counties. The town of Lincoln itself, once the hub of so much activity, "exists on the tourist trade. It's a quiet little town that they're trying to convert into the Western equivalent of Williamsburg."

Rasch will be glad to provide further information about Lincoln County or Billy the Kid. Contact him at 1839 Chandeleur Dr., San Pedro. CA 90732.

PAUL ROSENBERGER
SOUTHWEST INDIAN CEREMONIES

THERE ARE 6,000 HOPI, 10,000 Zuni, 20,000 Apache, 150,000 Navajo, and 300 Yavapai Indians, all within a few miles of Paul Rosenberger's home in Prescott, Arizona. Having been surrounded by Southwestern Indian culture most of his life, Rosenberger has become an expert in the religious ceremonies and tribal customs of the Indian people who are his neighbors.

Rosenberger's expertise has been acquired over a lifetime of studying the rituals "which are still practiced by the Indians living on the reservations." He is also the director of a museum that is called by many the "finest pre-Columbian collection in North America."

"I was raised on a ranch in the Verde Valley of Arizona," says Rosenberger. "In the part of our land we called the 'little pasture', really about 200 acres, lived a group of Yavapai Indians. I played with the kids as I was growing up, and that's where my interest first took hold."

Though he left the area for a time to attend the University of Arizona and live in Nebraska and California (even doing a stint as a car dealer in Beverly Hills), Rosenberger and his wife, Vonnie, continuously studied and photographed the Indians of Arizona.

In 1964, when he returned to Prescott as director of the Smoki Museum, his research on Indian ceremonies and dances took on greater importance.

His work has been aided by the fact that "we have friends on the reservations, who've told us a lot," says Rosenberger. In addition, Rosenberger has done considerable research into the relationships between the Indians of North America, Central America, and South America. "We've gone to the Mayan ruins in Mexico, and we find there is a connection between the religion of all the Indians in the Americas. Until comparatively recently, they all worshipped the snake. Now only about three Hopi villages do it."

There are a tremendous number of Indian ceremonies still practiced by the Southwest Indian tribes, says Rosenberger. "The Hopi have 15 ceremonies; the Zuni about 500; the Navajo maybe three dozen." He adds that white people attend these ceremonies infrequently. "The Indians rather resent tourists, and unless you're pretty well connected, you can't see the rituals or ceremonies at all," he says.

Rosenberger explains the differences in the religions of the Indians in his region: "The Navajo are earth worshippers. All of their ceremonies honor the Earth Mother or are connected in some way to the earth. The Hopi, on the other hand, worship the water and sun gods, as do the Zuni. The Apaches are a more warlike tribe, so they worship war gods."

According to Rosenberger, each of the Indian tribes has unique and fascinating ceremonies that distinguish it from the others. The Navajo, for instance have the "Big Sing." This annual social event goes on for three days. Also there are "curing ceremonies," with sand paintings and a medicine man/priest. "They lay the sick person on the painting, and chant, hoping to run the devils causing the illness out of the body," he says.

The major Hopi dance is the Snake Dance. "It originated out of a story similar to the *Bible*'s version of Noah's flood," he says. "It gives reverence to the snake, and thanks the gods for rain." Other important Hopi dances are the bean dance and the flute dance, both designed to promote the harvest.

The Shalako ceremony of the Zuni is a particularly fascinating ritual and one of Rosenberger's favorites. This week-long event, designed for "child training," features the "Kachinas, the ghost people who live in the peaks above Flagstaff." The Kachinas are "enormous costumed figures, 8- or 10-feet tall, who run through the village chasing, chastising, and rewarding the Zuni children."

For the Apaches, the major ritual is the "13 Mountain Chants," says Rosenberger. "You can trace this dance clear back to Mongolia and Tibet. It is the Apache equivalent of the *Bible*." As its name suggests, there are 13 different sections to the dance, which traces the history of the Apache people. "The 13 Mountain Chants ceremony would be so lengthy it would take all year to complete" if done all at once, so twice a year, certain segments of it are danced for three or four days at a time, Rosenberger says.

Watching the Apache ritual is quite interesting, he says. "They come out and dance like crazy for a half-hour or an hour, and then disappear. Then come back, two or three hours later, and begin dancing all over again," he says. "I don't know what the reason is for the way it is done, but it's very impressive and interesting."

By far the most unusual and secret ceremony Rosenberger has been allowed to observe is the Navajo's ritual regarding twins. "The Navajo believe that the gods are angry when a set of twins is born," he says. "So, they sacrifice one of the twins to the tree god. They decorate a tree, somewhat like our Christmas tree, tie the baby to it, and go away."

That's why, he says, "it's rare to see a pair of Navajo twins grow up. If you do, it's because the parents have become Christians."

All of these religious ceremonies, and many others, are faithfully practiced by Indians living on the Arizona reservations. "If they've stayed on the reservations, they haven't forgotten the rituals," he says. "If they go off the reservation, they turn their backs on the old ways."

Over the more than 35 years Rosenberger has been studying Indian dances and rituals, "we've seen an awful lot, and become friends with a great many of the Indian people."

The museum Rosenberger directs was founded in 1932 by the Smoki, an "organization of white people, like Rotary or Kiwanis, who were interested in civic improvement." In 1921, the group sponsored a re-creation of a snake dance to raise money for their annual rodeo. They got so interested in the Indian ritual, they dropped the rodeo, and concentrated on the snake dance from then on, Rosenberger said. Many of the members of the Smoki contributed Indian artifacts from their personal collections to help start the museum.

Rosenberger finds the Southwest Indian rituals, ceremonies, dances, and culture endlessly fascinating. "The more you dig into it, the more fascinating it becomes," he says. "Ancient history is a lot of fun, but you can't get your hands on it. But this is here right now, for observation and participation."

He'll gladly answer queries about Southwest Indian culture, or the Smoki Museum, directed to him at PO Box 1668, Prescott, AZ 86302.

RICHARD ROY
COVERED BRIDGES

THE STURDY COVERED bridges that carried generations of farmers and pioneers, travelers and vagabonds across the streams of America are fast surrendering to the demands of progress.

While he doesn't want progress to stop, Richard Roy of Manchester, New

Hampshire, doesn't want these unique pieces of Americana to totally disappear, either. So, he is trying to do something about it.

"I'm a sentimentalist," he says. "I look at a covered bridge and marvel at the architecture, at the skill of the people who built it. It always fascinates me to see what they were able to build, with the tools they had. Covered bridges get my blood circulating, just to look at them."

Roy's love affair with covered bridges began over 25 years ago. He was driving through the New Hampshire countryside with his wife, when they came across a covered bridge. Getting out to take a look, Roy noticed a small sign, which said, "'If you're interested in saving this span, contact so-and-so.' Well, I called the fellow up, found out about the bridge, and my interest grew from there."

Not content with visiting as many covered bridges as he could (although he's gone all over the Northeast looking at them), Roy has an oustanding photographic record of covered bridges in the U.S. and Europe. "I've got about 15,000 slides and 7,500 other pictures of covered bridges," he says. Some he took himself, others he obtained from fellow covered bridge buffs.

For anyone who might not have been lucky enough to ever see a covered bridge, Roy describes one: "To be an authentic covered bridge, it must be built in the old way. That means no iron supports, no bolts. Most covered bridges of the antique type are pinned together with wooden pegs." Of course, the bridges have a roof over them, hence their name. Roy says the bridges are covered "to protect the timbers of the bridge. If they're kept dry, the bridge will never rot."

The first covered bridge was built in Pennsylvania in 1805. Between 1850 and 1900, "probably more covered bridges were built than at any other time," Roy says. The bulk of covered bridges aren't to be found in the New England states, although those bridges get the most publicity. Roy says Pennsylvania, Ohio, and Indiana have more covered bridges than New England, and there are even covered bridges as far away as Washington, Oregon and California.

During the heyday of covered bridges, Roy says, the state of New Hampshire probably had about 345 ("and we're a small state"). Pennsylvania had "a couple of thousand. Today, there are only 1,000 left in the entire United States."

Keeping those 1,000 bridges alive is the job of several organizations, chiefly the National Society for Preservation of Covered Bridges. Roy is vice-president of that organization, and is active in the Connecticut River Valley Covered Bridge Society, for which he edits the quarterly *Covered Bridge Bulletin*. The eight-page publication has been going for 26 years, and "is intended to keep the members informed about the history of covered bridges and preservation efforts."

The oldest covered bridge still extant, in Sheffield, Massachusetts, is being saved with the aid of matching funds secured by the National Society for Preservation of Covered Bridges. Another famous preservation effort met with disaster, Roy says. The covered bridge between Haverhill, New Hampshire, and Newbury, Vermont, had been lovingly restored with some $240,000 raised for the purpose. In the summer of 1979, a sudden windstorm "took about three minutes to completely destroy the bridge." Fortunately, the eight people on the bridge at the time escaped with minor injuries.

Though Roy is fond of many covered bridges, the one at Swansea, New Hampshire, is his favorite. "It's a real nice one that has been very well preserved," he says. "It has a little more design than a lot of them do, with a Gothic arch that makes it unique. It's painted white inside and out, which shows that it's something special." Most bridges were constructed and maintained with less concern for beauty, Roy says.

It is important to preserve our covered bridge heritage, Roy insists, "because history should be recorded, and this is part of it. The architecture is special. I don't advocate stopping progress, but if it's feasible to do so, have progress and keep the bridges."

Roy advises the novice covered-bridge watcher to purchase *The World Guide to Covered Bridges* ($5, postpaid, from Richard Capwell, 526 Powers Rd., Pawtucket, RI 02860). Then, "start from home and work outward. If you don't want to take photographs, buy postcards or make drawings of the bridges."

Joining the national society is a good idea, too, Roy says. Contact Roger D. Griffin, 31 Federal St., Beverly, MA 01915. A $6.50 annual membership brings a 16-page quarterly *Covered Bridge Topics*.

Roy will gladly give information on covered bridges. He can be contacted at 73 Ash St., Manchester, NH 03104.

PAUL VAN REYEN
MEDIEVAL DUTCH CASTLES

A COLLEGE TERM paper on Dutch castles was the beginning of Paul van Reyen's involvement in controversial research in medieval Dutch architecture.

After writing this paper in his senior year at Hope College, in Holland, Michigan, says van Reyen, "I knew enough to object violently to the treatment of Dutch castles in a general book on European castles." Thus, it was not too surprising that when it came time to decide on a subject for van Reyen's master's thesis in history, he chose Dutch castles.

The book he reacted against so violently in college used Dutch texts as its basis for research, but the renowned author of the book "was a Scandinavian, who didn't read Dutch — so he just didn't get it at all." Van Reyen says the book was full of "gross misinformation" as a result.

Van Reyen's crusading spirit is still in evidence, today. He continuously corrects the many inaccuracies he finds in official records, much to the consternation of the Dutch government and many academics. "The biggest problem I've encountered ," he says, "is that the Dutch research people are exceedingly sloppy. I've been trying to get the attitude changed in Holland toward more careful research, but I'm having very little luck."

Improved research is necessary in this field, van Reyen feels, because "nonsense which I've already cleared up is still being taught to students. Most books are blindly repeating old errors."

Van Reyen has many examples of the kinds of inaccuracies he claims run rampant through Dutch castle history. On a trip to Holland in 1965, he spent a lot of time researching the 13th century Brederode Castle, located slightly north of the city of Haarlem. The castle has some 100,000 annual visitors, more than any of the other Dutch castles. The current structure was probably built around 1275, though van Reyen says there is evidence of five separate foundations of earlier versions of the castle.

"I went to the ministry of arts, which handles such things, and asked for the blueprints of the castle," van Reyen says. "What they gave me was totally wrong; not one dimension was correct." And he should know: "I made all the measurements again myself." Van Reyen blames the faulty blueprint on "make-work during the Depression of the 1930s. They just gave some laborer the job of making a blueprint, and no one ever bothered to check his work. This is typical of the way things are done."

Van Reyen traces the lack of interest in the more technical data about the castle to the fact that "the Dutch people are mostly interested in who lived in the castle. They can go into ecstasy about the woman who slept in the tower room of her castle, accompanied by a donkey which had to be lugged up innumerable stairs nightly by seven men," he says. "But I like to find out what was built, not who lived or fornicated there."

There are 300 castles still standing in Holland, says van Reyen, though they're not the storybook sort most people think of. "Actually, they're kind of disappointing," he says. "What we think of as castles are royal creations, built by monarchs with great wealth." In Holland, the castles were built by local nobility, often below the level of counts. Thus, the Dutch castles can't compete with the more magnificent castles of England and France because the "economics of their construction was so different," says van Reyen. "They're very small — comparatively speaking, of course." He adds that "people who have seen French chateaux are disappointed" when they view a Dutch castle.

Nonetheless, there are some interesting ones to see. Muiden "should be visited by everybody," he thinks. "It's in pretty good shape, you could almost live there." This castle, whose foundation dates to 1285, was rebuilt in 1369 and again in the late-14th century. "It is tremendously well-restored," van Reyen says.

Another not-to-be-missed Dutch castle is De Haar, near Utrecht, he says. This castle is still owned by the noble family that built it, and it was beautifully restored in 1892, when a Rothschild heiress married into the family. "This has become a Disney-sort of castle," van Reyen says, "It was never so grand when it was built. But it was restored to the style of what the Victorians thought was Gothic."

Van Reyen has written a couple of books (in Dutch) about the castles and their architecture, and hopes to eventually have a book published in English. When he's not studying castles or corresponding with people in Holland about them, he works as a translator for a New Jersey stamp dealer.

In researching medieval Dutch castles (or anything historical), van Reyen advises the student "not to trust anything that has been published so far. Go and check for yourself. If you have a different opinion, and you're sure of it, try to get it published."

Castle-watching for van Reyen is the ideal hobby. "I've never been able to get a job in history or fine arts," he says. "Castles are marvelous as a hobby so I can get back to my own field. And, too, you need something to do at night totally different from your work."

Van Reyen is happy to correspond with people about medieval Dutch architecture. He can be contacted at PO Box 555, Montclair, NJ 07042.

GORDON WENDT
GREAT LAKES STEAMBOATS

"**I**'D RATHER LOOK AT a picture of a steamboat than go to a beauty pageant," says Gordon Wendt. "Those boats are beautiful to me."

Wendt has spent most of his 62 years with the Great Lakes sidewheelers. These boats, with names like *The Chippewa* and *Good Time*, plied their daily trade on Lake Erie (and the other Great Lakes) for a little over 100 years.

A lifelong resident of the Lake Erie port city of Sandusky, Ohio, Wendt has made a study of the marine history of his hometown, especially the steamships that were prominent in commerce on the lake from 1818 to 1938. He's been interested in the maritime life of the Great Lakes "for so long I don't remember how it got started." He traces his interest to postcards his father used to send him of the ships he traveled on making business trips.

Wendt became a serious collector and researcher in 1946, after he came back from serving in the Army in World War II. He made the acquaintance of a couple of collectors in Detroit and Cleveland, and started collecting "artifacts, photographs, lithographs, anything to do with passenger boating on Lake Erie." A particular benefactor, a former passenger boat captain, left his collection to Wendt.

Wendt's current project is compiling a complete record of the maritime history of Sandusky. His primary source: local newspapers. "We're fortunate in that our town's newspaper files are on microfilm and go all the way back to 1822, when the paper began," he says. From his diligent reading of all the papers, he's obtained "a sheaf of notes that I hope to use to write a book."

Wendt has discovered that Sandusky was an important transportation center on Lake Erie. Many railroad lines came into the town, both from the Ohio Valley to the south and from the major cities of the East, he says. The railroads "pretty much sponsored their own steamboat lines until all the cities were connected by railroad," he says. The liners of the New York Central and the Erie Rail Road, among others, all came into Sandusky, where there was quite a bit of ore unloading and coal exporting.

"The saddest part is that Toledo and Cleveland, even though they developed much later than Sandusky, outstripped us in importance," he says, noting that Sandusky's shallow harbor made it difficult for many ships to get in.

Wendt says the Great Lakes steamships were made of wood (although latter day models did have iron or steel hulls) and their two paddlewheels were located amidships, rather than on the stern like the Mississippi River steamboats. Many of the ships were made by Frank E. Kirby, a Detroit designer. The ships were of all sizes, Wendt says, with the biggest about 160 feet in length. Two of the most notable sidewheelers were the *Rutherford B. Hayes* (named for the President) and the *A. Wherle, Jr.*. These 120-foot-long, beam engine boats "wound up in Lake Superior for most of their active service," says Wendt.

The sidewheelers "were nowhere near able to contend with bad weather," says Wendt, "and they couldn't be used when the lakes were frozen." Therefore, much of the work of the sidewheelers was for passenger trips and short freight hauls.

"They were used on all the Great Lakes," says Wendt. "There was a tremendous vacation trade betweewn Sheboygan, Wisconsin, and Mackinac Island on Lake Michigan, as well as fruit shipments between Benton Harbor and St. Joseph, Michigan." Lake Superior had its sidewheeler trade, too, "but it was primarily ships from the lower lakes coming up into Superior," he says.

"We have all the beauty of Lake Erie right outside our front door," says Wendt, noting that only near Sandusky are there any islands in the 241-mile long lake. Most of the marine activity was devoted to carrying passengers from Sandusky to several of these nearby islands, utilizing the sidewheelers of the Sandusky and Island Steamboat Company, which operated until 1938. For example, Wendt says, the ships "played a vital part in the life of the people of Kelly's Island, which is about 10 miles from Sandusky. It brought the sick to the mainland for treatment, it brought the dead home to bury them."

In addition, "Sandusky has a large waterfront resort, Cedar Point, which in the 1870s became a tourist Mecca," Wendt says. Sidewheelers came from Toledo, Detroit, and Cleveland daily to deposit tourists. "It made for a nice excursion," says Wendt, noting that today there are still "three little boats" that go to Cedar Point during the summer season.

Wendt's research has not been without some frustration. For one thing, he says, "there's a blackout between 1834 and 1843; the newspapers from that time all disappeared in a fire in the newspaper office." He's had to resort to the National Archives in Washington for information on the boats in those years.

He knows that Sandusky was a center of the steamboat building industry, but has had difficulty in finding the areas on the waterfront where the boats were built. "The newsmen of the time were frustratingly vague," he says. However, he has managed to locate much of the original waterfront, and pin down some locations where he feels ships were constructed.

"Mainly for my own edification," says Wendt, "I've built a number of models of Great Lakes ships." These he designed and built himself, many from period photographs or lithographs. His models are mounted on the wall of his den.

Wendt is a member of the Cleveland-based Great Lakes Historical Society and the Steamship History Society of America, organizations he commends to buffs. In addition, he says, "it's amazing how many marine museums there are" concentrating on the Great Lakes. Especially worth visits, he feels, are the Great Lakes Maritime Institute in Detroit, and the Bowling Green State University Marine Museum in Bowling Green, Ohio.

"When I first started collecting material on Great Lakes steamships," says Wendt, "there wasn't a lot published." His main sources, in the early days, were books by Dana Bowen, *Lore of the Lakes*, *Memories of the Lakes*, and *Shipwrecks of the Lakes*. These books, still in print, "are standard reading for people interested in the history of the Great Lakes."

Wendt looks upon his research as "a time-consuming labor of love. But another generation is coming along, and I'd like to see if I can't spread some of what I learned from my forebears " in Great Lakes history.

"Some days I can go down to our little yacht club on the lake and sit looking out, and think I can see the boats I used to see as a boy," says Wendt. "I guess it's a sign I'm getting old... but they sure were beautiful."

Wendt will gladly answer questions about Great Lakes steamships, or other aspects of Great Lakes history. Contact him at 121 44th St., Sandusky, OH 44870.

NATURE AND SCIENCE

ROBERT CAMPBELL
NUT GROWING

ROBERT CAMPBELL is crazy about nuts — of all kinds, shapes and sizes. What's more, he's attempting to turn nuts into bucks by making Canada a profitable nut-growing region.

For those doubters who think nuts don't grow well in the cold northern U.S. and Canada, Douglas is quick to dispel the misconception: "Many people underestimate how hardy and venturesome the species of the plant world are. Many items can be grown in the north, beyond most people's wildest imagination."

He has the nut trees to prove it. The two-acres he bought in 1969 near Niagara-on-the-Lake, Ontario, is "loaded right to the gills" with an estimated 500 Northern pecan, chestnut, and hickory nut trees. Most of the trees are from 15 to 20 feet high and are "just getting into the interesting stage," having produced about three 6-quart baskets in 1979. They will be producing an estimated 300 to 500 pounds of nuts annually in another five or six years.

Campbell, 41, became interested in nuts when he was six years old and had a collection of hickory and walnuts. "My grandparents took me hickory-nut hunting in the Windsor-Sarnia area of Canada, near Detroit. In those times, people used to pick up wild nuts, shell them, and use them for cooking."

He urges people to try growing nuts if they live in such places as Connecticut, New York, Michigan, Wisconsin, Iowa, and anywhere north of these states. One of the best kinds of nut trees to grow, particularly in the Northeast is the Chinese chestnut, Campbell says. They are resistant to chestnut blight (which the American chestnut wasn't). He also suggests raising English walnuts (the northern strain), hazelnuts, filberts, black walnuts, hickory nuts or Northern pecans in northern climates.

Nut growing doesn't require a lot of land, either, Campbell claims. "Even the relatively average-sized city lot could grow filberts," he says, adding that these nuts grow on bushes about 8 to 10 feet high which can be used as a hedge. Plant 10 or 20 of the bushes and "you'll produce a bushel or two of nuts in an otherwise wasted area."

Campbell is particularly interested in correcting the misconceptions he feels people have about growing nuts. For one thing, he says, it doesn't take the excessive number of years to produce a good crop of nuts that people think. Most trees take from two to ten years to bear fruit.

He believes that economic developments will make nut growing more popular. "One factor that is attractive now is the relatively high price for nuts. This
will increase, and California will seem to get farther away," he says, referring
to that state's corner on the U.S. nut market.

In addition, "nuts are very, very nutritious. There is a good variety of
nutrients in them that are important to health." Besides, says Campbell,
"there's just a lot of fun out of it."

People "have tried to relate nuttiness to growing nut trees, but when they
see the commercial return, they rapidly change their minds. Nut trees are as
durable and reliable as any you will get, so they make a nice type of shade tree,
too."

Campbell, who teaches vocational subjects for the extension division of
Niagara College, has banded together with other nut-growing enthusiasts in
his region. The Society of Ontario Nut Growers publishes a semi-annual
newsletter, of which he is the editor. He also serves as president of the 2,000-
member Northern Nut Growers Association, an international group that advocates the growing of nuts in northern climes.

Campbell feels nuts are an especially important crop to Canada, which
imports some $45 million worth of them annually. But he realizes that it will
take time — probably at least 35 years — before there will be a significant
nut-producing industry in the country.

Campbell is all for people getting into the growing of nuts. He recommends
purchasing nut trees, at first, from any of the 10-15 nurseries in the United
States that specialize in nut trees. Once the nut-grower has some experience
and some good stock to work from, raising trees from seed is the next step.

His group will provide, on request, a list of the nurseries. "Most lots have a
capacity of one or two trees, so, rather than planting an elm or maple, it's
equally practical to plant a nut tree." His advice for beginners: "Now is the
time to get started. Stick with it until you get the desired results." And he'll be
happy to help novice nut-growers along. Contact him at RR#1, Niagara-on-
the-Lake, Ontario, Canada, L0S 1J0.

GEORGE CHAPLENKO
ASTRONOMY

GEORGE CHAPLENKO HAS stars in
his eyes all the time, with the help of the telescopes he has designed and built.

One summer night in 1970, while watching "The Tonight Show" on television, Chaplenko heard host Johnny Carson "mention that he owned several
telescopes and that he had recently observed certain planets with them." The
statement aroused Chaplenko's curiosity, and being mechanically inclined, he
constructed a telescope to see if he could see what Carson was seeing. "I've
been making telescopes ever since," he says.

Chaplenko wasn't much interested in astronomy "until I built that first
telescope," though he had studied it in school, and had even, in high school,

built a simple telescope." But now,"I've got the bug real bad," he says, adding that telescope building is "very rewarding because you can build something useful that is probably better than what you could buy." Though building a telescope is a time-consuming operation involving many hours of concentrated work, he says his telescopes "have better optical quality, more convenience of handling, and are sturdier than most of those that are manufactured."

All of the telescopes Chaplenko has built have been reflecting, not refracting telescopes. "I build 4- to 12-inch telescopes," he says, "all from scratch, and even make custom models for other people." He likes to "build and rebuild" his telescopes. "I use one for awhile, then pull it apart and build it again." He is always tinkering with the telescopes, making little improvements as he rebuilds them.

The joys of astronomy are many, says Chaplenko. "The visual pleasures alone are fascinating. It's very hard to describe, unless you are one of us, why it's such a thrill to look at the moon. Once you see it through a telescope, the sky is never the same."

Of course, for ideal observing, Chaplenko says, "you have to catch a night when both the light pollution and air pollution from the surrounding city is low. You can see everything. We treasure those nights."

While Chaplenko feels that "anything you look at the first time is the most exciting thing you've ever seen," he does have some particularly favorite obser-vations. These include his first viewings of "the disk shape of Mars, the equato-rial zone of Jupiter, and the Andromeda Galaxy. My wife helped me find the galaxy: she has sharper eyes than I do."

Since 1977, Chaplenko has been president of Amateur Astronomers, Inc., a Cranford, New Jersey-based organization of some 350 astronomy buffs. The association's purpose, says Chaplenko, "is not only enjoyment, but also to introduce astronomy to the public." The group is extremely active, featuring regular lectures on astronomical topics, running annual seminars on telescope use and adult education classes in astronomical subjects, and holding "star parties" to which the public is invited to view particular astrophenomena.

The most extensive project of the group, however, has been the construction of a 10-inch refracting telescope, which it donated to Union College in New Jersey for its observatory. In exchange for the telescope, the group is granted the use of the college's observatory.

Making a telescope, says Chaplenko, can be a pleasant (though laborious) experience. "It all depends on your personality. If you have had experience building things from kits, you are probably best advised to use a kit to make your telescope. If you really are a do-it-yourselfer, by all means, build from scratch." He adds that a scratch-built telescope can take up to a year to complete.

Chaplenko admits, "I like to build anything." In constructing telescopes, he finds a great deal of satisfaction in knowing that what he's built "is an instru-ment as accurate as anything I could buy, and yet I can make it for a fraction of the cost of a commercial model."

Combining his professional interests as a reasearch and development engi-neer with his hobby, the 56-year-old Chaplenko wants to "design a completely new type of telescope mounting system and clock drive mechanism (which keeps the telescope turning at the same rate as the stars appear to move). I also want to have a hands-on experience with as many different 'scopes as possible."

For beginners, Chaplenko counsels, "Concentrate your attention on specific aspects of astronomy. Don't try to do everything at once." He also advises against getting "more telescope than you actually need. Consider the limitations in seeing of your area."

Chaplenko suggests amateur astronomers join a local astronomy club. The association with other people, many extremely knowledgeable, will make astronomical explorations "easier and more fun."

Chaplenko is always willing to counsel telescope builders and other people interested in astronomy. He can be contacted at 73 Alexander St., Edison, NJ 08817.

CHRISTOPHER COOPER
ALASKAN MALAMUTES

Dogs HAVE A HARD life sometimes, but if they're Christopher Cooper's Alaskan Malamutes, they're living the way nature intended. Cooper breeds and trains his dogs to be the sturdy, hard-working animals they are in their natural habitat.

Cooper's intense interest in malamutes dates from 1975. He first saw a malamute in a pet store in Albuquerque, New Mexico, and immediately fell in love with the breed. Unfortunately, "the pet store, as I was soon to discover, is the worst place to purchase any type of animal," he recalls. "I found this out much to the heartbreak of myself and the pain and suffering of the dog I purchased there."

A friend (and his current partner in a kennel), Bobbie Leslie, interested him in breeding in 1977, and since then, Cooper has been "breeding quality Malamutes with their intended purpose in mind." Their kennel, Maluk's Dianom Star Kennels, has produced 30 AKC registered puppies.

"We don't breed profusely," Cooper says. "We do it according to quality. If we find the right stud and dam for the betterment of the breed, we do it. We aren't like the puppy mills or backyard breeders" who breed indiscriminately, in his view. It is important to improve the strength quality of the breed, Cooper feels. "Malamutes are frequently bred for the show ring with features that a judge would like, or that will be worth more money at stud. This kind of breeding takes away from the workability of the breed. A little, flashy malamute can win over a powerful dog in the ring because that's what many judges expect."

What kind of malamute is Cooper interested in producing? "I'm looking for soundness — a well-structured dog that moves with ease, that is square, with fairly large bones, is well-proportioned, and who can pull over 3,000 pounds." Some dogs, Cooper says, have been known to pull 10,000 pounds. "I will never breed for the ring alone, but always for the type of dog that can and will pull the best, according to the standard," he says.

His dog, Maluk's Star Image, is well on her way to becoming a champion in record time. She won her "companion dog" rank in December of 1978, at the age of six months and 3 days, making her the youngest dog of any breed to achieve the initial ranking recorded by the AKC. She earned her "companion dog excellent" rank at 13 months, and is now working on the "utility" rating, the highest possible ranking for obedience.

The 30-year-old brick mason, who lives in Sunland, California (near Burbank), has become involved in training and racing sled teams of dogs. "You can't just put the dogs in harness and expect them to pull a sled," Cooper says. It takes over a year to train the dogs. Sleds require from one to five or more dogs, but he most often uses five-dog teams. The dogs have to have the right temperament to pull and race. Not all dogs can do it, he says.

He has also begun training some of his dogs for weight pulling competitions, where they pull sledges with heavy weights. Cooper also takes his dogs into the mountains near Palm Springs on backpacking trips. Here, Cooper trains them for carrying loads, giving each dog has its own backpack.

For the person interested in breeding malamutes (or any dogs), Cooper advises checking "the temperament of any breed before buying to see if it is compatible with you." Then, buy directly from a reputable breeder, not a pet store. Malamutes are adaptable to many situations, Cooper says, "but be sure you have time for a dog before buying."

Cooper will give further information on malamutes to anyone contacting him at 10635 Sable Ave., Sunland, CA 91040.

GORDON FORE
HIBISCUS CULTURE

Its COMMON RELATIVES are the Rose of Sharon, okra, and cotton. It usually grows in tropical climates, where it's known for its brilliantly colored, delicate flowers. It's the hibiscus, and of special interest to Gordon Fore, a leading authority on the propagation of a particular variety of the flower, Hibiscus Rosa Sinensis.

Fore wasn't always interested in the hibiscus. The 45-year-old salesman for an agricultural chemicals company from Ft. Meyers, Florida, first encountered the flower when he moved to Florida, in 1961.

"My father-in-law had just started a nursery," Fore says, "and with my professional background, I became interested from being around his flowers and watching them grow."

Today, Fore does a lot of growing of his own on his 2½- acre property. "I have a small nursery, " he says, "and grow some plants to sell, but my main interest is in breeding. It's really a hobby with me."

So far, through careful study and research, as well as propagation of plants, Fore has managed, through breeding and cross-breeding, to achieve "limited success in increasing the vigor of the plants, and the variety of color, texture, and longevity of the flower." His hibiscus have six possible blossom colors, both single and double blossoms, and many will live for as long as two or three days.

The first hibiscus came to the United States from Europe at the turn of the century, Fore says. Most of the cultivation of the hibiscus has been done in Hawaii, since the climate there is most favorable to the plants.

Much of Fore's work in hibiscus care and culture has been done in conjunction with the American Hibiscus Society, which was founded in 1950. Fore says the group has over 3,000 members in 43 states and 31 other countries. The emphasis of the society, according to Fore is on the Rosa Sinensis variety, and the general goal of producing hardier flowers.

The best hibiscus plants, says Fore, have a nice compact bush. The leaves have a heavy texture and the plant blooms profusely. "What we're trying to achieve is an all-around, good healthy plant."

Fore has won "many, many awards" for his work in hibiscus culture. In 1979, his variety "Bloomin' Blazes" was awarded the Seedling of the Year trophy at the American Hibiscus Society's annual convention. Fore has also written three editions of *What Every Hibiscus Grower Should Know*, the society's official guidebook for the novice hibiscus grower.

Growing hibiscus plants can be difficult, but it is rewarding, says Fore. "They're best grown outdoors, though you can grow them indoors in at least 65 percent light." The plants are susceptible to a variety of diseases, especially nematodes, which are soil-borne organisms that attack the roots. The plants have to be sprayed periodically, and guarded against cold weather. A cold snap in Florida almost cost him his entire collection.

"They are very touchy, but they're really not too difficult to grow if you fertilize them, care for them, and spray them regularly," he says.

"My goal is to continuously improve the hibiscus by hybridizing" he says. "It's a hobby that gives me a tremendous amount of satisfaction."

"I enjoy growing things, and I enjoy seeing the new flowers blooming. We have every color of the rainbow in our garden." He also enjoys surprising friends with flowers cut from his garden.

Fore advises anyone interested in growing hibiscus plants to purchase a copy of *What Every Hibiscus Grower Should Know*, available from the society for $5.40, postpaid. And, he says, joining the American Hibscus Society is also important, because it provides valuable contacts with other growers, who are a vital source of information about the proper way to handle the plants.

Fore can be reached at Rt. 1, Box 491F, Ft. Myers, FL 33905.

EDDIE FUJIMOTO
KOI

WHEN EDDIE FUJIMOTO describes his fish as koi, he's not talking about their personalities. His fish are an ornamental, intelligent (they even do tricks) Japanese variety of carp (kin to the common goldfish), which are very popular in Japan — and are developing great popularity in the United States, as well.

In a relatively few years, Fujimoto has become one of the country's leading experts in the complicated, but rewarding, field of koi raising, showing, and breeding.

"I always liked ponds and fish," Fujimoto says. When he was stationed for 12 years in Japan with the U.S. Air Force, he took note of "the pretty gardens many of the people had. They always had a pond, with these marvelous fish swimming in them."

After returning to the States, where he joined the security department of McDonnell Douglas, Fujimoto purchased his first koi from Japan in 1968. Since then, he has won numerous prizes for his fish at koi shows ("in many respects, they're just like dog shows," he says). He has nearly 130 of the fish, in varying sizes from two inches to 28 inches in length, swimming in his back-yard in Midway City, California.

Koi, says Fujimoto "are very beautiful and unusual fish." They are bred in any of several colors or color combinations, and with a slightly different body conformation from the traditional carp. With their white skin, and the definite, brightly-colored brocaded patterns on their skin, koi are at once astounding and unique.

According to Fujimoto, koi are bred to very strict standards of excellence. Chief among these (and counting for roughly 50 percent of a judge's score) is body conformation. The fish must look rugged in the "shoulder" area, he says, "and appear strong and healthy. In Japan, in fact, they are the symbol of strength and endurance, and that is why a koi flag is flown during Boys Day, the Japanese national holiday." The other 50 percent of koi scoring is based on intensity and pattern of the color.

Fujimoto keeps his prize-winning koi in a 4,500-gallon pond in his back-yard, and another 1,000-gallon pond in the atrium of his home. The water in the ponds is purified 24 hours a day, he says, so that "it's pure, like drinking water. Koi can't live in the murky water like most fish."

Since 1976, Fujimoto has published a bi-monthly newsletter about koi. "I began to see the need for information about koi to be available, and, at the urging of others began publishing the *Koi USA* newsletter," he says. From a somewhat shaky start, the 24-page publication now goes to 600 subscribers in 40 states, Canada, England, Japan, and Guam. Most of the subscribers are members of Associated Koi Clubs of America, a hobbyist group with many local chapters across the country.

Written in a lively, informal style by Fujimoto and a staff of fellow koi enthusiasts, *Koi USA* "is designed for the expert and the novice alike," he says. It contains information on such koi-related essentials as pond making, filter design, medical problems and their cures, and results of koi shows.

Fujimoto enjoys his koi because "they are like artwork. When you come home from work, and look at your pond, with its rock formation and waterfall, it really relaxes you just to see it. You can pet the fish, you can hold them. The whole landscape takes on a special beauty because of your fish."

The beauty of koi swimming in a well-designed pond has made koi keeping an international hobby, Fujimoto says. "It is my hope that someday, when the word koi is heard, everyone in the USA will understand what is being talked about."

For the beginning koi keeper, Fujimoto warns, "Never buy koi without having an adequate pond with a filter." An adequate pond would be no less than 2-feet deep, and about 3-feet-by-5-feet in dimension. It's also important to make sure the fish are properly sexed and color-keyed.

He also feels it is helpful to meet other koi enthusiasts before embarking on building a pond or getting too far into the hobby. The best way to do this, of course, is to join a local koi club. The Associated Koi Clubs of America can provide information on area clubs, Fujimoto says.

Fujimoto will also be glad to give advice and counsel to novice koi collectors, as well as trade shop-talk with seasoned hands. Both he, and Associated Koi Clubs of America, can be reached at PO Box 1, Midway City, CA 92655.

RONALD GATTIE
ASTROPHOTOGRAPHY

RONALD GATTIE'S PHOTOS are like a fascinating trip into the universe, as if the viewer were hanging suspended among the darting lights, zooming comets and meteors, and stolid planets glimmering in the endless darkness. He's made them all from right here on Earth — through astrophotography.

Just what is astrophotography? According to Gattie, it's photographing the stars, planets, the moon, anything in the heavens, with cameras used in conjunction with telescopes and other astronomical equipment.

Gattie has been at it since 1973, and already his pictures have achieved recognition for their excellence. Photographing those stars and galaxies so many millions of miles away "is one of the most spectacular adventures imaginable," he says.

How did the 37-year-old research technician from Plainfield, N.J., get involved with astrophotography? "When I was young, I went to the Hayden Planetarium in New York City and was so fascinated, I started to read all I could about astronomy," Gattie recalls. He bought his own telescope and became even more intrigued. "I didn't really know too much, but I sure was interested in watching the skies with it."

After several years, he tired of astronomy, until 1973 when he bought another telescope, joined an astronomy hobbyist organization, and started taking pictures using his telescope "to further enhance what could be seen with the eye. I was rather impressed to see what could be done with the simple equipment I had. I didn't think it could be done."

Gattie does not specialize. "I try to cover just about all the objects you can photograph," he says. These include "deep sky" photographs of galaxies, nebulae, and star clusters, in addition to the planets and the moon, as well as the sun.

Using special filters, he is able to capture "solar prominences that are usually seen only during an eclipse," he says. "I enjoy this kind of photography, because I am able to see changes in the prominences over a period of hours."

Often it does take hours, or at the very least, minutes, to take astrophotographs. This is where the specialized equipment comes in. To get started properly in astrophotography, Gattie says, the beginner "needs a telescope of sufficient aperture to see objects that are rather dim to the naked eye. Figure what your needs are. Get the largest aperture you feel you can handle, with short focal length."

A single lens reflex (SLR) camera is necessary, so the photographer can see the subject directly through the viewfinder. The camera must take time exposures. Use the fastest possible film. "You will be photographing for a few seconds up to a few hours," he says.

If the photographer lives in a location, as Gattie does, that is "very suburban, with a lot of light pollution, you will get fogged film unless you use professional film."

In addition, Gattie says, a "clock drive" which keeps the telescope in line with the rotation of the earth, is absolutely essential to astrophotography. Without it, the subject being photographed would "wander out of the picture. You would have a streaked image, as the earth turned."

His favorite photographic subjects are distant stars and star groupings light years away. "The Andromeda Galaxy, for example, is quite bright, with an estimated 100 billion stars, and can be seen with the naked eye. Yet it is 2.3 million light years away," he says. "What you are seeing is the past." And unlike some kinds of photography, "If I miss it tonight, I can always get it tomorrow."

The most distant object he has photographed? It's difficult to say. "I've gotten some objects from South Plainfield that are 15 million light years away, but that's still rather local". There are stars billions of light years away."

Some of Gattie's pictures have been published in *Night Skies* and *Astronomy Magazine*. In addition, several of his photos were used for the jacket of the jazz record, "Richard 'Groove' Holmes: Star Wars — Close Encounters".

Gattie's greatest delight in astrophotography is its enhancement of the object photographed. "You tend to see an object through the telescope as a little fuzzy ball. In photographing the object, many things are put on the film that your eye, even aided by the telescope, cannot see. What you saw as a little fuzzy ball really looks like all kinds of beautiful and interesting things on film," he says.

Gattie says personal satisfaction is hard to find."You try for a long time and the doing of it isn't easy. You develop a techinque and try for consistency, the object being to get better pictures. You strive for standout shots as your technique improves.

"There's also a feeling of camaraderie with others. You can learn from them. It's the kind of hobby that can get you together with other people.

Gattie recommends amateurs join a local astronomy club, of which there are many throughout the country. He is also willing to answer questions about astrophotography, addressed to him at 248 Pierce St., South Plainfield, NJ 07080.

ROBERT GATTUS
ROLLER CANARIES

BELIEVE IT OR NOT, they aren't some kind of brand new disco attraction!

"The roller canary is a mutation of the wild canary," says Robert Gattus, about the birds with the unique and beautiful song. He's been breeding and showing them since 1961, and has earned the distinction of being a "master breeder." One of only five certified roller judges in the United States, Gattus is also president of the 500-member Central States Roller Association, the largest American organization of roller canary enthusiasts.

The 47-year-old Gattus is a vulcanizer of rubber conveyors from Baltimore, Maryland. He lived in Germany from 1950 to 1953, while in the service, and married a German woman there. Her father raised the birds and was a famous judge in Germany. When Gattus returned to the United States, his father-in-law sent him some canaries and eventually taught Gattus how to be a show judge.

The roller canary was introduced into Germany at the turn of the century. "A few German breeders worked on getting the chops and chirps out of the birds's song," says Gattus, "leaving only the rolling 'tours,' like the purring of a cat." Though most birds sing through their mouths, with their beaks open, roller canaries are bred to produce "a canary that sings with his beak closed, through the portholes of his beak, thus producing the rolling 'tours.'"

These "tours," are a combination of musical notes. There are 12 possible variations of song that a bird can sing. In competitions, the birds sing in quartets, harmonizing with each other, Gattus says.

The training of the teams of canaries is unique. Only males born in the spring of the year are trained (the females are mute). The baby birds are put together in one cage and all sing merrily for a time until "you decide which will make a good team," he says. The four best birds are chosen, and separated from the rest, "to get to know each other."

After the chosen birds have had a chance to sing together for awhile, they instinctively develop their own vocal arrangements and begin to harmonize. Then, each bird is put into a separate cage. The cages are stacked, one on top of the other, Gattus says, and the birds are ready to be trained to sing on command.

The stacked cages are put into a dark-interiored cabinet, Gattus says. Then, through a process of gradually exposing the birds to varying degrees of light, they are taught to break into song the moment they are in bright light and to stop when they are in the dark; to be properly judged, they must begin singing immediately when they are in the presence of the official.

Gattus has 35 birds for breeding and showing purposes. There are 25 females and 10 males. The male will breed with any female, he says. All the contests for roller canary singing are held in November and December because "it is the time of the canaries' cycle of life that their song is most mature. By January, the song goes downhill; they become interested in breeding, and starting forcing their song, thus becoming worthless for shows."

In 1974, Gattus won the Grand Champion team award in the three largest shows in the country (Chicago, Minnesota and Ohio) and from 1975 to 1977, he produced champions annually. He has developed a strain known nationwide for their depth and hollowness of tone.

Gattus recommends the novice attend a roller contest, if possible, to learn quality song characteristics before buying any birds. He says that purchasing birds is expensive (males are $40-50 each, females $20-$25 each) because you need three hens for every male. "Purchase only quality contest birds and hens of the same strain — it's very important." Two males and six hens are enough to get started with.

The birds can be purchased only from the 2,000 people in the United States who breed and show the birds. They aren't available in pet stores. The best way to find a reliable breeder, Gattus says, is through the advertisements in *Cage Birds Magazine*, and by writing for catalogues of one of the 10 roller canary shows held in the U.S. annually.

Gattus is fond of his birds and fascinated by the hobby. "It's a real challenge to train them," he says. "It's fascinating to see what you can produce, and how you can train a little creature like a canary to do wonderful things."

Despite the work involved, Gattus finds his hobby a perfect way "to get away from the wear and tear of the world. It's relaxing of an evening to be with your birds. You're always entertained by rollers; there's always something going on."

Gattus would be glad to hear from anyone interested in roller canaries. He can be contacted at 2803 E. Joppa Rd., Baltimore, MD 21234.

PEARL GEORGE
PAPILLION DOGS

WHAT'S UNDER ONE FOOT in height, weighs five or six pounds, has ears that look like a butterfly, and a plumed tail?

Papillions, that's what. These diminuitive dogs, a favorite of Madame de Pompadour, are one of the rarer breeds that have begun to receive some attention in the United States in recent years. Certainly one of America's most prominent breeders and showers of these diminutive "butterflies" is Pearl George of Los Gatos, California.

In 11 years of breeding the dogs, Mrs. George has produced two best-in-show (all breeds) winners, the only U. S. papillion breeder ever to do so. This is considered to be an especially outstanding achievement, Mrs. George says, because it has been accomplished with a limited breeding program. But that's not all. Mrs. George's dogs have been awarded best puppy honors four times at the Papillion Club of America National Specialities Show (another record), and she has produced 25 home-bred AKC breed champions. In 1976, her dog Champion Kavar The Huntsman was named the number one papillion in the U.S., based on points accumulated in his show career.

Born in North London, England, Mrs. George "was raised with a wide assortment of dogs, like most English children. My father was always bringing home unwanted puppies. One day, he came in with a day-old border collie, and explained that the dam had to act as a 'foster mother' for a litter of English bulldog puppies whose mother was a 'show bitch.' I, of course, wanted to understand why a bitch could not raise her own puppies." That was when she began studying dog breeding, an interest she has carried all through her life.

Mrs. George didn't become seriously interested in showing dogs, however, until 1967, when she received Quinetta, a papillon, as a gift. Shortly thereafter, she went to a dog show, saw some other papillions on display there, and "I felt that the one I had compared very well with what was being shown." At her first show, "we won a third place ribbon, then a second — and I was hooked!"

Since her primary interest is in breeding the papillion, Mrs. George is anxious to "develop a strain that is an excellent breed type, sound in structure and temperament, that can consistently pass on their qualities." The dogs, of spaniel origin, have the friendly spaniel temperament and are highly intelligent. Really, says Mrs. George, "they are the ideal dog, not exaggerated in any way, designed so as not to be prone to problems" that afflict other show dogs.

A papillion can be best described as "a plain, basic, sensible, intelligent little dog, with large, rounded ears." They're hardy, too. Mrs. George's first pap is "still gorgeous" at 13 years of age (the average lifespan is 16 years).

Mrs. George says that there are several ways a "good" dog can be determined. First, it must conform to the breed type classification ("small, dainty dog") of the American Kennel Club. It has to have a sound body structure and move well. "We want a dog that can 'pick them up and put them down' when it moves," she says. Next in importance is the clarity of the color of the dog. Its mixture of brown and white or black and white must be definite and in proportion, she says. Finally, the large, beautifully flared butterfly ears must have good shape.

The best place to buy a papillion (or any purebred dog) is through a recognized breeder, says Mrs. George. For one thing, the breeder will try to match the personality of the owner to that of the dog; not all are compatible. In addition, by buying from a breeder, the purchaser knows something about the dog's history before purchasing it. This is especially important if the person wishes to breed or show the papillion.

When you buy a puppy from a pet shop, it usually comes from a "breeding farm," where no particular care is taken with it, Mrs. George says. All the pet shop wants is "a fluffy little puppy, and they rely on people to buy on impulse." This often results in people not getting the pet suitable for them.

By way of example, a papillion is not suitable for a house with small children, because the dog is too small to survive children's roughhousing. On the other hand, a papillion is "marvelous" for adult families and older people, according to Mrs. George.

For the novice breeder/shower/dog owner, Mrs. George has much advice. First and foremost, she believes, "All dogs, be they show dogs or not, should be family pets." Therefore, it's important to select the breed of dog carefully, considering such factors as available space, how much grooming is involved, the dog's temperament, and what kind of environment the dog will be living in.

For show dogs, Mrs. George says, the selection process is much more complicated, involving research into the background of the dog, medical exams, and the like. "Do keep in mind that show dogs are a somewhat expensive hobby, if done correctly," Mrs. George cautions." You do not make money...you're lucky to break even on the vet bills."

Mrs. George is nonetheless enthusiastic about showing dogs as a hobby. "Win or lose, there are a lot of benefits to this hobby. You will meet many people and make many new friends who have an interest in common with you. You will stimulate your mind in learning about such things as genetic inheritance, pedigrees, and so on."

Her sage advice to would-be dog showers:"Watch what wins and learn why it's winning."

Mrs. George is active in the Papillion Club of America, the breed group organization. She has been editor of their monthly newsletter *Pap Talk* since 1978, and writes a regular column on breeding and medical problems, along with occasional feature articles. She is a founder of the Papillion Club of Northern California and currently is president of the club.

Mrs. George's greatest reward has been "the marvelous people I've met. I've made meaningful friendships all over the world."

Breeding her dogs has been a source of considerable satisfaction for Mrs. George (who is a self-described "frustrated artist who can't draw a straight line"). The knowledge that she, through her dogs, "can produce something beautiful gives me a great feeling of pride, and believe me, breeding is not easy."

Anyone interested in papillions should contact the secretary of the Papillion Club of America, Mary Jo Loye, 5707 Hillcrest Dr., Detroit, MI 48236, or Mrs. George at 24750 Highway 17, Los Gatos, CA 95030.

ANTON GLASER
ANCIENT MATH PROBLEMS

THEN THERE'S THE STORY of the Persian king, who wanted to reward a wise man for all of his sage advice.

"What can I give you as a reward?" the king asked.

The wise man answered, "Give me a grain of wheat for the first square on the chessboard, and double the number of grains for each successive square." How much grain did the generous king have to give the wise man?

For most of us, a problem like that would cause some consternation if it appeared on a math test. But for Anton Glaser, a professor of mathematics from Southampton, Pennsylvania, problems like these are no problem — he "collects" mathematical mind-benders.

Glaser first ran across these ancient math problems (he doesn't have a date for the one cited above, but says it is "very old") while he was doing research for his doctorate in the history of mathematics. "Since I was specifically interested in the binary system, most of the problems I've collected involve the use of binary or non-decimal numeration," he says.

Many of these problems appear in his book *The History of Binary and Other Non-Decimal Numeration*, which grew out of his dissertation. "Even though my doctoral dissertation was completed in 1969, I still enjoy searching out the puzzles and researching their histories. I've never even counted how many problems I've uncovered," says Glaser.

The problems were popular among educated people in all eras, Glaser says. Most of them had been transmitted orally before the 18th and 19th centuries, when they were finally written down. They were created for recreation. Instead of watching TV like we do now, people would gather in groups and stimulate their minds with the problems." For a lot of people, Glaser included, working problems of this sort is "relaxing and a lot of fun."

Eventually, Glaser would like "to gather and publish a collection of ancient mathematics problems, together with a discussion of what implications we can draw about the social milieu that influenced those problems." But, he says, the press of his academic career keeps such a project "at least five years away, at present."

By now, one might be asking what the solution to the problem of the king and the wise man is.

"This problem can be solved with relative ease, just by thinking it through, and applying the binary system to your calculations," Glaser says.

There are 64 squares on the chessboard, and if the wise man were to receive one grain on the first square, two for the second, four for the third, and so on, the total amount "would exceed the world production of grain at present levels," Glaser says.

"Thus, it would have been impossible for the king to grant the wise man's request," Glaser says, proving the wise man was a wise guy.

This problem is one of Glaser's favorites because "it illustrates the futility of chain letters or pyramid sales schemes. The same mathematical principles apply to keep anyone from ever getting rich following that formula."

Glaser will be happy to give further information, and always is glad to receive ancient math problems from other people. He can be contacted at 1237 Whitney Rd., Southampton, PA 18966.

PERRY GRAY
BIRD DOGS

W HEN PERRY GRAY gave up track, football, and baseball upon graduating from college, he wanted a hobby that would keep him out of doors and in contact with animals. He settled on bird dogs. Today, he is one of America's leaders in field trials and the breeding and training of the dogs who participate in them.

"Back when I got started," he recalls, "there weren't great professional sports opportunities like there are now. I'm not saying I could have been a pro, but I chose bird dogs because of the thrill it gave me seeing the dogs going through their paces."

For 43 years, Gray, 71, a retired automobile dealer from Hillsdale, Michigan, has been vigorously pursuing the sport of bird dogging, and he's raised some championship caliber dogs himself.

In fact, one of Gray's dogs, Paladin's Royal Heir, in addition to being a consistent winner on the field trial circuit between 1955 and 1959, was elected to the Field Trial Hall of Fame for siring several national champions out of the 300 or 400 puppies he fathered.

What makes a good bird dog? Not all dogs are suited to be bird dogs, says Gray. "You have to work the dogs for awhile to determine whether or not they have the necessary talent." The field trial dog "is a super dog. He's got a great nose, speed, and stamina. Only a very, very few can make it." The most common breed is an English pointer (which is what Gray prefers), but he says other breeds, such as German shorthaired pointers, English setters, Irish setters, Brittany spaniels, and vizslas (a Hungarian breed) are also used as bird dogs. Whatever the breed, he says, it's vital that the dog "has a tremendous bird sense, a good nose, and speed."

The true test of the bird dog comes in the field trials, elaborate affairs which are usually conducted from horseback, says Gray. There are three classes of dogs: puppies (aged up to one year), derbys (one to two years), and all-age (three years and older). All the dogs in a particular class are grouped together, and "run in braces of two at a time, your dog with someone else's," says Gray. There are 30-minute, one-hour, and three-hour trials, which are held in various outdoor surroundings under prevailing weather conditions.

The three top dogs are selected by two judges on the basis of a subjective evaluation of the dogs' performance in the field. The idea is for the dog to track the game, "then mesmerize it enough without flushing it so that the hunter can come to it," says Gray.

Gray's winter home is in Somerville, Tennessee, near the site of the annual Grand Junction National Field Trial Championships. "These trials have been held for over 100 years, and they're the granddaddy of all the other events in the country," he says.

Currently, Gray has five dogs which he trains and enters in the field trials. "I do as much of the training and working of the dogs as I can myself," he says, "but age has stopped me from doing a lot of it." He now often has the help of a professional trainer.

Training the dogs can be an arduous process. "Most dogs don't get good until they're six to eight years old. That's when they hit their peak. By age 10, though, they're about through; they're pretty well burned-out," Gray says. Field trials "are a rough game. You're out in all kinds of weather and cover, and it tells on the dogs after awhile."

Incidentally, while female dogs "start earlier, they finish earlier." Males, while stronger, are not necessarily better bird dogs, Gray says, but if they're good they're more profitable to own, because "the stud fees can help you recoup some of your money."

It is expensive to raise and train bird dogs. In addition to the normal expenses of food and medical care, there are training fees (if a pro is used to train the dog) and the entry fees to the field trials themselves. "These can run anywhere from $200 to $300 most of the time," says Gray.

Gray advises the novice not to enter the bird dog game unless "you have a lot of ambition and desire. It's hard work." He also advises the beginner not to purchase a dog without being accompanied by someone already familiar with them. "Chances are, if you go by yourself, you'll pick the wrong dog."

Bird dogging, for Gray, has been a constant source of enjoyment for all of these years because "I enjoy being outdoors in the clean air. And I like to compete, and there's fierce competition in this sport." Mostly, though, Gray enjoys the other people he meets who, like him, "talk and live dogs."

Gray will be glad to advise novice bird dog fanciers, if they will write to him at 156 Barber Dr., Hillsdale, MI 49242.

WILLIAM HALLIDAY
CAVES

EVEN THOUGH WILLIAM Halliday says he has "a very high chicken factor," he has braved the dangers of over 800 caves around the world. He is an expert and author on the subject, as well as a noted cave conservationist.

Halliday, a physician and medical administrator who lives in Seattle, Washington, has been interested in caves for over 30 years. It all started back in Virginia, "when I was in medical school. In the summer of 1946, I was a counselor at a boys' camp, and there were caves all around the area, some of which I explored."

Since then, Halliday has traveled extensively, looking for caves. He also writes about caves, and directs the Western Speleological Survey. He's been the director of the "small volunteer organization that works systematically to locate, explore, scientifically study and conserve caves in the western United States" since 1955.

In doing all of the research and exploration, Halliday has, quite naturally, learned a great deal about caves and caving techniques. In the United States, most of the "important" caves are of limestone (Mammoth Cave in Kentucky is one of these), but Halliday has found the western United States rich in other types of cave structure, too.

There are "lava tube caves, the abandoned conduits of lava flows; there are geothermal caves, from the craters of the high volcanos in the West; and there are littoral caves and sea caves, made by the pounding of waves over the centuries."

The Pacific Northwest is particularly rich in important and unusual caves, he says. The world's longest mapped cave is Paradise Ice Cave on Mount Rainier, Washington, he says. "It's eight miles of cave that changes with the change of the glacier which surrounds it. It's dynamic ."

The longest lava tube cave in North and South America is Ape Cave, two-and-a-half miles long, also in Washington State. And both Mt. Rainier and Mt. Baker have important geothermal caves on their high peaks.

Halliday has become involved in cave preservation and exploration on a worldwide scale. In 1980 he attended a conference in Trieste, Italy, on the uses of The Karst, an area of caves on the Italian-Yugoslav border. "Currently, we are gravely concerned about the effects of industrial pollution on the caves," he says, "and we are trying to get the Italian and Yugoslav governments to create Karstic national parks to save them."

Studying caves, and being involved in efforts to conserve them, are just small parts of Halliday's interest. He prefers to get down inside a cave and explore it himself. "There's a whole psychology of cave exploration," he says. "A mountaineer who wants to climb a mountain has a fixed point at which he will be successful. The speleologist, on the other hand, is always looking for something beyond a certain point, because you're never quite sure if you've found all of a cave."

Of the 800 caves he has visited, "every one has been fascinating in its own way," he says. He once spent 33 hours in the deepest cave in the United States, in Neff Canyon, Utah, and he's also become quite fond of "geothermal caves, with the hissing steam vents surrounding you as you explore them."

Cave exploration "is basically hazardous to both the explorer and the cave," says Halliday. "Everybody gets banged up a bit." Fortunately, Halliday has never been badly injured, though he did "bang" himself up while on a mapping expedition in an Oregon cave when he tripped and fell over an outcropping.

Adequate instruction in both emergency and conservation procedures is essential for anyone exploring caves, Halliday emphasizes. A good source for the proper information is the National Speleological Society, which has members all over the United States "who are very anxious to work with anyone interested in exploring caves." According to Halliday, among the absolute musts for any cave exploration are "three sources of light, emergency gear to use in getting out of the cave, and a knowledge of how to handle ropes correctly."

Halliday says the National Speleological Society even has its own private cave, that has been the subject of an "intense conservation effort, for it contains a unique collection of small, cave-adapted animals" including various varieties of salamanders and blind fish. This cave, Shelta, is "right in the middle of Huntsville, Alabama — right under the First National Bank." It's a limestone cave, and not a terribly big one, but "interesting to explore if you don't mind mud."

Halliday has written three books, all published by Harper & Row, based on his exploration and research. The first, *The Adventure Is Underground*, details explorations of caves in the western United States. *Depths of the Earth*, is about U.S. caves, in general. His latest book, *American Caves and Caving*, covering the caves of the North American continent, was published in 1974.

"I've scratched my head for along time to figure out why I like caves," says Halliday. "I guess it's just that there's always more to discover both physically and psychologically each time I explore a cave."

He'll be glad to advise novice spelunkers, or provide further information on caves, to anyone contacting him at 1117 36th Ave. E., Seattle, WA 98112.

CHARLES KAPRAL
LUNAR PHENOMENA

BY MEASURING THE brightness of certain portions of the craters on the moon, on a special 20-step brightness scale, amateur astronomers like Charles Kapral feel they will be able to determine whether the moon is an active planet — or the dead orbiting appendage of the earth that many scientists have labeled it.

By day, Kapral is an engineering systems coordinator for the Fedders Corporation; by night, he's out staring at the moon, looking for these so-called "lunar phenomena."

There have been over 2,000 cases of the phenomena reported, Kapral says. Whenever there is a significant change in the brightness of a particular feature of the moon's surface, a phenomenon is said to have occurred.

According to Kapral, the moon could be "like the earth, and these changes in brightness could occur when the pressure builds up and steam escapes." Other possible lunar phenomena include color change and obscuration (a surface phenomenon such as fog that obscures other happenings).

"Nobody really knows why these changes occur," says Kapral. "It might be something for the next crew that goes to the moon to work on." One thing is certain, however: "There are too many of these 'phenomena' to be optical illusions."

Looking at the stars and the planets — and wondering about them — has been an important part of Kapral's life since childhood. In eighth grade, he says, he began reading books about astronomy and the universe. By the time he was in high school, he had a small telescope, and he has been observing the heavens ever since. That first telescope, however, has been replaced by a 2.4-inch Unitron refracting telescope, with 300-power magnification.

In all of his observations, Kapral has seen some unusual — and beautiful — things. "An eclipse of the sun is, without a doubt, the most spectacular thing you can observe with a telescope," he says. You see the edge of the moon...a profile of the mountains...the corona of light shooting out of the sun. It's fantastic!"

The lunar transient (they are called transient because the changes are, apparently, temporary) phenomena program, operated under the auspicies of the Goddard Space Flight Center, is a long-term observing project which is operational every night the moon is visible, according to Kapral. He is one of a network of observers across the country who take to their rooftops and backyards nightly to record data and observations. He reports his findings to the Goddard scientists every few months.

The observation process is complicated somewhat, Karpal says, by the quality of the earth's atmosphere at any given time. "If there is a lot of heat and turbulence, the atmosphere is 'wavy' and it tends to obscure what you are trying to observe." Therefore, to standardize the observations of all the people involved in the project, "you have to know the quality of the atmosphere at the time and get a statistical mean. You have to determine how much turbulence exists."

The major question for researchers in transient lunar phenomena is, ' Is it an optical illusion or is it an actual physical change?" says Kapral.

Kapral feels that research of this sort is very important, and could eventually lead to substantial benefits for earth. "If the moon is geologically active, for example, there may be a way of tapping lunar sources of energy that could be used to alleviate our energy problems," says Kapral.

It is surprisingly easy to get started in the observation of lunar transient phenomena, or in other areas of astronomy, Kapral says. Of course, it is important to have a good (but not necessarily top-of-the-line) telescope. An adequate telescope will cost $125 to $150. Binoculars will also do for beginners, says Kapral, although they are less precise.

While it is essential for the beginning observer to learn the constellations and have a good moon map, Kapral says it's also important to learn correct observing and recording procedures before attempting serious projects "so you don't waste a lot of time on worthless observations."

All that mooning over the lunar surface is "satisfying" to Kapral. "I'm a computer programmer, and it's very relaxing to go out and spend a lot of time getting a closer grasp of the universe," he says, "I'm seeing things the average person probably never will see — and certainly will never visit. It's a real firsthand experience with the universe."

Kapral will be glad to give information about the lunar transient phenomenal program, or about astronomy. He can be contacted at Building 28, Apt. 3, Skytop Gardens, Parlin, NJ 08859.

STEWART MacKENZIE
SHORTWAVE RADIO

STEWART MAC KENZIE HAS been to a lot of different places in his life, many of them without ever having to leave the comfort of his Huntington Beach, California, home.

MacKenzie, 46, is one of several million people worldwide who explore foreign lands and other cultures in a much more direct and interesting way than just by reading about them in books — he does it by shortwave radio listening.

MacKenzie became interested in shortwave radio in 1953, while he was in the Army stationed in Korea during the Korean War. "Over there, the programs for servicemen on the Armed Forces Radio Network were only on shortwave, so you had to have one to listen," he says. He obtained a Hallicrafters S-38C receiver and "that receiver gave me the world to listen to."

Currently, MacKenzie owns a Collins R-392, a U.S. Army surplus digital receiver. He has owned this radio for seven years, having had other Hallicrafters equipment in the interim.

The hobby involves listening to shortwave radio bands. "You can hear everything on the whole radio spectrum from two megacycles to 30 megacycles," MacKenzie says. Shortwave is below the AM broadcast band, and above FM, he adds.

MacKenzie has fixed up part of his garage as a shortwave listening room. All of his radio gear, his library of books, and other items are out there "so I don't disturb anyone else in the house while I'm listening to the radio."

MacKenzie says his two antennas, one a long, horizontal wire, the other vertical (30-feet above his roof) "are used to switch back and forth, from vertical to horizontal, depending on the conditions. "Whether a signal is received vertically or horizontally depends on 'propagation,' a condition of the upper atmosphere that bounces radio signals back to earth. When propagation is intense, a radio wave may circle the earth several times, bouncing back and forth between the atmosphere and earth and growing steadily weaker.

According to MacKenzie, the best time to listen to shortwave radio is "between sunset and sunrise. Not only are the listening conditions the best, but that is the time when most of the countries have their English language programs on the air."

He has heard more than 200 countries, so far, he says. "Distance is really meaningless. You can virtually get the whole world — and beyond."

MacKenzie, like many short wave listeners, collects "QSL cards." These are "cards you can receive when you write to a station to verify you have heard their program." The listener is supposed to give details of the program he heard, plus the time of day. When it is verified by the station, they will send "a card in acknowledgement. They're usually quite colorful, often depicting a scene from the country."

MacKenzie is a member of the American Shortwave Listening Club, a nationwide group of nearly 1,000 dedicated shortwave listeners. He is also the publisher of its monthly bulletin, which contains information members submit about various geographical areas, he says. "A member, when he hears a particular program, sends in a report to a regional correspondent," says Mac-Kenzie. "This way, we keep abreast of what's happening in the various countries." Currently, he is also serving as general manager of the club, which moved its base of operations to his home.

MacKenzie says his biggest thrill as a listener had to be the Friendship 7 flight to the moon. "I heard it both going out and returning, as well as the whole landing. In fact, I have everything on tape."

Often, shortwave listening can be informative about important events, says MacKenzie. "When the Russians invaded Czechoslovakia, we heard it first. We heard the news that the Pueblo crew was released by the North Koreans a day before regular newscasts told us the same thing."

The shortwave listeners represent "a wide segment of society. There are a lot of retired people, especially, in the hobby," he says. "Many of them can't afford to travel, but with shortwave they can go wherever they want, and it's a good way to keep busy."

Shortwave listening is not a particularly expensive hobby, either, says MacKenzie. "There's a receiver to fit any pocketbook," from $50 for a beginning outfit to over $3,000 for the most advanced set-up. The average cost is about $300, including antennas, he says. People used to build their own receivers, but MacKenzie says that advanced technology has made it too complicated for people to build their own kits.

"The first thing you should do, once you have a receiver, is to check the library for books. Then, locate a club in your area, and join it. Without some kind of guidance when you start, you can really be lost."

MacKenzie says "it's hard to say" why he enjoys shortwave listening. "It is a good alternative to listening to domestic radio stations, with all the loud music and commercials, and TV is not too exciting anymore." With a shortwave radio, "you can be on top of the news as it's happening," he says. In short, "You can listen to exciting events, get other views, and lots of stations have good music with no commercial interruption - if you don't mind a little propaganda from the government."

The radio stations are mostly government-sponsored, he says. The US has only one shortwave station, the Voice of America, plus three stations belonging to religious broadcasters.

MacKenzie suggests that beginners (and more seasoned veterans, too) join the ASWLC. For membership information, simply write to MacKenzie at 16182 Ballard Ln., Huntington Beach, CA 92649.

DAN MARTIN
FIRE APPARATUS PHOTOGRAPHY

IN 1930, AT THE age of four, he visited the Evanston, Illinois, fire department with his nursery school class. At age eight, he got his first camera. Today, at 54, Dan Martin's still involved with fire departments and photography.

Martin, of the Chicago suburb of Naperville, Illinois, is a noted photographer of fire apparatus, a skill he puts to good use as the co-publisher of a fire apparatus buff publication called *Visiting Fireman*.

"That visit to the fire station was a memorable experience," he says. "It was a fairly large fire station. But I didn't get to ring the bell on the fire engine. That honor went to a cute little girl who happened to be the fire chief's niece."

For a long time, he says, "I was interested in antique cars and fire engines, in that order. Then I met some antique car people — and decided to favor fire engines."

Martin developed his photographic skills with his first camera, and by 1941 had begun taking pictures of fire equipment. He kept on with it until 1959, "never getting to show any of my pictures to anyone, until I discovered there were other people with the same interest." From then on, Martin says, "I had a marathon correspondence that I've never been able to keep up with."

He had "always been interested in the apparatus as machinery, but when I realized that some of the equipment from the 1930s, which seemed to have been around forever, was being replaced by new and shiny machines I was skeptical of, it became my hobby to collect and preserve the old pieces of equipment in photographs."

His collection consists of "thousands and thousands of photos. I have 100 albums full, and that's just a fraction of what I have." In his quest to add to that collection, Martin has traveled to Los Angeles, Maine, Richmond, Seattle, and all over the Midwest. He's supplemented his collection by borrowing negatives from other enthusiasts and making prints of their photographs. "I have been able to reconstruct much of the history of this equipment through these photos," he says.

He's had some help in the vigorous pursuit of his hobby. "In 1951, I married the only girl in the world who would go to work to buy a fire engine for me," he says. It's a 1926 American La France engine, 24-feet long, weighing 11,000 pounds, with a pumping capacity of 750 gallons per minute. It sits in his backyard and, while he still enjoys it, "I've outgrown blowing the siren every New Year's Eve."

Like much of the rest of his hobby, Martin's participation with *Visiting Fireman* is also largely the result of happenstance. Again, it was his wife, Mae, a dedicated fire buff herself, who gave him a push.

"We knew that the man who had operated the publication was selling out, and my wife urged me to buy it and run it." So, in partnership with a friend, Jeffrey Schilke, Martin purchased *Visiting Fireman* in 1977.

"The major purpose of *Visiting Fireman* is to serve as a directory of fire buffs," he says. "They all keep in touch by letter, though some go in for telephoning." Sandwiched in this directory of some 2,000 names, which are updated annually, is "editorial matter concerning various projects, museums, a list of local and national fire buff organizations, a listing of the radio frequencies used by fire departments across the nation, and the like," he says.

Martin is proud of his work with the publication: "It gives me a great feeling of accomplishment to be providing a service that leads to the preservation, or at least the remembrance, of fire days gone by."

"The photographic aspect was always a means to an end for me," says Martin. "I wasn't into the technical aspects of the photography; I was more interested in the picture. And I just kind of accidentally got some good results."

Martin says, "I want pictures of all the fire apparatus I've ever seen, plus the many things I never had a chance to see. It seems the more pictures I get, the more I want."

He advises novice fire apparatus buffs to pick up a copy of *Visiting Fireman*. It's $6.50 postpaid, from Visiting Fireman, 203 N. Washington St., Batavia, IL 60510. Martin will gladly answer queries directed to him at 1024 Elizabeth, Naperville, IL 60540.

PATRICK MILLER
MODEL ROCKETRY

N̲OT ONLY THE National Aeronautics and Space Administration (NASA) sends up rockets; so does Patrick Miller.

Miller, 31, a mathematician and educator from Albuquerque, New Mexico, is an expert and educator on model rocketry, as president of the National Association of Rocketry.

"I was always interested in astronomy and space science as a kid," he says. "So, it was only natural" that he became fascinated with model rockets. He began flying them in 1967 when he purchased one from a company that made the items in kit form. The single-stage, six-inch Astron Scout "flew all right the first time out," says Miller. His interest blasted off as well, and for the next three years he built and flew many model rockets.

Since 1970, however, the main focus of Miller's attention has been in the research side of model rocketry, rather than in flying. Armed with an M.A. degree in mathematics from the University of New Mexico, he has done intensive research into the flight dynamics of model rockets, and has been heavily involved with educating young people about rocketry.

Among his important educational/research projects is a program using rockets and mathematics which he has designed for high school students. Under this program, students study the ballistics of model rockets, using a computer and other aids, and do mathematical predicting of flights, in addition to testing their hypotheses with actual experiments. The summer program is conducted on the University of New Mexico campus, says Miller, and has been "very successful, with much favorable response on the part of the students."

Another important educational effort with which Miller has been involved is the National Model Rocket Program for Schools. This program, primarily for teachers of seventh- to twelfth-grade students, has been a popular aspect of the National Association of Model Rocketry over the last several years. Teachers of these students receive packets of materials which include activities using model rockets. "The program has been a great success, and I am busy revising it for the 100 or so schools that use it."

Another of the programs that the National Association of Model Rocketry, the leading hobbyist group, sponsors is a model rocket competition. According to Miller, "one of the more popular and intense events" in the competition, among representatives from 10 to 15 nations, is the scale modeling of real rockets. "The model rocket builders do amazingly detailed work," he says, "reproducing down to the last scratch of paint" real rockets used by NASA or the military. Another competitive aspect of model rocketry is in distance flying. The world's record for a model rocket flight is an altitude of one mile, according to Miller. Many model rocketers are extremely interested in this aspect of the hobby.

Miller is enthusiastic about model rocketry as a hobby for anyone, and especially young people. "It's very safe, really, " he says, adding that since 1960 an estimated 150 million rockets have been flown and there have been no deaths (and few injuries) as a result.

Children also learn something from model rocketry, he says. "You can illustrate many principles of physics, and constructing a model rocket is so simple that even a fourth grader can do it. "Besides, it's a lot of fun." He adds that children can now buy model rockets that are not only scale-model duplications of real Saturn 5's, Nikes, and other missiles, but also rockets from *Star Wars*, and *Star Trek*.

Miller's main satisfaction in model rocketry "has been working with the people who fly rockets, although I am not really interested in flying them myself. And I have enjoyed being involved with the administration of the association, and working on the educational programs, too."

For the novice rocket builder or enthusiast, Miller recommends joining the National Association of Rocketry and participating in its many conferences, conventions, and competitions.

Information on the association can be obtained from PO Box 725, New Providence, NJ 07974. Miller can also be contacted at that address.

SUSIE PAGE
CATS

CAT FANCIERS ALL over the country know Susie Page — she's called the "Ann Landers" of cats!

Through her column "Help!" in the monthly *Cats* magazine, and her work in setting up spay and neuter clinics, as well as judging, breeding, showing, and registering cats, Mrs. Page is a one-woman dynamo of cat expertise.

Mrs. Page bought her first cat, a Burmese, in about 1960, "and began breeding and showing, eventually getting into judging." Since 1972, she's written the column that's made her famous in the cat world. "It was my idea and it caught on," she says, adding that she's received (and individually answered) more than 14,000 letters since the column began.

The most common questions that Mrs. Page receives have to do with the health of the animals. For example, neutered cats "will spray, contrary to popular belief. The best way to clean the carpet after that is to use baking soda and water." Another hint Mrs. Page offers is that "brewer's yeast tablets control fleas. Feed your cat three or four, and it will change the taste of its blood so that fleas will no longer feel welcome."

Like a lot of their owners, cats are overweight. "The solution is a long process of dieting," she says, based not so much on the amount of food, but on its content. "Cats who are overweight need more protein, and smaller quantities of food, to be sure." She suggests feeding an overweight cat (or any cat, for that matter) "more human food." She cites a study of 900 cats which proved that the cats "who ate raw meat had less sickness, were less overweight, and lived longer" than cats who ate commercial cat food.

Another function of her column, Mrs. Page says, is to clear up popular misconceptions people have about cats. For example, "Cats do not always land on their feet. If they do, it's just luck. They also don't find their way home if you abandon them or move away." The equivalent human age of a cat "is not seven times its own age. When it's one year old, that's the equivalent of 20 years for a human; each year thereafter is equivalent to four human years." Finally, there's no truth to the rumor that "male calico cats (which are very rare) are worth $50,000 if you can find one. Most of them are sterile and aren't worth anything to anyone," she says. Research is being conducted into why calico cats are predominately female. It is "thought to bear some relationship to Mongoloidism in human beings."

One problem Mrs. Page is personally concerned about is birth control for pets. And she's been a strong advocate of community clinics to deal with the problem. These spaying and neutering clinics are easily set up, says Mrs. Page. "It's just a matter of getting people together to talk local veterinarians into participating." The next step is to raise money. "Usually, the group pays for half of the operation, the pet owner the other half," says Mrs. Page. She has personally been involved in setting up 11 community clinics since 1972.

While spaying has apparently made a dent in the general cat population, it's a small dent, according to Mrs. Page. "It's true there aren't as many kittens being born, but the reduction is so minimal that there is still one kitten being born every 20 seconds in this country." The ground that has been gained, she adds, comes from "responsible pet owners who take their animals to be altered, but it's the irresponsible people we need to reach if we're going to significantly arrest the problem of over-population among pets."

While Mrs. Page shies away from saying that certain people shouldn't own a cat, she does say that "it depends on you. You have to pick a breed and the animal within that breed that fits you the best." She advises careful study before purchasing a cat, to determine whether or not both cat and owner will be happy with the new living arrangements.

"I like cats because you can pick them up. They do fit in apartments. Also, they're easy to care for," she says. "Unless they're piggy, you can leave them alone for the weekend quite nicely, with a supply of dry food and water."

Anyone who has a cat "that doesn't go outside will notice that the cat is much more dependent and responsive," says Mrs. Page, citing the fact that the winding around a human's leg that some cats indulge in is a sign of insecurity.

Her new book, based on questions from her column, is called *Let's Talk Cats* (Stephen Greene Press, 1980). She compares it to the "Dr. Spock book for children."

Mrs. Page can be reached at 10065 Foothill Blvd., Lake View Terrace, CA 91342, for further information.

MARY SANDERSON
GREENHOUSE GARDENING

NOT SO LONG AGO, only the wealthy could afford greenhouses in which to grow their plants. Today, given less expensive materials and the greater affluence of the average consumer, small home greenhouses are cropping up all over the country. People are discovering not only the joys of gardening year-round, but a fun way to save energy, as well.

One of the leaders in the greenhouse movement — as a hobby and a way in which to conserve energy — is Mary Sanderson, of Wallingford, Connecticut. Mrs. Sanderson helped organize the Hobby Greenhouse Association, the first national organization for home greenhouse enthusiasts, which has some 3,200 members in every state, Canada, and "one lady in Japan, who we feel adds something to the group, since the Japanese are such renowned gardeners." Needless to say, Mrs. Sanderson is a dedicated greenhouse gardener herself.

"We have an 8½-by-13½-foot lean-to greenhouse on the side of our home," she says. "We use it for growing plants that will stand colder temperatures." Among the varieties she grows with great success are primula, geranium, certain varieties of orchids, bird of paradise, and cyclamen.

"There are just too many out there to count," she says. "We have a great many plants, because we've had the greenhouse since 1970."

Mrs. Sanderson and her husband "started greenhouse gardening for the same reason everybody else does: we had so many plants in the house, we had to have some place to put them all and care for them properly.

Fortunately for the Sandersons, the greenhouse faces south, and is equipped with passive solar energy systems to take full advantage of the sun's rays. This greenhouse, because of its location, has furnished the Sandersons with an additional source of heat. "It can certainly be a help when there's lots of sunshine," she says, "Sometimes, it's like living in the Southwest."

The advantages to having a greenhouse are many, Mrs. Sanderson thinks. "You can garden 12 months a year," she says. "You can grow your own bedding plants for the outdoor garden, or grow tropical plants you ordinarily wouldn't be able to grow in our climate."

Naturally, a successful greenhouse garden is the result of a good deal of hard work on the owner's part. Mrs. Sanderson says she spends at least half an hour per day working in her greenhouse. "You have to look the plants over, to make sure there are no bugs, and feed and water them properly. There are all kinds of chores to be done in the greenhouse," Mrs. Sanderson says. "I'm lucky to have a built-in gardener; my husband is retired."

It makes a difference, she says, where the plants are placed in the greenhouse. For example, "You can't put a geranium out of the sun, but there are other plants that would die if they were exposed to direct sunlight." And you have to adjust the heat and air flow for the plants daily.

When she's not working in her greenhouse, or admiring some new blooming example of her handiwork, Mrs. Sanderson is likely to be working on projects for the Hobby Greenhouse Association or its bimonthly journal, *The Planter.*

"We are an educational organization," Mrs. Sanderson says. "We have an advisory board of people within the organization who help other members with their greenhouse gardening problems. Sometimes, the amateurs have better ideas than the experts do."

For anyone wanting to build a greenhouse, Mrs. Sanderson stresses that the most essential step is selecting the proper location. "It's a very poor idea to build a greenhouse facing north," she says. "The very best location is facing southeast, followed by south, southwest, east, and west."

Once you've picked your site, you're ready to begin to build the greenhouse. There are a number of firms around the country that sell prefabricated greenhouses or the gardener can build one from scratch. Mrs. Sanderson suggests a careful investigation of all the manufactured models before deciding to build from scratch. "Sometimes it's cheaper to buy a prefab."

While some people have been able to build greenhouses for practically nothing by knowing what to look for in junk heaps, Mrs. Sanderson says most greenhouse builders can expect to spend between $800 and $2000.

Some kind of heating system is necessary, but Mrs. Sanderson says the cost of heating can be minimized. "You can cut down on heating by using insulation in the greenhouse, for example," she says. "Thus, you'll be able to take advantage of the natural solar energy pouring in through the windows."

Once the greenhouse is built, the enjoyment begins. "It's a lot of fun for the whole family," Mrs. Sanderson says. "It's very relaxing." Having a greenhouse "gives people a sense of achievement," Mrs. Sanderson thinks. "And it gets you away from the hustle and bustle outside. It's like a different world when you're inside a greenhouse."

Mrs. Sanderson's most enjoys "raising seeds. I like to plant the seeds and watch them grow." A pet project she is working on with a friend, the crossing and development of new colors of Christmas cactus, has been particularly absorbing. "We've gotten seed pods with no seeds in them, so far," she says. "We haven't been able to figure that one out yet."

Mrs. Sanderson will gladly provide further information on greenhouse gardening, the Hobby Greenhouse Association, or *The Planter*. She can be contacted at PO Box 951, Wallingford CT 06492.

SAM SCHEER
SIAMESE CATS

SAM SCHEER, AT 85, probably spends more time on Siamese cats than anyone else in the United States — and he wishes that he had time to do more!

Scheer, of Aurora, Colorado, has been the secretary of the 600-member Siamese Cat Society of America since 1960, as well as the editor of its quarterly journal. In addition, he serves on the board of directors of the Morris Animal Foundation as chairman emeritus of the feline division. He and his wife, Lily, are the proud owners of six champion Siamese cats.

He wasn't always a cat fancier. Says Scheer, "I was strictly a dog man. I could take cats or leave them, but my wife loved them." But Christmas Day, 1953, changed all that.

He had chanced to remark once to his wife that "If I had a cat, I'd want a Siamese," so when he "came downstairs that Christmas morning, there was a shoebox under the tree," he recalls. "The card read 'For Daddy'. I opened the box, and out jumped a little sealpoint Siamese, right onto my shoulder. I was hooked from that time on."

Soon thereafter, Scheer and his wife began to breed and show Siamese cats. They were very successful, Scheer says, raising many champions and grand champions while they lived in Syracuse, New York (where Scheer worked for the Philco Corporation), and later on in Florida, after his retirement. "We've won dozens and dozens of prizes for our cats," he says, "but we retired from showing and breeding in 1970."

Nowadays, the Scheers keep "a few senior citizens" around the house. The oldest cat is 17 years old, the youngest, 13, and Scheer says there's no trouble at all keeping several cats around the house.

The cats are all neutered or spayed, says Scheer, and "they all behave themselves. When we were active in breeding and showing we had 14 or 15 cats around the house at a time and never had any difficulty, either."

Though Siamese have a reputation in some quarters for being strange and unfriendly, Scheer scoffs at the notion. "Sure, they're strange and unusual and everybody thinks they're smarter than any other breed. But, and maybe I shouldn't be saying this, cats is cats."

After all, he points out, "All human beings are human beings — but some are lousy and some are wonderful. It's the same with cats. Why, we even have a plain alley cat that's the most beautiful thing you've ever seen."

Siamese cat fanciers say their cats are "bright, intelligent, and good companions. They aren't any more unfriendly than any other cat," Scheer says. "Actually, I think all cats are wonderful."

Scheer has been credited with revitalizing the Siamese Cat Society of America. When he took over as the national secretary in 1960, the 50-year-old club had only about 70 members and was dying on the vine. In the succeeding 20 years, Scheer "just worked at it, writing to every Siamophile I could find." Now the club is celebrating its 70th anniversary with members in every state of the United States and many foreign countries.

The *Siamese News Quarterly* was his idea as well. The lively 32-page journal is put together entirely by Scheer and his wife, who do everything but the printing at home.

As if all this weren't enough, Scheer has been active since 1965 in the work of the Morris Animal Foundation, the Colorado-based organization involved in funding animal health research. The feline division of the foundation has been involved with some two dozen projects at 12 veterinary schools since 1955, making important financial grants to aid in the fight to keep cats healthy.

Says Scheer, "It has sometimes been an uphill climb getting cat lovers enthusiastic about supporting research into health problems. If they could see the tragedy involved, they would appreciate the vital necessity for funding research into diseases that affect our beloved cats."

Scheer is very supportive of people who might be interested in breeding and showing Siamese cats. But he urges careful study and research before getting deeply involved. "Do a lot of studying. Get all the books you possibly can and read." His own "felibrary" of some 450 books on cats has proven invaluable to him.

"Then, go to shows, walk around, talk to people, and observe the judging," he says. "It's vital to learn something before you jump in. Too many people have gotten burned by jumping right in."

Scheer will be glad to provide further information about Siamese cat showing or breeding, as well as membership in the Siamese Cat Society of America. He can be contacted at 2588-C So. Vaughn Wy., Aurora, CO 80014.

ILSA STERNBERG
SHOWING DOGS BY THE HANDICAPPED

ILSA STERNBERG SPENDS all her waking hours in an electric wheelchair, crippled by a form of muscular dystrophy. But that hasn't stopped her from becoming a leading competitor in the obedience training, breeding, and showing of dogs.

Miss Sternberg, 30, of Hartsdale, New York, is the first person in a wheelchair to get a championship or tracking degree in American Kennel Club history. And she has been instrumental in changing the AKC regulations to accommodate the handicapped.

Dog obedience training became the focus of Miss Sternberg's life in 1969 when she was given a dog as a gift. It "proceeded to chew up a complete set of dinette chairs, rip off wallpaper, and refuse to come when I called," she says. So, in self-defense, she enrolled her pet in an obedience course, and "became hooked on the sport."

In 1969, when Miss Sternberg began showing her dog, "officials were reluctant to allow people in wheelchairs to show in the ring." The AKC felt "it would be a distraction for other dogs and exhibitors, which has since been proven to be an erroneous assumption."

"There had been complaints in the field trials, previously," she says. "Several judges refused to judge me, it was a matter of principle; judges who didn't feel like judging me didn't have to."

Finally, in 1974 the AKC changed the rules to allow "handicapped people to compete on an equal basis." According to Miss Sternberg, "there is now a specific rule that while the dog must conform to the exercise, the handicapped person can adjust ring procedure according to disability."

She gets "calls and letters from all over the country now. I've been told there are many handicapped people competing. There is even a blind girl who trained to be a judge."

The difficulty in training the dogs depends on the handicaps of the person, she says. "Each requirement for each person has to be altered." Since she is confined to a wheelchair, Miss Sternberg can't reach the dog. So, "I put it on a table. I can't run and chase the dog, so it must be trained to come when called. The dogs sometimes realize that I can't get to them."

"Though I have some friends that help, I do most of the training myself." When she was training her first championship dog, a Chesapeake Bay retriever, Calbak Dark Cloud of Bo-Jib (known as "Cloudy"), she discovered that "my electric wheelchair wouldn't go fast enough in the ring. The dog has to go both fast and slow. Unfortunately, I have to take substantial reductions on the score. When the dog has to jump, I go around the jump in my chair, while the dog goes over."

Training the dogs to jump hurdles is something of a problem for Miss Sternberg. The hurdle is 3-feet high, and "just getting the dog to make that kind of jump takes careful, slow training to build him up to it." It's very important to start out with "making it fun. But I could not get him to go fast enough to make the hurdle," she says. So, she used pieces of string at graduated levels to encourage the dog over.

It took her several months to train Cloudy, spending 10 or 15 minutes a day at the task. "Since he was going to be a big dog, I had to make sure his house manners were good, too," says Miss Sternberg. "It's most important to make the dog a good companion as well as a champion." All of her dogs "pick up anything I drop, and they're taught to speak on command."

Cloudy won his first championship, Companion Dog Excellent, in 1971, and went on in short order to take an AKC breed championship, a tracking degree, and field trail win, all firsts for a dog handled by a handicapped person. She's also had a golden retriever and now concetrates on papillions, with which she has taken three championships.

Miss Sternberg says she got "great help" from other people in her efforts to be allowed to compete in the show ring. The professional handlers "were lots of help, too, in making it apparent to the judges that my presence in the ring was no interference to them." This, she believes, was what softened the position of the AKC.

Dog obedience showing and training "is a sport where we who are handicapped can compete on the same level as anyone else," says Miss Sternberg. "There's no favoritism shown, and it's worth the effort to compete with someone who has no disability. There are very few opportunities, after all, for handicapped people to compete with those who are not."

"Being with the dogs, something that returns your affection" is the most rewarding aspect of her hobby for Miss Sternberg. "I also enjoy the chance to get out and meet people." For herself, she has found dog training and showing "good physical therapy and exercise."

For the handicapped person thinking of entering the sport, Miss Sternberg suggests "getting a young dog you can manage. Don't get a big dog if you aren't strong. Then, go to training class just like anybody else." Unfortunately, she says, since there is little literature at the moment on the subject of the handicapped and dog handling, the novice has to learn from experience.

Miss Sternberg suggests contacting the American Kennel Club, 51 Madison Ave., New York, NY 10016, for rules and information. She'll also be happy to give advice and offer encouragement. Contact her at 29 Marion Ave., Hartsdale, NY 10530.

BARBARA STREBEIGH
AIREDALE TERRIERS

THE FIRST AIREDALE terrier Barbara Strebeigh owned, nearly 60 years ago, came into her life by accident.

In those days, the San Francisco dog pound had a yard fronting on the street, and Miss Strebeigh happened to be walking past when a number of dogs were put out into it. Among the dogs was one "great dog, all skin and bones, but, even so, obviously a dog of quality breeding. The other dogs all frisked about the attendant, but not this one. He sat up in a corner and begged."

Miss Strebeigh unhesitatingly walked into the pound and took him home, and for many years, the dog, Rowdy, was her "protector and companion, who crossed the continent with me many times and went on all our camping trips."

"Some family must have grieved very much to have lost him," she says. "He was a loyal and wonderful dog who was careful to see that he would not lose me and again be a lost dog."

When Rowdy died, Miss Strebeigh wanted to get another Airedale, "the best that could be bought." So, she went to a leading kennel, got a dog, "and since then I have never been without an Airedale."

Since 1924 Miss Strebeigh has bred and shown Airedale terriers from her kennel in Birchrunville, Pennsylvania. She was inspired, she says, by the fact that Rowdy "had turned out to be the greatest, and I decided he could only be followed by the best. So I determined to breed the best. I have had many champions."

Though she's bred and shown many dogs through the years, a couple of them particularly stand out in her mind. One of them, Champion Birchrun Ricochet, "helped create a line that produced six champion Airedales in two litters." Miss Strebeigh was co-owner of another noted dog, Champion Bengal Sabu, one of the top Airedales of the 1950s. He was a leading Airedale sire between 1958, when he retired from dog shows, and 1971. On the show circuit, Miss Strebeigh says, a winning Airedale "shouldn't be too big, no more than 24 inches high, and must be sturdy, good looking, and have a good wire coat."

Miss Strebeigh has been involved with the Airedale Terrier Club of America, the national Airedale breeders group, for many years. She's edited their *Newsletter of the Airedale Terrier Club of America* for some 30 years.

What makes Airedales so appealing to Miss Strebeigh and other fanciers is "their personality: they're very sensitive yet aggressive. They have a lot of sweetness in their character. They're very perceptive of feelings." Yet, because the Airedale combines the strength of an otterhound with the powerful bite of a bull-terrier, she says, "the dog makes a wonderful watchdog."

For the novice wishing to raise Airedale terriers, Miss Strebeigh feels it is essential to select a dog with top bloodlines. This, of course, requires a study of pedigrees, as well as much observation and conversation with breeders. "This is really most important," she says, "because you must have a proper understanding of the background of the animal, his temperament, and his hereditary characteristics, both good and bad, in order to make an intelligent choice."

Miss Strebeigh, a sportswoman (a champion field hockey and squash player) and sculptor in terra cotta, is in her late 70s, and extremely deaf. Yet, with the help of a friend who has lived with her for 19 years, she's still able to maintain the kennels and her lively interest in Airedales.

She credits her durability in the Airedale field to her enjoyment of "sharing a hobby with the congenial, fun-loving Airedale owners I've met through the Aierdale Terrier Club. Secondly, I've always been active in sports, and if it's done properly dog breeding and showing should be, and is, a sport."

Of course, "it goes without saying" that the Airedales themselves have always been "very much a part of my life. They went everywhere with me."

Miss Strebeigh will be glad to give further information to anyone who might be interested in breeding Airedales, or in just knowing more about the breed. She can be reached at Birchrunville, PA 19421.

VOLTA TORREY
WINDMILLS & STEAM ENGINES

Lᴏɴɢ BEFORE AMERICANS had gasoline and heating oil supplies or nuclear power plants to worry about, there were two splendid natural sources of power that were important to American life, and may be again — wind power and steam.

The landscape was once dotted with windmills, which were used from early Colonial times as a means of creating energy to pump water. Steam engines, a later development, harnessed water power and heat to make machinery run in the embryonic factories of the early 19th century.

Both of these important components of early American prosperity are the interest of Volta Torrey, a 75-year-old Washington, D.C., man who has spent a lot of time studying windmills and steam engines, mainly as alternative sources of energy.

Torrey's interest in windmills and steam engines came rather late in life. "I grew up in Nebraska, where there were many windmills," he says, "but I never paid too much attention to them, since they were so common." But while he was working for the National Aeronautics and Space Administration (NASA) as a writer and historian, it became part of his job to be concerned with windmills. Today he is an expert in the fascinating topic of "molinology," the study of mills.

"In the 1970s, NASA became interested in developing wind as an alternate energy source," Torrey says, "so I began doing research in the Library of Congress and the Smithsonian Institution, and enlisted the help of friends across the country to track down old windmills for me." Pretty soon, Torrey was traveling around the country, studying the windmills and "growing very interested in their operation and history."

Torrey says there are still several thousand windmills left standing in this country. "Some are preserved for some historical reason," he says. "The others are still used for pumping water or generating power."

What Torrey has been concentrating on in his research (which has continued despite his retirement from government) is the history of the use of windmills for power.

According to him, the first windmills in the United States appeared in the 1600s, in Virginia. "Very quickly after their arrival in New Amsterdam [present day New York City], the Dutch erected windmills, too," Torrey says. Windmills continued to spread across the country, marking the farmyards of the cattle ranchers and wheat farmers of the Great Plains and Rocky Mount in states and the rich farmlands of the Midwest.

In recent years, says Torrey, windmill-generated power has been considered "too expensive. But now with fuel prices rising so fast, it has become economically more attractive."

A visit Torrey made to a major manufacturer of windmills in Beatrice, Nebraska, shows why windmills have been considered obsolete. "I told them I wanted to buy a windmill," Torrey says. "So they took me right out to a salesman, who very politely told me a windmill would cost $2,000, but they could sell me an electric pump for $200. If there was a power line near where I wanted to put the windmill, I would be wiser to buy the pump, he said."

The anecdote illustrates why windmills haven't gotten greater use as alternate sources of power, Torrey explains. "Rural electrification, the greater convenience of a constant source of current, made reliance on the whim of the wind an unattractive alternative." Thus, he adds, the use of windmills drastically decreased, particularly after World War II, when they were no longer used as alternate energy sources for the war effort.

Torrey feels that the windmill has a place in our energy-conscious society. "The wind can be a very valuable supplementary source of energy," says Torrey. "The Department of Energy has been spending a lot of money on wind power development lately, and it's probably a wise investment." A windmill can generate electricity, pump water, and "still grind grain, which was one of its original purposes."

He is so enamored of windmills that he wrote a book *Wind Catcher* (Stephen Greene Press, 1976), which has sold "extensively around the country to libraries and researchers," Torrey says.

Along with Torrey's fascination with windmills, comes his interest in the steam engine. "In a way, steam and mills are connected," he says. In the late 1700s, Oliver Evans "started automation in this country by automating a flour mill, using a steam engine more powerful than the one invented by James Watt." Evans is particularly intriguing to Torrey, because he was an ingenious inventor who accomplished many "firsts" with steam power.

One of Evans' particular coups was the construction of "the first self-propelled vehicle ever seen on the streets of Philadelphia." It was "a huge contrivance that was used to clean out the river."

Unfortunately, the plans for most of Evans' inventions were lost over the years, says Torrey, but "I've dug up enough information in the Library of Congress and the Smithsonian to write a biography of Evans, which is now in manuscript form."

"The origins of American technology fascinate me," Torrey says simply. "I think Evans, a friend of Washington and Jefferson, by the way, was responsible for bringing the Industrial Revolution to America."

In explaining his fondness for his avocation, Torrey says, "I think it's important we know how things like automation and mass transportation, which are such important parts of our lives today, got their start. There's educational value to history, as well as nostalgia."

Torrey will gladly answer inquiries about windmills or steam engines addressed to him at 616 G Street SW, Washington, DC 20024.

WILLIAM VALAVANIS
BONSAI

THE FIRST BONSAI TREE he ever had died shortly after he bought it, but that didn't discourage William Valavanis.

"I just kept going," he says. "I still killed trees, but not as many. Besides, everybody loses trees, especially when they're starting out." After that initial disappointment, when he was 11 years old, Valavanis was determined to become a bonsai expert. He attended the University of New York Agricultural and Technical College in Farmingdale, and went to Japan in 1970 to study briefly with Kyuzo Murata and other bonsai masters. Graduating from Farmingdale in 1971, he returned to Japan for a one-year apprenticeship in bonsai culture. Later, he obtained another degree, in ornamental horticulture, from Cornell University.

Today, at the age of 28, Valvanis is a nationally known bonsai expert who teaches and lectures around the country. In addition, he has his own bonsai school and arboretum at his Rochester, New York, home and publishes a lavish magazine, devoted exclusively to bonasi art and culture. "It's my goal to expand and promote classical bonsai art, through my magazine, through my lectures, and through the propagation of unusual, little known plant material," says Valavanis.

He specializes in dwarf pines and maples, with rough bark. "These are unusual in the whole field of bonsai in America," he says. "Most people have selected trees for fast growth and color. Mine are horticultural curiosities."

Valavanis hurries to correct misconceptions he feels most people have about bonsai, the horticultural art form imported from Japan. "It's not an ancient art; bonsai is only 150 to 250 years old," he says. Another common misconception is that "bonsai are houseplants. They are not. They have to be kept outdoors." Naturally, like many growing things, bonsai must be protected from the severest winter weather, but basically they should be allowed to live like the trees they really are.

To properly grow a bonsai, Valavanis feels, it is vital to understand the symbolic nature of the art. "You are keeping the tree alive. It is a symbol of the spirit, trying to keep part of nature alive in a container."

There are many different methods for creating a bonsai work of art, according to Valavanis. Obtain "container-grown nursery stock. Study its form, decide on what the tree will look like, and prune or eliminate all unnecessary branches." The remaining part of the tree, wired into position with soft copper wire, is transplanted into an appropriately-sized bonsai container.

Then it's simply a matter of letting time — and nature — take its course, Valavanis says. "Many Americans are in a hurry and want their bonsai to be, too." In the spring it's time to check the growth and shaping of the tree. "Prune away one-half to two-thirds of the tree," says Valavanis, "letting it grow slowly in the correct position and form." If the grower fertilizes the tree once a month, and transplants it every one to three years (depending on its root growth pattern), "he should have a beautiful and healthy tree."

The average life expectancy of a bonsai tree? "A couple of hundred years, " says Valavanis. "They outlive their normal counterparts in nature because they have better care. The trees "require constant dedication — like a pet," he adds.

Valavanis firmly believes that bonsai "is a hobby anyone can enjoy." He teaches everyone, from professional people down to a 12-year-old who has been studying with him for three years. "Finding a good instructor is very important," he says. "I've been at this for 17 years, and I'm still learning from others."

For the beginner, Valavanis recommends *The Japanese Art of Miniature Trees and Landscaping* by Yuji Yoshimura Halford (Chas. Tuttle, 1957, $13.95) as the best basic book in the art of classical bonsai.

Valvanis is especially proud of his magazine, *International Bonsi*, which he began in 1979. It is the first independent (not organization-affiliated) bonsai magazine in English, and he sends it to some 2,000 subscribers in 47 states and 19 foreign countries. "I make a special effort to have all the information contained in the magazine valid," he says, "and it is professionally produced, so it is as attractive as it is informative."

Valavanis feels he's found his niche. "It's my life," he says without hesitation. "I've been trained to do this 24 hours a day. It's the only thing I do. Through bonsai, I am trying to give pleasure and enjoyment to others. I enjoy expressing myself through the trees. Each bonsai is a living, sculptural art work."

He will gladly answer questions or give advice on the art of classic bonsai, as well as provide further information on his bonsai journal. He may be contacted at 412 Pinnacle Rd., Rochester, NY 14623.

BEATRICE WARBURTON
IRISES

IF ANYONE COULD improve on nature, Beatrice Warburton could. She's been growing irises for years, and she's created more breeds of the flower than nature intended.

Mrs. Warburton (or "Bee, as I'm known around the world"), has been growing irises for 66 of her 76 years. And she's loved every minute of it! "When I was a child, there was a clump of irises, of the variety named 'Princess Beatrice' that grew under the downspout of our house in Brighton, Massachusetts." Since the lovely flowers "sort of bore my name," Mrs. Warburton was fascinated by them.

That interest has carried through her life. Wherever she lived after that, if she could, she grew irises. When she settled in Westboro, Massachusetts, with her family at the end of World War II, "I planted irises long before the house was finished."

Today, "there are rows and rows of them," and Mrs. Warburton has become one of the world's leading experts in the growing and hybridizing of the flowers, often called "flags."

The iris, a native American flower that grew in swamps and wild places all over the country long before it was cultivated, has changed a lot over the years, she says. "The garden irises of today are far, far different. They're larger, with more colors, a better shape, and they live longer. They're just much more beautiful."

Mrs. Warburton has bred and hybridized the iris into nearly 90 new varieties. For her efforts, she's "won a bowlful of medals," and numerous plaques and other awards, along with the respect of fellow iris growers worldwide. "Everybody involved with irises knows who I am," she says, for she has traveled all over the world showing irises, judging shows, and doing research.

She's proudest of "Brassie," a variety of iris that she created. The plant, which stands about one foot tall, with bright yellow flowers, is "a hardy, reliable, useful garden plant," says Mrs. Warburton. Among the other breeds she has created, she is also especially fond of "Blue Denim" (named for its brilliant color) and "Scented Air," (because "it's so fragrant"). "A lot of the new irises are too fancy, and too large. What I breed are real gardener's plants."

Breeding irises is, of course, a time-consuming process. Mrs. Warburton has experimented with many types over the years, in her search for the right kinds of flowering and growing characteristics. Her success is a tribute to her perseverance, as much as anything else.

Contrary to what the uninitatied might think, it is not terribly complicated to grow irises. "Hell no," exclaims Mrs. Warburton. "They're not difficult. Oh, they have their troubles like any other plant," but basic care and loving attention make them flourish.

Mrs. Warburton has worked closely with the American Iris Society, the leading national organization for iris growers, and has spent some 25 years judging irises in many contests around the world. She is also active in the Median Iris Society (named after a particular type of iris that she specializes in) as an officer of the group and editor of their publications.

While Mrs. Warburton is enthusiastic about breeding and growing irises, she is especially enamored of the people she comes in contact with through her hobby. "They're some of the most wonderful people in the world," she says. "There's no occupation I can think of where you can be friends with 12-year olds and senior citizens at the same time——friends with everyone from scientists to dolts," she laughs. "Really, it's great. Everybody should have a hobby, and ride it hard, as someone once said."

Mrs. Warburton feels self-education is a necessity before attempting to grow or breed the plants. The many horticultural magazines on the market, Mrs. Warburton says, will instruct the novice on sources of iris bulbs and where to write for catalogues. By reading and studying these catalogues, it is possible to build up some expertise on the plants.

Mrs. Warburton advises care in choosing the plants to be grown because "sooner or later you will want to cross them." Take the time to find out which plants are most fertile and make the best parents because "you wouldn't want to start breeding purebred dogs with mutts."

The American Iris Society booklet, *Iris: An Ideal Hardy Perennial*, which she wrote, is a good place to find information on the care and growing of irises.

Mrs. Warburton's greatest satisfaction in her hobby is "the joy of creation. Can you imagine walking out in the garden and seeing something ready to bloom, something that you, in a real sense, created, nutured and cared for? "There's no thrill on earth like it — except having a baby", she says.

Mrs. Warburton will give advice or information to anyone writing her at 2 Warburton Ln., Westboro, MA 01581.

REBECCA WINGERT
ALPINE PLANTS

IT MAY BE HARD to believe, but many plants grow above the timber line on most high mountains. They are called "alpine plants," and a Victoria, British Columbia, housewife has become expert on the growing and breeding of these plucky plants.

"Even though they're called alpine plants because they grow in the Alps," Mrs. Wingert says, "the term has come to be more generally applied to include plants growing at altitudes of 7,000 feet and up, as well as certain woodland and seaside plants in western North America."

Alpine plants are commonly found in rock gardens, says Mrs. Wingert, and are a common sight to anyone who hikes in high mountain areas. Some varieties, like primula or "rock plants" are particularly well-known. The rhododendron is also considered an alpine plant, she says.

Mrs. Wingert has always loved gardening. Her interest in alpine plants and rock gardening "evolved over the years," she says. "I was always interested in the plants that grew high up on the mountains." In 1970, however, Mrs. Wingert plunged into the study of alpine plants. She joined several alpine plant-related groups, and began studying the many varieties.

"Since our weather in Victoria is very mild and very good for growing things," she has been quite successful with her plants. "We have just a regular city lot, 60 feet wide by 120 feet deep," she says. Her collection of 250 alpine plants is grown behind the house, "under the sundeck, where they are sheltered from the winter rain, and get a nice southern exposure." The plants "don't like to be soggy," says Mrs. Wingert.

"A great many of these plants are difficult to raise," she says. "You have to create the right climate. I do the best I can, but sometimes I have to improvise." Since the plants grow well among rocks, Mrs. Wingert has her specimens planted in pots with a top dressing of rocks. "It keeps the roots cool," she says.

Mrs. Wingert is modest about her garden: "Really, it's nothing at all. I don't even encourage visitors; it's simply a neat, suburban garden in a subdivision." Yet, it's one that produces champion plants. Several of Mrs. Wingert's plants have won best of genus, best of show, and best North American plant in alpine plant shows.

Mrs. Wingert says that some alpine plants are "becoming endangered species. In Canada, for example, the government is trying to look after trilliums, dogwood, and some ground-growing orchids which are on the verge of extinction."

To keep these endangered plants and others like them from disappearing, Mrs. Wingert and other alpine plant buffs "try to bring into cultivation those that are becoming extinct in the wild." This is done without attempting to hybridize the plants, thereby creating new strains. "We try to keep the species pure," she says. "It spoils things to do otherwise."

Alpine plants flourish more easily in some areas of North America than in others. "It's not too easy on the eastern coast," Mrs. Wingert says. "Believe it or not, the plants can't stand too much winter freezing." Alpine plants do especially well in the Pacific Northwest, she thinks.

Since the cultivation of alpine plants can be somewhat complicated, Mrs. Wingert thinks it's a good idea for novices to join their local chapter of the American Rock Garden Society. "Attend their meetings," she says, "and you'll get to know more about the plants, and meet other people in your area who are growing them." The society also offers many informative books and pamphlets, she says. Joining a club will also provide access to the club's "seed exchanges," through which members trade home-grown seeds with other members.

Alpine gardening means a lot to Mrs. Wingert. "Without it, I'd be a very dull old lady," she says. "The joy of producing something beautiful from a small seed is wonderful. And the glory of being out in the fresh air and up on a mountainside searching for plants is worth experiencing."

Mrs. Wingert will gladly answer questions about alpine plants, directed to her at 1715 Llandaff Pl., Victoria, BC, Canada V8N 4V2.

GEORGE YINGLING
PENSTEMONS

THE MOST prolific wildflower in the United States is the penstemon. Commonly called "beard-tongue," the penstemon is country cousin to the snapdragon and the foxglove, and exists in more than 200 varieties and another 50 or so hybrids.

While they are attractive as a garden flower, many of the varieties are in danger of extinction. The penstemon has become the object of concern to a group of people in the U.S., among them George Yingling, of Dayton, Ohio, who is interested in the care and breeding of the plants.

Yingling, a retired U.S. government engineer, is a leading expert on this uniquely American wildflower, as a well-known breeder and as the editor and publisher of the *American Penstemon Society Bulletin*, the journal of the nationwide organization concerned with their cultivation and growth.

Yingling came to penstemons in the late 1950s, when he "saw an article in a gardening magazine about them. They were beautiful things, and I got interested and joined the American Penstemon Society."

Yingling now grows close to 45 varieties of the flower in his home garden. He's also started a penstemon breeding program at the Cox Arboretum in Dayton, with another 35 to 40 varieties.

One of the crosses he is working on involves the species *penstemon digitalis*. "This is a hardy, disease-resistant plant, with white blossoms, that stands quite tall," he says. Yingling is trying to develop brighter colors in the flowers by crossing the digitalis with the Western variety of penstemon, which he says is much more colorful.

Hybridizing penstemons is "kind of tricky," says Yingling. "Sometimes they'll take and sometimes they won't."

He describes the cross-pollination process: "You have to be careful. Just before the bloom opens, pull it off so that the pollen is exposed. When the bloom begins to curl down, that means it's fertile. Then pull the pollen sacks from the other plant you wish to cross, and dab them on the stamen of the flower. Cover the stamen in a glassine bag, and when it takes, the ovary will swell." It's just a short time to appearance of a seed pod, which is plucked from the plant, shelled, and the seeds planted. "It really doesn't take a great deal of skill to do this," he says. "The most important thing is patience."

Even though they are so prolific and indigenous to America, penstemons are not too well known," says Yingling. In fact, he adds, there are only about 250 people in the world interested in the propagation of these plants. Yingling thinks every American gardener ought to plant penstemons, mainly because they are a hardy, attractive flower. They are also easy to grow. In general, the plants like "poor, gravelly soil, and no fertilizer. In fact, if you fertilize them, they'll flower so much they'll bloom themselves to death.

Penstemons are also adaptable. "If you put out 50 varieties, from different areas of the country, the first thing you know, you'll have a plant that's indigenous to somewhere else growing in your garden. Penstemons are funny this way: some adapt, and some will not. You can never tell."

He suggests planting the digitalis, the Ruby King (hybrid tall red plant), the Rose Elf (another hybrid), the many colored *penstemon barbatus* (the oldest variety on record, grown in Colonial days) that grows in many colors, and *penstemon smallii*, which has a deep rose or lavendar flower.

While the seeds for these plants are available in some nurseries, Yingling says the best source is the American Penstemon Society's seed exchange program. There are 100 varieties available, donated by the organization's members, and they can be purchased, at cost, for 20 cents per package.

"I am fascinated by penstemons," Yingling says, "mostly because of the unique opportunities for breeding the plants. There are very few people dealing with penstemons, and there's such a wide variety of material, that I enjoy the opportunity to develop something unique."

Yingling thinks it's a good idea, since there's not much written about penstemons, for the beginner to join the society. Contact Orville Stewart, PO Box 450, Briarcliff Manor, NY 10510. Memberships are $5 per year for a regular member, $5.50 per couple, and $7.50 for a sustaining membership.

Yingling will gladly answer questions or give advice on penstemons. He can be contacted at 399 Cheltenham Dr., Dayton, OH 45459.

ARTS AND CRAFTS

JAMES ANDREWS
REED ORGANS

ONE OF THE MOST delightful musical instruments imaginable is the reed organ. A popular fixture of many homes, particularly from 1870 to 1920, reed organs today are unusual antiques, often collected as much for their quaint beauty, as for the intriguing musical sounds that emanate from them.

James Andrews, of Troy, New York, knows all about the charm of reed organs. He grew up with them as a youngster, and today he's an expert in the restoration of these interesting music makers.

Andrews went to high school in Mount Herman, Massachusettts, just 17 miles south of Brattleboro, Vermont, which was the home of one of the most famous reed organ manufacturers, Estey Organ Co. "In those days, the 1930s, Estey still made reed organs, as well as the pipe organs which they make to this day. I was interested in music, and I worked for the Estey factory during two summer vacations, so that was my first exposure to reed organs."

Today, Andrews and one of his three sons have a collection of four reed organs, three of which they have restored. Included are a two-manual Estey from the 1920s, "one of the larger reed organs ever made," a one-manual organ made by Lyon & Healy in 1871, and a Woodbury organ from 1881. The fourth organ, "is in pieces, and we don't even know who built it," Andrews says.

Andrews doesn't restrict himself to restoring and playing reed organs; he's also been studying their history as well. The earliest reed organs were not the ones everyone commonly associates with the term, says Andrews. "They first had organs," he says, "that were held on the lap, while a bellows was squeezed by the person's knees." The foot-pump mechanism did not appear until the 1860s.

"Many companies built reed organs," says Andrews, "particularly in the late 1800s." He notes, however, that many of the companies who sold reed organs under their own company names didn't really make them themselves. Manufacturers like Estey or Lyon & Healy constructed the organs for the companies whose labels appeared on them.

Restoring a reed organ is quite easy, according to Andrews. "The mechanism is pretty simple," he says. "Anybody who has a modest knowledge of woodworking and what not to do, can do it."The most delicate parts of the reed organ are, rather obviously, the reeds. Though they are made of hardened brass, they must be "handled with extreme care."

The reeds in the organs are "free reeds," Andrews says, meaning that they vibrate up and down, without touching any hard surface. The organ works on the "principle of suction," says Andrews, which is produced by pumping the foot pedals, sucking in the air which vibrates the reeds.

The exterior of the organ is less sensitive, Andrews says. Since the organs were wood-machined, "things fit very well together, so it's a matter of regluing and rescrewing, in most cases."

Unlike a piano, or many other musical instruments, reed organs don't have to be tuned. The reeds are "very sensitive to dirt and abuse. So to keep them functioning, it is necessary to take a fine tissue, or onion skin paper, or a camel's hair brush, and clean them off." That will keep the tune intact, and, besides, "no one should ever put his hands on the reeds," says Andrews. For the novice reed organ restorer, Andrews recommends the publications of Vestal Press, Vestal, New York, which can be ordered by mail.

Andrews says good reed organs can still be found today, and relatively easily. Prices, of course, are rising steadily. "I bought a reed organ for $17 a few years ago," says Andrews. "You can still find a bargain like that occasionally." Now, however, he says it is much more common to find organs which previously sold for $100 or $150 going for $600-$700. Andrews says a prime source for these organs is auctions, though they can sometimes be found in secondhand stores, flea markets, and antique stores.

"It's interesting to note that today reed organs are frequently bought more as a piece of furniture than as a functioning musical instrument," says Andrews. He thinks it is the unique appearance of the organs with their fine wood-carved cabinets that interests antique buffs.

For Andrews, the most fun to be had from a reed organ is restoring and playing it. "They're interesting, a relic of the past. There was very little serious music written for them, but they're an entertaining bit of nostalgia."

Andrews will answer queries about reed organ restoration, directed to him at PO Box 246, Troy, NY 12181.

DAVID BECK
ANTIQUE MUSIC BOX RESTORATION

THE MUSIC GOES ROUND and round, and it comes out of David Beck's music boxes, antique gems he carefully restores in his basement workshop, to bring back the delicate tinkling of the marvelous machines that were popular from 1810-1910 in the United States and abroad.

That many of these music boxes have a chance to play again is due to the efforts of Beck, who has been a full-time music box technician since 1972 and is one of the best in the nation at this time-consuming, intricate work.

Dissatisfaction with his job propelled Beck into full-time music box restoration. "I was working in the electronics industry, which fell apart in 1972," he says. "I got kicked from pillar to post, and when I got laid off the last time, I just decided to heck with it." He and his wife had collected and restored music boxes since 1967, so he did not embark on the new venture a complete novice.

Beck's interest began when he obtained some antique music boxes from an auction sale. They needed fixing, so he tinkered with them himself and soon discovered that he liked it. "I guess I'm a frustrated musician and they fulfill some kind of need. Plus, I am mechanically inclined and like to take things apart and put them back together." He gets plenty of opportunity to do that. Not only does he have a sizeable collection, but he fixes music boxes for people all over the country as part of his business.

The music boxes Beck deals with are of two types. The cylinder music box is what one traditionally thinks of as a Swiss music box. The other, larger and far more complex, is the disk music box. These music boxes (really music machines) play metal "records" and have a deeper, more sonorous tone.

Each kind of music box is collectible, but for different reasons, says Beck. "The cylinder music boxes were made by families, and each is unique, so you can't swap parts from one music box to another. The disk boxes, on the other hand, were manufactured, thus many parts could be swapped between machines of different manufacturers, but each manufacturer had a characteristic sound."

According to Beck, most of the cylinder boxes were made in Swtizerland or Germany, while the bulk of the disk music machines (and the best of them) were manufactured by Regina, a Rahway, New Jersey, concern.

Among the items Beck is particularly proud of in his personal collection is a symphonium disk music box, from Leipzig, made in 1902 or 1903. This music box stands 7 feet tall, and plays disks that are 21 inches in diameter. "Only about eight of these machines have survived," says Beck.

Restoration of antique music boxes is "intricate work that takes quite a bit of time and skill," says Beck. "You have to be a machinist, and have perserverance and a good musical ear." If a part needs replacement, Beck has to make it himself. Most of the boxes have to be "pulled down and put together again" by Beck before they are in proper working order. Once the mechanism of the music box is working, it's necessary to musically tune the box, as well.

Beck's wife helps him. "Her speciality is dampering the cylinder boxes to get the squeaks out," he says. "This requires patience and time, and is a real acquired skill, which she has to keep practicing as much as possible to retain her ability." She can also "pull down and pretty much put together" a complete music box herself, Beck says.

"Music boxes are not as rare as you think," says Beck. "There are plenty of them around. We always have a batch to work on." He estimates that it costs anywhere from $200 to $2,000 to have a music box put in perfectly restored playing order.

While it is sometimes difficult for novice music box collectors to find items to collect, it's not impossible, says Beck. But he cautions the would-be collector to be wary. "Unfortunately, a lot of stuff at the bottom of the barrel is around. It certainly isn't worth what it's being sold for." Though it is possible to get a good antique music box for as little as $100, it's most common to pay anywhere from $500 to $5,000 for one, Beck says.

Beck admits that the prices are high. "The investment potential is hard to believe. Music boxes increase about 36 percent a year in value. It kind of boggles the mind." He suggests a collector buy a music box anyway, even if it is expensive. "Try to find a good machine and buy it. You'll be glad five years from now you did."

One purchase Beck is glad he made is of a 15½-inch disk Regina. "To have a collection and not have a Regina, you'd be really missing something," he says. Though he bought it in Atlanta, the box retained an original shipping label routing it to a Savannah, Georgia, hotel. Even though Beck is only the third person to own it, "it was a typical basket case" when he bought it. Now, it's worth a great deal.

Music boxes have been good to David Beck. "I really like being my own boss," he says, 'and I have a real interest in, and love for, these machines. I'm the kind of person who doesn't want to know a little bit about something. Being able to pull them down and examine them closely gives me an experience I wouldn't have if I were just a collector."

Beck is happy to provide advice or appraisals on music boxes, as well as fix them. He can be contacted at 230 Lakeview Ave. N.E., Atlanta, GA 30305.

TERRILL BORNE
MUSIC ROLL CUTTING

As THE HEYDAY of the nickelodeon and the player piano fades into the distance, it would be nice to think that the wonderful music of that era will linger a bit longer. To this end, Terrill Borne, a journeyman organ builder and musical instrument restorer from Louisville, Kentucky, has taken his career into an interesting sidelight: the making of music rolls.

Borne was always interested in how things worked, particularly pianos and organs. He assembled a reed organ from used parts while he was in high school. On graduation from Hanover College, he went into the Army, spending his hitch with the Army Band at Ft. Bliss, Texas. After his discharge, he served an apprenticeship in a pipe organ factory, before going into full-time restoration of organs and other instruments. "From a beginning like this, my interest spread like crabgrass to all related facets," he says.

Borne's interest in making music rolls became serious in 1968, when he acquired his first nickelodeon. "When I was young I had seen one somewhere, and I wanted to own one someday. Finally, I could afford to acquire one and start to restore it." Right away, he discovered the machine required a rare type of music roll. "I got one roll with the nickelodeon," he says, "but I went for a long time without another.

With his musical background and mechanical skills, Borne decided to begin making his own music rolls, punching them out laboriously by hand. "It takes about 20 hours to punch out a typical nickelodeon roll," he says. The songs are first arranged on paper, and Borne draws lines on the roll where the holes should be punched. Using an arch punch and a hammer, Borne says he "makes the holes the proper size. It is just the most tedious type of work imaginable, but not really very difficult. After you observe how music rolls play, it becomes apparent how to make one."

Borne discovered that he was not the only one having problems obtaining music rolls, so he began producing them for fellow collectors. Now, he makes 10 copies of each roll at a clip and sells them.

There is now a machine that copies old music rolls, Borne says. He does a pencil tracing of the music on the paper, and sends it to a friend who owns such a machine. "That machine is more accurate and will put the holes wherever they belong."

Nickelodeons went out in 1929, when the last units were made, says Borne. "When they stopped making them, they stopped making the music rolls, too. In the 1940s, the last company quit making the rolls. Today the collector has to try to find them."

The difference between a player piano and a nickelodeon, says Borne, is slight, but important. "The piano, used in the home, was pumped by foot pedals, though some of the later models were electric," he says. Nickelodeons, on the other hand, "were made for commercial use. They were entirely automatic and operated when a coin inserted in the slot turned on the electricity." Also, nickelodeons were frequently a combination of musical instruments, with violins, organs, and drums "making a monster unit."

Borne says he has arranged six music rolls from scratch, but he has copied several dozen original rolls. Nickelodeon rolls have ten songs per roll. Some of the rolls he makes are composites, taking songs from several rolls and putting them on a new roll.

The arranging takes 10 or 15 hours, depending on the complexity of the work, and Borne sells each roll for $50-$55, depending on its type.

He enjoys this avocational sidelight to his vocation because it always means a new supply of music for his machines. "A new music roll is different from what you've got. I like to have as many as possible."

Borne will be happy to counsel piano roll cutters, musical instrument restorers, or anyone interested in the general subject. He can be reached at 204 N. Madison, Middletown KY 40243.

ERWIN CALDWELL
WOODCARVING

HE KNOWS HOW TO whittle time away — and make it pay! Erwin Caldwell devotes eight to ten hours per day to carving wood in his garage workshop and has become a well-known craftsman in the process.

He grew up in Cleveland, Ohio, where he began carving on peach pits at the age of 10. "We didn't have TV," he says, "so we made up our own entertainment."

In the early 1930s, he entered a carving contest cosponsored by *Youth's Companion* magazine and a cutlery company. He won the $25 fourth prize ("that was really a lot of money in those days," he laughs) for his carving of a prisoner in a cell, with a ball and chain. He developed technical proficiency with those first peach pit carvings, and soon moved on to wood.

In the 57 years he's been carving, he estimates he has made thousands of pieces; and he's sold hundreds of them. He's been at it full-time since he retired in 1971, after working as a designer for the Bailey Meter Co., of Wycliffe, Ohio. He now lives in Gainesville, a town 60 miles north of Dallas on the banks of the Red River.

Caldwell has carved out a name for himself in the field, mainly through his "carving within a carving" work. Few woodcarvers ever attempt this difficult task, Caldwell says. The pieces carved in this way take him about nine or 10 months, and a lot of wood, to complete. One of his most notable, prizewinning carvings is of a cowboy sitting in a jail cell, with a dog and a broom in the cell with him.

Caldwell prefers working in basswood (called linden in some parts of the country) because it is straight-grained, relatively soft, and doesn't split easily. He still does most of his carving with a long-bladed pocket knife, although for some of the more elaborate and larger pieces, he has to use chisels.

He has won many prizes for his efforts in carving within carving, mainly at the International Woodcarvers Congress in Davenport, Iowa, and the International Woodcarver's Exposition in Toronto, Canada.

By far his most complicated piece was something he carved over 40 years ago. It took him two years, but whenever he exhibits it, his exact replica of a 4-wheeled carriage (modeled on Napoleon's coach) draws praise for the careful attention to detail and the intricate work that went into its execution.

Caldwell sells his pieces for anywhere from $10 to $1,500, but he doesn't work on commission: "I start when I want and do what I want."

Woodcarving is one of the fastest growing hobbies in America, says Caldwell. The National Woodcarvers Association boasts some 16,000 members. His own group, the North Texas Woodcarvers Guild, has had a real boom in membership, with 140 members, many of them retired people.

"People are getting tired of TV," Caldwell says. "They like to make something, they like to get out and meet people." The woodcarvers association's meetings are very social, and "more people just keep coming all the time." He also teaches classes at local extension centers on woodcarving, as well as giving slide shows and demonstrations throughout Texas and in other areas.

Caldwell believes "anyone can become a woodcarver. It's just a matter of practice." He suggests beginners start with a knife that is easy to handle and some fairly soft wood. Then, get one of the several books available in libraries that provide step-by-step procedures for carving. Start with a simple project, he cautions, like carving a dog or a cat, because it's something "everybody sees every day."

Caldwell is always happy to counsel novice woodcarvers. He can be contacted at 1909 College, Gainesville, TX 76240.

Woodcarving is a surprisingly inexpensive hobby, the only major expense being the knife, Caldwell says. Any kind of wood will do, and can be picked up anywhere either free or for little money (unless you are using a special kind of wood or a "luxury" wood like mahogany or teak). The low cost of the hobby makes it especially attractive for people on fixed incomes or young people.

TANYA CHAPLENKO
EGG DECORATING

FROM 1884 UNTIL the Russian Revolution of 1917, the bejeweled, solid gold Easter eggs designed by the Moscow jeweler Peter Carl Faberge were the delight of the Russian royal family. When Faberge was exiled after the Revolution, many of the eggs disappeared, never to be seen again.

The custom of decorating eggs is a tradition in Russia and the Ukraine. From primitive days, colored eggs have signified important events in the religious life of the people. The elaborate decoration practiced by Faberge, was but an extension of that ancient practice.

Today, the art of egg-decorating is enjoying renewed popularity. Tanya Chaplenko, a New Jersey housewife who came to the U.S. in 1949 from Kiev in the Ukraine, is one of the modern-day artists reviving this centuries-old craft.

Mrs. Chaplenko first became interested in egg-decorating in 1973. "My husband gave me a book, by Rosemary Disney, called *The Splendid Art of Decorating Eggs*, which was all about this craft. I thought they were pretty, and decided to try it for myself."

Although she doesn't use the solid gold eggs of Faberge, Mrs. Chaplenko has created some very beautiful eggs, indeed. The most common egg to decorate is a goose egg, but she's also used quail eggs, turkey eggs, and duck eggs in her art.

As Mrs. Chaplenko explains it, the art of egg-decorating is intricate and time-consuming. "You have to clean the egg shell completely, inside and out," she says. "Then lightly draw your design on the outer shell with a pencil." If the egg is going to be a "jewel box" (one that opens), the next step is to prepare that opening.

"Make a mark on the egg where you want the little hinge to go, and cut a tiny slit with a small razor-sharp knife. Insert the hinge, and glue it with epoxy, allowing the egg to dry over night," she says. The next day, cut around the egg, and open it up, "hoping the hinge will work," she says.

After cleaning the inside of the egg thoroughly, Mrs. Chaplenko says it can either be painted with gesso or an entire scene can be constructed in both halves of the shell.

Mrs. Chaplenko enjoys creating eggs that are thematic in conception. For example, she's made a Halloween egg. "It's green, with a pumpkin shaped door. When you open it up, there's a witch and two black cats inside, with another witch flying to the moon in the background." She's even carried the theme as far as the stand the egg sits on: it's made to look like two scarecrows.

Another egg she is particularly proud of is her Mona Lisa egg, which is "a very feminine, light blue egg that opens in a scallop shape, with dark blue velvet inside. On the outside, are four openings, each containing a cameo of an old-fashioned lady."

Each egg takes from one to three weeks to do, Mrs. Chaplenko says. Goose eggs are the best "because they are big enough for complicated scenes, and they're much sturdier than other eggs."

One of Mrs. Chaplenko's eggs (many of which she sells) went all the way to Budapest, Hungary. The decoration was based on the Crown of St. Stephen, the sacred symbol of the Hungarian monarchy. "It was beautiful, in colors of gold, red and green, with double doors leading to a red velvet chamber on which a replica of the crown sat, and it was decorated with jewels." She first made the egg for the Hungarian Ball in New Brunswick, New Jersey. It was raffled off, and the winner was so delighted that she wanted another one to send to her parents in Budapest. So, Mrs. Chaplenko made one just like it.

She's only kept 22 of the eggs for herself, selling the others to friends or at craft shows. "I've been amazed by one thing at the shows," she says, "Boys about 10 to 15 years old are the people most fascinated by the eggs. They just look and look at them, and keep coming back for another look."

Mrs. Chaplenko says, "It isn't very hard to learn to decorate eggs." She thinks the Disney book is an invaluable aid to the beginner. In addition, she counsels, "Be persistent, don't give up. And don't be afraid to be different or to experiment."

For Mrs. Chaplenko, "Egg decorating gives a great feeling of tranquility. It's nice to be able to produce something that you can really admire, and which brings so much pleasure to others."

Mrs. Chaplenko will gladly answer questions about egg-decorating, addressed to her at 73 Alexander St., Edison, NJ 08817.

DE LORES DE RYKE
OLD TIME FIDDLING

D E LORES DE RYKE'S DONE a lot of fiddling around in her day. All over her native Nebraska, and even all around the world. Mrs. DeRyke is a fiddler, of the old-time variety — and she's one of the best!

Mrs. DeRyke, who has lived in Lincoln, Nebraska, all her life, has been an old-time fiddler for the last 42 years. She became interested in fiddling because her grandmother, Bertha Draper Crandall, was a fiddler, as were two of Mrs. DeRyke's uncles. Mrs. De Ryke studied the classical violin as a public school student (she teaches the violin today), so it was a fairly easy transition.

She started by studying her grandmother's music. Since she could read music, she thought that would be the easiest way to learn fiddling but what she was able to play "didn't sound like any fiddling that I'd ever heard." What was missing, of course, was the unique rhythm and technique, something Mrs. DeRyke says can only be learned from another fiddler. So, she studied with a fiddler named Floyd Swearingen in her hometown.

After she had been fiddling about 20 years, "I got tired of having the older members of the family ask me when I was going to learn Uncle Gene's special tune 'Lost Indian'. The thing they forgot was that no one was alive in the family who still fiddled it." Her search for the missing tune was the beginning of her expansion into the world of fiddling.

"I started hunting the tune by writing every fiddler I could locate, asking about fiddling and, especially, this tune. Finally, in early 1978, I located a tape of the tune, which the family says probably is the one I'd been seeking," she recalls. Not only had Mrs. DeRyke found the "Lost Indian," but "I had made friends with hundreds and hundreds of fiddlers, and had enough information for a book about fiddling around the world."

One of the joys of Mrs. DeRyke's life is performing. She plays with two groups, "Fiddlin' De and Friends" and "Old Time Fiddlers," both of which specialize in traditional Nebraska fiddling of the period prior to 1911. That is a "very simple fiddling style because by the time they'd been plowing the fields all day, they didn't have enough strength to do anything fancy."

The group frequently performs at nursing homes, hospitals, and other institutions in Nebraska, and she feels it is "some kind of therapy" for the people who listen. There were people who were thought to be too senile to speak who have suddenly opened up when they heard the fiddle music, she says.

"When you go into a nursing home, and they come down the halls barely able to walk, then you look up awhile later and the same people are dancing without their canes and crutches," it's a rewarding moment, Mrs. DeRyke says.

Mrs. DeRyke is the founder and president of two fiddling organizations, the Nebraska Old Time Fiddlers Association and the American Old Time Fiddling Association. In addition, for the last 15 years, she's edited *American Fiddlers Newsletter*, which is distributed internationally. She's also written and published a book, *Fiddlin' De's Beginning Fiddler's Notebook*. She also gives instruction in how to judge fiddling contests, and since 1976 has even had time to teach fiddling at nearby Southeast College.

"I've been fiddling for over 42 years," Mrs. DeRyke says. "There's a lot to learn, but few people who really can teach fiddling technique." Still, Mrs. DeRyke encourages beginners in the field. Learning fiddling is "10 percent inspiration, 90 percent perspiration," says Ms. De Ryke. She advises not studying "with anyone who plays with a stiff bowing wrist. A fiddler must have a nice flexible wrist as well as nimble fingers on the fingerboard."

"Also, don't study with someone who never fiddled with the older fiddlers," she warns." Fiddlers who learned to fiddle entirely from records are not really fiddlers, because they lack the experience and have not had the traditions, styles of fiddling, or even the tunes, passed to them as the fiddlers know them," she says.

Mrs. DeRyke would like to devote more of her time to historical research about fiddling. She is trying to put together an archive of items she's gathered in over 40 years of fiddling. She has mountains of letters, tapes, records, and publications, many of which, she says, are unavailable elsewhere. In addition, she is also looking forward to publishing several books of fiddle tunes (like "Lost Indian") that are in danger of being lost forever.

Mrs. DeRyke is always glad to exchange letters with fiddlers and fans. "I run a fiddling clearinghouse," she says. She can be reached at 6141 Morrill Ave., Lincoln, NE 68507.

JOHN EDWARDS
PLAYER PIANOS

Not so many years ago, the player piano was the staple of many a well-appointed middle-American living room. They came in all shapes and sizes — from uprights to grands — and they brought musical entertainment to people in a radio-less, phonograph-less age. Besides, as John Edwards will tell you, they're a lot of fun!

Edwards was born in 1943, well after the heyday of the player piano, and grew up with radio, records, and television. But, "in 1974," he recalls, "my wife's grandmother gave me a piano, with a Marque/Ampico playing mechanism in it, and I wanted to get it playing again. So, after asking around and not finding anyone who knew much about them, I 'dove' in and started anyway."

Fortunately for Edwards, after he got his piano apart, he found that a friend of his also had rebuilt a player piano, and had some spare parts, which he gave to Edwards. Edwards also got the book *Rebuilding Player Pianos* by Larry Gibbons (Vestal Press, Vestal, NY), "the Bible for anyone getting started in rebuilding a player piano," he says.

With a lot of work (about 300 hours, he estimates) and the aid of the book, Edwards was able to successfully rebuild and restore his piano.

"When it was finished, it played well, so I decided to look around for another one and rebuild it. It's been going on ever since," he says.

Edwards' work on his first player piano didn't go unnoticed and unappreciated. When the tuner came to tune the piano for the first time, he was so enthusiastic that "he asked me to be a partner at his shop and do player restoration work there," Edwards says. For the 37-year-old systems analyst and programmer in Emerson, N.J., it was an exciting opportunity for an interesting and absorbing part-time job.

Edwards has since participated in the restoration of many player pianos (pianos which play each note without difference of expression) and reproducing pianos (pianos which reproduce the "dynamics the original artist put into the making of the roll"), as well as nickelodeons, hand organs and similar instruments. His expertise in restoration now enables him to complete most major jobs in about 80 hours.

Edwards owns 11 reproducing grand pianos, and a great many uprights

("I've lost count," he says). Since space is a problem in his home, most of them are kept in the piano shop. The rarest player piano mechanism he has owned was a Model B Ampico, "considered to be the most sophisticated and accurate in reproduction," and used in such pianos as Mason Hamlin, Chickering and Knabe. In addition to the pianos, he has several thousand rolls of player and reproducing piano music "that take up a lot of space in my basement."

Edwards also collects other automatic musical instruments. He has a hand-crank barrel piano from Spain that was built about 1875. This instrument, which was mounted on a donkey cart, plays 10 different Strauss waltzes.

For the person interested in player piano reconstruction, Edwards says it is still possible to obtain an instrument for less than $250 "as is, meaning just about everything has to be done to it." He urges the do-it-yourself enthusiast not to attempt to fix the piano part without some experienced help. "The player piano is only as good as the piano," he says, emphasizing the need for professional assistance, such as his shop can provide.

"After years of disuse and neglect, people are rediscovering just how enjoyable these pianos are," Edwards says. "I really like bringing back something that so much thought and care went into. These instruments have a quality of workmanship and materials that lend themselves to restoration, and I just find pleasure in doing it."

Edwards will be happy to give advice and counsel to player piano restorers. He can be contacted in care of Associated Piano Craftsmen, Inc., 19 Emerson Plaza, Emerson, NJ 07630.

RALPH HENLEY
INLAID FURNITURE

HIS GRANDFATHER WAS a sea captain. Along with four brothers, who were all also sea captains, Grandpa sailed out of Portland, Maine, around the Horn to Japan in the late 19th century. But, like many a brave captain before him, Ralph Henley's grandfather was lost at sea off Honolulu, in 1884.

The captain's wooden sea chest remained in the family, and was used by Henley as a tool box when he was a boy. But many voyages and many years had taken their toll on the chest, and, in 1965, Henley decided to "either remake it or throw it out." The inlaid top panels were broken through, so he bought a kit and replaced the panels. All of a sudden, he was on his way to becoming an expert in the fine and precise art of building wood inlay furniture. Since then, the 65-year-old retired industrial artist from Orange, Massachusetts, has produced a sizeable collection of hand-crafted inlaid furniture.

Henley does all his own furniture designing, too. His art background makes it possible. He gets an idea for a piece of furniture, "usually traditional Colonial," purchases the materials, and then spends many hours putting it together. For the inlay designs, he uses different colored woods, "fitting them together like a jigsaw puzzle." He has used over 100 different kinds of wood in his furniture-making, but favors mahogany, cherry, holly, maple and lacewood.

"I've made between 40 and 50 pieces, big and little,"Henley says. He is especially proud of a pair of secretaries that are inlaid all over — even inside the drawers. He spent 18 months making the two, one of which he gave to his daughter.

The inlaid design on these pieces features sailing ships on the top, and an Arctic scene on the front of the lid. The writing surface is Moroccan leather. The piece stands about 6¼ feet high, 30 inches wide, and 16 inches deep.

Henley is firmly convinced that anyone can learn to make inlaid furniture. "It's really just a matter of patience and selecting the right woods," he says. "There are plenty of books that can be consulted on the subject." He also advises that some drawing ability can help the beginning inlaid furniture craftsman.

The expense of the hobby is not particularly prohibitive. For example, the two secretaries he made cost him about $150 in materials. That might seem like a lot, until one realizes that furniture in stores is much more expensive and "this you couldn't buy for love nor money."

"I enjoy getting the results and seeing my work improve," says Henley. "I just like to do it. It's nice furniture to live with; we get use out of it, and other people like it."

Henley is happy to offer assistance to beginners in the field of inlaid furniture. He can be reached at 295 Pleasant St., Orange, MA 01364.

ALICE KASPARIAN
ARMENIAN LACEMAKING

I AM TRYING to pass this knowledge to the next generation before I die,"says Alice Kasparian about the skill of Armenian lacemaking. "That will be my contribution to my adopted USA, the country that gave me and thousands of my countrymen asylum and freedom from persecution."

Mrs. Kasparian, a retired pharmacist from Belmont, Massachusetts, has known persecution in her life. She is a survivor of the 1915 genocide of an estimated 600,000 Armenians by the Turks, in which 18 of her relatives perished. Even though she has been in this country since 1920, Mrs. Kasparian has never forgotten her homeland — or the wonderful heritage of its crafts.

Armenian lace is "a unique, individual, traditional lace," says Mrs. Kasparian. It is worked with a sewing needle and fine cotton or highly twisted silk thread. The technique involves making loops of various sizes, with knots in between them at equal distances. The size and variety of the loops determine the pattern, which Mrs. Kasparian says "resembles a fishnet, and is very beautiful when completed." Some of the lace is similar in appearance to macrame, another Armenian handcraft, Mrs. Kasparian says.

Mrs. Kasparian first learned the techniques of making Armenian lace when she was six years old, living in Angora (present day Ankara, Turkey). "I learned from my mother," she recalls. "A girl wasn't considered educated unless she learned how to make lace. I learned it along with reading and writing." It was important to know how to make the lace because "every bride must have lace edging on her wedding head scarf." Women often spent years creating the ornate and complicated lace for their bridal veil.

Ever since Mrs. Kasparian has been in the United States, she has taught lacemaking. She is continuously working on pieces of her own, too. She now has about 50 items of lace, including doilies, squares, and lace-by-the-yard.

The craft of Armenian lacemaking has been perfected and refined over many centuries since its first appearance in 1900 B.C. Each culture that has come in contact with Armenian lace has altered it in some way. Armenian lacemaking appeared in Europe in the 16th century, Mrs. Kasparian says, and was taught to Belgian, Dutch, and German nuns by Armenian nuns. Thus the craft was passed down through generations, through cultures, each adding individual touches to it. "Now I'm teaching the craft to ladies in the United States," says Mrs. Kasparian. "It's a perfect illustration of how we transmit knowledge to other countries."

Interestingly, the craft of Armenian lacemaking is not particularly popular with contemporary Armenians, Mrs. Kaspairan says. "Of course, after the massacre of our people, much of our knowledge was scattered. The older generation knew it (Armenian lacemaking), but the new generation doesn't want to learn sewing."

Mrs. Kasparian credits the resurgence of interest in Armenian lacemaking to the "new trend in the United States of trying to re-create all the different needle arts." Teaching the craft remains her major interest. She teaches classes in nearby towns, and has taught all over the United States. "It's really not difficult to learn," Mrs. Kasparian says. "But if you want to do fine work, you have to be patient."

To achieve the best results, Mrs. Kasparian says, a lacemaker must be prepared to pay close attention to the process, counting the number of knots and loops, and carefully making loops of equal size. "If you learn when young, you can master it," says Mrs. Kasparian, who hastens to add that it's possible, nevertheless, for anyone to learn how to make the lace.

Mrs. Kasparian has written a book, filled with step-by-step instructions, for making Armenian lace. Titled *Armenian Knotted Needle Lace and Heritage Embroidery*, the book is awaiting publication.

Novice lacemakers who would like to know more about this unusual and intricate craft, can contact Mrs. Kasparian at 124 Oakley Rd., Belmont, MA 02178.

LINDA MOSS
VICTORIAN COOKING TECHNIQUES

CUISINARTS, BLENDERS, instant mixes, and microwave ovens aside, "all I knew how to cook was a TV dinner," says Linda Moss of her early culinary skill.

Miss Moss still shuns those marvels of 20th century convenience, but she's now a fabulous cook — a real maven in the preparation of food in a 19th century style.

"I was a weaving major at Virginia Commonwealth University, and had my Bachelor of Fine Arts degree," she says. "I had done a lot of children's workshops in weaving, when, in 1976, a friend of mine asked if I'd like to set up a children's educational program on Saturdays at the Valentine Museum," a home with an operational Victorian kitchen in Richmond, Virginia.

In such an environment, cooking seemed a natural part of the program. Today, she has 20 to 25 students at each weekly session, aged five to 13 years, and "I give them the opportunity to see what happens when you cook."

All of the cooking is done in the Valentine Museum's kitchen, "which features a beautiful coal stove." Miss Moss and her students churn butter, use a hand-turned ice cream freezer, and squeeze lemons by hand for lemonade, as part of the course. "They get so excited doing it, that they don't care how it tastes, just so what they make resembles a cupcake to take home to their mothers. It's a treat to teach the kids to cook. If you could see them grin when the food comes out of the oven! They might be covered with chocolate from head to toe, but they've had a grand time!"

"The major difference between Victorian cooking and ours is the equipment," says Miss Moss. "They had no food processors, blenders or microwave ovens." Food preparation machinery was not, however, totally absent from the Victorian kitchen.

"They were the first people who started to get lazy about cooking," she says. "They came up with all these crazy inventions to try to make cooking easier, but they never worked." For example, the museum has a large cherry pitting machine, which Miss Moss describes as looking like "a space insect." The cook was supposed to drop the cherries in, and the machine would cut them in half, extract the pit, and spew out the pitted cherry. "You put in the cherry, turn the crank, and instead of doing the job, the machine just mashes up the cherry something awful," she laughs.

Some of the Victorian gadgets were a bit more useful. "They made wonderful apple corers and peelers," she says, "and a neat winged thing to keep flies off of food." She's also partial to the museum's butter churn and cast iron waffle irons.

Today's cooking techniques aren't necessarily improvements over those of the Victorian era, says Miss Moss. "Fire stoves, rather than gas or electric, are much better, for example. It's an acquired talent to learn how to damper these stoves, but once you have it down, bread and cookies taste a whole lot better."

The major difference, as she sees it, is that "cooking was about a zillion times more work."

The Victorians did eat somewhat differently from us, she says. "They had more game foods than we do now; more game was available. It was as easy for them to go out and kill deer, quail, rabbit, or opossum, as it is for us to go to the market for hamburger today."

Thanks to the imperfections of refrigeration, "their eating habits were much more restricted than ours. Their diets were more bland, with lots of starches. Everything, of course, was fresh, so there were no preservatives or additives to worry about," she says.

One of the more unusual delicacies of Victorian cuisine is "beaten biscuits." "They're kind of weird," says Miss Moss, adding that they are made by beating the dough (after it has been run through a special ringer) "for two hours, to get the bubbles out. It ends up creating something more on the order of a flat cracker than a biscuit. It is really not very tasty."

Miss Moss gained her cooking expertise by "practicing and doing a lot of reading," consulting both contemporary and Victorian-era cookbooks. *Fannie Farmer's Boston Cooking School Cookbook* is invaluable, she says, as an authentic source for recipes of the time. Consulting another Victorian cookbook, *The Ladies Housekeeping Book*, is somewhat confusing. "It didn't use conventional measurements. A recipe would suggest using 'half a cone of sugar,' and I discovered that meant half of the container of sugar they used in those days."

She stresses Victorian techniques of cooking, even outside her classes, using all the authentic implements and ingredients. She does make modern-day substitutions if necessary.

Miss Moss advises anyone interested in Victorian cooking techniques to "study and practice." She'll be glad to provide information to anyone writing her at 3126 Floyd Ave., Richmond, VA 23221.

JOYCE ODELL
HISTORIC COSTUMING

A FARTHINGALE is not a coin or a storm. And a cranach isn't a painting. They are both elements of medieval and renaissance clothing, and Joyce Odell knows more about them than almost anybody else. She makes them as part of her interest in historic costuming.

A member of the Society for Creative Anachronism (SCA), a California-based historical reenactment group, Miss Odell wears the authentic costumes in the guise of Lady Joscelyn Fitzharry of Gillyflower at SCA events. The SCA, with its two to six costume events per month, offers the "costume person scope for literally full-time involvement. And I," says Miss Odell, "am a costume person."

Miss Odell, a 34-year-old cartographer with the City of Los Angeles Department of Planning, has been interested in costuming since 1970, when she created a costume for "an exotic Halloween party" at the Westercon science fiction convention. At the time, she was involved with a fantasy group, the Mythopoeic Society, where she also had the opportunity to make an occasional costume. After three years at this she discovered the SCA, whose members concentrate on the entire spectrum of medieval history from 800 to 1650.

The most frequent event sponsored by SCA is the tournament, Miss Odell says. "They're largely for the purpose of simulated combat, but the spectators are dressed as people of the times. There are also contests for the spectators in handicrafts and the performing arts."

In the SCA, a costumer "clothes himself or the person the costume is intended for," she says. "The costume is not presented to an audience, but only to the other attendees at the event. Without the buffer of aesthetic distance, detail is of the utmost importance."

"The accuracy of the material used, and the general silhouette of the costume are important. It's vital that the detail is credible from close-up," says Miss Odell, commenting on the necessity she feels for accuracy in all the costuming she does. "You are not on a stage performing for someone, where the costumes don't have to be as authentic because they're far away. When you're wearing a costume in the middle of a crowd of other people who have the same expertise as you do, it will be noticed whether or not your costume is properly executed."

It is "impossible to estimate how many costumes I've made over the years," says Miss Odell. "My costuming skills have developed since I first became involved, so a lot of the older things I've made have been taken apart and used in new projects, or scrapped."

She's "most pleased" with a 16th-century Italian costume she made in 1978. "It was the first one I made from the skin out," she recalls. She had to make the farthingale, corset, and shift (the underwear of the period) from patterns she cut herself, after doing research on how these garments were constructed. The costume was "very pretty, in dark green taffeta, with a velvet stomacher and knot work in silver and green cord. The bodice was made of vertically-striped taffeta, with a matching green brocade smocking on the sleeves." She says the dress was reminiscent of the costumes in Franco Zeffirelli's film *The Taming of the Shrew*.

"That costume, I can say with great certainty, took one solid week to make." She had the flu at the time and was able to spend most of the week at home working on the costume. The underwear, because it was difficult, took several days in itself.

According to Miss Odell, the SCA was founded in 1966, at a backyard tournament party for one of a group of friends going into the Peace Corps. "They all liked it so much they kept on doing it," she says, and brought in other people from the Berkeley-Oakland, California, area. "The group just grew from there, branching out to the East Coast, and much of the rest of the country, in the early 1970s." For a $10 annual membership fee, the SCA participant gets a newsletter from the local "kingdom," and a subscription to the SCA journal *Tournaments Illustrated*.

For most people, Miss Odell feels, the major attraction of the SCA is "very definitely the 'blood sport' of single combat. But since SCA's basic stated purpose is historical education, virtually any human endeavor is applicable." Members engage in a great many arts and crafts. "Whoever is interested can find others who are more than willing to participate in a particular art or craft."

She, however, likes the "opportunity to learn the different forms of crafts. I'm an incorrigible dabbler and there's somebody who knows how to do just about everything in the SCA." She has studied and written articles on English dances of the time, and designed a set of Regency-era paper dolls crafted after characters in the period novels of Georgette Heyer. "My goals are always to amuse myself, expand my knowledge, and develop skills," says Miss Odell.

Miss Odell cautions beginners in the field of historical costuming to strive for accuracy, above all. "If the costume requires a special foundation garment, get one," she says. "Or find some way to at least make the line of the costume follow the line of the period." Finally, "a proper headdress or hairdo amounts to a full third of the total effect."

Miss Odell suggests anyone seriously interested in historical costuming should read any of the good books which cover technical costuming aspects. Stage costuming texts, however, "are not a good idea, because they don't stress accuracy and precision in costuming," she says. The best idea, Miss Odell thinks, is joining the SCA and learning from other members.

The address of the organization is Society for Creative Anachronism, Inc., Office of the Registry, PO Box 594, Concord, CA 94522.

LOUISE PASS
MEDIEVAL ARTS

H ER SPECIALITIES ARE Elizabethan costuming, cloisonne enamel and calligraphy. Louise Pass is a young 20th century woman with a decidedly medieval turn of mind.

Through her involvement with a unique group of medieval history and craft mavens, the Society for Creative Anachronism (SCA), Miss Pass has developed professional skills in crafts that have been neglected for hundreds of years.

"Along with a natural inclination toward art," Miss Pass says, "I became acquainted with the SCA, and got involved in it, with a group of my college friends." That was in 1969 and Miss Pass has steeped herself in the history of the Middle Ages and its arts and crafts ever since.

Miss Pass, a 31-year-old civil engineering draftsman who lives in San Diego, California, says that her connection with SCA "has given me a place to learn things that I enjoy and an opportunity to display what I've done." Though many of the SCA's events revolve around medieval battling in re-created tournaments, Miss Pass says that there's plenty of room for other aspects of medieval life to be studied and reenacted at the same time.

"When you have a tournament, it's like a little world. It includes cooking, clothing, dancing, singing, and music. We try to bring in all the aspects of the Middle Ages," she says. She has found her niche in three different arts and crafts of the time.

In costuming for instance, "I specialize in Tudor and Elizabethan period clothing. I've made fairly authentic Elizabethan clothing for myself and for most of the men in the group. The challenge of making a costume, from the underwear out, for a particular period is considerable," she says.

Making her own costumes is a time-consuming job, she says. It involves "owning a large library of books and often going to a university library to find paintings or first-person accounts of the clothing of the period in which I'm working." She estimates that, depending on the amount of detail work involved, "it takes from 30 to 70 hours to make a costume properly."

If the clothing is made correctly, she says, "it's usually not uncomfortable. You don't have to wear a tight corset to be authentic." Men's costumes are quite comfortable, too, she says, adding that some of the men in the group not only make their own costumes, but "do some of the most incredible machine embroidery I've ever seen."

Cloisonne enamel requires a lot of concentration, and some specialized materials, Miss Pass says. Cloisonne is the glazing of melted colored glass powder onto metals. It is different from the usual enameling process "because you create a design on the metal in silver wire, then pour the color in between the wires. It produces a depth and translucency unlike anything you've ever seen." Miss Pass has her own kiln, in which she heats the items she makes to temperatures of 1,400-1,500 degrees Farenheit.

Cloisonne dates back as far as the Celts, more than 2,500 years ago, she says, and was particularly popular during the Middle Ages "as jewelry or to ornament book covers or reliquaries in place of jewels."

She uses her cloisonne skills to make awards for the SCA and jewelry, which she both sells and enters in shows. She has created a special necklace, the three-piece "Gothic Madonna," which is a modern interpretation of a madonna pose, with two angels. "It's not something you'd want to wear to work. It's a fairly large piece, that probably weighs no more than a pound."

Finally, Miss Pass has become proficient in three forms of calligraphy, "so-called 'beautiful handwriting.' Many people do Italic, which I hate — it's too modern." So, she concentrates on Batarde, Black Lettering, and Round Gothic. "Black Lettering is similar in appearance to what you might call 'Ye Olde Englishe' calligraphy. Batarde is a more fluid form of that, and Round Gothic is a Southern European version of Black Lettering, " she says.

Perhaps the most astounding thing about Miss Pass's accomplishments in these three rather difficult crafts is that she is mostly self-taught.

"I knew how to sew already, thanks to my mother. As for constructing the patterns for dresses, I studied to be an architect, so it doesn't seem difficult, by comparison. Designing a skyscraper is a lot more scary."

Her calligraphy skills were attained largely through studying books and hour after hour of practice. She was inspired to tackle enamels by a woman she knew in Phoenix. "She made really incredible stuff," says Miss Pass. "Her classes (to say nothing of the jewelry she made) were too expensive for me." So, again, Miss Pass studied on her own, and, after moving to California, discovered other people who were involved with enamels and learned more from them.

Miss Pass's favorite of the three crafts she pursues is cloisonne. "I like it because it is so beautiful when you get it done and so frustrating while you're doing it. It really demands concentration, for even the teeniest mistake can ruin the piece." She sells much of the enamel jewelry she makes, in order to raise the money to continue making enamels. She says the price of materials, especially the silver used, has increased a great deal recently.

"A lot of people say SCA is an escape, but it really isn't, she says. "It's a hell of a lot of work. I enjoy it because of the people I meet. They tend to be very intelligent, interested in history and crafts, willing to take the time to find out what they don't know." The most striking feature of the people she's involved with in the SCA is that "they are people who haven't quit learning."

Miss Pass will be pleased to assist beginners in the fields of cloisonne enamels, medieval calligraphy or Elizabethan costuming. She can be reached at 4751 Bancroft, Apt. 2, San Diego, CA 92116.

LORRAINE POPHAM
DECOUPAGE

I WAS SEARCHING for an art form that had permanency, not just a fly-by-night, throwaway appeal," says Lorraine Popham. "And I found it, in the art (not the craft) of decoupage."

Mrs. Popham, of Marysville, Michigan, has been deeply involved in a variety of arts and crafts since 1953, when she became a Girl Scout leader.

"I had to learn about trees and flowers in order to teach my group," she says. From that, she branched out into flower arranging, Ikebana, and other Oriental arts. She had her own florist business for awhile, as well as a Christmas House shop which featured handmade items designed and made by area residents.

But it is decoupage that most intrigues Mrs. Popham. Her approach to decoupage may seem a bit unconventional, particualry for those who think it's limited to "plaques and purses."

"Decoupage is a whole lot more," says Mrs. Popham. It is the art of applying paper cut-outs, usually of colored art prints of some kind, to a surface. The coloring of the cut-outs is an artistic skill, as is the proper application. The art was developed in the late eighteenth century.

Mrs. Popham says that in the late 1700s, China and Japan were producing ornamental furniture with raised gold leaf. This was brought to the Italian and French courts and was so popular that the ladies of the court began making their own version, which was decoupage. They made papier mache furniture, mirrors, chests, secretaries, all with decoupage.

The proper technique is to "select a print compatible with the period of the piece of furniture or item you are working on," says Mrs. Popham. The print is then hand-colored (preferably), cut out and glued onto the surface. Then it is "buried in multi-coats of varnish, lacquer or acrylic, and sanded to a mirror finish."

The techniques have changed a bit over the centuries, says Mrs. Popham. "In the 18th century decoupage was ornate and fussy, and the craftsmen tried to copy the Old Masters. Today, the designs are contemporary, though there is still some use of more classic designs and artwork."

It's not difficult to learn decoupage, Mrs. Popham says, "but it's very time-consuming." It takes some 25 to 30 coats of varnish over the surface before the piece is completed, and coloring the prints can take six months or more.

"Everybody can learn," she says. "It's especially good for young people. They can go to a garage sale, and pick up a table for two dollars, bring it home, strip it, refinish it, decoupage it, and it can be worth $3,000 to $10,000, based on their skill."

The "purses and plaques" school of decoupage knows little of the work Mrs. Popham and other decoupage artists undertake, tackling whole roomfuls of furniture or accessories, instead of knicknacks. "When decoupage was introduced into this country, it was an art form," she says, "but people looking for a fast-buck have cheapened it."

Mrs. Popham has a master's degree from the National Guild of Decoupage, the leading school of the art, and she has conducted seminars all over the United States and Canada since 1968. She also teaches the art of decoupage and other crafts in her studio near her home. She keeps the studio open only six months per year, spending the rest of her time in "travel, education, or creating something new."

Mrs. Popham advises beginners that "no matter what phase of the art field you follow, you should start with a well-qualified teacher and read everything written on the subject." The artist can become familiar with the techniques of the art form by visiting museums and galleries. Then, says Mrs. Popham, "design, create, and accomplish your own piece of art that is representative of your thinking, your personality, and tells the story you want it to."

The most rewarding aspect of decoupage for Mrs. Popham is that "When you create a beautiful piece, you won't throw it away. It becomes an heirloom, it decorates and enhances your home, and it brings out artistic instincts in other people."

Mrs. Popham is always glad to answer questions or give advice on the art of decoupage. She can be contacted at PO Box 325, Marysville, MI 48040.

ROBERT ROSENBAUM
MUSICAL INSTRUMENT RESTORATION

R OBERT ROSENBAUM HAS always enjoyed music. He was a musician in his college days, and now he's a leading restorer of musical instruments, and an authority on their history.

"I've long been intrigued by technology and history," he says, in explaining his interest in musical instrument restoration. "I find this to be a happy combination of the technical aspects with the historical development of instruments. Technology and history "go hand in hand" in Rosenbaum's quest for the

essential perfection needed to properly restore musical instruments. "You have
to restore with traditional materials, methods, and the intent of the times when
doing this kind of work, " he says.

Rosenbaum, 53, a scientist for Revlon's pharmaceutical division, has been
restoring musical instruments, chiefly woodwinds, since 1960. He has restored
instruments from as early as the mid-16th century to as late as the early part of
the 20th century. "Each project is a challenge, I have to concentrate to do it
fully and properly," he says.

He applies quite sophisticated scientific methods to his work. To determine
what an instrument or one of its component parts is made of, Rosenbaum uses
spectroscopy to determine the chemical content, then works backward from
that to find the exact substance used. For example, while he was restoring a
keyboard instrument made in England about 1800, he came across some black
material that was used as a spring to operate the keys. He couldn't replace it
with the hog bristle that is found in contemporary harpsichords, so he had to
determine what the material was.

"It took an awful lot of conjecture and research" before Rosenbaum discovered that the substance was baleen, a hair-like bone from the mouth of a sperm
whale. "It was used in corsets," he says, "and is a very resilient material. When
I discovered what it was, it was a relatively simple matter to find a replacement."

American instruments from 1800-70 are particularly interesting to Rosenbaum. Currently, he is working on the complete restoration of a flute made by
Asa Hopkins, of Litchfield, Connecticut, around 1828. "He founded a factory
in Litchfield, and I've been concerned with following through his history and
comparing his technique with other instrument makers," says Rosenbaum.

Rosenbaum notes that "more and more American-made antique instruments
have been uncovered over the last few years." He says they have been neglected
by collectors, who, by and large, prefer European instruments.

European instruments determined "most of the basic patterns for American
instruments. The Americans imported them, and improved on them, trying to
make them simpler because American musicians were not as proficient as the
Europeans." This resulted in instruments that were "primitive and could fool
you into thinking an 1850-60 U.S. instrument was made in Europe between
1810 and 1820."

Rosenbaum has been heavily involved with the work of the American Musical Instrument Society (AMIS) since 1971. AMIS is a nationwide organization
of 500 musical instrument collectors and historians. He was president of the
group from 1971 to 1977, and is on the board of editors of the *AMIS Journal*,
the society's scholarly publication.

Rosenbaum also works on the Visiting Committee of the Department of
Musical Instruments at New York City's Metropolitan Museum of Art. It is
Rosenbaum's task to advise museum staff on technical items relating to the
restoration and preservation of the instruments in their collection.

For the novice interested in musical instrument restoration, Rosenbaum cautions that "it's not work for an amateur. A novice can do more damage than
good to an instrument. It is difficult, time-consuming work, that can only be

learned through trial and error, and by asking a lot of questions. It doesn't hurt to be somewhat mechanical, too."

Rosenbaum says, "I'm reasonably skilled with my hands, and you acquire general skill as you go along. But the most important thing is to get a lot of advice, for that's how you learn. Don't hesitate to ask questions."

He also stresses the importance of accuracy in restoration — and of indicating on replacement parts that they are replacements. "Any responsible person does that in restoration," he says.

Rosenbaum feels there are only "three institutions in this country that are in a position to give sound advice: the Boston Museum of Fine Art ("they have a school and workshop for musical instrument restoration"); the Metropolitan Museum in New York City ("they are generous with their time"); and the Musical Instrument Department of the Smithsonian Institution in Washington, D. C.

AMIS is an excellent source of information, Rosenbaum believes. Write to Dr. Andre Larsen, American Musical Instrument Society, U. of S. Dakota, PO Box 194, Vermilion, SD 57069.

DENNIS SOLDATI
JUGGLING

IT'S A TOSS-UP whether Dennis Soldati is prouder of his accomplishments as a juggler or of his personal collection of juggling memorabilia.

It really doesn't matter, because he's achieved expertise, recognition, and pleasure from both areas of the art that he describes as "beautiful magic."

Soldati, 40, of Rego Park, New York, traces his interest in juggling to his days as a student at Montclair State College in New Jersey. He was an English major and a gymnast, and liked to put both skills to work on the stage.

"Whenever the drama club needed someone for an athletic role, I always tried out," he says. Naturally, when someone asked him if he could juggle for a part in a production of *The Madwoman of Chaillot*, Soldati hastened to say "yes" — even though he had never juggled before in his life.

"I like to say that that was the best lie I ever told," says Soldati. "I set out to learn how to juggle. I practiced 10 hours a day for two weeks, and by the time of the tryouts for the play, I could do a juggling routine with three balls and a dozen tricks." He landed the part of a street juggler, and his career was on its way.

"The most amazing thing is that, during the entire run of the play, I made only one miss," says Soldati. "It was a virtually flawless performance, and you don't come up against that too often. I'm very proud of it."

His interest was piqued and he began collecting items relating to juggling. His collection today, perhaps the largest in private hands, is a virtual treasure trove of the history of juggling going back over 50 years. "I really haven't been able to count how much material I have," says Soldati, who has his collection stored neatly all around his apartment.

The collection includes books, pamphlets, brochures, photographs, letters, posters, catalogs, magazines, newspaper articles, props from famous jugglers, films, and business cards, to name just a few of the items. Soldati's particular favorites are the "props," the items used by jugglers in their acts. These range from clubs, rings, and straw juggling hats, to exotic aluminum cannon balls, battleaxes, knives, and spinning plates.

He specializes in collecting items from famous figures in the world of juggling, including Bobby May, George DeMott, Lottie Brunn, George Lerch, and Ben Beri.

Three battleaxes, for example, were part of an act Bobby May did in the Skating Vanities shows in the 1940s. May appeared on roller skates, "doing tricks at 30 miles per hour that no one else can do standing still," as the ads boasted. "He's retired now," Soldati says, "but he is considered one of the world's best jugglers."

Another of Soldati's most treasured possessions is a ring signed by the Russian star, Ignatov. It is one of 11 that Ignatov juggles in his act (the most objects juggled by anyone, says Soldati). When Ignatov visited New York with the Russian Circus a few years ago, Soldati and a friend presented him with a membership in the International Jugglers Association, and Ignatov "autographed the ring all around the edge. That's something almost any juggler would give his right hand for."

Soldati's collection is so highly thought of that the Donnell Branch of the New York Public Library turned over their display facilities to him in the summer of 1977, for an exhibition of juggling memorabilia. The exhibit covered three floors. "I just about took over all of the library's available cases. I could have done the exhibit another 50 times over without duplicating the items," he says.

Soldati enjoys watching other jugglers work, and learning from them. "There's a beautiful kind of magic to being with the performers and seeing them work, sometimes under adverse conditions. To see a flawless performance literally brings tears to my eyes," he says.

Juggling, Soldati says, is considered by circus performers "to be the most risky kind of act to do, because it is so difficult to do a perfect performance." Most jugglers, though, are pretty adept at covering up misses, and only another expert can tell, much of the time, that a mistake has been made. The juggler "learns every trick twice: once in practice and once before an audience," says Soldati.

One of the "nice things about juggling is that there are no distinctions between the sexes." There are many women jugglers who have achieved fame. Lottie Brunn, for example, still performs with the Ringling Brothers Circus, is one of the living masters of so-called "build-up tricks," tricks where the juggler is balancing, spinning, and juggling objects all at the same time. For practice, she does her entire seven-minute act over and over again, says Soldati. "She's been doing that every day for the last 35 years, and she does it until she does it perfectly," he says.

As a juggling historian, Soldati wants to know more and more all the time about juggling. "I wanted to catalogue all the tricks, until I realized it was an impossible task...If I lived to be a thousand I could never accomplish all of the tricks that exist."

Juggling "has been around for thousands of years, and yet jugglers are still astounding us with new tricks. It's a hobby that just has no end of fascination," Soldati says.

Soldati insists that anyone can learn to juggle three balls in less than an hour. To prove it, he has taught a number of his co-workers at the corporate headquarters of J.C. Penney how to juggle.

"Learning the basics is easy," he says. "To go beyond the basics takes much more time," and Soldati suggests finding a competent teacher. "Unless you're a natural juggler, your mind doesn't have a wide-enough scope" to work on the additional moves without help.

"If you see what other people have accomplished — the great variety —your thoughts suddenly expand and you just keep trying. The only true limitation is your mind," he says.

Soldati is active in the 1,000-member International Jugglers Association, the leading association for amateur jugglers.

As the historian of the group, Soldati likes doing research into the lives of jugglers, famous and not-so-famous. "I like the idea that I haven't let a juggler pass through this world and not be remembered."

Soldati will be glad to provide further information on juggling or juggling history. He can be contacted at 97-40 62nd Dr., Apt. 8-E, Rego Park, NY 11374.

DORIS SOUTHARD
BOBBIN LACEMAKING

BOBBIN LACE PROVIDES some of the most intricate and beautiful contemporary examples of the needleworker's art. This fine needlecraft, largely neglected over the last few generations, has enjoyed new life under the aegis of Doris Southard, a New Hartford, Iowa, housewife, who is a leading teacher of this fine and delicate art.

Bobbin lacemaking is the art of weaving lace using many individual threads, each attached to a bobbin. Pins hold the stitches as they are worked over a pattern already pricked out on a piece of cloth, fastened to a "pillow," a special frame. She says that at least a dozen, but frequently many hundreds, of the 4-inch long wooden bobbins are used to hold the thread.

Mrs. Southard, 60, started making bobbin lace in 1950. Intrigued by a how-to magazine article, she learned the basics, using makeshift equipment and clothespins for bobbins. But it was not until 1966 that she was able to get enough free time to pursue her lacemaking seriously.

"With the help of some old books and through much trial and error, I gradually gained expertise," says Mrs. Southard. "While I was never too concerned with what I made, the intricacies of the craft fascinated me utterly, and I couldn't rest until I had unravelled its secrets." she says.

She "mostly made hankies or strips of lace for trimming, because I was more interested in the fine linen threads, some as thin as hairs." This thread, imported from Europe, is becoming more and more popular among bobbin lacemakers. "Some people go into heavy threads, but soon come back to the fine ones," she says. Mrs. Southard "likes handwork of all kinds" and finds bobbin lacemaking "the most fascinating form because it requires more skill than any of the others."

Unfortunately, "it's a dying craft. It has been reviving a good deal lately, but it still hardly rivals knitting as a popular needlecraft," Mrs. Southard says. Bobbin lacemaking was "an enormous cottage industry for hundreds of years," she adds, "and during the 1600s, when bobbin lace was most popular on the ruffs and cascades of the time, lacemakers produced extremely fine, beautiful lace that nobody even attempts to duplicate today."

Almost as soon as she knew how herself, Southard began teaching and demonstrating lacemaking to others. She's been at it ever since. She even taught classes by mail for several years. "I wrote all my own material for teaching since almost nothing else was available in the way of books," she says.

Nowadays, Mrs. Southard is "trying to get out of teaching. I find it too exhausting." She teaches classes at her local YWCA, and the Weaver's Guild in her area. "The only reason I teach at all anymore is that it is a dying craft, and it deserves to be better known. There's almost no one to teach anybody in this area if I don't," she says.

People who don't live near Mrs. Southard can benefit from her talent and expertise. A series of articles in *Shuttle, Spindle and Dyepot*, a periodical for handweavers and spinners, led to a contract with Charles Scribner's Sons for Mrs. Southard to produce an instructional book. *Bobbin Lacemaking* was published in 1977 to reviews "favorable without exception."

"There was a need for the book," she says. "I was always surprised that no one had written one before I did." She says her book is one that "any beginner can use to learn the art of bobbin lacemaking, with no teacher at hand." The craft "is not hard to learn. I had no trouble teaching a 10-year-old grandchild how to do it. If you can read and follow directions, you can learn to make lace. It's just a matter of step-by-step learning."

Anyone with questions about bobbin lacemaking can write to Mrs. Southard in New Hartford, IA 50660.

ABRAHAM TAUBMAN
MODEL SAILING SHIPS

IHAD NO REAL intention to become a ship modeler," say Abraham Taubman, "but a visit to Mystic Seaport, the historic Connecticut sailing port, helped to change my mind."

Taubman, 68, a retired businessman from Jersey City, New Jersey, has been building model sailing ships ever since he stopped by Mystic Seaport on his way to a Cape Cod vacation in 1972.

At the time, he was interested in whaling, particularly the harpoons used by whale-hunters. "I thought I'd stop off at Mystic Seaport and pick up a harpoon to put on my wall with some other artifacts I had collected," Taubman says. While he was there, he became interested in a model of the *Charles W. Morgan*, a whaling ship berthed at Mystic Seaport. He bought a kit for building the model ship.

"I had a neighbor who was a ship modeler, who told me that building a ship like the *Morgan* would be very difficult. He suggested I start small and work my way up," Taubman says. So, he purchased a small kit of a New Bedford whaling boat, and started by building it.

Since 1972, Taubman has built four model sailing ships. "While that might not seem like too many, it's important to bear in mind that each kit takes one to three years to complete," says Taubman. The work is so intense and demanding of concentration that 10 hours per week is the maximum time most people can devote to building the detailed, intricate wooden models.

In addition to the New Bedford whaling boat, he also has modeled the *Kate Cory* (a large whaling ship), the *Charles W. Morgan*, and the schooner yacht *America*. Currently, he is hard at work on the Norwegian sailing ship *Norske Nov* (Norwegian Lion).

All of the boats Taubman has built have been from kits. In fact, he says, that is the way most people build model ships, although the most advanced modelers, with many years of experience, build them from scratch. "It takes a great deal of experience and skill to do that," he says. "I don't feel I have that proficiency yet, but it's my dream to be able to do this someday."

Even though they are kits, Taubman says, there is a great deal of work involved in the construction. The ship models are made from wood (usually pine and basswood, he says, although some, like the *Norwegian Lion* are made from oak or other hardwoods), and are anywhere from 2 to 3 feet in length. The kits have been carefully designed, down to the last tiny detail, to an exact scale replication of the actual ship. "Some of the detail is really amazing," says Taubman, "from genuine coppering of the hulls right down to tiny deck furniture."

Building ship models "could be expensive," says Taubman, "if you get carried away." Though most people "start with just a knife and a pair of pliers, they generally acquire a big supply of tools" which can be costly. The kits themselves vary in price from $25 to $1,000, he adds.

Taubman is apparently an excellent craftsman. Two of his models are on display in ship museums. The *Kate Cory* is on permanent display at the National Maritime Historical Society (2 Coleman St., Brooklyn, NY) and the *America* is on long-term loan to the Stevens Institute of Technology in Hoboken, New Jersey.

Taubman is secretary of The Shipcraft Guild, an international organization for model shipbuilders. He also edits the guild's monthly journal *The Binnacle*, which is sent to the 190 members. The major purpose of the group, Taubman says, is to provide opportunities for model shipbuilders to teach and learn from each other, and to have a place where people interested in the same hobby can get together. The guild meets every Tuesday at the National Maritime Hall in Jersey City, for an afternoon of swapping information and model building.

In order to improve the authenticity and quality of his work, Taubman has done extensive research on sailing ships in general and the ships he has built, in particular. To this end, he "sets aside one hour each and every day for reading on the subject." He's built up a library on sailing ships as a result of his hobby.

Taubman finds his hobby "very, very relaxing. After a day of work, you're all tense and nerved up. Building a model ship, you can relax in a world by yourself." Not only that, but "you get a lot of pleasure out of seeing something that has really been created with your own hands."

Taubman is enthusiastic about model shipbuilding as a hobby for all. "You might be surprised, but there are a lot of women who go in for it, " he says. "And it's great for senior citizens, too."

He will be glad to provide any information he can on model shipbuilding. Contact him at 11 College Dr., Jersey City, NJ 07035.

ESTHER WOJCIK
POLISH PAPER-CUTTING

BY FOLDING IT just so, and making a number of carefully planned cuts, Esther Wojcik can turn an ordinary piece of paper into a lovely work of art.

She is an expert practitioner of paper-cutting, a traditional craft of her Polish heritage,and produces elaborate pictures, entirely cut from paper.

Mrs. Wojcik, 70, has been cutting paper in one form or another, much of her life. "I think it's a hand-me-down," she says. "I'm sure my grandma cut paper, because she always did cross-stitch embroidery and lots of other handwork." Anyway, Mrs. Wojcik has been cutting paper herself ever since she was a schoolgirl.

Her repertoire of paper-cutting projects was pretty much limited to fancy Valentines. One day, when she was a schoolteacher, she tried making a cross for Palm Sunday. "I did some experimenting with different folding and cutting," she says, "and finally ended up with a lacy cross that looked like a church window."

She continued to experiment and was soon on her way to expertise in this intricate craft, in which she is largely self-taught.

Paper-cutting originated in Poland in the late 18th century, she says. "The peasants did all kinds of labor in the manor house, and saw the fine laces and works of art there. They wanted those things, too."

Initially, paper was in short supply, so the people used animal skins. Then they started with single-fold cutting of paper, doing "stylized trees, geese, horses; what they saw, they cut."

As paper gradually became more readily available, the people used it more. When Mrs. Wojcik visited Poland, she saw some country houses that had the original paper curtains, cut to resemble lace. "They were gray and dirty with age," she says, "but they were beautiful."

According to Mrs. Wojcik, there are several regional styles of Polish paper-cutting. "The experienced person can recognize, by the subject of the picture and the way it is made, what region it is from," she says, adding that she is able to recognize only the few techniques that are known in this country.

One important type of Polish paper-cutting comes from the town of Lowicz. There, people used colored paper to make their projects. Not only were the pieces more elaborately cut, but different pieces were pasted together to form pictures.

The favored motifs of Polish paper-cutting revolve around nature, Mrs. Wojcik says. The rooster is particularly popular, as is what the Poles call a "star." "It's not the five-pointed star that we think of, " Mrs. Wojcik says, describing the elaborately cut "star" as anything that is folded and cut on the round. "Sometimes there are as many as 64 sections to the 'star,'" Mrs. Wojcik says.

In Poland, a popular way to display these paper works of art is to mount them on small paper plates. "I visited a house in the country that had them mounted at window-level, a series of pictures all around the room. They're used mainly for Christmas and Easter decorations."

Mrs. Wojcik has spent many years teaching Polish paper-cutting to people around Chicopee, Massachusetts, where she lives. "I really enjoy teaching others how to do Polish paper-cutting," she says, "They're all so pleased when the project turns out."

She never lets anyone fail. Her classes are very detailed and progress step-by-step so that any student can learn. "No matter who they are, they're artistic when it comes to paper-cutting."

She draws a diagram on the blackboard of how she wants the paper folded, and lines to show where the cuts should be made. Then, she asks her students to follow her directions exactly.

"Often, they come out with too many folds, or they've cut big places where they should have little places," she laughs. "But I tell them everything is going to look nice...and it usually does."

Believe it or not, the Poles use "sheep shears to cut with. I tried to find a pair, but I guess they're not sold here anymore — so I just stick with embroidery or nail scissors."

Mrs. Wojcik thinks Polish paper-cutting is an ideal craft for just about anyone, from fourth grade on up. Somewhat surprisingly, "the pasting is a lot harder than the cutting. You have to be very exact."

She uses gift-wrapping paper for making her fancy pieces, although any kind of paper will do. In class, she uses newsprint. "The Poles have a wonderful kind of paper, specially made, but they won't share it with anybody," she says.

The craft of paper-cutting means a lot to Mrs. Wojcik. "I'm not an excellent housekeeper," she says, "and I hate the kitchen. So, I get a greater satisfaction out of people seeing the things that I make and commenting favorably on them."

Mrs. Wojcik will be glad to provide further information on the history and technique of Polish paper-cutting. She can be contacted at 53 Marion St., Chicopee, MA 01013.

MABEL WOOD
COBWEB PAINTING

A LOT OF PEOPLE might think Mabel Wood is a bit unusual. After all, how many 78-year-old ladies do you know who paint pictures on cobwebs?

Mrs. Wood doesn't pay much attention to the doubters, because she knows that she is reviving a unique folk art that originated over 200 years ago in the Tyrolean Alps. And cobweb painting is just the latest creative adventure of the self-taught artist from Horseheads, New York.

Actually, Mrs. Wood doesn't really paint on cobwebs (although the original German artists did), because they are so fragile. She uses the sturdier (and more plentiful) webs of the tent caterpillar for her pictures.

The art form was invented in the mid-18th century by Elias Punner, and it was practiced only from about 1765 to 1825, with a brief revival in the 1870s. Mrs. Wood says there was some experimentation on the part of a Fayetteville, Tennessee, woman in the 1890s, but cobweb painting had pretty much disappeared until a historian rediscovered it and published an article about it in *Natural History* magazine in 1956.

According to Mrs. Wood, "Religious devotion was the motive that inspired these people to develop a technique for painting on one of the world's most fragile materials — cobwebs — gathered from their homes or gardens." It was the desire of the peasants who first practiced the art "to prove their religious devotion by giving the best of their talents in the creation of pictures of religious subjects painted on such frail material," she says.

Originally, the webs used in the paintings came from the "funnelweb" spider and the large brown grass spider (which is not known in the United States), as well as the common house spider. But, Mrs. Wood says, the painters turned to tent caterpillar webs because they liked "the fine silky gossamer" appearance and greater durability. "However, in the scarce old writings about these paintings, the term 'cobweb' is used to describe all of them," she says, adding that of the 100 known paintings to have survived (in both museum and private collections around the world), the bulk of them are on tent caterpillar webbing.

Mrs. Wood's own interest in the paintings began in 1977, when her brother, Meredith, a painter and sculptor from Oregon, sent a few pages torn from the *Natural History* article, with the notation "This sounds right up your alley."

Well, "it did sound intriguing" to Mrs. Wood, and she spent the next two years experimenting. Although it was too late in 1977 for her to begin gathering and painting the webs, she was able to obtain 75 webs in 1978. These have allowed her to continue with her experimentation. Mrs. Wood taught her daughter, Barbara Smith, how to do web painting, and now the two scour the nearby woods, searching for the webs.

"Before I even start to paint, the preparations are a task in themselves," says Mrs. Wood. First, she must cut the frames on which the webs are gathered. "The average size of picture is about 1½-by-1½ inches square, though they can be as large as 2½-by-3 inches," she says.

There follows several hours in fields and along highways where the tent caterpillar webs are found. The light wooden frame that Mrs. Wood constructs ("not more than 3 inches long"), is "glued onto the 'nest,' as the tent caterpillar web is more properly called, and allowed to dry." After it dries, Mrs. Wood cuts the frame and the web down and takes it home. Finally, many hours are spent with round-pointed tweezers, carefully removing dirt and worm residue from the web. Only after this process is complete can Mrs. Wood begin the delicate work of painting with a soft brush and acrylic paints on the web.

"I tried using oil paints when I first started," she says, "but oils seem to follow the pattern of the webbing too closely and interfere with the picture." She also notes that in order for the webs not to be ruined during the painting process, "they have to be elevated off the table or else they stick."

Extreme care must be taken all during the gathering and painting of the webs. "If you collect 60 webs, you're lucky to get 20 paintings out of them," she says. "You ruin 20 cleaning them, and then, while you're painting, it's easy to poke holes in them and you ruin another 20." When the picture is completed (she usually paints landscapes or other scenes from nature), Mrs. Wood mats the picture and encases it in glass.

Mrs. Wood and her daughter each have their own technique for the paintings, Mrs. Wood says. "My daughter discovered that by using colored backing, the picture can be made to appear three-dimensional. I, on the other hand, am striving to paint a picture that can be seen through both sides of the web."

Mrs. Wood began seriously pursuing painting as a hobby after a heart attack in 1939. Through the years, as a busy farm wife (she raised four children and tended to all the household and farm chores on a 200-acre cattle farm), she kept right on with her artwork "whenever I could steal the time."

She enjoyed experimenting with making paintings on various small items, like buttons, plates, pin and earring sets, and wooden plaques. A number of her paintings were done on commission for people who had seen her work and liked it, she says.

Although Mrs. Wood has developed cataracts and "my eyes are beginning to bother me considerably," she plans to continue with the web painting as long as she can. "I'm working hard to get as far as I can while it is possible," she says.

She and her husband "are collectors of everything, and have filled this old farmhouse with so many interesting items that folks call this our private museum." Her web paintings occupy a place of honor in the house.

"Many people come to visit and they like to see something new and different," she says. "So, there's never a dull moment. I don't like TV, and I spend my evenings reading, writing, or working on my web paintings."

Mrs. Wood will gladly give advice and instruction to novice web painters, or provide further information about this intriguing artform. In addition, she has pictures which are completed that she would like to sell. She can be contacted at 3950 Chambers Rd., RD 3, Horseheads, NY 14845.

AND SO FORTH

JIM ALLAN
ELVISH LANGUAGE

THE FANTASY EPICS of a British university professor, J.R.R. Tolkien, have captivated readers the world over. His *The Hobbit* and *The Lord of the Rings* stand out as two of the 20th century's most popular novels.

Hidden in the delightful world of Tolkien's Middle Earth, are fragments of Elvish, a "language" he invented. The leading researcher into this language is probably Jim Allan, a 35-year-old Canadian.

Ever since he was "utterly overwhelmed" by *The Lord of the Rings* in 1965, Allan has been fascinated with Tolkien's use and invention of languages.

"I've always had an interest in mythology and legends," says Allan, "so Tolkien was right up my alley. Like most people who read and love the books, I wanted more,".

Since Allan has " the kind of mind that likes compiling obscure bits of data into a whole," he began studying the fragments of Elvish in the Tolkien books. He compiled lists of words and their meanings, which led him, in 1972 to write and publish a pamphlet, *A Glossary of Eldarin Tongues.*

There are two Elvish languages, "Quenya" and "Sindarin," says Allan. Quenya in sounds and grammar is based on Finnish, while Sindarin is more like Welsh. The two have distinctive characteristics: Quenya is "sonorous and mellifluous," he says, "with the use of liquid consonants and nasals predominating (liquids are *l, r,* and nasals are *m,* and *n,* for example). In Sindarin, there is a greater use of the voiceless and fricative sounds, like *th, f, s, ch (k).* "Both languages are very musical. There is a high ratio of vowels and voiced sounds to consonants and unvoiced sounds."

Quenya was spoken by the "High Elves of the West," Allan says. "It is no longer a tongue in Middle Earth; it is a dead language, the equivalent of Latin." Sindarin, on the other hand, "was spoken by the Gray Elves (or Sindar), and would have been used for daily conversation by many of the characters in Tolkien's books."

Tolkien began inventing languages "when he was still a child. It was a lifelong interest." Allan says the author made up the languages "before he invented the mythology to go along with them."

Allan discovered that among the legions of Tolkien fans, many were challenged by the invented languages. There were Elvish passages in both *The Hobbit* and *The Lord of the Rings* that "begged to be deciphered. It's very normal for people taken by the books to make a list of names" and through those names begin to trace the Elvish derivations and thus come to an understanding of the two languages.

This perception led to the compilation and publication, in 1978, of a massive volume *An Introduction to Elvish*, which Allan edited. The book is a collection of writings by Allan and other researchers about the various dialects of Elvish, and the relationships of each to the other and English, along with glossaries and other linguistic data.

The book was "a compendium of all the evidence" on the Tolkien languages. Though little was published by Tolkien on the Elvish tongues, Allan had a chance to spend a day with Tolkien's papers at the Marquette University Library, in Milwaukee, Wisconsin. "I treated the research as a puzzle. You have to put together possible meanings by running back and forth between texts and discovering the commonalities of letters and words."

In 1971 Allan, and other like-minded Elvish language buffs, began putting out "an irregular journal," *Parma Eldalamberon* (Book of Elvish Tongues) as a scholarly publication devoted to research into the subject. Thus far, only five issues of the journal, which Allan describes as "very technical," have been published and sent to its 200 subscribers. Currently, Allan is involved with another publication of his invention, *Caer Pedryban*, a monthly bulletin of fantasy, folklore, and mythology, which he sends to 150 people.

Allan's interest in languages is partly the result of his academic background. He earned an M.A. in Near Eastern Studies from the University of Toronto, specializing in ancient history and languages. He taught himself medieval French by reading the entire seven volumes of *The Vulgate Cycle of the Arthurian Romances*, a landmark series edited by Oscar Sommer.

Not only is Allan active on the Tolkien fantasy fan scene (he writes articles for many publications and appears at science fiction and fantasy conventions), but he also has a strong interest in the Arthurian legends. He is writing a book about the origins and development of that epic. "It will use pieces of evidence previously overlooked," he claims, to prove that there is more of a continuous tradition in the stories from 5th and 6th century Britain to the present than is normally supposed.

An Introduction to Elvish is available for $13.80 from Brann's Head Publishing, 45 Milk St., Frome, Somerset, England. Allan can also be contacted there with queries on the Elvish languages and other Tolkien matters.

DONALD ALLURED
HANDBELL RINGING

THE BELLS ARE always ringing for Donald Allured and he doesn't mind it a bit. He's the leading U. S. expert on the musical marvel known as handbell ringing.

"Actually, they're properly known as *English* handbells," says Allured, who lives in Birmingham, Alabama, when he isn't traveling "60,000 or 70,000 miles per year teaching and conducting handbell choir concerts."

Allured didn't start out ringing bells. He was an organist and choir director for many years, until one day in 1967 when a member of a church in Lansing, Michigan, where Allured was working offered to donate some money to start a handbell choir. "That's how I got started," he says, "and I soon grew to love it." So much so that in 1976, he began to devote his time to teaching and directing handbell choirs all over the country. He spends each fall at Princeton University, instructing and leading the handbell choir at the famed Westminister Choir School.

"The bells are English in origin, and derive from the practice of 'change ringing' the bells in the church tower." he says. Along about the 1500s, somebody discovered they could do the same type of thing with bells held in the hand, and the new musical form was born.

Handbell ringing first appeared in the United States in the 1920s, says Allured, but it wasn't until the 1950s that "handbells really began to take off." And take off they did. Today, Allured says, there are some 30,000 bell choirs all across the United States, and more are cropping up all the time.

"Handbells are precisely tuned musical instruments," says Allured. The brass bells with leather handles come in sets, from two octaves with 25 bells to five octaves with 61. They are constructed with the clapper rigidly mounted and hinged "so it can ring in only two directions, with a restraining spring that prevents the clapper from lying against the bell." When the bell is rung, it vibrates, producing a mellow, resonant sound, says Allured. Between rings, the bells are kept on small tables which are covered with two to four inches of foam padding.

Most handbell ringing in this country is done in institutional settings because of the expense of a set of handbells (in the thousands of dollars). The usual size of an American handbell choir is 10 people, with a five octave set. Allured says there are as many as 16 or 17 people in some five octave bell choirs, seven or eight in two octave groups. Ringers are usually children.

Handbell ringing "is not really difficult to learn," says Allured, "but takes a fantastic amount of technique and practice these days. The material most bell choirs are working on now is very, very advanced musically, and it requires much training. There is also a gracefulness to it that has to be taught."

Allured, in addition to his activities as a handbell instructor and choir director, has also had time to compose some 75 pieces for handbells and has arranged many classical works for handbells. "You can use the bells for any kind of music," says Allured. "You can use them in church or in the circus."

Allured is president of the American Guild of English Handbell Ringers, which has been of "great help in promoting the art of handbell ringing," says Allured. It's a professional organization of choir directors, and has some 3,200 members.

Allured thinks that his bellringers are athletes of a sort. "A good handbell choir makes the Pittsburgh Steelers look like a kindergarten," he says, noting that the vigorous motion with which the bells are rung requires a great deal of precisely used strength to achieve proper sound and tempo.

"A good handbell choir," Allured adds, "can be inspired and inspiring. Handbells have a very different sound. You can't reproduce their sound on any other instrument. They're just fantastic."

Allured will gladly answer inquiries about handbell ringing in general or about the American Guild of English Handbell Ringers. He can be contacted at 221 95th St. N., Birmingham, AL 35206.

REINHOLD AMAN
PROFANITY & CURSING

WHEN HE SWEARS TO IT, you'd better believe him. He's Reinhold Aman, he founder/leader/resident expert of the only organization in the world dedicated to offensive language — The International Maledicta Society.

Operating from his home in Waukesha, Wisconsin, the 44-year-old former professor of languages and literature has built a veritable empire of cursing. Not only is there the society, but there's also Maledicta Press (of which he's president), and its major publication, the twice-yearly journal *Maledicta: The International Journal of Verbal Aggression.*

Aman got into the study of insults, curses, swearwords, slurs, blasphemy, stereotypes, and graffiti (to name just a few of the types of language included among the society's concerns) in 1965 while translating a word list that had been circulated by a German professor in 1876. The professor had asked some 40,000 people to put the words and phrases into their regional dialect.

When Aman was translating this list into English, he found the threat, "I'm going to knock you on the ears with a cooking spoon, you monkey," and he wondered "Why call a human being a monkey? That night, I compiled from memory a list of 200 other animal metaphors in my native Bavarian language."

Over the past 15 years, he has collected many thousands of insults in over 200 languages and dialects, representing the last 5,000 years of history. Aman himself speaks six languages, and can read, with the help of dictionaries, another 25. "I look for words with negative connotations, terms of abuse or words with negative value," he says, in explaining his research.

Not surprisingly, Aman's interest in offensive language and its serious study has also been a curse. He began devoting himself full-time to his interest in 1972, after leaving the University of Wisconsin in Milwaukee, where he was an assistant professor of German. "I was in basic disagreement with the low quality of teaching, which they didn't want to improve." He also felt that academic circles gave little credence to his research.

Today, he works at home, doing everything connected with the publishing and distribution of his journal himself. He sends 2,000 copies per year to people in 52 countries, and last year netted $3,700 from his enterprise (which keeps him occupied 16 hours a day, seven days per week) to feed, clothe, and house himself, his wife and daughter. "We've had to live on 50 percent of what the regular welfare screw-off gets," he says.

He does all the work himself on a typesetter in his house, because he doesn't feel he can trust anyone else to do it. "I want a beautiful product," he says, "and that's what I get."

And he does. *Maledicta* is printed on quality paper, with a thick paper cover. Inside, the layout is dignified, and the articles (by Aman and other contributors) are well-written and surprisingly restrained for a journal devoted to topics that are often considered offensive.

Aman's journal is a cornucopia of forbidden verbal delights. Included in a recent issue were articles with the following tantalizing titles: "The Cockney's Horn Book: The Sexual Side of Rhyming Slang";"How to Hate Thy Neighbor: A Guide to Racist Maledicta"; "On Swearing Apes"; "Talking Backward about Sex (etc.) in Thai." Aman's writing is a witty combination of scholarship and blasphemy, making the journal a diverting read for even the most stodgy.

The popularity of profanity, cursing, and insulting results from the fact that "the whole world is one offensive stimulus. It's terrible how many stupid people there are in this world, who make us angry," Aman says.

The golden age of verbal abuse was in Shakespeare's time, Aman feels. "Shakespeare could cuss and insult in very eloquent language," he says. For example, Shakespeare's phrase "Thou loathed issue of thy father's loins" translates today into "you crud" — certainly not an elegant change.

The best insults, says Aman, are Yiddish, because not only do the speakers have three languages (German, Slavic, Hebrew) to draw from, but "for 2,000 years the Jews have been on the dirty end of the stick, persecuted and pushed around, with no way to fight back physically, so they've had to resort to words." A favorite Yiddish insult: "May all your teeth fall out except one, so you can have a toothache."

For obvious reasons, some of Aman's more provocative items couldn't be published here, but among the most interesting is an insult from Ghana: "'You stink like a river tortoise,' which doesn't sound like much, unless you know that the river tortoise emits such awful gas that it would knock you over," he says.

Why does Aman keep on with his work? " I love it. It's my mission in life," he says. "A labor of love. I don't care about the money."

As for advice to anyone out there interested in the study of offensive language, Aman urges purchasing *Maledicta* (individual subscription and membership in the society is $15 for one year), and counsels researchers to be "bold, unafraid of intimidation and ridicule," and to be persistent in research, "even if it causes financial and other suffering for one's beliefs."

Aman, and the International Maledicta Society, can be reached at 331 S. Greenfield Ave., Waukesha, WI 53186.

GEORGE BARBER
BIG BANDS

WHAT DOES A MAN do with 74,126 78-r.p.m. records? Well, if he's George Barber of Riverside, Connecticut, he uses them on three weekly radio programs saluting the Big Bands. And he keeps them in a carefully catalogued collection, which makes him a leading expert on that exciting musical era.

During the 1930s and 1940s, Big Bands were musical news. Barber's love affair started in 1942, when he was a high school student. "I liked the interesting sound of the Big Bands," he recalls. "They had 16 to 25 men, and it's just amazing what a wonderful, unique sound came out."

Barber stresses that "you can take the same song, and have as many bands as you can find record it, and you'd never find any two recordings alike." He credits the arrangements of the tunes that each band made, as well as the high caliber of the musicians, for the unique sound of each band.

Naturally, as the owner of over 74,000 records, Barber is somewhat hard-pressed to name his favorite. But he does have two recordings that he is particularly fond of. He owns the first recording by Big Band great Paul Whiteman, "Japanese Sandman," which was cut in 1920. "That's so rare that a lot of discographies don't even list it," Barber says.

Barber's other favorite record has a mystery connected with it. It is a 1936 recording of Benny Goodman playing "Popcorn Man." "Somehow, and no one knows why (not even Benny, because I've asked him), the record was never released by RCA," says Barber. He adds that 10 copies are known to have slipped out of RCA's hands, and now belong to private collectors. Barber checked into why the record wasn't released with a long-time RCA employee and "even she had no idea what happened."

The more unusual and less well-known of Barber's records are kept in a specially-built, temperature-controlled room in his basement. Barber also has a complete music listening room, with turntables, tape recorders, amplifiers and speakers, on the main floor of his house, which is where he keeps most of his records. The entire collection is thoroughly catalogued in 12 volumes, Barber says.

The Big Bands made the most popular music of their day, Barber believes, because "people wanted to dance closer together in ballrooms." The smaller bands (those with less than 10 musicians are not considered Big Bands) "just couldn't be heard in the big ballrooms, and besides, they mostly played Dixieland or jazz, music that couldn't be easily danced to."

Records by the Big Bands could be phenomenally popular, Barber says. For example, a recording of "Green Eyes" by the Tommy Dorsey orchestra, featuring singers Bob Eberly and Helen O'Connell sold 800,000 copies the first day it was released in 1941.

Though there are a fair number of Big Bands playing today, Barber says they don't hold a candle (for the most part) to the bands of the 1930s and 1940s. A combination of economic factors including rising prices and unionization, among other conditions, caused a decline in the popularity of the bands after World War II.

The 53-year-old Barber is a quality control worker in a Connecticut defense plant, but his proudest accomplishment has been as a radio disc jockey. Late in 1974, at the urging of his wife, Barber contacted the management of radio station WGCH in Greenwich, Connecticut, near where he lives. "They were very interested when they heard about my collection," Barber says. In March, 1975, he went on the air on Sunday from 4:05 to 6:00 p.m., and has been spinning records ever since.

The show is popular, according to Barber, so popular that during one of his New Year's Eve Big Band dance party broadcasts, people who were having trouble receiving the show from the low-wattage radio station "were calling up and saying that they had been driving their cars all around the area, just so they could listen to my show."

In 1979, Barber branched out, and began conducting a weekend morning radio show on WNYC-AM in New York City. Titled "Sunrise Serenade," (after the famous Frankie Carle piece, which is another of Barber's favorites), the show is broadcast on Saturday and Sunday mornings from 9 a.m. to noon.

On his shows, Barber frequently features interviews with the greats of the Big Band era, many of whom have become Barber's close friends. Frankie Carle, Sammy Kaye, Ray McKinley, Bob Eberly, Tommy Tucker, and many more of the famous Big Band leaders and musicians have been guests on his shows. Barber has recorded each show, creating a priceless resource for people interested in the history of Big Bands.

Barber thinks that it's possible the Big Bands will see a renaissance, in the not too distant future. Already, he says, there are a number of programs on radio that are devoted to the music. What's more, he feels the popularity of disco and rock is declining.

"A lot of record stores are getting stuck with rock and disco records, " he says. "The kids who ordinarily buy them just don't have the money." Besides, Barber feels, "once the kids are exposed to Big Band music, they love it."

Barber would be glad to hear from anybody interested in the Big Bands. He can be contacted at 25 Juniper Ln., Riverside, CT 06878.

OWEN DARNELL
TRADITIONAL JAZZ

T HE CRADLE OF JAZZ, New Orleans, has been his home for so many years, it's no wonder Owen Darnell is a jazz buff. But his interest and fondness for traditional jazz began many years ago in his native Colorado. "I loved jazz music from early childhood," he says, "and commenced collecting records in the mid-'30s."

Today, Darnell, a safety director for a steamship company, puts all of his expertise and his 13,000-record collection into his two weekly jazz programs on radio. One has been heard since 1979 over WWNO, the National Public Radio outlet in New Orleans; the other program, which he co-hosts with another jazz buff, has been a presentation of the New Orleans Jazz Club on WWL-AM radio since 1976.

Traditional jazz "just struck the right chord in me as a child. I loved it from the first time I ever heard it, and I've never gotten over that love," says Darnell. The first record he remembers hearing was Bix Beiderbecke's "Somebody Stole My Gal."

When, as a teenager, he went away to sea as a merchant seaman, he took his jazz recordings along with him. "When we hit port, I'd go out hunting jazz wherever we were. My search for authentic jazz led me into some interesting byways and situations during my seafaring years." When his maritime days were over in 1958, Darnell continued his quest for the best jazz in the land.

Darnell defines traditional jazz as "fairly close to basic New Orleans jazz, with some refinements." It is not "modern jazz which is 'free' or sans meter," he says. Traditional jazz was popular from 1917 until the early 1930s, when it was replaced in popularity by swing. Currently, says Darnell, after a period of decline, traditional jazz is enjoying a revival.

Traditional jazz (also called "Dixieland," a term Darnell says most buffs reject as "too limited and regional a description") zoomed to popularity thanks to The Original Dixieland Jazz Band, which played New York in 1917. "They had a three-day engagement as a relief band at a club called Risin' Weber's Cafe" says Darnell, "and they ended up staying there a year, before going on a long tour of Europe." This landmark group, led by trumpeter Nick LaRocca, was all white. But, says Darnell, New Orleans blacks also contributed much to the genre.

During the same period, many of the New Orleans black jazz musicians "emigrated to Chicago, and began their own form of traditional jazz, sometimes called 'Chicago style,'" says Darnell. "It was more staccato, pronounced, less emotional and gutsy than the pure New Orleans sound." So-called "West Coast jazz" also originated from the traditional jazz mold, again with regional refinements.

Darnell specializes in researching and collecting the records of the legendary Beiderbecke, a trumpeter considered "the Beethoven of traditional jazz." In his regrettably short career (he died in 1931 of "alcoholic pneumonia",) Beiderbecke "influenced every jazz musician who came after him, as well as all of his contemporaries," Darnell says."He founded a new style of jazz, which was much more lyrical and imaginative, with more interesting harmonics and unexpected (but musically logical) improvisations."

Darnell has over 300 recordings representing "every known side Beiderbecke ever cut," including second and third takes in some instances. "Some of these recordings are still in the vaults of the record companies and haven't been released to the general public yet," he says. "Every so often, though, they'll issue a 'new' Beiderbecke recording."

The other major forces in traditional jazz, Darnell thinks, were Louis Armstrong, Jelly Roll Morton, Fats Waller, and Jack Teagarden. "They were truly the giants of jazz, along with Beiderbecke." Today, jazz is as popular as ever, says Darnell. There are nearly 400 jazz buff organizations across the nation. Darnell credits *his* continued interest in traditional jazz to two factors. "The emotions produced by the music itself are very stimulating. Listening to jazz can cure my ills. In addition, the people who play and who played it are interesting, good, and charming."

According to Darnell, even classical music buffs are not immune to the charms of traditional jazz. Arturo Toscanini, the great conductor, was a fan. He once parked in his limousine outside a New Orleans jazz club to listen to the music coming from within, Darnell says. "Most people who understand classical music have an affinity for jazz," he says, providing no explanation as to why this might be so.

There are still great traditional jazz players today, he says. Among the performers Darnell particularly recommends are Red Balaban ("he has one of the best bands in existence"), Eddie Polser, Pewee Irwin, Vic Dickinson, Jim Beebe, and Turk Murphy (who has a nightclub in San Francisco called "Earthquake McGoon's"), among others.

He advises would-be jazz buffs to attend all the live performances they can, and read up on the music and its makers. "That's really the best way to develop an appreciation for any kind of music."

PAUL DREXLER
ART DRECO

IT SHINES AND STINKS, like a rotten mackerel by moonlight.' To the novice it may appear offensive, deformed, bizarre, hideous, homely, ill-made, ill-shaped even repulsive," says Paul Drexler.

What is the 33-year-old San Francisco art dealer describing? Perhaps the most unusual development in the art scene in many a year — Art Dreco.

For the unititiated, Drexler (who coined the term in 1973) explains further. "In a classic piece of Art Dreco, one sees ugliness transformed into beauty, a kind of beauty that can elude all but the most sensitive and observant." Some 85 of these unusual and bizarre pieces of art have formed the basis for Drexler's Art Dreco Institute, a museum/art gallery he has established in San Francisco.

How did Drexler discover this exciting new art form? It all began innocently enough. As an antique dealer in Massachusetts, "I kept seeing pieces at auctions I couldn't classify" as antiques belonging to a specific period.

Finally, he found the item that became the basis for his entire collection and the Art Dreco Movement: Blanche DuBois. Blanche DuBois is a doll-shaped lamp, dressed in a tattered oilcloth gown, with frizzy hair and an incredibly vapid expression on her face. She was part of a "tray lot" of miscellaneous items at an auction. "It was just an amazing piece," Drexler says, so he bought it and took it home.

From there, Drexler's collecting began to take shape. He found pieces of

Dreco under every rock. "It's been with us since the beginning of time," he says, although the late 19th century and the 1930s, 1940s, and 1950s have produced it most prolifically. After showing and selling his Dreco art around Deerfield and Amherst, as well as in Boston, Drexler moved his base of operations to San Francisco in 1979.

According to Drexler, Art Dreco is going over big in the City by the Bay. "A lot of people strongly identify with Art Dreco," he says. "One of the most common reactions is 'That looks like something in my grandmother's house.'"

But, after all, "there is a kind of beauty to it — a folk art, naive quality." Drexler is quick to explain and expound on the place of Art Dreco in the art world. It combines some elements of kitsch and camp, though he stresses that neither one of those well-worn terms adequately describes Dreco.

There are the manufactured items that, "through decay and changing times" have become Dreco. An excellent example of this kind of Dreco is the Atomic Bomb Game, manufactured in 1946 by the A.C. Gilbert Co. This prime bit of Dreco is a hand-held steel ball game, with a map of Japan as the background, and holes marked "Hiroshima" and "Nagasaki." The object of the game: to get the bomb-shaped steel balls into the holes.

The major and most definitive works of the drecoist movement are those by the "name" artists: Augustus Scheissmacher, Clarice Henry (pronounced "Ahn-ree") and others. Drexler claims that Schiessmacher, working in a rural setting at the turn of the century, created many of the monumental works of Art Dreco, which frequently feature stuffed rodents.

Mrs. Henry, a Lousiana housewife, according to Drexler, is especially noted for her works with stuffed frogs, including the immortal "Spirit of '76" which was created for our nation's bicentennial: three frogs, in Colonial garb, with fife, drum and Old Glory. Truly inspiring. And Drexler says Mrs. Henry's tribute to the Marines who raised the flag at Iwo Jima, a replication of the famous statue, is in the works.

Drexler isn't planning to confine himself just to taxidermy, in his quest for the best of dreck. Films are a particularly vital area, he says. He'd like to organize an Art Dreco Film Festival. "These are films that were so badly done that they're hardly ever seen," he says.

Heavily represented in the festival would be the films of Vera Hruba Ralston, and such science fiction/horror epics as *Robot Monsters From the Moon*." In this noteworthy cinematic exercise, he says, the director apparently "had no money...so he dressed the monsters in gorilla suits and space helmets." Another important Dreco film is the 1968 *Skidoo*, featuring Groucho Marx and Jackie Gleason in a film Drexler describes as "a real turkey."

How do you tell if you have encountered a piece of Art Dreco? Drexler has devised a simple test. "Go to a rummage sale. If a particular item lies untouched for a few hours, that's a pretty good sign it's Art Dreco. But if not only that piece remains untouched, but every piece around it within 5 to 10 feet remains untouched as well, that's a sign of enormous drecocity."

Drexler walks a very thin line between put-on and reality in his promotion of Art Dreco. "Obviously there's humor involved," he says, "but a real case can be made for Art Dreco, and I'm trying to do it in an entertaining fashion."

He offers this further inducement to potential Dreco patrons: if you have what you consider to be a piece of Art Dreco, "get in touch with me, and I will try to authenticate it." He can be reached at Art Dreco Inst., 323 Noe St., San Francisco, CA 94114.

JAMES EARLEY
MEDIEVAL WARFARE

FOR DUKE JAMES GREYHELM of the Kingdom of the West, there are many battles to be fought and won, particularly if he wants to maintain his rank in his kingdom, and have the opportunity to be crowned king. Dressed in his medieval suit of armor, Greyhelm sallies forth to glorious combat on the battlefields of Oakland, California.

The noble Greyhelm is really 28-year-old public school science teacher, James Earley. As one of the more than 10,000 members nationwide of The Society for Creative Anachronism (SCA), Earley has been involved with re-creating the Middle Ages in pageantry and battle for the last 12 years.

"I came to the Middle Ages through a totally different period," Earley says. While attending a science fiction/fantasy fan convention in California in 1968, "I saw a medieval tournament put on by the members of the SCA. It looked like fun, so I joined a short time later."

Lest you be worried about the wear-and-tear on these 20th century Lancelots, Earley hastens to add, "We're not into getting ourselves hurt." Earley and his compatriots have at each other with a variety of ugly weapons, from swords made of rattan (that weigh just enough to handle like steel, but don't inflict injury or shatter) to battleaxes and maces made from wood or leather. They dress in period costumes, and armor, to make it all look even more authentic.

Most of the fighting carried on by the members of the SCA is in the re-creation of medieval hand-to-hand combat. "There's a skill to this kind of fighting," Earley says. "Unless you have previous martial arts experience, it can take a year or so of practice to become really proficient."

There are marshals who watch the fights for safety, Earley says. The fights are scored on the basis of strength, effectiveness, and location of hits. Each participant is "obligated by the Code of Chivalry and on his honor to decide fairly how hard a hit is."

SCA members occasionally gather "in territorial teams and have a war," Earley says. "It's fairly realistic. You just have a great time. It's a team sport."

Surprisingly enough, "serious injuries are rare," he says. "It's certainly safer than football." Besides, "wearing armor is a gas," Earley says, but admits that it can be very hot! Though the suit weighs about 85 pounds, it's "not the weight that gets to you." It's the heat." There's no ventilation, and Earley says it was not uncommon for "knights to die right there in the saddle from heat prostration."

He makes all his own armor and sells some pieces to other people in the group. He estimates it took him about 50 to 60 hours of "trial and error, plus taking metal shop courses and reading a lot of books" to create the protective gear, which is worth more than $1,000. "I just keep getting better and better," he says, adding that he is considered one of the best armorers on the West Coast.

Most of the competitions are fought to determine who will be "king" of the "kingdom" for a certain period of time. Earley's knightly battles have earned him the coveted West Kingdom crown four times since he's been in the organization. What's more, he's participated in four inter-kingdom wars, and "numerous rebellions, battles, melees, and so forth."

"Being a king is great," Earley says. "People give you lots of goodies, you get the privilege of knighting people, all the things medieval kings got to do. But you have to be a good king. That's the difference between now and the Middle Ages. If the other people don't think you're a good king, they can just leave." So far, Earley says, everybody has been a good king.

Women are beginning to participate more in the combat aspect of SCA, Earley says, "so I expect that someday there'll be a Queen of the Kingdom of the West." There's "no stigma attached to losing in combat. Even if you know you're going to lose, because you're not as good as someone else, it's okay. It's your chance to look good for a few minutes. Everybody's a winner when it's done right."

Earley emphasizes that the SCA is interested in promoting the "positive" aspects of the Middle Ages. "We try to live up to the really beautiful parts — the chivalry, the manners — and get rid of the draggy stuff, like plagues and famines." What he and his fellow medieval buffs are trying to do, Earley says, "is become courtly, gentle and glorious people doing noble things, and about half the time, it works."

Certainly, Earley thinks, the medieval form of battle is more desirable than the 20th century alternative. "It's a lot more glorious way to go off to die than with guns or the atomic bomb," he says. "How long would Vietnam have lasted if Nixon had to go out there with a sword and lead the army?"

Earley credits the popularity of groups like SCA (which is spread out all over the United States in seven separate "kingdoms") with modern man's desire to "escape the drudgery of the 20th century. For a few hours, you don't have to worry about the atom bomb or pollution."

Not only that, but Earley feels participation in these events changes the people involved. "The society really inspires people to do wonderful things. They learn and do things they never thought they could do. The people are generally better behaved, too. Chivalry and honor rubs off on them in everyday life."

For Earley, particpating in the SCA and its re-creations of medieval life have had an additional enjoyable aspect. "I met my wife at a medieval dance class," he says, and now both of them are heavily involved in the organization.

Earley recommends anyone interested in the SCA or medieval battling should contact the group's main office, PO Box 594, Concord, CA 94522. In addition, Earley will be glad to answer questions, directed to him at 6509 Hillmont Dr., Oakland, CA 94605.

GORDON GREEN
TV & FILMS OF 1940S & 1950S

As a youngster growing up in Longview, Texas, Gordon Green "didn't have the benefit of the opera, the ballet, or any sort of cultural activity of that nature." Like millions of other young Americans, he relied on the movies and television to provide some cultural stimuli.

Today, Green is a physician and consultant with the U.S. Department of Health and Human Services in Dallas; he is also an expert in the films and television shows which were a big part of his life in the 1940s and 1950s.

What Green has collected over the years is "mostly intangible, a stockpile of knowledge that might be described as trivia." Occasionally, he will research a particular aspect of films and TV shows, but "I can't afford to indulge my passion for collecting" by gathering memorabilia related to his interest.

Green's emphasis in his study of films and television shows is "on the less-than-major characters, the people who served in supporting roles, who created very minor characters, or had less dominant personalities." The programs of the DuMont television network and "grade B" films of the era are two of Green's favorite subjects of study. "Frankly, these old TV shows were more interesting than 'I Love Lucy' was on the network."

The most striking fact about the minor actors for Green is that "they played a multitude of characters, but could always be identified as themselves. Maybe they weren't good actors, but you got to know them, to recognize their faces and their styles." Among the memorable actors of this time Green lists Kane Richmond, Dick Foran (a singing cowboy), Roy Barcroft, Lane Bradford, and even George Reeves, familiar to millions as Superman. "Reeves did a lot of interesting things, from appearing in *Gone With the Wind* right on down," says Green, but he was always a recognizable person. "Ditto for Clayton Moore, TV's Lone Ranger."

Though Green says it is somewhat difficult to select his top five favorite films and TV shows, he makes a stab at it. His favorite film was *The Third Man* with Orson Welles and Joseph Cotten. "I liked it because it was pure escapism and a good spy story," he says. The other movies he really likes are *Loss of Innocence* with Kenneth Moore; *I'm All Right, Jack*, a lively British import; *Diplomatic Courier*, a Tyrone Power starrer; and *Quo Vadis*, "entirely for the performance of Peter Ustinov."

In television, the serials "Winning of the West" and "Brick Bradford" are his all-time favorites. He also likes more esoteric shows, he says, like "The Hunter" (starring Barry Nelson) and "The Crusader" (with Brian Keith), because their adventures took place in European capitals. Kent Taylor's performance in "Boston Blackie" is another favorite of Green's, in addition to "Space Patrol," and "Tales of Tom," as well as Ernie Kovacs's shows.

The DuMont Network which existed only from 1946 to 1956, "was always the underdog. Even today, I prefer to watch the UHF channels because they are working harder," says Green. While it is true that "most of the programs on the DuMont Network were absolutely wretched, they did have one great program, a situation comedy called "Col. Flack," which starred the noted British comic character actor, Alan Mowbray, says Green.

He thinks the films and TV series from the 1940s and 1950s were appealing "because the people making them had to be creative. They weren't producing fine art, and they knew it. They were looking for a fast buck." To Green, "art can have several purposes. It can promote and uplift the human spirit or it can lift the spirit of daily life. Each of us quests for something outside the daily routine, something to be enjoyed for the pure escape it offers."

Says Green of his dual interests in television and film, "I saw the two as virtually interchangeable. The difference in the two media was whether I wanted company or not." He "always went to the Saturday matinee in my hometown, which cost nine cents. From age eight until I was in high school, that was the admission for the afternoon's show, and it left me a penny to buy candy with."

Perhaps Green's interest in the films and TV shows is the result of "cultural deprivation as a youngster," he says. "Had I been exposed to fine arts sooner, the appeal of these shows and movies might not have been so strong. But after awhile, actors came to be like close friends."

Green will be glad to answer questions about TV or films of the 1940s and 1950s. He can be contacted at 1200 Main Tower Bldg., Dallas, TX 75202.

HELENE HOVANEC
WORD PUZZLES

YOU MIGHT SAY Helene Hovanec is a lady with all of the answers — or at least she isn't puzzled by them. For Mrs. Hovanec is thrilled by crosswords, tantalized by brain teasers, and attracted to acrostics. In short, Mrs. Hovanec is a word puzzle maven of the first order.

It's been that way ever since she was a kid in Brooklyn. "I grew up in the pre-television era," the Kingston, New Jersey, woman says, "and I was hooked on puzzles by the time I was six years old. My mother used to buy me activity books and I would devour the word puzzles." Her favorites as a youngster were the rebuses, puzzles that used pictures or symbols to represent words.

When she was 16, she learned how to do the *New York Times* crossword puzzle and "I've been an addict ever since."

Not only does Mrs. Hovanec enjoy solving puzzles, particularly crosswords (which she says are her favorites), but she likes to create them, as well. "I've constructed a lot of children's puzzles," she says, "including rebuses, and codes, a real variety." She also enjoys making up puzzles that are slightly offbeat. "Some of these ideas just come to you," she says.

Puzzle history also fascinates Mrs. Hovanec. She says the first puzzles were actually riddles, and that the oldest known riddle is the famous one the Sphinx told Oedipus: "What has four legs in the morning, two in the afternoon, and three at night." (The answer: man, as a child, an adult and an old man.) There was "lots of word play, in Greek and Roman times," she says, thus, puzzles were a popular way to indulge that quirk.

Another great era for puzzlers was in the 19th century, Mrs. Hovanec says. "There were many puzzle books published in the 1800s," she says, "but the puzzles were more related to poetry and literature than most are today."

The most enduring "fad" in puzzledom has been the crossword puzzle. It originated in 1913, and represented the first time that a word puzzle was "disseminated to the masses," she says. Doing crossword puzzles literally became a fad when Simon & Schuster published a crossword puzzle book as part of its initial list of books in 1924.

"I think puzzles are an integral part of our culture. They are as old as mankind, and will undoubtedly continue forever," she says.

Her latest passion has been the English cryptic crosswords. "After years of not really understanding them, I've begun to get the hang of it," she says, explaining that the word clues in the cryptic crosswords usually are a play on words. "It's a lot of fun doing these puzzles," she says. "The very difficult English cryptics are probably the most challenging puzzles in existence today."

Mrs. Hovanec has also started publishing her word puzzles. *Marvel Word Games* (Simon & Schuster, 1979) is a book of children's puzzles based on the famous superhero characters from Marvel Comic Books. She also wrote *The Puzzler's Paradise* (Paddington Press, 1978). This book traces the history of puzzles from antiquity to the computer age, and includes anecdotes, unusual puzzle facts, biographies of noted puzzlers, and more — a potpourri of useful material for the puzzle fanatic.

Mrs. Hovanec recently formed her own small business, H Squared, Inc., for which she has written and produced a slide show about puzzles for fourth-to-sixth graders, and she has begun selling puzzle T-shirts. She'd like to expand her business into a full-time operation some day.

Puzzles "stimulate my brain," Mrs. Hovanec says. "They're something you can do anywhere. Believe it or not, doing puzzles keeps me organized. I work a puzzle sometime during every day."

Through puzzles, "I've met a lot of people. Puzzles used to be thought of as a solitary pursuit," she says, "but I've found it's like card games or backgammon as a hobby to pursue with others."

She is active in the National Puzzler's League, a nationwide organization of puzzle buffs, founded in 1883. "We have almost 300 members," she says, "of all ages and from all backgrounds." The league also publishes a newsletter called *The Enigma*, which features puzzle news and "esoteric, really difficult, challenging puzzles" in each issue.

For novices in the puzzle game, Mrs. Hovanec suggests reading as many puzzle books as possible. Then, "start constructing your own puzzles. And don't be afraid to be innovative." She says word search puzzles are the easiest for beginners to construct.

She also suggests joining the National Puzzle League. For a mini-sample of

The Enigma, write to Mrs. M. Friedman, 325 Middlesex Rd., Buffalo, NY 14216.

Mrs. Hovanec is also glad to hear from fellow puzzle fans (or would-be puzzle fans), who can write to her at 5 Spruce Ln., Kingston, NJ 08528.

HELLMUTH KORNMULLER
SAUNTERING

IF SOMEONE TOLD Hellmuth Kornmuller to take a walk, he would — happily. Kornmuller is an exponent of sauntering, a new mode of exercise that threatens to send joggers running for the hills.

"From the time I could crawl, I had an interest in sauntering," says Kornmuller, now a 57-year-old philosophy professor at Lake Superior State College, Sault Ste. Marie, Michigan. "I am probably the first one to develop the 18-week saunter-crawl."

Sauntering, or leisurely, essentially purposeless walking, is gathering popularity. Already there are more than 6,000 members in The World Saunter Society, founded by Kornmuller and several colleagues in 1975. Kornmuller says that sauntering is but one of the rather unusual activities popular at Lake Superior State College. They also have organizations devoted to such esoteric (but entertaining) practices as stone skipping (see page 321), unicorn hunting, and word censuring, among others, he says.

"One thing led to another, until we ultimately codified sauntering as much as an uncodified activity can be regularized," he says. There's even an annual August saunter on the front porch of the Grand Hotel at Mackinac Island, "reputed to be the longest porch in the world."

According to Kornmuller, the essence of sauntering is that "speedy walking is frowned on; purposeful movement is also to be avoided. Anything but leisurely strolling would interfere with the diversionary experience. But it hasn't been clearly established what that is. Sometimes we don't know the difference between ambling, sauntering, and just walking."

Unlike jogging, or other forms of physical activity, Kornmuller says sauntering requires no special equipment. "If you know how to saunter, you will know what is proper to wear," he says. Walking sticks, umbrellas and the like are popular with saunterers, as aids in the enjoyment of the stroll.

Sauntering is a legacy from the ancient Greeks, according to Kornmuller, who says that Aristotle lectured students during relaxing outdoor walks to stimulate thought. Nineteenth century European philosophers popularized the method, he says, but sauntering was primarily an attraction on the decks of passenger liners and the sidewalks of cities after dinner or theater. The sauntering group, incidentally, has a hall of fame for saunterers, including such worthys as Oliver Hardy and Maurice Chevalier.

What made Kornmuller decide to take up sauntering? "I have never been in a hurry to get anywhere, and probably my training in philosophy strengthened my sauntering instinct." he says.

Kornmuller says that sauntering "may easily outlast jogging. Joggers seem to have all kinds of rituals and special equipment." The nice thing about sauntering "is that you can do it anywhere without any special equipment. With sauntering, you just go out and do it." It does have benefits. "Like walking, its good for your circulation, and it's fun. At least it proves to you that you are still alive" while you are doing it.

For the beginning saunterer, Kornmuller advises, "Start slowly, saunter slowly, stop slowly, live longer."

For further information on sauntering (or to join the worldwide fraternity of fellow-saunterers) write Kornmuller, at Lake Superior State College, Sault Ste. Marie, MI 49783.

LOUIS KRUH
CRYPTOLOGY

As A YOUNGSTER, Louis Kruh was spellbound by Edgar Allan Poe's short story, "The Gold Bug." The main character in the chilling tale found a parchment bearing a cipher which gave coded directions to finding a treasure supposedly buried by Captain Kidd.

Cryptology — the science of creating and deciphering codes — has fascinated Kruh ever since. During World War II, he studied cryptography at New York City's Hunter College, thinking it would be useful when he joined the armed forces.

While he didn't have a chance to use what he learned, he retained an interest in the intriguing science, and now specializes in collecting the ciphering devices and machines used by governmental agencies involved with cryptography.

Kruh has "a dozen or so" items in his collection, which might not sound like a lot, but he claims it is "the largest collection of its kind in private hands." Most government equipment of this nature is destroyed as soon as it is no longer being used (to guard the secrecy of the coding system), and collectors face a formidable task in locating this equipment. What makes it additionally fascinating is the research the collector must do to obtain the history of the equipment he has collected, Kruh says.

These machines don't really have a monetary value, according to Kruh. "It's rare that you find them and rare that you find anyone who wants them," he says, adding that there are probably no more than a dozen people who collect the devices.

The most interesting cipher device Kruh has is an M-209. This machine was used by the U.S. Army in World War II and the Korean War. It featured a series of 25 silver dollar-sized disks mounted on a spindle. On the rim of each disk, Kruh says, is a 26-letter disarranged alphabet. "The secret to the code is knowing the order in which the disks are mounted on the spindle," he says.

Kruh discovered through his research (which took five years to complete) that this type of device was apparently a popular one in coding operations. It's invention was credited to a U.S. Army colonel, in 1922. But Kruh found evidence that Thomas Jefferson had invented a similar device over 100 years earlier. Not only that, but the same device had been "invented" by a French Army major in 1891.

"Everybody got their 'original' idea from the 'letter lock,'" says Kruh, "an 18th century French combination lock which used letters instead of numbers."

Kruh also collects all manner of books and other printed material about cryptology, including code books. He has code books in German, French, Japanese, Swedish, and several other languages.

He also has a copy of the first U.S. book on cryptoanalysis, written in 1916 by a Lt. Col. Parker Head. "Think about that," Kruh says. "We've only used code for about 64 years. The French and Italians had it hundreds of years before us. We were naive."

Kruh, who works in the public relations department of New York Telephone, admits that his hobby "is pretty consuming." He is working on a 212-page paper on public relations and secrecy in the United States government. The result of his research: "frustration, which led me to file some lawsuits under the Freedom of Information Act, which forced the government to release certain documents I needed to complete my research."

"That is just an illustration of how deep I go in the pursuit of my interest," he says.

Kruh is one of 800 or so amateur cryptologists who are members of the American Cryptogram Association. He's also set up a special cryptographic study group for Mensa, the international organization of persons with genius IQs, of which he is a member. The code group has 50 participants, and a quarterly newsletter (which Kruh compiles) that contains difficult and challenging cryptograms for members to solve.

"One thing I enjoy is that the subject is not that widespread, so it's possible to get your hands on the machinery," he says. "It's esoteric and intriguing and enables you to be involved with historical and intellectual pursuits."

Kruh recommends that persons who think they might have an interest in cryptology read *The Codebreakers* by David Kahn (Macmillan, 1967). This is one of the few books on the subject, and Kruh feels it is a good introduction to the field.

Seriously interested persons should join the American Cryptogram Assoc., 9504 Forest Rd., Bethesda, MD 20014, and subscribe to *Cryptologia*, a quarterly magazine ($20 per year, Albion College, Albion, MI 49224).

Kruh will be happy to give advice or further information about cryptography or the cryptographic equipment in his collection. He can be contacted at 17 Alfred Rd. W., Merrick, N.Y. 11566.

JUDITH MARTIN
ETIQUETTE

IF YOU'RE EVER dining in a swank restaurant, and you see a woman calmly eating her asparagus with her fingers, don't stare at her impolitely or make rude remarks. It'll be Judith Martin, eating the vegetable properly, as etiquette dictates.

Though she's usually to be found writing for the "Weekend" section of the *Washington Post*, Mrs. Martin has another guise, that of "Miss Manners," a syndicated columnist who specializes in answering readers' questions about what is and isn't proper in this chaotic age of runaway personal freedom. She's been writing her witty columns, filled with sensible advice, since 1978.

But back to the asparagus: Mrs. Martin says, "It is absolutely correct to eat asparagus that way, but it drives people berserk. So berserk, I hope, that they will go home and look it up and discover it's proper. I think picking up asparagus with your fingers is a wonderful gesture." You could wager there are few people in the United States who know the "proper" way to eat asparagus.

How then did Mrs. Martin become an etiquette maven? "That's a good question. I just suddenly found I had a tremendous storehouse of information in my mind. I don't know how I got it, but I suspect it came from the fact that I lived in the diplomatic community abroad as a child, where they were much more formal. Also, I read lots of 19th century novels." She realized that "from my reading, I had picked up the modes of behavior of the people in the books."

Also, "while my colleagues were covering the poverty beat, I covered the wealth beat," she says. She used to report on "the embassy and the White House social scenes for the *Post*, and I got very interested in diplomatic history and protocol. Actually, protocol is an advanced form of etiquette."

In her composed way, Mrs. Martin is a quiet crusader for a return to the days when "you didn't scare horses on the street" (as the Victorian saying goes) by behaving with impropriety or rudeness. "Manners are coming back. People have really had it." Walk around Washington (or any large city, she'd wager), and "you find people screaming obscenities at each other at the slightest provocation. Rudeness has accelerated to the point where no one can stand it anymore. If we'd all just take control of ourselves, life would be much improved."

This mean-spiritedness has apparently infected all elements of society, she says. " Even the little old ladies have gotten rude. And if they're rude, what's left?" This state of affairs, Mrs. Martin feels, has its genesis in "the contemporary feeling that it is more important to express our own feelings than to have consideration for another's. That, coupled with the philosophy 'It's not my fault,'" spells disaster for good manners in our time.

For example, Mrs. Martin spent two days in New Orleans trying to straighten out a problem with a room reservation. "The hotel had overbooked, and a group of us were without rooms. I must have spoken to 20 hotel employees and no one felt responsible for the mixup; no one even apologized."

"As Miss Manners, I was much too polite to stand in the middle of the hotel lobby and scream until I was attended to properly, but I found myself hoping one of the other people who had been similarly abused would fight back." What really happens in these situations, she says, "is an escalation of the amount of rudeness. Each person feels he is not responsible, so he does nothing to correct the problem. The individual wronged strikes back in socially unacceptable ways."

Mrs. Martin faults "the general pop psychology view that people's prime concern should be their own feelings" as the cause. "People are so busy exorcising their guilt, they don't have any even when they should."

This new attitude has "overrun basic 'common sense' etiquette, which always dictated that if you see someone is distressed, you say you're sorry and ask what you can do to help."

"I have always been polite and well-mannered," she says. "I may have cracked once or twice over the years, as my colleagues on the paper could probably tell you, but I'm raising two polite children with lovely, if somewhat archaic, manners." Basically, she enjoys the "ritual and tradition" that manners and etiquette provide. "Also, it's fun to speculate on what's the proper form of address for the Holy Roman Emperor to use when he looks at himself in the mirror."

With rudeness running rampant, it's interesting to note that there are still people who are cognizant of etiquette. Unfortunately, a lot of them have got it all wrong, says Mrs. Martin, "and are using etiquette incorrectly to make other people miserable." For example, she frequently gets letters from elderly widows, questioning what their "friends" told them: that once her husband dies, the lady is no longer "Mrs. John Doe" but "Mrs. Mary Doe." This is "just not true," says Mrs. Martin, and she explains that fact forthrightly to the anxious questioners. "You have to ask, 'Why are they doing this?' Probably just to rub it in to the woman that she's a widow."

The most common question she receives as Miss Manners is "What do I call a person I live with who's not my spouse?"

"I haven't figured an answer out yet," she says. "This particular problem arises because in the 'old' morality you used to have public relationships (that is, you were either married or engaged); everything else, was kept private." Thus, people weren't at a loss as to how to introduce themselves and their friends.

Nowadays, Mrs. Martin says, "we are in an in-between stage of people sharing homes and not being married. There's slowly developing a body of rules." The safest way to go, she thinks, is to "treat any couple of this sort as a married couple."

As to what to call the individuals involved, Miss Manners is perplexed. "A lot of people think 'partner' is good, but that conjures images of two old guys in business suits, smoking cigars and cheating each other. As for 'lover,' it's too graphic: who cares about their sex lives? Why does the distinction have to be made clear anyway?" Socially, "invite both parties by name. Don't seat people together who live together, married or not. They tend to tell the same stories, contradict each other on the facts, and start arguing."

Mrs. Martin enjoys writing her column. Unfortunately, "the volume of mail it generates is enormous. It's the bane of my life, because, being polite, I want to answer it all personally."

"There's an important difference between manners and morals," she says. "The Victorians and the Edwardians made a big distinction between what you do and what you say." Miss Manners finds that desirable. "In fact," she says, "I get very annoyed if a perfect stranger starts telling me, in the middle of dinner all about his private life." The Victorians and Edwardians "were doing the same things we do: they just kept quiet about it."

Another neglected area of manners these days is food. "I'm a great believer in sensuous eating," she says. She thinks dining should be "time-consuming. **People complain so much about slow meals, but they're wonderful. Eating** should be made an experience. The more interesting and complicated it is, the better."

When it comes right down to it, "the only perfectly packaged food is the banana. It comes in its own matching case, has a handle, and everything. But most foods are designed for spending time with; they're marvelous, sensual, and delightful."

Manners are important, ultimately, "because they provide a sense of order. They illustrate that there is a right and wrong, and a rational, preferred way of doing things in a chaotic world."

Mrs. Martin/Miss Manners welcomes tasteful inquiries about questions of etiquette and manners, addressed to her c/o United Features Syndicate, 200 Park Ave., New York, NY 10017.

WILLIAM RABE
STONE-SKIPPING

HOW MANY TIMES have you stood next to a small pond, a lake or a river, absorbing the beauty of a summer's day, and absent-mindedly skipped a stone across the sparkling water?

Have you ever thought you were participating in an organized sport?

Well, if William Rabe, and some 500 other avid stone-skippers have their way, stone-skipping might become the hottest national pastime since the Frisbee.

How did Rabe, college relations director for Lake Superior State College in Sault Ste. Marie, Michigan, become the maven of stone-skipping?

"It all started in the summer of 1968," he recalls. "We were living on Mackinac Island for the summer, as we do each year. My son, John, who was about three at the time, noticed a lot of people skipping stones and wanted to try it himself." Stone-skipping was popular on the beaches on Mackinac, which are filled with small, flat stones, just right for skipping.

The next summer, Rabe wrote a feature article on stone-skipping for the island's *Town Crier* newspaper that included "just a passing reference to a tournament to be held on July Fourth, which I'd just made up totally."

He mailed a copy of the story to the University of Detroit (where he was then employed), and it was sent out to a special mailing list.

"We're kind of isolated on the island," Rabe says, "and all of a sudden I started getting phone calls from all over about the tournament. So, I figured, 'Why not?'"

That first tournament drew 75 entrants who tossed 225 stones in the Mackinac Straits, and the Mackinac Island Open Stone Skipping Tournament was born. "The cream of the jest," says Rabe, "is that the *Town Crier* never has published a report of the event."

Checking later into the history of stone-skipping on Mackinac Island, Rabe found out that "back at the turn of the century, there was an annual tournament among two or three families, so we were just reviving a tradition."

Currently, about 500 people pay a 50-cent entry fee to toss plinks, pittypats, plunkers, agnews, and skronkers, with the flat stones from Windermere Beach, in front of the island's Windermere Hotel. "With a ferry dock right there where the competitors skip, we like to look on Winderemere Beach as a sporty course," says Rabe.

Whoever gets the most skips during the course of the tournament wins the coveted "Little David Trophy," a 75-pound mounted rock, and a year's supply (52 pounds!) of Ryba's Fudge, a Mackinac Island delicacy.

Incidentally, for the uninitiated, Rabe explains that "plinks are clean-cut, long skips; pittypats are short skips at the end of a run; a plunker is a stone that sinks; an agnew is a stone that lands in the crowd; and a skronker is a stone that never hits the water."

The competitors of all ages tend to come back year after year, often in family groups, like "the skipping Loys of Flint," an entire family of ardent stone-skippers, led by their son Glenn, who is one of three men tied for the world record, 24 skips.

There are other important personalities in the world of competition stone-skipping, Rabe says. Each tournament officially gets underway when "the Grand Old Man of Stone-Skipping, U.S. Navy Cmdr. E. M. Tellefson (Ret.), shouts, 'Let he who is without Frisbee cast the first stone,'" Rabe says.

Never forget the immortal Rolf Anselm. "He's the pioneer in the use of drip-dry trousers to wear while skipping knee deep in water, which is the favorite stance of a number of skippers," says Rabe.

Rabe says anybody can enter the tournament: "All you have to do is show up." Age is of little importance. "Parents are constantly berating me for not having a separate category for children, and I always say, 'Right, to protect the adults.'"

As the tournament grew, so did the organization surrounding it. Rabe and his stone-skipping associates, with their tongues planted firmly in their cheeks, have the World College of Stone-Skipping Jurisprudence to codify stone-skipping rules and certify the judges who officiate at the tournaments. Last, and perhaps least, there's the august publication *Boulder: The Avant-Garde Journal of Stone Skipping*, which Rabe publishes.

It's Rabe's intention to "leave no stone unskipped" and to "bring to public attention what has always been the case in private: stone skipping is a natural sport, a true gentleman's avocation."

Interestingly enough, for all of his association with the sport, Rabe confesses he hasn't had much time (or inclination) to actively participate himself. "I just really enjoy the organizing of it," he says.

For the novice stone-skipper, Rabe asserts "it's all in the foot and the arm." To skip according to regulation, "swing from the shoulder, keep the stone low, breathe deeply, and let 'er rip." He also advises the novice, "Don't hesitate to skip knee-deep when necessary on rough or sporty courses."

And, Rabe adds, it's a good idea not to choose stones which are too large or too small.

"Remember, even the Grand Old Man of Stone Skipping, who hurled the great 17-skip stone in 1932, started as a youth with three- and four-skip stones."

It's Rabe's view that stone-skipping is one of the most ideal competitive sports. "It's very common and something everyone knows how to do; whether they do it well or badly, everyone can do it." He also finds competitive stone-skippers "approach it sincerely. There are no arguments. It's a much cleaner sport than Frisbees."

Rabe can be contacted at Lake Superior State College, Sault Ste. Marie, MI 49783, for further information on stone-skipping or the stone-skipping tournament.

WILL SHORTZ
ENIGMATOLOGY

THE WORD "HERE" reverses meaning if you add the letter "t" in front of it. The word "ever" reverses meaning if you place an "n" at the start. What four letter word reverses meaning if you prefix it with the letter "y"?

This tricky little puzzle was made up by Will Shortz, a 27-year-old Stamford, Connecticut, man who has the world's only college degree in enigmatology — the study of puzzles.

Shortz, who is associate editor of *Games* magazine, and a freelance puzzler whose work has appeared in many major newspapers and magazines, has been interested in puzzles since childhood. "I was motivated, in part, by my mother who is a writer and taught me to appreciate language. We were always interested in words around our house," he says. "Also, I liked mathematics."

At a tender age, his hero was Sam Loyd, "America's renowned puzzlist from the turn of the century." Loyd, Shortz says, was "one of the most noted American chess experts," but he is most widely recognized as the inventor of the popular sliding-square puzzle that has the 14th and 15th squares out of order, the purpose being to get all the squares in numerical order.

By the age of 15, Shortz was already writing a puzzle book, and selling his work to national magazines. The first puzzles he sold were to Dell Publishing, and they were what he called "Time Tests," five-part tests with questions about words and a time limit to solving them.

Shortz's fascination with puzzles continued into college. Through the independent learning program at the University of Indiana, he created his own college curriculum in enigmatology, the study of puzzles. "The people at IU were pretty skeptical at first," says Shortz, "but they came around."

Shortz was able to find professors who were willing to work with him on courses of his own devising, in various disciplines, all related to puzzles. He obtained his degree in 1974, after completing courses such as "Creation of Mathematical Puzzles," "Word Puzzles in the 20th Century," and "The Psychology of Puzzles." His thesis, on American word puzzles before 1860, was published in a national journal of recreational linguistics.

Shortz feels that "the big value of puzzles is entertainment. The best puzzles are the ones which challenge you. They are also a great means of stimulating the brain and keeping it active."

He started out liking (and still favors) "variety puzzles, little word teasers particularly," but gradually became interested in crossword puzzles. His greatest interest right now are British cryptic crosswords. These puzzles, which involve plays on words as the clues, are "intelligent and challenging," he says.

Ancilliary to his puzzle constructing and solving, Shortz has also established a collection of puzzle-related books and magazines. He has over 3,000 of them, dating back to the 18th century.

The oldest puzzle book in his collection, from 1798, is a book of charades, entitled *Amusing Recreations*, but Shortz's favorite is *Key to Puzzledom*. This book, published in 1906 by the Eastern Puzzlers League, "is a collection of all the best puzzles made up to that time, with instructions on how to write puzzles, how to solve them, and something about puzzle history."

Shortz has published a puzzle book of his own, *Brain Games*, a collection of 175 brain teasers (Simon & Schuster, 1979). Four other volumes of puzzles are in process, including *Brain Games II* and three books of crosswords.

Since 1977, Shortz has directed the annual American Crossword Puzzle Tournament, sponsored by the Stamford (Connecticut) Marriott Hotel. It's a whole weekend of crosswords, where participants work the puzzles and are given points based on speed and accuracy. At the end of the contest, Shortz says, the top three contestants solve one last puzzle for the championship. In 1979, over 160 people participated.

Shortz thinks some people have "a natural bent" for doing puzzles. "To be sharp at them, you have to be intelligent; but just because you're intelligent, you're not necessarily going to be sharp at puzzles." He says puzzle expertise comes from an enjoyment of "letter play," seeing how letters work, rather than how words work. "Actually, it's amazing how close mathematics and word puzzles are," he says.

For the novice puzzlist, Shortz says "a good knowledge of puzzle history is an invaluable asset in puzzle-making." He suggests reading puzzle books and old magazine puzzle articles at the library, as well as looking at newspaper puzzles, new and old.

Probably the easiest puzzle for a beginner to create, he says, is a crossword, because "once you start, you can just plunge ahead. Just remember two basic rules: the black squares are to be symmetrical, and two-letter words are frowned upon." Shortz says that if the puzzle doesn't seem to be working out, "just go back and erase words, if necessary. I know it doesn't sound very scientific, but that's the way it's done."

Puzzles "appeal to my mind," Shortz says, in describing why his childhood hobby has become the focus of his life. "I love to think and exercise my brain. Puzzles are very satisfying because they take you into almost every other field of endeavor, and you learn something about history, art, music, any subject you can think of."

Oh — by the way — the answer to the puzzle in the first paragraph: the word is "ours," which with a "y" is transformed into "yours."

Shortz will be happy to answer questions about puzzle history, or anything related to puzzles. He can be contacted in care of *Games* Magazine, 515 Madison Ave., New York, NY 10022.

ALBERT SIKORSKY
CLOWNS & CLOWNING

ALL THE WORLD LOVES a clown, the saying goes. Certainly, Albert Sikorsky does.

Sikorsky, 47, a former Internal Revenue Service fraud investigator, has spent much of the last 13 years clowning around, both as a performer and as a historian of clowns and clowning. He is also the administrator of the nation's only organization for clowns, Clowns of America.

Clowning is a family affair for the Sikorskys. He got involved in 1967. "My brother-in-law has cerebral palsy, and he was going to a special school at the time. They needed someone to dress up in a costume to work their bazaar, and my wife volunteered me."

Sikorsky enjoyed it so much the first time out that he became an enthusiastic volunteer clown. Today, his entertainment agency and tax accounting business, along with the management of Clowns of America, has taken him off the tanbark and put him behind a desk fulltime; he hasn't actively clowned since 1977.

Sikorsky did both the more dignified whiteface clowns and "augustes," clowns with painted faces who are usually the butt of the humor. He had to work hard at being a clown, he says, because "I'm a serious businessman type, and it didn't come naturally. I enjoyed it because I could do things I couldn't do in real life. When you're performing in a hospital, the kids appreciate what you're doing. We're doing something for society, making people laugh."

His interest has affected his family. "It was one of those family affair hobbies that turned into a full-time thing," Sikorsky says. Two of his sons, aged 18 and 21, have a juggling act that appears around the country with circuses and in nightclubs. In addition, a third Sikorsky son is a partner in another family business that sells juggling equipment. "I like challenges. A year ago, I said, 'Who's going to buy juggling equipment?' Today, schools, colleges, recreation centers are all just gobbling it up."

From the top clowns at Ringling Brothers and Barnum & Bailey Circus to Ronald McDonald, most every American clown, amateur or profesional, belongs to Clowns of America or one of its local "alleys" in cities across the country. The group has 4,100 active members, out of a total membership of 8,000 people. "We really have been taking in new members in the last few years. It's been an avalanche," Sikorsky reports. In addition, he edits and publishes the organization's monthly magazine, *The Calliope*, which "is always coming out late because I'm so busy. But the members are pretty tolerant and don't seem to mind."

An interesting development in clowning, says Sikorsky, "is the ministerial clown. That's got to be about the biggest thing happening." He gets four or five letters a week from clowns who utilize their skills for religious purposes. "Even the Catholic Archdiocese of Baltimore has several," he says.

Sikorsky has an extensive library of research materials relating to clowns and clowning history. "I'm a good source of historical information," he says, noting that he often supplies the answers to queries by researchers interested in some aspect of the subject.

Clowning "goes back to the cavemen. There's always been somebody around who was funny," he says. Clowns have also been detected in ancient Egypt, according to Sikorsky, who says that a pharaoh preserved his life for many years by performing incognito as a clown until he was able to gain the throne.

In America, one of the most important clowns was Dan Race, who performed in Abraham Lincoln's time. "He was the model for Uncle Sam," says Sikorsky, "and Congress actually adjourned to watch him perform."

If you want to be a good clown, Sikorsky recommends that "you study all the related arts: magic, juggling, Italian commedia dell'arte, mime, and so forth. If you want to be the top clown, you want to know about all of those things. Study and work. You don't really have to go to a clown college, or the courses put on by the local Clowns of America alleys. You can do it yourself." Remember, "clowning is hard work. Although it comes out funny, there's really skill and expertise behind it."

Incidentally, Sikorsky says, there's not much truth to the traditon that clowns are laughing on the outside and crying on the inside. Sure, "some clowns aren't jovial all the time. After all, they're only characters; behind the funny whiteface is a human being. Every clown I know is a pretty happy person. Most get more out of life than most other people."

Sikorsky and Clowns of America, can be contacted for further information at PO Box 3906, Baltimore, MD 21222.

MARTIN SLOANE
COUPONS

ANYONE CAN SAVE $1,000 a year on their grocery bill. Martin Sloane says it's all a matter of knowing what to cut out — of the newspaper.

Sloane, a Long Island attorney turned entrepreneur, is the nation's leading coupon maven. And he's managed to turn a hobby into an astonishingly effective business that has netted him a syndicated newspaper column, a published book, and an organization of 30,000 members, all in three short years. Clipping coupons and taking the advantage of the refund offers made by many manufacturers has been Sloane's abiding passion since 1975.

"My wife had to go out of town for awhile to help her sister who was ill," says Sloane. "So I had to do the family shopping." While he had clipped some coupons to take with him to the store, he was "very frustrated" because he could only take advantage of 50 cents-worth of the $10 in coupons he had with him.

He determined then and there that he had to work out a system to make effective use of the cents-off coupons and manufacturers' refund offers. The combined use of coupons and refund offers can save the consumer as much as 60 percent on any given product, Sloane says.

Expertise in coupons, he found, came simply from organizing them into 12 product groups. He then built up a "coupon inventory of 2,000 coupons and refund offers." Now, when Sloane goes to the supermarket (he still does most of the family shopping), "I have one to four discounts for each product I buy."

Though most everyone is familiar with cents-off coupons, Sloane says, "most people don't know about refund offers, because the stores don't like to display the tear-off forms" needed to secure the refunds from the manufacturers.

"The successful refunder trades by mail," says Sloane. "There are at least 100,000 people all across the country who regularly trade refund offers with each other." What the refunders do is gather all the offers available to them in their area, and arrange trades with other refunders who have a selection of different offers.

The American Coupon Club, the center of Sloane's coupon empire, was founded in 1977, and its growth has been phenomenal. He publishes *The National Supermarket Shopper*, a monthly magazine that, in a typical month, provides club members with information on more than 200 refund offers of $1.25 or more, as well as information on coupon clipping. Membership in the American Coupon Club, which includes a subscription to the magazine, is $15 per year.

The best way to obtain cents-off coupons, Sloane says, is to clip them from the weekly food section of the newspaper. "The smart couponer gets more than one copy of the food section to get all the coupons needed."

Coupon collectors speak their own language, reminiscent of sportstalk. A "double play" is having a discount coupon and a refund slip for a particular product. "The ultimate achievement is the 'triple play,'" says Sloane. For instance, if the supermarket advertises french fries on sale at the supermarket for 89 cents, and the customer also has a 50-cents-off-coupon and a $1 refund offer, "you see that you can start making money" by taking advantage of these offers.

The rapid rise of inflation has done little to diminish the enthusiasm of manufacturers for creating coupons and refund offers, according to Sloane. In 1975, he says, there were some 35 billion coupons; by in 1980, some 90 billion will be issued. Manufacturers also will make more than 7,000 refund offers in 1980, he says. "You can turn almost every boxtop or package label into cash."

According to Sloane, it isn't possible to determine the actual amount saved by savings at the cash register. "Rather, you have to consider how much you can save each month at the register *and* in the mailbox," he says. He estimates that the person who "really wants to save," and follows his organizational scheme, "will save $50 to $100 per month under the plan."

Additionally, if "a refunder sends off two sets of trades, each with a batch of 10 or so offers each week, that's an average of 80 to 100 new offers per month, for the four or five hours of work it takes to gather up all the offers in your area and send off the letters," he says.

An estimated 60 million people will use at least one coupon a year, says Sloane, and there are about 10 million confirmed coupon clippers who do a lot more than that. "So, clip all the coupons. What you don't use, you can trade."

"It is my purpose to help the consumer save in any way possible," says Sloane.

So popular is couponing that Sloane's book (based on his column, syndicated by United Features Syndicate) *The Supermarket Shopper's 1980 Guide to Coupons and Refunds* (Bantam, 1980), sold out its initial printing of 200,000 copies!

Sloane thinks that clipping coupons is beneficial in other ways than just saving money. Among more than 4,000 letters he gets weekly was one from "a woman who told me she was very depressed after her children had left home, and she wasn't interested in anything — until she got started couponing and refunding." Now, says Sloane, the woman "has taken a new interest in life."

Couponing, Sloane says, "is just like any other hobby or pastime. When you get experience, there's a great deal of enjoyment and satisfaction in pursuing it. In the world of coupons, there is the opportunity to meet people and make new friends."

As an attorney, Sloane was "always looking for a cause." When he found that "I had something to offer a lot of people who needed help," the prospect of turning his private couponing interest into a full-time occupation "was very exciting."

To get started in couponing, Sloane suggests joining the American Coupon Club. Soon, he says, local chapters will be in operation in 28 states. For a sample copy of the magazine (send $1.50) or further information (send a stamped, self-addressed envelope) write to the American Coupon Club, PO Box 1149, Great Neck, NY 11023.

Sloane can be reached c/o United Features Syndicate, 200 Park Ave., New York, NY 10017.

ROB SUNDE
OENOLOGY

I LEARNED BY DRINKING," says Rob Sunde of his interest in oenology — the study and appreciation of wines. A more convivial hobby can scarcely be imagined.

Sunde, 43, a news executive with WCBS Radio in New York City, has developed such an expertise in wines that he's hosted a weekly radio program, "News From the Grapevine," since 1977.

He discovered wines in 1958, while serving in the U.S. Army in Europe. There, drinking the vintages of France and Germany, he started developing a taste for wines that continues to this day. "I'm still in the process of becoming expert in wines," he says.

When he got back to the States, "I had a good liquor dealer who was a tremendous wine expert, and he helped me out by introducing me to various wines. That's how you build up expertise over the years, by rooting around various wine shops and liquor stores," experimenting with wines and listening to the wisdom of people more experienced in the field. "Then you start collecting, bottle by bottle."

For the wine buff, there's nothing more important than his wine cellar. Sunde has a splendid one in his Norwalk, Connecticut, home. He estimates that he has between 500 and 600 bottles in his collection, representing "wines from all over France and California, along with some Italian and German wines, many of them good vintages which I couldn't afford to buy at today's prices."

Perhaps his most precious wine (and the oldest in his collection) is a bottle of 1937 Chambolle Musigny, a French Burgundy. "She's a very fragile old lady," says Sunde. "Once the cork is pulled out, the wine would last no more than 45 minutes."

Sunde has specialized in vintages of the 1960s and 1970s, which "were available basically at a fair price before the French got out of hand in their pricing."

His cellar ("a real cellar, surrounded by earth and mortar, with racks for the bottles of wine and no windows") is kept at a temperature of 55 to 65 degrees Farenheit at all times. "The optimum temperature for wine is 60 to 65 degrees," he says, "so that is what we shoot for." The cellar is the perfect place to keep the wines "so they can age gracefully, without disruption, undue sunlight, and the like. "The wines can mature at a predictable rate, so they can be consumed at the optimum time. That's the great benefit of a wine cellar. You can buy wines when they are young and immature and cheap, and consume them when they're mature, highly drinkable, and impossibly expensive."

In his cellar, Sunde has wines that he won't be drinking for a long time yet: his 1975 Bordeaux, for example, "will probably be in the cellar after I die" but won't be ready to drink until, at the earliest, 1990. The wines of 1970s vintages, he'll start drinking around 1985. Right now, "I'm drinking the wines people want to drink wine right away." Indeed, it's possible to drink most common wines today, "because they're made to drink young."

For the dedicated oenologist, however, time is the essence of wine — as well as experimenting to determine what the individual's taste is. "The more you branch out, the more sophisticated your taste gets," Sunde feels.

While there is a good deal of talk of collecting wine as an investment, Sunde tends to downplay that aspect. While sales statistics show that wines are growing in popularity "by leaps and bounds," Sunde says that the problem with buying wine for an investment is "that you're assuming you'll have someone to sell it to on the other end." Since it's against the law for one individual to sell a bottle of liquor to another, it seems unlikely that there's much practical chance of wine being a good investment. Besides, looking at wine as an investment takes a lot of the joy out of it, he says.

While Sunde is partial to French wines, saying "The French are still the mark by which all other wines are judged," he has other favorites as well. He feels that many of the California wines are excellent, "There are more than 320 vineyards and winerys in the state," he says, "and they all offer products. There's more wine in California than we can possibly consume."

What does Sunde like best to collect and drink? "There's nothing like a good French Burgundy. I say that advisedly, because there are lots of bad ones, too." Since his favorite wines are red, he's also partial to Bordeaux, California Cabernet Sauvignon, and California Zinfandel. In the whites he would recommend Pinot Chardonnay, or Chardonnay Le Montrechat. In addition, "some from the 1960s."

To be a wine collector "takes tremendous patience," says Sunde. "Most great bargains are to be found among Spanish and Italian wines." The cheapest wine he recommends is Romanian wine. "For $2.50 a bottle, you can't do better."

For the would-be oenologist, Sunde doesn't recommend rushing right out to start a wine cellar. "It's a much better idea to find a dealer who's knowledgeable in wines and willing to spend time in advising you, giving you the benefit of his expertise."

"The person should be led into it gently," Sunde thinks. "He should be encouraged to buy affordable wines, and let his tastes come up to a level of understanding of wine." Starting with a wine the person likes is a good way to begin, even if it's not the most sophisticated wine available, he adds.

Wine is Sunde's favorite drink "because, of all the natural things you can drink, only wine is a combination of something pleasurable and something good for you, at the same time. Wine, in proper quantities, of course, is healthful. It does wonderful things to the soul and spirit."

Sunde will be happy to answer questions about wines, addressed to him at WCBS Radio, 51 W. 52nd St., New York, NY 10019.

BJO TRIMBLE
STAR TREK

SHE DESCRIBES HERSELF as "a natural-born yenta, professional noodge, and all-around, well-known local flaming whacko," but Bjo ("pronounced 'B-Joe'") Trimble is really only wild about one subject: "Star Trek." And she has carved out a favored niche for herself in science fiction fandom as a result.

Mrs. Trimble, 47, a Los Angeles artist, writer, magazine publisher, convention organizer, wife, and mother, has devoted 14 years to "Star Trek," the ground-breaking science fiction television series that captured the hearts and minds of a large and ever-growing (thanks to program syndication) legion of ardent fans. As the unofficial den mother of this crop of "Trekkies," Mrs. Trimble is probably the leading historian/activist of the "Star Trek" movement, and an influential science fiction buff.

She was already a science fiction fan in 1966 when the show first came on the air, so "it was a fairly easy step to enjoying the only adult science fiction on TV," she recalls. So impressed was Mrs. Trimble with the quality of the show that she wrote a fan letter to producer Gene Roddenberry ("knowing how important such letters are to keeping shows on the air") and, to her surprise, was invited with many other "Star Trek" fans to visit the set.

After meeting the stars and production personnel of the show, Mrs. Trimble's interest really caught fire, and "kind of got out of hand."

"A friend and I started keeping notes on the show," she says. "She lost interest and went off to get married or something. I was already married, so I just kept watching the show." Soon, her notes had filled many notebooks, forming a valuable reference authors later used in compiling most of the myriad of books about "Star Trek," making Mrs. Trimble *the* "Star Trek" maven.

All was not well with "Star Trek," however. There was a major move afoot, after its second season on NBC, to cancel the show. Mrs. Trimble was the organizer of the "Save Star Trek for a Third Season" movement, a nationwide letter-writing campaign that flooded the network with over one million pro-"Star Trek" letters and successfully saved the show for another year.

"As a long-time science fiction fan, I hoped that by keeping "Star Trek" alive, programming executives might consider putting more such programs on."

Unfortunately, even the love of the fans was not enough to save the show, which fell from the network lineup after the third season, with no effort being made to save it. "Frankly, " says Mrs. Trimble,"what killed the show was that the people put in charge of the third season were simply not competent."

Mrs. Trimble achieved national prominence as the author of *The Star Trek Concordance* (Ballantine, 1976). The book, which features complete synopses, and cast and crew listings for each of the 78 episodes of the show, is a compendium of facts, trivia, and scholarship about "Star Trek," its stars, themes, and technical achievements.

How does Mrs. Trimble account for the appeal of "Star Trek," which still has legions of devoted fans?

"I read much of the fan mail," she says, "and I think it is largely because it postulated a future for mankind 200 years from now. We hadn't managed to blast ourselves off the planet, and there were attempts being made to understand fellow creatures. The show was suggesting we had a good future, where people were working together to try to solve problems."

Also, Mrs. Trimble says, the fact that the show had "many characters that people could identify with," was a major factor in its appeal.

"Star Trek" also had a liberating influence on women in the male-dominated world of science fiction, Mrs. Trimble feels. "The old story 'men don't like girls with brains' was disproven. Suddenly, it was okay to be a woman on a space ship. Women really came out of the woodwork and admitted for the first time that they read, understood, and enjoyed science-fiction, too."

The show had a revival of sorts in 1979, through the Paramount film *Star Trek: The Movie*. How did a dedicated Trekkie like Bjo Trimble like it?

"Well, for most of us the film was a large disappointment," she says. The reason, Mrs. Trimble feels, is that the production was "rushed along by Paramount, who wanted it out by Christmas, and then sold it as a G film, which means (Gene) Roddenberry had to take out all the good parts. It ended up being dull." She appeared in the movie, as an extra in a scene on the flight deck of the U.S.S. Enterprise.

Not only has Mrs. Trimble been deeply involved with "Star Trek," but in several other areas of science fiction fandom, as well. With her husband John, Mrs. Trimble originated and operated FILMCON/EQUCION, a popular science fiction and fantasy fan convention in Southern California from 1973 to 1976. At these conventions, which featured stars of science fiction and fantasy films and TV shows, authors of science fiction, and collectors of all kinds, as many as 5,000 people immersed themselves in the weekend-long schedules of seminars, speeches, and special events.

"The conventions were wonderful," Mrs. Trimble says, "but we simply couldn't continue doing them. The demands on our time were adversely affecting our family."

Mrs. Trimble then turned to publishing, with a "fanzine" (so-called because it is a publication put out by and for fans) *Megamart*. This magazine, which features articles on "every facet of science fiction and fantasy fandom, along with some very good amateur art," is sent all over the country to people who are interested in many science fiction and fantasy subjects. *Megamart* is published out of the Trimbles' Los Angeles home, by a dedicated, volunteer staff.

Mrs. Trimble is an energetic person (she'd have to be, to get all this accomplished), who says "I've never been bored more than five minutes in my whole life — I do something about it." She advises would-be Trekkies or science fiction fans to "be interested in anything. It's not really sophisticated to act blase in a world of wonders."

Mrs. Trimble, who'll be glad to answer questions about anything relating to "Star Trek," science fiction, or fantasy, can be reached at Mathom House, 696 S. Bronson Ave., Los Angeles, CA 90005. For further information on *Megamart*, write to the magazine, PO Box 1248, Inglewood, CA 90308.

JACK VAN GILDER
KITE BUILDING & FLYING

WHEN HIS TWO stepsons asked him to make them a kite in 1971, little did Jack Van Gilder suspect that someday he would be one of America's leading kite-flyers and an authority on their construction.

Van Gilder, a 58-year-old life insurance salesman from Seattle, Washington, has made a nationwide reputation for himself in the organization of kite-flying events and by teaching kite-building to groups in his home state.

"The first kite I made was a miserable failure," he remembers. It was a replica of a triangular-shaped French military box kite, of the kind used by the French for reconnaissance at the turn of the century. Unfortunately, Van Gilder says, "I didn't know it needed to be made out of something stiff, and I made it out of bamboo, which is flexible."

Undaunted, Van Gilder found the book *Kites* by Wyatt Brummitt (Golden Press), and made a successful "delta" kite from a design in the book. From that point, he just took off.

These days, Van Gilder still likes to experiment, but has two specialties in kite-building. One is kites with Northwest Indian totem designs. One of the most successful, he says, is a Thunderbird shaped kite.

His other specialty is somewhat more spectacular. "I build kite trains," he says. A kite train, Van Gilder explains, is a string of kites (in this case, 108 deltas, each 48 inches wide), made of lightweight plastic, stretched along a string at 10-foot intervals. Van Gilder says every 10 kites are a different color, and the train "makes quite a splash" as it soars high over the University of Washington football games, for which Van Gilder originally created the kite train.

Altogether, since he began kiting, Van Gilder estimates he's made 500 kites of varying shapes, sizes, and materials. "The bottoms of Lake Washington and Elliot Bay here in Seattle are pretty much papered with my kites," he jokes. Ironically, his stepsons have "outgrown" kites, "but that's okay, kitemaking is really serious business; you can't leave it to a bunch of kids."

As a founder of the Washington Kieflier's Association (sponsored by the Pacific Science Center), Van Gilder has organized numerous kite projects, including such diverse happenings as half-time kite displays at professional basketball games ("Yes, kites will fly indoors; merely walk them around the floor at 4 mph"), dedications of new parks, the opening of Seattle's new waterfront aquarium, greeting the first tour ship of the year to Canada, and so on. Van Gilder and 85 fellow kiters in the Puget Sound area, are kept busy with kiting events, demonstrations, and kite-building all year long.

The club, which every Sunday afternoon has a kite fly at Gasworks Park ("the Mecca for kite-flyers in Seattle"), makes a special effort to bring kiting to the community at large, Van Gilder says. A recent project was a day of kite-flying from a tour boat in the Sound for 150 children from the Children's Orthopedic Hospital in Seattle.

He's done some flying of his own, too. "I even won a fighter kite contest in 1979," he says. Fighter kites, 14- or 24-inch-square and framed on pieces of bamboo, "are just about the national sport in India," Van Gilder says. The kites' strings are run through a mixture of glass fragments and glue, and are used to cut opponents' strings. "The kites are constructed so as to be highly controllable," he says. "It was supposed to be a deep dark secret how to do it, but some of us have figured it out."

Building a kite is easy, says Van Gilder. There are many books available that give step-by-step instructions. And, "it's just a whole lot of fun." There's no secret to successfully flying a kite, either, he says. It's simply a matter of adapting the kites to their surroundings. "In Seattle, the breezes are so gentle we have to make our kites out of tissue paper or balsa wood, so they can take the 3-to-4- mile an hour breeze we generally have."

It's Van Gilder's secret ambition to "be pulled aloft by a string of kites.The dream of silent locomotion is always there in most people. I'd like to look down from, say, 200 feet." But, he adds, "I'm too much of a coward to take up hang gliding. Besides, my wife is a registered nurse and she says 58-year-old men don't belong on hang gliders."

So, he has to be content "to dream of flight, standing on the ground, feeling the string pull and hearing it hum in the wind."

Van Gilder is really high on his hobby. "It's the most perfect hobby because it doesn't take much money (most of us learn to be pretty good scroungers for materials), and it satisfies our creative instincts by putting a kite together and our artistic instincts by decorating it."

Kite-making and flying has been an ideal interest for him, Van Gilder says, "because something in me always wanted to make something with my hands." When he was 10 years old, "I asked for, and got, a coping saw instead of a baseball bat. Soon I was turning out wooden Thompson submachine guns for the whole neighborhood."

Kiting "brings you into contact with young people, young parents, children, and youthful older folks. It encourages companionship with other people," Van Gilder says.

He'll be happy to offer advice, counsel or good wishes to novice kiters. Van Gilder can be contacted at 1925 Walnut S.W., Seattle WA 98116.

EDWARD WEBER
RAILROAD BUILDING PHOTOGRAPHY

WHEN HE WAS A KID, Edward Weber used to love to watch the steam locomotives around his hometown of Chatham, New Jersey. He also liked photographing them.

"But, all too soon, they started disappearing," he recalls. "And like the great trains they serviced, the railroad buildings began to disappear too, at an alarming rate. So in 1948, I began taking pictures of stations and other railroad buildings."

So far, Weber has taken over 3,500 interesting and unusual photographs of train stations, the signal towers that guided the trains, and other buildings constructed on the railroad right of way, "often way out in the country, on the worst roads possible."

He's covered most of the Middle Atlantic region, and the states of Pennsylvania, Virginia, Ohio, West Virginia, Kentucky, Maryland, and Illinois, in his quest for subjects to photograph."

His most memorable railway picture-taking experience resulted from pure luck. One fall day in 1954, Weber and a friend decided to take a ride on the Ontario & Western Railroad. It left Weehawken, New Jersey, every day, bound for the Catskill Mountain resorts. "We thought it was just the last day of the season," says Weber, "but it turned out to be the very last passenger train they were going to run." So, Weber and his friend had a great ride in the outdoor observation car, and "took pictures of the crew, and the train, and everything."

"As many as 20 percent of the old stations and buildings have now disappeared. At least another 25 percent are in terrible condition," he says. "Since passenger service has disappeared, for the most part, these buildings haven't been maintained at all." Many stations, if they have been saved, are used for other purposes now. It is imperative, therefore, for the person who is interested in photographing these old buildings to "be aware of what's going on, and get a picture before the building is gone entirely or before another use changes its railroad flavor."

Unfortunately, even with the all the energy difficulties the United States is experiencing, Weber doesn't look for a resurgence in train travel. "I'd like it, of course," he says, "but my feeling is that the public doesn't want to be regulated by a timetable anymore. They like their cars too much. There would really have to be a pretty hard pinch to get people to give up their cars for public transportation." Realistically, says Weber, "I don't think you could attract riders even if the ride was free!"

At the moment, Weber says, "I take my own pictures, rather than trading or buying from others. The reason is that I have limited time, and really no time to correspond with other people who do what I do, even though I'd like to. I've only been able to devote about 20 hours a year, lately, to taking pictures, so when I do have some free time, I like to go out and take what pictures I can."

Weber uses "nothing exotic" when he takes his pictures. He has a Crown Graphic 2 by 3 press camera, and he uses only black and white professional Plus-X film. He also develops everything in his own darkroom.

Weber is a member of the Railroad Station Historical Society, a group of 600 people around the country who like to look at each other's pictures. "We are not a preservation group," he says, "but a group that is keenly interested in observing stations while they are still around."

In addition to photographs of steam locomotives, and railroad buildings, Weber also has an interesting collection of old railroad timetables, which he started in the mid-1940s. About 200 different railroads are represented. "This collection really helps me in my picture-taking," he says. "I have a lot of employees' timetables that can provide clues to the locations of telegraph offices and other railroad buildings out in the country, that aren't on the ordinary timetables." Since Weber always maps out a photographic junket specifically before embarking, these timetables are "a big help in efficient planning."

Weber's all for people taking pictures of railroad buildings. "If you can afford the gas to go traveling around, get as many pictures as you possibly can," he says. The most important thing for the beginner: "Just be aware of what's around. And take that picture before it disappears."

Weber is happy to counsel the novice railroad picture buff. Contact him at 142 New Hampshire Dr., Ashland, KY 41101.

INDEX